Perl
from the Ground Up

About the Author

Michael McMillan is a software engineer with expertise in Perl, C/C++, Visual Basic, and Microsoft SQL Server. A savvy Web site developer and Internet/systems administrator for various companies, Mike has coauthored several programming books on Visual Basic and writes the "Inside the Box" column for *Windows NT Systems Magazine.*

Dedication:

To my father, who through nature and nurture helped me become a writer.

Perl
from the Ground Up

Mike McMillan

Osborne **McGraw-Hill**

Berkeley   New York   St. Louis   San Francisco
Auckland   Bogotá   Hamburg   London   Madrid
Mexico City   Milan   Montreal   New Delhi   Panama City
Paris   São Paulo   Singapore   Sydney
Tokyo   Toronto

Osborne **McGraw-Hill**
2600 Tenth Street
Berkeley, California 94710
U.S.A.

For information on translations or book distributors outside the U.S.A.,
or to arrange bulk purchase discounts for sales promotions, premiums, or
fund-raisers, please contact Osborne/**McGraw-Hill** at the above address.

Perl from the Ground Up

1234567890 AGM AGM 901987654321098

ISBN 0-07-882404-4

Publisher
Brandon A. Nordin

Editor-in-Chief
Scott Rogers

Acquisitions Editor
Meg Bonar

Project Editor
Heidi Poulin

Editorial Assistant
Stephane Thomas

Technical Editor
Dan Camper

Copy Editor
Gary Morris

Proofreader
Rhonda Holmes

Indexer
Valerie Robbins

Computer Designer
Roberta Steele
Jean Butterfield
Sylvia Brown

Illustrator
Brian Wells

Contents

v

Contents

Acknowledgments

The first person I have to thank is Larry Wall for creating such a useful and fun programming language. Larry comes from a school of programming that has all but died out—the solitary programmer who creates something neat as much because doing so is fun as because some boss somewhere told them to. This school of programming began with Ken Thompson and Dennis Ritchie and their creations, Unix and C respectively. Hopefully, as scripting languages become more and more prevalent in today's computing environments, more programmers will join this school to create their own scripting languages for us to use.

My wife, Terri, and my three children, Meredith, Allison, and Mason really just want to see their names in print, but I would like to thank them for supporting me through the long hours I put in writing and programming.

Having a great set of friends helps take some of the pressure off when deadlines are looming. I especially want to thank Jim and Joanne Colebank for providing us with food and entertainment on a few weekends when I really needed a break from the work.

The people I work with at T4 Systems, particularly Larry Plummer, Frank Barber, and Philip Cole, provide me with a challenging and fun work atmosphere and are very supportive of my writing.

Finally, the staff at Osborne/McGraw-Hill have helped in ways too numerous to mention. Megg Bonar, my acquisitions editor, deserves some sort of award for patience in shepherding me through this project. Her editorial assistant, Stephane Thomas, did a great job organizing all the final details as I finished up the book. My technical reviewer, Dan Camper, provided many great insights into both the technical aspects of Perl and in how to best present them in the book. Matthew Trunnell and Shelly Powers contributed great content which helped to make this a much better book. I also want to thank Heidi Poulin for her help in reviewing the chapters to make sure they were stylistically and logically consistent.

Introduction

Scripting languages have become an important component of the programming language community. Though scripting languages have been around for a long time (the first scripting language I learned was Job Control Language, JCL, which I used to submit WatFor/WatFive programs to an old IBM mainframe back in college in the late 1970s), they have only recently come into their own as worthy of respect from experienced computer programmers.

Scripting languages have become popular for several reasons. First, as computers have become faster and faster, it is less important to program in low-level languages such as C or C++. More powerful processors can now take the place of more efficient, low-level programming languages. Another factor for the increased use of scripting languages is the increased complexity of today's applications. Scripting languages help control complexity in several ways, but in particular they help the programmer by allowing him or her to use the scripting language to prototype the application. I have actually used Perl several times to prototype a concept and sell it to my boss before moving on to another language to actually implement the application. Scripting languages also help control complexity by being used as a "glue" language to bind different components together into a single application. In today's programming environment, it is not uncommon to use C++, Java, and Visual Basic as the programming language for different components of a client/server application. A scripting language such as Perl can be used to glue these components together into a cohesive whole.

Finally, scripting languages have become popular because of their use in Internet and Web programming. I have seen estimates that say Perl is used in over 80 percent of all interactive Web sites and other scripting languages are also used quite often for Web applications. This is because, as you will learn in this book, you can learn to use a scripting language like Perl very quickly and get good results with a minimum of effort. Then, as you begin to learn more about the language, you can move up to more complex problems.

Of the scripting languages in common use today, Perl is arguably the most popular. One estimate pegs the number of Perl programmers in the United States at 600,000. Of course, Perl is not the only language most of these programmers use, but I'm sure a vast majority wish it were. As you will discover as you read this book, Perl not only provides efficient and powerful solutions to your programming problems, it is also a blast to use.

Who Is the Audience for this Book?

The ideal reader of this book is someone who has had previous exposure to a computer programming language. While you don't need to be an expert in any language to benefit from this book, it doesn't teach the basics of computer architecture or the fundamentals of computer programming. If you've had even just a little exposure to Basic or C, or even JavaScript or VBScript, than you have a good enough background to benefit from this book.

You will get the most out of this book if you have some sort of programming project or problem to work on as you read along. The most ideal projects will be the kinds of things Perl is best at solving: text processing, data manipulation, and Internet programming. If you are a Web master and you've been copying Perl scripts onto your Web server, you can use this book to figure out how those scripts work. If your latest assignment at work is to massage that old mainframe data for use in your new client/server environment, the chapters in this book on pattern matching and data manipulation will help you tremendously. Finally, if you just enjoy computer programming, you will discover even greater joys learning the power and flexibility of Perl.

What's in this Book

This book consists of 22 chapters that will teach you everything from the basics of Perl to the specialty areas of network and CGI programming. The first ten chapters present Perl's building blocks, from how to form Perl expressions to writing regular expression pattern matchers. The final twelve chapters introduce you to specific application areas where Perl can create an efficient and powerful solution.

Perl can be used in both the Unix and Windows environments, and in many cases, the same Perl expression or function will work on either platform. Some Perl functions, however, will only work in Unix (or Windows), and where these functions occur in the text, it is pointed out which platform supports which function.

Perl is fairly new to the Windows platform, and because of that, there have been few books published about using Perl in Windows. Several chapters address specific Windows applications areas, such as Windows NT administration and database programming in Windows. Unix hasn't been completely ignored, of course, and there are several sections that address the Unix environment exclusively.

What You'll Need

Unlike other computer programming languages, which often require a substantial investment if you want more than the language's "learning edition," the complete Perl is free. Regardless of the platform on which you use Perl, you need to get Perl from the same place—the Perl Web site. The URL is **http://www.perl.com**. To get the latest version of Perl, whether for Unix, Windows, or Mac, go to **http://www.perl.com/latest.html**. At this site you will find complete instructions for downloading the right Perl for your computing environment. And did I mention it's free?

While you're at Perl's Web site, be sure to spend a little time there getting familiar with the resources available to you. One of the nice things about Perl, which you'll soon be reading about, is the way many people have contributed to making Perl a better and more useful language. The Perl Web site is the jumping-off place for finding that special Perl library to solve your problem of the day.

CHAPTER 1

An Introduction to Perl

Unless you've been programming in a monastery high in Tibet for the past ten years or so, you've no doubt heard something about a programming language called Perl. What you've heard about Perl depends on how you spend your time with computers. If you're involved in the Internet and the World Wide Web, you've heard that Perl is often used to write CGI scripts, those programs that take your name and credit card information off of a web page and send them to a database somewhere (and hopefully nowhere else). If you're new to Unix systems administration, you've probably heard the senior administrators talk about how Perl has helped them perform the latest magic needed to get some chore done in a fraction of the time it would have taken them to do manually. If you're a systems or application developer, you've probably heard that those nasty data transformation programs that are taking you many hundreds of lines to write in C or Visual Basic can be written in just a few lines using Perl.

Perl does all these things and more. This chapter will introduce you to Perl. You'll learn why it was invented, what it is used for, and why so many programmers and systems administrators have found it an indispensable tool for getting their work done. In fact, some people find Perl so powerful that they swear off whatever language or languages they've been using and use Perl exclusively for all their programming projects.

A Short History of the Perl Language

Perl is the creation of Larry Wall, who was a systems administrator for a West Coast company when he developed it. Larry was given the task of creating a configuration management and control system for 12 computers and workstations divided between the West Coast office and the East Coast office. To solve this problem, Larry used a program he had already written, **rn**, which is used to read Usenet news, and he added an append command and a synchronize command. This solved the configuration management and control system problem, but then Larry's manager asked for the system to produce reports. Larry's first thought was to use **awk** to produce the reports, but **awk** couldn't handle all of the requirements Larry needed, so Perl was born.

Perl wasn't named Perl at first. After several readings of the dictionary, looking for an appropriate three- or four-letter word, Larry settled on "Gloria," his wife's name. Knowing this would cause too much trouble around the house ("Why won't Gloria ever do what I ask her to?"), Larry first picked the name "Pearl" (for Practical Extraction *And* Report Language). He found out that there was a graphics language of the same name, so the name became "Perl," as it is to this day.

The first versions of Perl had pattern matching, file handles, scalars, and formats, but the language only handled limited regular expressions, it didn't have associative arrays, and there were very few functions. The features of Perl grew as Larry discovered more and more uses for it. Perl also grew after Larry unleashed Perl on the Internet. As people began to use Perl in their day-to-day programming and administration tasks, they asked Larry to add this feature and that feature. Larry hated to turn anyone down, and Perl has grown to the size it is today.

Another factor in the history of the Perl language is the growth of Perl library modules. While Perl certainly lives up to its reputation as the Swiss army knife of programming tools, the language simply can't be expected to do everything. To fill in the holes, independent programmers have written modules of Perl code that can be included in Perl programs to extend the functionality of the language. In fact, for many systems administration purposes, the Perl modules are as useful as the language itself. The growth of these modules has led to more and more people finding Perl useful for their work and has led to the overall growth of Perl itself.

A Tour of the Perl Language

The best way to learn a computer language is to dive right in and start working with examples of the language. This section presents an overview of Perl that will lay a foundation for studying the details of the language. The examples in this chapter will focus on the *what* of Perl—what features it has and what you can do with it. The *why* of Perl—why Perl works the way it does—will be the focus of Chapters 2-12.

A Simple Perl Program

Compared with other computer languages, such as C++ or Visual Basic, it is easy to write simple programs in Perl. It is also easy to run complex programs in Perl. Perl is an interpreted language, so you don't have to go through a lot of gyrations with a compiler to run a Perl program. All you have to do is make sure you have Perl installed on your computer system, write your program, and run it.

The simplest Perl program you can write is a one-line program that you run from the command line. Here is the classic "Hello, world" program in Perl, entered completely at the command line:

```
perl -e "print 'Hello, world!';"
```

Once you have typed this line and pressed ENTER, the following text is displayed on the screen:

```
Hello, world!
```

Let's examine in detail the command line entered to produce this text. First, the command to invoke the Perl interpreter, perl, is written. Next, the Perl command-line switch, -e, is written to tell Perl to look for a line of code and not to look for a file of code to execute. Following the switch is the line of code that we want to execute: "print 'Hello, world!';". The line of code is surrounded in double quotes to identify it as the code. The Perl function, **print**, tells the interpreter to take whatever text that follows and display it on the standard output device, normally the screen.

NOTE: A *keyword* is a special word in Perl representing a function that Perl is to perform. A keyword is also called a *reserved word*, meaning that the word is special to the interpreter and cannot be used for any other purpose, such as a variable name.

Following the **print** keyword is the text to be displayed, surrounded in single quotes. The **print** keyword expects its input (the text to be displayed) to be surrounded in quotes. Normally, you will use double quotes to mark text that is to be printed, but since we are already using double quotes to mark the line of code for the -e switch, single quotes are used to mark the displayed text. **print** will accept either type of quotes.

A single-quoted string is simply a string, meaning that if you put special characters inside single quotes, such as \n, they will be interpreted as a backslash and a letter "n", not as the newline character. However, a double-quoted string acts more like a C string, so that if you have the characters "\n" in a double-quoted string, they will be interpreted as a newline character.

Following the text to be displayed is a semicolon. This semicolon is used to mark the end of a Perl statement and is used just like it is in C or C++. Every Perl statement must end with a semicolon, even statements that are entered on the command line. Finally, another single quote is entered to denote the end of the text to be displayed, and a double quote is entered to mark the end of the code being sent to the Perl interpreter.

Another way to run this simple program is to enter the Perl code into a text editor and save it as a file. Perl programs written this way must have the file extension .pl so the interpreter will recognize it as a Perl program.

The first lines of code of your Perl programs will depend on what type of operating system you are using. For example, Perl programs that are run in the Unix operating system always start with some version of the following line of code:

```
#!/usr/bin/perl
```

This line identifies the location of the Perl interpreter, which is usually found in the directory /usr/bin. If you are running Unix and aren't sure where the Perl interpreter is located, find someone knowledgeable about your system to tell you.

If you are running Perl on some version of the Windows operating system, you cannot use the #! (pronounced "shebang") directive. To run Perl programs in Windows, you can use one of two methods. One way is to set up a file association so that when you click on a Perl program icon, Windows will associate the Perl interpreter with the Perl program file. The other way is to run your program from the command line. For example, if your Perl interpreter is located in C:\Perl\bin, you can run a Perl program like this:

```
c:\perl\bin>perl hello.pl
```

The name of the Perl program that created the text displayed here is hello.pl.

```
C:\WINDOWS>cd\perl\bin

C:\Perl\bin>edit hello.pl

C:\Perl\bin>perl hello.pl
Hello,World!
C:\Perl\bin>
```

The code in this file is simply the line:

```
print "Hello, world!";
```

Getting Input from the User

Many Perl programs require that the user provide information to the program in the form of user input. Getting input from the user in Perl involves using the *<STDIN>* operator, which (in this instance) gets a line of input from the standard input device—the keyboard. This input has to be placed somewhere, and like most programming languages, input in Perl is placed into a variable. Now let's look at a simple program that lets the user decide what information to display on the screen.

NOTE: From this point on, the programming examples in this book will not include the #! directive. If you are programming in the Unix environment, don't forget to include this directive.

```
Print "Enter some information to display on the screen: ";
$input = <STDIN>;
print $input;
```

When this program is run, you will see the following on your screen:

```
Enter some information to display on your screen:
```

If you typed the words "Perl from the Ground Up", your display will look like this:

```
Enter some information to display on your screen: Perl from
         the Ground Up
Perl from the Ground Up
```

Two aspects of Perl need to be pointed out in this program example. First, the variable that receives the user's input starts with a dollar sign ($). There are several different types of Perl variables (as you will discover later), and each Perl variable type is denoted with a special character. The most common Perl variable type is a scalar variable, which is denoted with a dollar sign. A scalar variable can hold either a string or a number, and that is all a scalar variable can hold.

The dollar sign ($) is a mnemonic for the "s" in "scalar", just as an array variable in Perl is denoted with the "at" sign (@). The Perl variable types will be discussed in depth in Chapter 2.

The other aspect of Perl that is new in this example is that the **print** function can take a variable as well as a text string. When a variable is passed to the **print** function, no quotes are needed, since Perl knows that the variable is a text string. Actually, there is another argument that can be passed to the **print** function in this example, STDOUT, but it is the default and can be left out when printing to the display. STDOUT, the file handle name for the standard output device, if used, is placed right after the **print** keyword, so that the **print** function in the previous code could look like this:

```
print STDOUT $input;
```

Making Simple Decisions

All Perl programs will have to make decisions based on the data the program processes. One simple form of decision making in Perl is the **if** statement. The **if** statement evaluates a conditional expression and executes a statement if the conditional expression is true. For example, the following *if* statement evaluates a numeric expression and prints "True":

```
if (10000 > 9000) { print "True";}
```

In this example, the conditional expression is 10000 > 9000. The expression is enclosed in parentheses primarily to make the code easier to read. The statement part of the **if** is enclosed in curly braces. These braces denote a statement block and are required. This **print** statement is only executed if the conditional expression is true.

The following program is another example of the **if** statement. This example gets two numbers from the user and prints "True" if the first number is greater than the second number. Here is the code:

```
print "Enter the first number: ";
$num1 = <STDIN>;
print "Enter the second number: ";
$num2 = <STDIN>;
if ($num1 > $num2) { print "True"; }
```

This example shows that the conditional expression can consist of variables and not just data. In fact, the conditional expression can be any expression that Perl can evaluate to True or False. More on this in Chapter 2.

Repeating Program Statements Using a for Loop

Many programs require a statement or set of statements to be performed a specified number of times, performing what is called a *loop*. One of the ways to write a loop in Perl is to use the **for** looping construct, which looks like C's **for** loop.

A **for** loop is constructed by providing an initial value, a condition to end the loop, and an increment value. Here is the format of the **for** loop:

```
for (initvalue;condition;increment) {
    statement block
}
```

A simple example, printing the numbers 1 through 10, will make the **for** loop construction clear:

```
for($number = 1; $number < 11; $number = $number + 1) {
    print "$number ";
}
```

The output of this program is

```
1 2 3 4 5 6 7 8 9 10
```

This **for** loop begins by assigning the value 1 to the variable $number. The program then checks to see if the value of $number is less than 11. Since it is, the program prints the number 1. Then $number is incremented by 1 ($number = $number + 1), and the loop is run all over again until, finally, $number is equal to 11. This makes the conditional expression ($number < 11) false, and the loop ends.

This **for** loop can be written in a more efficient manner by changing the form of the increment step. If you are familiar with C or C++, you know that you can increment a variable using the ++ operator. This operator increases the value of the variable it is associated with by 1. The operator can be placed either immediately before the variable or immediately after it. Deciding where to put the ++ operator will be discussed in Chapter 2. Using the ++

operator instead of explicitly calling the variable name changes the **for** loop like this:

```
for($number = 1; $number < 11; $number++) {
    print "$number ";
}
```

Perl's Built-in Functions

Perl has almost 200 functions built into the language. You have already used one built-in function, **print**. There are many more, obviously, and they can be used to simplify your Perl programs by cutting down on the amount of code you have to write yourself.

A *function* is a set of statements that perform some action on the inputs to the function, called the *arguments*. For example, one of the **print** function's arguments is the text string, or variables, placed next to the function in a line of code, as in:

```
print "this";
```

or

```
print $this;
```

Remember that there is actually another argument to the **print** function, STDOUT, which is the default and can be left out.

The set of statements inside the function perform the proper operations to display "this" or $this to the standard output device. Since you don't actually see the set of statements that make up a function, functions are often referred to as *black boxes*. A black box is something that performs a certain "function", though it isn't known exactly how the function is performed. The important point to remember is that you shouldn't really care how the function does its job, just so long as it does it properly. Your "function" as a programmer is to make sure you give the function the proper arguments so it can do its job properly.

When the set of statements that make up a function finish executing, a final value is calculated and is passed back (or returned) to the program where the function was called. All functions have a return value, even if that value is a null or empty string. Some functions, such as **print**, will return a numeric value based on whether or not the function is successful. **print** returns a 1 if it was able to print its argument, and it will return a 0 if it isn't successful.

Many of Perl's functions will be familiar to you if you are coming from another computer language such as C or Basic. For example, this next small program calculates the length in bytes of a text string using the **length** function:

```
print length("This is a test of the length function");
```

This program will print the number 37.

You can also assign the return value of a function to a variable. Using **length** again, here is an example of this use of a function:

```
$StrLen = length("This is a test of the length function");
print $StrLen;
```

This example will also print the number 37, but this time it prints the number because 37 is the value of the variable $StrLen.

Creating Your Own Functions in Perl

You are not limited to the functions that are part of the Perl language. If you need a function and it is not built in, you can write the function yourself. User-written functions can also be called *subroutines* to distinguish them from the built-in functions, which is what they will be called in this book.

To create a subroutine, use the keyword **sub** followed by a name for the subroutine, followed by a left curly brace. After this, add the Perl statements that will perform the operations that make up the subroutine. End the subroutine definition with a right curly brace. You are now ready to use this subroutine in your program.

To refer to the subroutine, preface the subroutine name with an ampersand (&). Here is a sample program that uses a user-built subroutine to sum a list of numbers:

```
print &sum(2,2);
sub sum {
    $sum = 0;
    foreach $num (@_) {
        $sum += $num;
    }
    return $sum;
}
```

There are several things in the preceding program example that might look a little strange to you. The **foreach** keyword is a looping construct that works with a list of items, such as an array. Each item of the list is stored in a variable (the argument right after the **foreach** keyword) and then is used in the set of statements that make up the loop. The oddest construction in this program is the list argument to **foreach**, @_. Perl has special variables that represent standard groupings of data. In this case, @_ is an array that represents any list of arguments that are passed to a function. As you noticed in the preceding example, the contents of the @_ array are (2,2). The other special Perl variables will be covered in Chapter 2.

Finally, the previous example uses a funny-looking operator, +=. If you are familiar with C or C++, you already know what this operator does. If you come from another language, such as Basic, you may be able to guess what this operator does. It is a shortcut operator for incrementing a variable. The line of code that uses the += operator could have been written "$sum = $sum + $num", but this is considered bad programming style. The += operator is more efficient and has come to be accepted as a standard coding convention in Perl.

Working with Data in Files

Perl works very well with files. It is easy to open files, read data in from files, write data out to files, and close files in Perl. In fact, if you're used to working with files in another language, you will probably find that Perl handles files in a much cleaner way than other languages.

The following program example works with a file consisting of company names, their stock prices, and the number of shares held. The data in the file looks like this:

```
ABC Co., 123.50,1034
XYZ Inc., 23.43,2565
```

The next program simply reads in the two lines of data, multiplies each stock price by the number of shares held to get a value for each company, prints the total value of the stock holding, and then sums the two values to get a total value of stock holdings. Here is the code:

```
$sumtot = 0;
open(STOCKDATA, "compdata.txt");
while($line = <STOCKDATA>) {
    chomp($line);
    ($compname,$price,$shares) = split(/,/,$line);
```

```
    $totval = $price * $shares;
    $sumtot += $totval;
    if ($totval > 0) {print "Total value of $compname holdings:
            $totval\n";}
}
print "The total value of all stock holdings: $sumtot\n";
close(STOCKDATA);
```

The **open** statement in the second line of the program is used to open a file. The first argument to **open** is a file handle, which is a name for the I/O channel between Perl and the file that is being opened. The second argument to **open** is the name of the file to be opened.

The next line is another kind of loop, a **while** loop. A **while** loop loops through a set of statements "while" the conditional expression that follows the **while** keyword is true. In this example, the conditional expression is the assignment of the current line of data, represented by the <STOCKDATA> operator, to the variable $line. As long as there is data in the file, the conditional expression will evaluate to True. When the file is empty, the expression will evaluate to False.

The fourth line introduces a built-in Perl function, **chomp**, that removes the end-of-line character from the line of text. You can end up with some very strange results if you don't remove the end-of-line character.

The next line uses a very powerful Perl function that makes many programmers drool the first time they see it—the **split** function. The **split** function breaks up a line of text based on the first argument passed to it. In the preceding program example, the right-hand side of the assignment statement is

```
split(/,/,$line)
```

The first argument to **split** is the pattern matching operator //, which contains the pattern the operator is supposed to match—a comma. The second argument to the function is the variable $line, in which each line of data is stored. The result of this function is that each line of data is divided into separate data items, based on the position of the comma delimiter.

The left-hand side of the line is a list of variables that will hold the data divided up with the **split** function. The data divided up by the **split** function is assigned, in order, to one of the variables on the left-hand side. So, in the example, the variable $compname gets the first piece of data, the variable $price gets the second piece of data, and the variable $shares gets the last piece of data.

Now we're at the sixth line of the example, which simply calculates the value of the stock holding using the variables created in the previous line. Next, a grand total is calculated by adding the value of one stock holding to the total value of all stock holdings. Finally, if the value of the stock holding is greater than zero, it is printed on the display. You will notice that the variables are mixed in with the text string, a style very foreign to C and Basic programmers. In Perl, double-quoted strings are *variable interpolated,* meaning that you can mix scalar variables with quoted text and the values of the variables will be interpreted when the string is evaluated. This is really just a fancy form of string concatenation. This **print** line also includes an operator you may not be familiar with if you don't have a background in C or C++—the \n operator. \n is used to force the computer to perform a carriage return and linefeed, or, in Perl parlance, a newline.

At this point the program loops back to the beginning of the **while**, continuing until there is no more data. When there finally is no more data, the program continues with the line past the closing right curly brace, printing the total value of all the stock holdings.

Using the Perl Modules

The Perl modules, also called library modules, are collections of Perl code that can be used for specialized purposes. There are two sets of library modules: the standard library that comes with every distribution of Perl, and the rest of the modules, which are located on the Internet at various sites and are known collectively as the Comprehensive Perl Archive Network (CPAN). The contents of the standard library are discussed in detail in Appendix B, and CPAN is discussed in Appendix E.

The modules that come with the standard library and the modules on CPAN perform a wide variety of functions, from error handling to file access to handling network and interprocess communications. Chapter 19 look at many of these modules in greater detail. In this section, a few basic modules will be examined to understand how they are called and used in Perl programs.

The first module we will examine is Cwd( ). This module gets the pathname of the current working directory. To use the module in your Perl program, you declare it with the **use** function. **use** imports the Perl code supporting the module into your program. Here is an example of the Cwd( ) module:

```
Use Cwd();
$dir = cwd();
print $dir;
```

```
chdir ("..");
$newdir = cwd();
print $newdir;
```

On my Windows 95 system, this program produces the following output:

```
c:\Perl\bin;
c:\Perl
```

The line of code that reads chdir ("..") is a Perl function that changes the working directory based on the argument given to the function. The argument "..", if you don't already know this, moves the working directory up one level in the directory structure.

Let's look at another example using an arithmetic module—*integer*. Normally, when Perl does arithmetic, it does floating point operations if the hardware will allow it. The integer module forces Perl to use integer operations from the point where the module is imported into the program. Here is a simple example that shows the difference between Perl's floating point operations and importing integer operations with the integer module:

```
print 11/6 . "\n";
use integer;
print 11/6;
```

This program produces the following output on my computer system:

```
1.83333333333333
1
```

A final example of a Perl module will make use of one of the modules found on CPAN. This module, called Service, is designed to work with Perl for Win32 on the Windows NT operating system. This particular module, unlike the two standard library modules in the previous examples, is made up of more than one module. Here is a Perl program that utilizes the Service module to get a list of the services running on an NT server and the status of each service:

```
use Win32::Service;
$hostName = 'MCM1';
$serviceName = 'Server';
Win32::Service::GetServices($hostName, \%services);
```

```
foreach $srvc (%services) {
   Win32::Service::GetStatus($hostName, $srvc, \%status);
   print $srvc . " " . %status . "\n";
}
```

The output for this program will be something like this:

```
Alerter 4
Computer Browser 4
Directory Replicator 4
Event Log 4
Locator 4
Messenger 4
Netscape HTTP Administrator 1
```

The output lists the service and its status. If the status is 4, the service is running. If the status is any other number, the service is currently not running.

The main difference between this program and the other Perl programs that utilize a module is how this program calls different functions within the module. For example, the **GetServices** function is called in the following line:

```
Win32::Service::GetServices($hostName, \%services);
```

The first part of the line, Win32::Service, tells Perl that the Service module is located in the subdirectory Perl\lib\Win32. Then the actual function is called. Using the double colons in this way is known as using the function's fully qualified name, and this method has to be followed for calling Win32 modules using Perl for Win32. The second argument to this function (\%services) is a reference to a *hash*, which is an associative array in which each element is made up of two parts: a key and a value associated with the key.

A Taste of What's to Come

This brief tour is meant to give you some taste for the power and flexibility of Perl, both as a language and as a systems administration tool. There are many more details to the Perl language and they will be covered in Chapters 2-10. There are also many more uses for Perl, and those will be covered in Chapters 11-24.

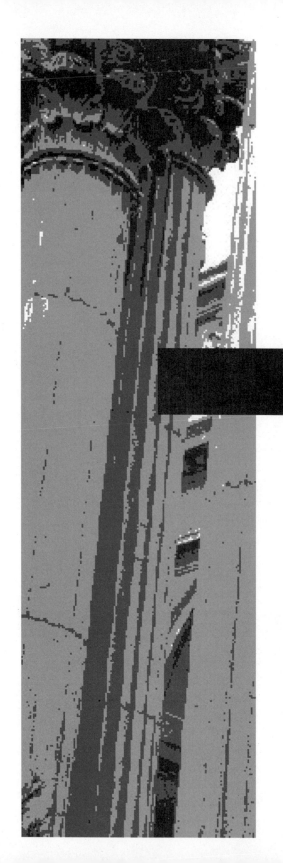

CHAPTER 2

Perl Language Basics—Data Types and Operators

A computer program consists of a series of expressions that taken together perform some sort of function, like a word processing program or an algebra calculation program. Expressions are made up of data and operators that manipulate the data. This chapter introduces the Perl data types and operators that are used to create Perl expressions, which in turn become Perl programs.

Perl Data Types

There are five data types in Perl. Each data type has an identifier so Perl will recognize what it is. The identifier is placed at the front of the variable name. These data types, their identifiers, and what kind of data each type contains are listed in Table 2-1.

Perl is what is known as a *weakly typed* language. If you are a C or C++ programmer, you are familiar with a *strongly typed* language, in which each variable and its data type has to be declared before its use. A weakly typed language simply means that you don't have to declare a variable and its type before you use it in your program. Most, if not all, interpreted languages share this characteristic. Perl is not really an interpreted language, since Perl code is first compiled into an intermediate form before a program is run; but because the compile-link-run cycle is so short and quick, Perl feels like an interpreted language.

Now that the Perl data types have been introduced, the next sections will explain them in detail and show you how to use them in your programs.

Scalar Data Types

The *scalar* data type holds a single value, which can be either a number or a string. A variable that holds a scalar value will be prefaced by a dollar sign ($),

Type	Identifier	Data Contained in Variable of this Type
Scalar	$	Number or string
Array	@	List of values, indexed by number
Hash	%	Group of values, indexed by string
Subroutine	&	Subroutine callable by Perl
Typeglob	*	Reference to anything of that name

The Perl Data
Types
Table 2-1.

which is a mnemonic for "scalar." For example, $example is a variable that holds a scalar value.

To assign a value to a scalar variable, you use the equal sign (=) as an assignment operator (operators are discussed in depth later in this chapter). To assign a string value to a scalar variable, you write an expression similar to the following:

2

```
$question = "What is the date today?";
```

NOTE: Remember, as you learned in Chapter 1, to put a semicolon at the end of every +expression.

A number is assigned to a scalar variable in the same way:

```
$pi = 3.14159;
```

A scalar variable doesn't care if the number is an integer or a real number, so the following assignment will also work:

```
$number = 17;
```

You can also assign a scalar variable the value of another scalar variable, like this:

```
$number = $pi; # $number receives a copy of the value of $pi
```

Scalar variables can be used within strings in different ways depending on how you write the string. For example, if you put a scalar variable inside a string created with double quotes, Perl will perform variable interpolation and put the value of the variable inside the string. The following Perl code listing presents an example of variable interpolation.

```
$name = "John Doe";
print "Hello, my name is $name.";
```

The output of this simple program is: Hello, my name is John Doe. If, however, you use single quotes instead of double quotes to print the string, like this:

```
$name = "John Doe";
print 'Hello, my name is $name.';
```

Perl will output this: Hello, my name is $name. This occurs because Perl will not perform variable interpolation on strings that are written within single quotes.

Writing strings in double quotes is also useful in doing what is called *backslash interpretation*. Here is an example of the newline character, first discussed in Chapter 1:

```
print "After Perl prints this line, it will print a newline.\n";
```

The characters "\" and "n" represent the newline character, which prints a newline to standard output. As long as "\n" is within double quotes, the Perl interpreter will print a newline when it comes across these characters. If, however, you write the following line of code:

```
print 'After Perl prints this line, it will print a newline.\n';
```

Perl will print the line with the "\n" instead of a newline. Single-quoted strings will not support backslash interpretation.

Perl can understand the context a scalar variable is used in and will handle the variable accordingly. Here is a Perl program where the scalar variable is used in more than one context:

```
$millennium = "2000";
print "The new millennium starts in the year $millenium";
print "Or does it really start in the year ", $millennium + 1, "?";
```

This program produces the following output:

```
The new millennium starts in the year 2000.
Or does it really start in the year 2001?
```

In the first **print** statement, Perl recognizes that $millennium is in string context because the variable is within double quotes. Perl uses variable interpolation to substitute the value of the variable for the variable itself. In the second **print** statement, Perl works with $millennium in number context because the variable is outside the double quotes and is being combined with the addition operator. Perl converts the value of the variable to a number, adds 1 to it, and then converts the variable back into a string in order to print it. Variable interpolation can occur only when the variable is inside double quotes.

Array Data Types

Perl has the ability to store a list of data in a variable. This variable data type is called an *array*. An array variable in Perl is identified by an "at" sign (@), which is a mnemonic for "array."

2

To create an array variable, a list of data elements is enclosed in parentheses and is assigned to an array variable, as in:

```
@grocerylist = ("bread", "milk", "eggs");
```

This example creates an array of strings. You can also create an array of numbers, such as:

```
@prices = ( .98, 1.52, 1);
```

Just as with scalar variables, Perl can accept a mixture of numeric data types, so real numbers can coexist in an array with integers (as well as strings) without causing system errors.

Once you have created an array variable and assigned data to it, you can retrieve the elements by referring to its *index number* (also called *subscript*). Like arrays in other computer languages, Perl arrays are indexed by numbers. Again like most other computer language arrays, Perl arrays are zero-based, meaning the first element of an array is number 0, the next element is 1, the next is 2, and so on.

To retrieve an element from a Perl array, you use a scalar identifier with the array name and the index number, enclosed in brackets, like this:

```
$item0 = $grocerylist[0];
```

which assigns the element "bread" to the scalar variable. It may seem strange to use a scalar identifier to retrieve an array element, but remember that you are actually working with a scalar item, the string "bread". You will learn more about arrays as a data structure in Chapter 3.

You can also assign scalar values to an array by using a scalar variable with an array subscript. The following Perl program can be used to re-create the grocery list array created earlier:

```
$grocerylist[0] = "bread";
$grocerylist[1] = "milk";
$grocerylist[2] = "eggs";
```

These statements will create the array even though there is no specific reference to @grocerylist. However, because it has been created, you can reference the array using array context if you wish. Again, operations using arrays will be discussed in more detail in Chapter 3.

Hash Data Types

The *hash* data type is an unordered set of scalar data indexed by a string scalar data item. A hash is also called an *associative array*, but because this data type is implemented using a hash table algorithm, hash is the name Perl programmers prefer.

A hash is created by creating a hash variable by prefixing the variable name with a percent sign.

To assign a set of scalars to the hash, create a list of scalars using a key/value relationship. This means, for example, that if you want to create an itinerary hash for your next business trip, and you want to view the itinerary by day, you would create the following key/value relationships:

```
%itinerary = ("Monday", "Meetings", "Tuesday", "Give talk",
              "Wednesday", "Slide show",
              "Thursday", "No plans", "Friday", "Return
                              home!");
```

The first string in the list is the key, and the second is the value associated with the key. S the first hash relationship in this example is: "Monday," "Meetings."

To access the associated value of the key of a hash, again use the scalar identifier with the hash name and the key for the element you want to access, this time using curly braces instead of brackets to identify the key. To retrieve the itinerary for Tuesday, for example, write the following Perl code:

```
print $itinerary{"Tuesday"};
```

which will print "Give talk."

Hashes are a very powerful data type/structure that will be discussed in much greater depth in Chapter 3.

Subroutine Data Types

Perl, like most other modern computer languages, allows you to create *subroutines* (or *functions*) that extend its functionality. Subroutines are identified with an ampersand (&) and a name.

To use a subroutine in your Perl programs, use the subroutine name prefaced by an ampersand wherever you want the subroutine to execute. Here is a Perl program that calls a subroutine to find which of two variables has the maximum value:

```
$first = 123;
$second = 124;
$largest = &max($first, $second);
print $largest;
sub max {
    my $max = shift(@_);
    foreach $arg (@_) {
        $max = $arg if $max < $arg;
    }
    return $max;
}
```

Don't worry about not understanding the actual code that makes up the **max** subroutine. These constructs will all be explained in the coming chapters.

The subroutine that calculates the maximum is identified with the **sub** keyword. In this example, the subroutine is written after the code that uses it, but it could have been written before the code that uses it, and a subroutine can be called from another file. All of these details and much more about creating and using subroutines will be explained in Chapter 7.

Typeglob Data Types

The *typeglob* data type is used to store a whole symbol table entry, such as an array or a hash.

In previous versions of Perl, typeglobs were used to pass arrays to functions. Perl Version 5 has references that are used to do this, so typeglobs aren't used in this manner much anymore. There are, though, other uses for typeglobs that will be discussed in Chapter 3.

Typeglobs are identified by an asterisk (*) since a typeglob represents everything. One way to use a typeglob is to alias a data structure, like an array. Here is a line of Perl code that does just that:

```
*list = *grocerylist;
```

Now you can access the grocery list using references to $list just as you could by using references to $grocerylist.

Declaring Perl Variables—Global, Lexical, and Dynamic Scope

Only one type of variable has to be declared in Perl programs—the subroutine data type. Other variable types can be declared or not declared, depending on your preference. As has been mentioned, if you don't declare a variable and then make a reference to it without providing it with a value, the variable will have a null or 0 value.

Subroutines, since they are declared, have global scope, meaning that any part of the program the subroutine is running in can reference the subroutine.

Any other variables that are declared or defined by assigning a value to them are normally considered global variables, available to any part of the Perl program the variable was declared in.

There are, though, other scopes within which variables can be defined. These scopes are dynamic and lexical. A dynamically scoped variable, declared using the *local* operator, is visible only to that part of the Perl program within the block of code the variable is declared in. Lexically scoped variables, declared with the *my* operator, are also visible only within the block of code they are defined in, but the difference is that local variables are visible to functions within the defining block, while lexically scoped variables are not visible even to functions.

The difference between dynamically scoped variables and lexically scoped variables is not to be taken lightly. You are less likely to redefine variables if you use lexical scoping, and lexically scoping variables is faster as well.

Here is a demonstration of how the same variable name can be used more than once using the proper scope:

```
$num = 2;
print &power($num,2);
sub power {
   my $num;
   if ( $_[1] < 0) { return;}
   $num = 1;
   for ( ; $_[1]; $_[1]--) {
      $num *= $_[0];
   }
   return $num;
}
```

2

In this example, the first time the variable $num is used, it has global scope. The variable is declared again, but this time within the subroutine **power**. Because it is declared with the *my* operator, this variable has lexical scope and it can only be recognized by Perl code inside the subroutine. Perl creates a symbol table for each subroutine and stores that subroutine's data in the table. Variables within a subroutine that are declared with the *my* operator can be found only on that subroutine's symbol table.

Now that you know what Perl's data types are and how to declare them in your programs, you are ready to learn how to use Perl's operators on these data types to create Perl expressions.

Perl Operators

Data types have to be modified and manipulated in order to create useful programs. Computer languages use operators to perform manipulations and modifications on data. Perl contains a rich set of operators for doing arithmetic, logical, and relational manipulations of data, as well as for doing the things Perl is especially good at, such as pattern matching and text processing. The following sections discuss these operators and how they are used. You will also learn about other Perl operators that will be used in your Perl programs.

Arithmetic Operators

For addition and subtraction, Perl provides the + and – operators. If these operators are used with numbers, they calculate a result in the normal way. If they are used with scalar variables, they first convert the scalars to numbers and then calculate the result.

For example, the pound sign (#) is used in Perl to denote comments that are not executed:

```
print 2 + 2; # prints 4
print 2 - 2; # prints 0
$two = "2";
print $two + $two; # prints 4
print $two - $two; # prints 0
```

To put strings together to make one string, an operation called *concatenation,* use the *dot* (.) operator. For example, here is an example that concatenates two strings together, putting a space between them:

```
$firstname = "John";
$lastname = "Doe";
print $firstname . " " . $lastname;
```

This little program outputs: John Doe. Concatenation is sometimes called *string addition,* and, in fact, early versions of some languages actually put strings together using the + operator.

The *multiplication* (*), *division* (/), and *modulus* (%) operators perform in the standard way. If you are doing modulus arithmetic, the % operator first converts its operands to integers before calculating the result. The / operator performs floating-point division by default. You can use the integer module to do strictly integer division (see Appendix C for details on using modules).

Here are some examples of multiplication, division, and modulus arithmetic in Perl:

```
print 2 * 2; # prints 4
print 2 / 2; # prints 1
print 5 % 2; # prints 1
$two = "2";
print $two * $two; # prints 4
print $two / $two; # prints 1
print 5 % $two; # prints 1
```

Perl also has a special multiplicative operator for strings, the *x* (lowercase) operator. *x*, or the *repetition* operator, returns a concatenated string that consists of the left operand repeated the number of times specified by the right operand. For example:

```
print "a" x 10; # prints aaaaaaaaaa
print "\n" x 5; # prints five newlines
```

You can also use the *repetition* operator to initialize the elements of an array, as in:

```
@allb = ('b') x 10;
print $allb[5]; # prints a "b"
```

2

When initializing an array this way, you have to put the character you are initializing the array to in parentheses to let Perl know you are working in an array, or list, context.

Exponents are calculated in Perl with the ** operator. This operator calculates its result using logarithms, so you can work with fractional powers. But this also means the results of the operation may be different than if you were calculating using multiplication.

Here are some examples of calculating exponents in Perl:

```
print 3**3; # prints 27
print 2**2; # prints 4
print -2**2; # prints -4
```

The last example shows that the ** operator has a higher precedence than the − operator, which used in this context changes the sign of a number. The order of precedence simply indicates which operator will take effect first when there is more than one operator in question. In the example above, the exponent is calculated before the sign change is performed; thus the result is −4 instead of 4. The order of precedence of the Perl operators is listed here.

Terms and list operators

- ->
- ++ − −
- **
- ! ~ \ and unary + and −
- =~ !~
- * / % x
- + −
- << >>

Named unary operators

◆   < > != <=> eq ne cmp
◆   &
◆ | ^
◆   &&
◆ ||
◆   .
◆   ?:
◆   = += − = *=, etc.
◆   , =>

Rightward list operators

◆   *not*
◆   *and*
◆   or *xor*

Perl has operators to automatically increment and decrement variables, the ++ and − operators, also called the *autoincrement* and *autodecrement* operators. If you are a C or C++ programmer, you are already familiar with these operators; if you're coming to Perl from some other language, such as Basic, an explanation of these operators is in order.

The ++ operator is placed either before or after a variable to increment it by 1 automatically. If it is placed before the variable, the variable is incremented before returning a value. If it is placed after the variable, a value is returned before the variable is incremented. Some examples will clarify this.

```
$value = 1;
$new_value = ++$value; # $value is incremented 1 and $new_value is
                assigned the value 2
$value = 1;
$new_value = $value++; # $new_value is assigned the value 1 and
                $value is incremented 1
```

The same order of execution occurs when using the − operator. For example:

```
$value = 2;
$new_value = --$value; # $value is decremented 1 and $new_value is
             assigned the value 1
$value = 2;
$new_value = $value--; # $new_value is assigned the value 2 and
             $value is decremented 1
```

2

If you have trouble remembering the order of evaluation when using the autoincrement and autodecrement operators, the most obvious rule is that when the operator comes before the variable, perform the operation first. When the operator comes after the variable, perform the assignment first.

Relational Operators

Relational operators compare how data items in Perl relate to one another, such as whether or not two data items are equal to each other or whether or not one data item is greater than another data item.

Perl has two different groups of relational operators—one group for string values and another for numeric values. Perl's relational operators for numbers are shown in Table 2-2.

When comparing two data items using a relational operator, Perl will return either a 1 if the comparison is true, or a null string if it is false. The *comparison* operator (< = >) returns –1 if the left operand is less than the right operand, 0 if the left operand is equal to the right operand, and 1 if the left operand is greater than the right operand.

Operator	Meaning
>	Greater than
>=	Greater than or equal to
<	Less than
<=	Less than or equal to
==	Equal to
!=	Not equal to
< = >	Comparison, with signed result

Perl's Numeric Relational Operators

Table 2-2.

Here are some examples of the numeric relational operators:

```
print (5 > 4); # prints 1
print (10 > 20); # prints " "
print (10 >= 10); # prints 1
print (4 < 5); # prints 1
print (4 <= 4); # prints 1
print (4 ==3); # prints " "
print (3 == 3); # prints 1
print (3 != 4); # prints 1
print (3 != 3); # prints " "
print (4 < = > 4); # prints 0
print (4 < = > 3); # prints 1
print (3 < = > 4); # prints -1
```

Perl has similar relational operators for string values. Table 2-3 shows these operators and their meanings.

Here are some examples of using Perl's string relational operators:

```
$item1 = "String";
$item2 = "string";
$item3 = "strung";
$item4 = "Strung";
$item5 = "4";
$item6 = "3";
$item7 = "String";
$item8 = 4;
print ($item1 gt $item2); # prints " "
print ($item5 ge $item6); # prints 1
print ($item1 eq $item7); # prints 1
print ($item3 ne $item4); # prints 1
print ($item5 eq $item8); # prints 1
print ($item1 < = > $item8); # prints -1
print ($item1 cmp $item8); # prints 1
print ($item1 cmp $item2); # prints -1
```

Relational operators, both numeric and string, are often used in conjunction with control structures to determine how Perl programs carry out their execution. You saw the use of a relational operator (<) in the section on subroutines, where the **max** subroutine assigned a value to a variable if one of the arguments was less than the other argument. You will learn more about how to use relational operators with control structures in Chapter 4.

Operator	Meaning
gt	Greater than
ge	Greater than or equal to
lt	Less than
le	Less than or equal to
eq	Equal to
ne	Not equal to
cmp	Comparison, with signed result

2

Perl's String
Relational
Operators
Table 2-3.

Logical Operators

Logical operators are used to test the truth or falsity of two data items. You can also combine relational tests using logical operators. The logical operators used in Perl are && (*And*) , || (*Or*), and ! (*Not*). The *And* operator returns true if both operands in the test are true; otherwise the test return False. The *Or* operator returns the left operand if the left operand is true; otherwise the test returns the right operand. The *Not* operator returns True if the negative of the logical is true; otherwise it returns False.

The logical operators are often called "short-circuit" operators because they determine the results of the logical test using as few of the operands as possible. For example, if the left operand of an *And* test is false, the operator returns False without actually testing the right operand because there is no way the test can be true.

Here is an example of using the *And* operator in Perl code:

```
$a = 1;
$b = 2;
$result = ($a > 0) && ($b > 0);
print $result;
```

The output of this program is 1, or True. The *And* operator (&&) first evaluates the left operand ($a > 0) and since it evaluates to True, the right operand is then evaluated. It is also true, so the result is True and a 1 is assigned to the variable $result.

Here is an example using the *Or* operator:

```
$a = 11;
$result = $b || $a;
```

In this example, the value of $result will be 11 because $b is not defined and thus will evaluate to False. $a does have a value, however, so its value is assigned to $result.

Finally, here is an example using the *Not* operator:

```
print "Not a" if !$a; # an alternate if...then form
```

This example will print "Not a" because the variable $a is not defined.

You can also use the operators *and*, *or*, and *not* instead of &&, ||, and !. They work the same but have lower precedence.

Assignment Operators

You have already seen many examples of the basic *assignment* operator, the equal sign (=). Perl has many, many more assignment operators, copying all the C *assignment* operators and adding a few of its own. All of Perl's *assignment* operators, with examples, are shown in Table 2-4.

As you can see in the examples, each *assignment* operator requires the following elements: a left-side value (called an *lvalue*), the *assignment* operator, and a right-side value (called an *rvalue*).

You can also make more than one assignment in a single expression in Perl, unlike some languages. For example, the following line of code is perfectly legal:

```
$a = $b = $c = $d = $e = "Nothing"; # all variables are set to
                "Nothing"
```

Bitwise Operators

Perl has a full set of operators to perform *bitwise* operations. The *bitwise* operators are & (*And*), | (*Or*), and ^ (*XOR*, or *exclusive Or*). These operators perform in the same manner as their C (or even Basic) equivalents, if you're

Operator	Example
=	$a = "Hello, world\n";
+=	$sum += 2; same as $sum = $sum + 2;
-=	$sum -= 2; same as $sum = $sum - 2;
.=	$string .= "more"; same as $string = $string . "more";
*=	$product *= 5; same as $product = $product * 5;
/=	$real /= .5; same as $real = $real / .5;
%=	$mod %= 3; same as $mod = $mod % 3;
x=	$string x= 5; same as $string = $string x 5;
|=	$a |= $b; same as $a = $a | $b;
^=	$a ^= $b; same as $a = $a ^ $b;
<<=	$a <<= $b; same as $a = $a << $b;
>>=	$a >>= $b; same as $a = $a >> $b;
&&=	$a &&= $b; same as $a = $a && $b;
||=	$a ||= $b; same as $a = $a || $b;

Perl's
Assignment
Operators
Table 2-4.

working with integers. The following lines of Perl code provide a few examples of using the *bitwise* operators.

```
print 4 & 2; # prints 6
print 4 | 2; # prints 0
print 4^2; # prints 6
```

Perl's *bitwise* operators perform differently when the numbers are stored in string values or when they are operating on a string value and a numeric value. When the *bitwise* operators work with two strings, the result will be another string. When they work with a string and a number, the string is first converted to a number, both values are converted to integers, and the result is evaluated. Here are some examples:

```
print "4.50" & "2.50"; # prints 0.50
print 4.50 & "2.50"; # prints 0
```

Bitwise operators always evaluate to True unless they return the string "0", which means the expression is False. For example:

```
print "True" if (4.50 & "2.50"); # prints a null string
```

Shift Operators

The *bit-shift* operators take the *lvalue* and return its value after it has been shifted to the left (<<) or the right (>>) by the number of bits specified in the *rvalue*. If the *lvalue* or the *rvalue* is a real number, the result will still be an integer, in keeping with the nature of the operation. Here are some examples:

```
print 2 << 4; # prints 32
print 16 >> 3; # prints 2
print 16.5 >> 3.23; # prints 2
```

The Arrow Operator

The *arrow* operator (->) is used to dereference references to arrays and hashes. Creating and using references is covered in Chapter 3 and discussion of the *arrow* operator will be deferred to that chapter.

Binding Operators

The *binding* operators (=~ and !~) are used to bind the results of a pattern match, a substitution, or a translation to a variable. These topics are discussed in detail in Chapter 5, but you can get a feel for how the *binding* operators work with some simple examples.

```
$a = "Perl";
print $a =~ /Pe/; # prints 1 meaning True
print $a =~ /No/; # prints a null string
print $a !~ /No/; # prints 1
```

The first *print* expression matches the pattern "Pe" against the value of $a, "Perl." Since the pattern is found within the value of the variable, the result is True and the value 1 is printed. In the second *print* expression, the pattern "No" is not found in the variable, so the value " " (an empty string) is printed. Finally, the last *print* expression uses the negate binding operator to make a True expression, resulting in 1 being printed.

The Range Operator

The *range* operator (..) is used in two different ways. The first way is to refer to a range of numbers, as in 10..20, which refers to all the numbers from 10 to 20. Using the *range* operator in this way is using it in list context. When you use the *range* operator in scalar context, it takes on a boolean value, as in ($a .. $b). If the left operand is False, then the value of the expression is False. If the left operand becomes True, then the expression also becomes True. Here are some examples of using the *range* operator:

```
print (10..20); # prints 1011121314151617181920
print (a..z); # prints abcdefghijklmnopqrstuvwxyz
print "True" if ($a .. $b); # prints " " because $a and $b are
                undefined
```

The Comma Operator

The *comma* operator (,) is also used in two different ways, depending on its context. In scalar context, the *comma* operator is used to throw away the argument that precedes it. C's *comma* operator works just like this, but if you're not familiar with C, you may not understand how this works. An example will clarify this use of the *comma* operator:

```
$var = (256, 640); # the value 640 is assigned to the variable
```

In a list context, the *comma* operator simply separates the items in a list. For example:

```
@var = (256,640); # array var gets two values, 256 and 640
&max(1,2); # calls the subroutine max with two arguments, 1 and 2
```

These uses of the *comma* operator are quite straightforward and you should have no problem using them the proper way in the proper context.

The Conditional Operator

The *conditional* operator is used as a replacement for the if-then-else construct you'll learn about in Chapter 4. The syntax for this operator looks like this:

```
Test_Expression ? If_True_Expression : If_False_Expression
```

The *conditional* operator works like this: the Test_Expression is evaluated. If the test expression is true, the first expression after the operator is evaluated. If the test expression is false, the expression after the colon is evaluated. Here is an example:

```
$a = 20;
$b = 35;
($a > $b) ? (print "a is greater than b") : (print "b is greater
          than a");
```

In this example, the program will print "b is greater than a", since the test expression is False.

You can also use the *conditional* operator in assignment statements, like this:

```
$a = 20;
$b = 35;
$c = ($a > $b) ? $a : $b; # assigns the variable $c the value 35
```

Summary

Data types and operators are the nuts and bolts of any programming language. One of Perl's greatest strengths is its high-level built-in data types and the number of operators you can use to perform operations on those data types. Using these operators in conjunction with Perl's control structures (the subject of Chapter 4), you can write Perl programs that solve complex problems.

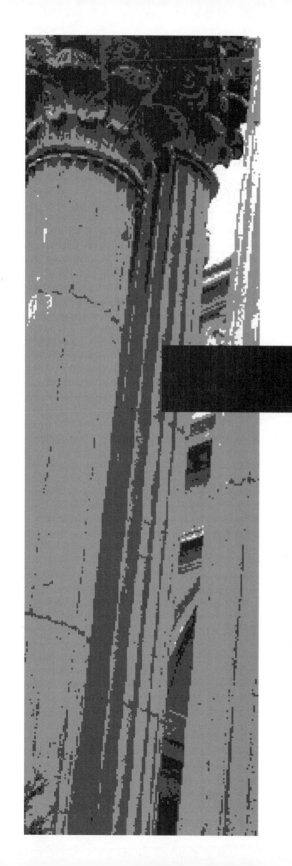

CHAPTER 3

Basic Perl Data Structures

In order to solve programming problems of any complexity, a Perl programmer has to be able to create structures of data. Creating data structures allows the programmer to avoid worrying about the inherent messiness of data and concentrate on creating a program to solve the problem at hand. Chapter 2 introduced the basic data structures of Perl— arrays and hashes—as data types. This chapter shows you how to use arrays and hashes as data structures; it also introduces references, which can be used with arrays and hashes to create more advanced data structures, such as arrays of hashes, hashes of arrays, and other types of nested data structures.

Arrays

The *array* is probably the most fundamental of all data structures and is present in almost every programming language in some form or another. The array is considered a fundamental data structure because it so closely mimics how data is stored in the computer's memory. Unlike arrays in most other computer languages, arrays in Perl are dynamic, meaning that they are automatically sized and resized. In other languages, an array must be declared as being of a particular size, and then if more storage space is needed, the array must be explicitly resized. In Perl, an array doesn't have to be declared before it is used, and when a Perl array needs more storage space, it is dynamically allocated.

Creating Arrays

An array is an ordered list of scalar data, called *elements,* that are accessed using a numeric subscript, sometimes called the *index.* The first subscript, or index, of a Perl array is 0, as it is in C and most other languages. As you learned in Chapter 2, a Perl array variable is created by prefacing an array name with the "at" sign (@).

Here is an example of creating an array consisting of the numbers 1 through 10:

```
@numbers = (1,2,3,4,5,6,7,8,9,10);
```

The elements that are assigned to an array are separated by commas and surrounded by parentheses. When you are creating an array of numbers like the example above, you can use the *range* operator as a shortcut to listing all the numbers, like this:

```
@numbers = (1..10);
```

Since Perl arrays are lists of scalar data, you can mix numbers and strings in arrays. For instance:

```
@grades = ("John, 95, "Bill", 88, "Mary", 76, "Joan", 100);
```

Other languages, such as C, require that array elements be of the same data type. Actually, that's true in Perl also, but the scalar data type includes both numbers and strings.

There is no requirement that an array actually contain any elements, so the creation of an empty array is legal in Perl:

```
@nothing = ();
```

You can also use an existing Perl array in creating a new array. For example:

```
@glist1 = ("milk", "bread");
@glist2 = ("eggs", "cheese", @glist1, "soda", "crackers");
```

The second Perl statement creates an array that has the following elements: ("eggs", "cheese", "milk", "bread", "soda", "crackers"). When Perl sees an array name as part of a list being assigned to another array, it expands the array in the list and adds a copy of its elements to the new array list.

You can also string array assignments together on the same line if you want more than one array variable to get the same elements. Here is an example:

```
@students = @names = ("Mary", "John", "Joan", "Bill");
```

Both arrays now have the elements ("Mary," "John," "Joan," "Bill"), though each array has its own copy of the elements.

Once an array is initialized, if you assign the array variable to a scalar variable, the scalar variable will get the length of the array, as in:

```
$len = @names;
```

The value of $len is 4, which is the length of the array @names. Notice that when this form is used, no subscripts or brackets are used when referring to the array name.

Finally, if you put a scalar variable in list context (by surrounding it in parentheses) and assign an array variable to it, the scalar variable will get the first element of the array, like this:

```
($len) = @names; # $len is assigned "Mary"
```

Accessing Array Elements

As you learned in Chapter 2, when you are accessing an individual array element, you have to refer to the array in scalar context by putting a $ in front of the array name. To refer to the array element you wish to access, put the element number inside brackets after the array name, like this:

```
$name = $names[0]; # $name gets the value "Mary"
```

Remember that Perl array indexing begins with 0, which is the index number of the first element of an array.

You can use the array name in scalar context to assign new values to an array. Here is a short program that adds a name to the @names array, placing the name at the end:

```
$len = @names;
$names[$len+1] = "Jane"; # @names now is ("Mary", "John", "Joan",
                         "Bill", "Jane")
```

Another way to do the same thing, eliminating the first assignment statement, is to use the @names array directly, like this:

```
$names[@names+1] = "Jane"; # same as the array assignment statement
                           above
```

How you choose to write statements like this depends mostly on your programming style because either way is correct.

A very common access method used with arrays is looping through an array to perform some operation or set of operations on the elements of the array. While Perl's looping constructs will be discussed in Chapter 4, the **for** loop will be presented here because it is such a common means of accessing the elements of an array. Here is a simple loop that prints the contents of the @names array:

```
for ($x = 0; $x < @names; $x++) {
   print $names[$x], ;
}
```

Many of the operators you learned about in Chapter 2 can be used with array access. For example, here is a short program that creates an array of the numbers 1 through 10 and then loops through the array, incrementing each array element by 1:

```
@numbers = (1..10);
 for ($x = 0; $x < @numbers; $x++) {
   $numbers[$x]++;
}
```

This program changes the @numbers array to (2,3,4,5,6,7,8,9,10,11).

You can also increment just one element of an array like this:

```
@numbers = (1..10);
$numbers[3] += 3; # this changes element 3 from 4 to 7
```

This permanently changes the @numbers array to (1,2,3,7,5,6,7,8,9,10).

If you try to assign an array element to an index number that is beyond the current range of index numbers, Perl will extend the array to accommodate the value. For example, if the @numbers array has 10 elements (indexed 0 – 9), assigning a 12th element the value 100 will create the following array:

(0,1,2,3,4,5,6,7,8,9,undef,100)

The 11th element, which has not been assigned explicitly, is given the value *undef*, or undefined. If you try to access this element, you will also get *undef*, which appears as an empty string or null value. It also serves as the value "false" in a conditional expression.

Array Slices

An *array slice* is a special way of presenting a list of elements from the same array. Here is an example of printing the first two elements of the @numbers array as a slice:

```
print @numbers[0,1]; # prints 12
```

The same effect can be gotten by writing the following line in Perl:

```
print $numbers[0], $numbers[1]; # not a slice, just regular
        array access
```

If you are a C programmer, don't confuse Perl's slice syntax with C's multidimensional array syntax. A *slice* is just a number of array elements taken together, still in array context. Perl does not have a true multidimensional array.

You can change the order of the elements of arrays using slices.

Here is an example that swaps the first two elements of the @numbers array:

```
@numbers[0,1] = @numbers[1,0];
print $numbers[0], $numbers[1];
```

The output of this example is 21. The first line uses two array slices to swap the elements of the array, and the second line accesses the array in scalar context to determine that the swap did work.

Array Operators—Push and Pop

One common use for an array in many programs is as a stack. A *stack* is a list of data where new values are added to and taken from the end of the list. Imagine the trays at your local cafeteria and how they are stacked. When you go into the cafeteria, you take a tray off the top of the stack, and when you leave, your tray is returned to the top of the stack (after it's been washed, hopefully). Stacks are used extensively in systems programming (operating systems, programming languages) and are a useful data structure for modeling many real-world problems.

Perl has a set of operators—*push* and *pop*—that perform stack operations on an array. *push* takes a scalar and an array name and pushes the value onto the array, at the array's end. *pop* takes an array name and returns the top, or last, element of the array (stack), removing the element permanently from the array. Here are some examples of these operators:

```
@numbers = (1,2,3); # initializes an array
push(@numbers,4); # assigns the scalar 4 as the last element of the
                    array
$top = pop(@numbers); # takes the last element (4) and assigns it
                        to $top
```

You are not limited to pushing just one value onto an array. A whole list of
scalars can be pushed in the same way one scalar is pushed, as in:

```
push(@numbers,4,5,6,7,8,9,10);
```

Array Operators—Shift and Unshift

Another common data structure that can be modeled using an array is a
queue. A *queue* is a list of data that is operated on by adding and taking away
elements from the bottom of the list, or the first of the array. The *unshift*
operator adds an array element to the first of an array, and the *shift* operator
takes an array element from the first of an array. If you think about it,
shift/unshift work very similarly to *push/pop*, just from different ends of the
list. Here are some examples:

```
@numbers = (1,2,3);
unshift(@numbers,0); # @numbers array becomes (0,1,2,3)
shift(@numbers); # @numbers becomes (1,2,3)
```

Just like the *push* operator, the *unshift* operator can take a list of scalars to add
to the array.

Array Operators—Reverse, Sort, and Chomp

The *reverse* operator takes a copy of an array and returns the reverse order of
the elements in the array. Because *reverse* works with a copy, the original
array (and its order) is preserved. Here is an example:

```
@numbers = (1,2,3,4,5);
@srebmun = reverse(@numbers); # the array @srebmun gets the list
            (5,4,3,2,1)
```

If you don't want to preserve the old order of the array after doing a reverse
operation, simply assign the reversed array to itself, like this:

```
@numbers = reverse(@numbers);
```

The *sort* operator takes an array and sorts it into ASCII ascending order. Here
is an example:

```
@names = ("Mary", "John", "Joan", "Bill");
@names = sort(@names); # @names is now ("Bill", "Joan", "John",
                  "Mary")
```

Beware using the *sort* operator with numbers, however. The ASCII values of numbers are not the same as the numeric values of numbers, so that the list (3,1,5,4,6,25,32) becomes (1,25,3,32,4,5,6) after being sorted.

The last *array* operator to look at is *chomp*. This operator removes newline characters from the end of a string, so that if you have an array of strings with newline characters attached to them, you can use *chomp* to get rid of the newlines at the end of strings. Here is an example:

```
@names = ("Joan\n", "Jane\n", "Mary\n", "Bill\n");
chomp(@names); @names becomes ("Joan", "Jane", "Mary", "Bill")
```

Hash Arrays

A *hash array* data structure is similar to an array, except the hash uses a scalar as an index instead of a number (subscript). A hash array is called a hash because it stores data using a hash table; another name for a hash array is an associative array. Because Perl does store the data in a hash using a hash table, the data aren't in any certain order (as an array is) and you cannot force order on a hash array.

A hash array variable is created by prefacing the hash array name with a percent sign (%). Data in a hash array are stored using a key/value pairing. For example, to create a hash array that consists of a teacher's gradebook, the student would be the key and the student's grade would be the value. This association between a key and a value is why hash arrays are also called associative arrays.

Here is the code to create a gradebook hash array:

```
%gradebook = (
    Mary => 100,
    John => 93,
    Joan => 88,
    Bill => 97,
);
```

Another way to perform hash array data assignments is like this:

```
%gradebook("Mary",100,"John",93,"Joan",88,"Bill",97);
```

Either way will suffice, but the => operator is easier to read when there is a lot of data to assign at one time.

To retrieve data from a hash array, you will use the hash array name in scalar context along with the key of the value you want to get. Here is an example using the hash array from the previous example:

```
print $gradebook{"Mary"}; # prints 100
```

Notice that the key is separated by curly braces instead of square brackets, as with regular arrays.

If you evaluate the hash array variable alone, Perl will print the entire hash array, like this:

```
print %gradebook; # prints Joan88Mary100Bill97John93
```

You probably noticed that the hash array data didn't print out in the order the data was entered into the hash. Remember that Perl stores hash array data using a hash table algorithm, and the order the algorithm selects may not (in fact, probably won't be) the order in which you entered the data.

Using the above example as a guide, creating a second hash array from an existing hash involves assigning the hash variable to a regular array variable, and then assigning the array variable to another hash variable. Here is an example:

```
@grades = %gradebook; # @grades gets Joan88Mary100Bill97John93
%grades = @grades; # new hash gets old hash data
        print $grades{"Mary"};
        # prints 100
```

If you assign an entire hash array to a scalar variable and then evaluate the scalar, you will get a funny result that will tell you absolutely nothing at all about the hash array you assigned. Here is an example, followed by an explanation:

```
$gr = %gradebook;
print $gr; # prints 2/8
```

The value of the scalar $gr is 2/8. This value represents a metric of Perl's hashing algorithm, so evaluating a hash array in scalar context is useful only if you are a Perl porter or implementor and you want to check the efficiency of the hashing algorithm.

Like regular arrays, Perl has a set of operators for performing special functions on hash arrays. The following sections will discuss these operators.

Hash Array Operators—keys

The *keys* operator returns the list of keys of a hash array. This operator is useful if you want to loop through a hash array, accessing each value of the hash by its key. Here is a simple example that prints out all the keys of a hash array:

```
%gradebook = (
    Mary => 100,
    John => 93,
    Joan => 88,
    Bill => 97,
);
print keys(%gradebook); # prints JoanMaryBillJohn
```

As was mentioned above, you can use the *keys* operator to loop through a hash array. Here is another example, using the *keys* operator to print out all the data in the gradebook hash array created above (see Chapter 4 for an explanation of the **foreach** construct):

```
foreach $key (keys $gradebook) {
    print $key . ": " $gradebook{$key} . "\n";
}
```

This code prints the following:

```
Joan: 88
Mary: 100
Bill: 97
John: 93
```

If you use the *keys* operator in an assignment statement, it will return the number of keys in the hash array. For example:

```
$num_keys = keys(%gradebook);
print $num_keys; # prints 4
```

Hash Array Operators—Values

The *values* operator returns the values assigned to a hash array. Here is an example that takes the grades from the gradebook hash array and assigns them to a regular array:

```
%gradebook = (
    Mary => 100,
    John => 93,
    Joan => 88,
    Bill => 97,
);
@grades = values(%gradebook);
print @grades; # prints 881009397
```

A more useful way to use the *values* operator with the gradebook hash array is to use the operator to sum the grades to get a class average. Here is the code to do this, using the *keys* operator from the section above and the gradebook hash array:

```
@grades = values(%gradebook);
$sum = 0;
foreach $grade (@grades) {
    $sum += $grade;
}
$num_grades = keys(%gradebook);
$avg = $sum / $num_grades;
print "The class average is $avg."; # prints The class average is 94.5.
```

Hash Array Operators—Each

In the section above, the *keys* operator was used to loop through a hash array to access each key/value pair of the hash. A more efficient way to accomplish this task is to use the *each* operator. This operator returns each key/value pair of a hash array as a two-element list. To use *each*, you will have to create some looping structure so that the operator is able to iterate through the whole hash array. When the last key/value pair of the hash array has been accessed, *each* returns an empty list.

Here is an example of using *each* to print out the names and grades from the gradebook hash array, much like you saw in the section on the *keys* operator:

```
%gradebook = (
    Mary => 100,
    John => 93,
    Joan => 88,
    Bill => 97,
);
while (($name, $grade) = each(%gradebook)) {
    print "$name: $grade\n";
}
```

The list of names and grades is printed from this code just like the earlier example using the *keys* operator, until the hash runs out of elements and a null assignment is given to the variable list.

Hash Array Operators—Delete

The last function you will need to be able to perform is deletion. Perl provides an operator to delete key/value pairs from a hash array—*delete*. You delete items from a hash array just like you look up an item, except you preface the reference with the *delete* operator, like this:

```
delete $gradebook("John"); # deletes John/97 from the hash array
```

The hash array now has the value Joan88Mary100Bill93.

References and Multidimensional Arrays

Unlike other languages, Perl's array capabilities do not include multiple dimensions. For historical as well as practical purposes, Perl has always relied on mainly flat data structures, such as one-dimensional arrays. However, for some applications, such as matrix mathematics, multidimensional arrays are a more natural data structure. You can build multidimensional arrays in Perl with just a little bit of work, and the following sections will describe how to do just that, using an advanced Perl feature called a *reference*.

Creating Anonymous Arrays Using References

In Perl, you can create two types of references—*symbolic* and *hard*. A symbolic reference is when you assign a scalar variable to another scalar variable, like this:

```
@students = ("Mary", "John", "Joan", "Bill");
$students = $students[0];
```

The second assignment statement, where $students is assigned the value of $students[0], is a symbolic reference, where the variable $students refers to the variable $students[0], which is actually just a placeholder, or container, for the value "Mary". A hard reference refers to the actual value itself, without storing the value in a scalar variable.

Internally, Perl, like most languages, stores scalar variables and their associated values in a symbol table. Normally, when you call a scalar in your program, Perl looks up the value associated with the scalar variable being called. The scalar variable and the value are tied together by a hard reference. If you assign a scalar variable to another scalar variable, they are tied together by a symbolic reference, the symbol being the scalar variable being assigned to the other scalar. However, there is still a hard reference to the underlying value, so that when the new scalar variable is called, an associated value can be pulled in.

What all this reference talk has to do with multidimensional arrays is this: when you create a multidimensional array in Perl, you are actually creating an array of references to array. This happens because the only built-in Perl array is a one-dimensional array, but we're jumping ahead of ourselves here.

To understand how references work in Perl, we will look at the simple example of creating an anonymous array, which actually involves creating a reference to an anonymous array.

An *anonymous* array is an unnamed array that is assigned to a scalar variable. This is done by surrounding the data of the array in brackets. Here is an example:

```
$students = ["Mary", "John", "Joan", "Bill"];
```

Notice that the variable being assigned the array data is in scalar context, so we are not creating an actual array, but a hard reference to array data.

Getting at the data in a referenced scalar variable is called "dereferencing" the variable. The best way to dereference the data in a referenced array is by using the *arrow* operator (->).

The *arrow* operator works by putting it after the scalar variable and then adding the array subscript you are actually trying to get. To get the first element of the anonymous array created above, you can write this line of code:

```
print $students->[0]; # prints Mary
```

Another way to dereference the array data is to use variable name ($students) in a scalar context. First, it is important to know that when the anonymous array data is assigned to a scalar variable, that scalar cannot be used in scalar context. If you do use a scalar variable this way, the value of the variable will be an internal Perl representation of the anonymous array, as in:

```
$students = ["Mary", "John", "Joan", "Bill"];
print $students; # prints ARRAY(0xc70858)
```

Trying to get at the data as you would a regular array results in the empty string:

```
print $students[0]; # prints the empty string
```

However, the following statement will print the first element of the anonymous array:

```
print $$students[0]; # prints Mary
```

The first dollar sign, instead of being an identifier for a scalar variable, is the dereferencing operator. For very simple anonymous arrays, you can choose to use either the -> operator or $.

Now that you understand the basic concepts of referencing and anonymous arrays, we can discuss using these features to create multidimensional arrays in Perl.

Creating Multidimensional Arrays in Perl

A multidimensional array is created in Perl by creating a list (array) of anonymous arrays. The best way to explain how to do this is to actually create the array first, and comment on what has happened afterwards; so here goes:

```
@gradebook = (
    ["Mary", 100, 94, 88, 92],
```

```
        ["John", 93, 79, 89, 96],
        ["Joan", 88, 92, 91, 99],
        ["Bill", 97, 98, 96, 100],
    );
```

The multidimensional array is set up just like a regular array, with the elements of the array being themselves anonymous arrays. To access an element of the array, you can use a syntax that looks like the syntax you would use with multidimensional arrays in C. Here is an example:

```
print $gradebook[1][3]; # prints 89
```

You are probably wondering why the above syntax works, when you just learned that to dereference anonymous arrays you should use the -> operator, as in:

```
print $gradebook[1]->[3]; # prints 89
```

You can use the double-bracket notation because there is an implied -> operator between every set of adjacent brackets. So, again, you can use either construct for getting the elements of a multidimensional array.

To print out the whole multidimensional array, you will have to loop through the array, using some sort of looping structure. Here is a simple way to do this, using a **for** loop:

```
@gradebook = (
    ["Mary", 100, 94, 88, 92],
    ["John", 93, 79, 89, 96],
    ["Joan", 81, 92, 91, 99],
    ["Bill", 97, 98, 96, 100]
);
for $array ( @gradebook ) {
    print " @$array \n";
}
```

The **for** loop will print the following output:

```
Mary 100 94 88 92
John 93 79 89 96
Joan 81 92 91 99
Bill 97 98 96 100
```

There are, of course, other ways to print the elements of a multidimensional array, but those will be left as exercises for the reader (I've just been waiting to say that).

Now that we've seen how to print out the elements of a multidimensional array, let's look at a method for creating one from a file. The file contains the data of the gradebook, with one student and their grades per line, like this:

```
Mary 100 94 88 92
John 93 79 89 96
Joan 81 92 91 99
Bill 97 98 96 100
```

The following program will read in a line from the file and assign it to a row in the array. A more thorough explanation follows the code:

```
open(IN,"grades");
while(<IN>) {
    @tmp_array = split;
    push @gradebook, [ @tmp_array ];
}

close(IN);
```

The first line opens the file that contains the data to put into the array. The **open** function takes two arguments—a filehandle name (IN) and the file to open. The next line starts a loop that will run while there is something in the file. When **while** comes to an empty line, it will transfer control to the line after the closing curly brace. The next line creates a temporary array and assigns the results of the **split** function to a row. The **split** function normally splits a line of text into substrings based on a pattern given to the function, but in this case, because no pattern is given, **split** just returns the whole string, the result of which is assigned to the temporary array.

The next line takes the row just added to the temporary array and pushes it onto the gradebook array.

To end the chapter, here is an example that reads the grades file into a multidimensional array and sums the grades for each student. This program can then be used as a basis for averaging grades, ranking students, etc.

```
open(IN,"grades");
while(<IN>) {
    @tmp_array = split;
    push @gradebook, [ @tmp ];
}
for $x ( 0 .. $#gradebook ) {
    for $y ( 1 .. $#{gradebook[$x]} ) {
        $sum += $gradebook[$x][$y];
    }
    if $sum > 0 { print $sum . "\n"; };
    $sum = 0;
}

close(IN);
```

Summary

This chapter showed you how Perl structures data so that you can perform operations on it. Perl provides you with very powerful data structures that can go a long way in helping you to solve even the most complex programming problem. Successful programming is often dependent upon choosing the most appropriate data structure for the problem at hand.

Now that you have an understanding of Perl's data structures, you are ready to learn to manage the flow of execution of your Perl program so that you can efficiently work with the data stored in your data structures. Chapter 4 discusses the various control structures you can use in Perl to control the execution of your programs.

CHAPTER 4

Control Structures

Only simple programs are executed strictly in linear order. More complex programs require that conditions be tested and acted upon appropriately. Some conditions will require that a statement or block of statements be executed based on the boolean value of the condition (often an expression). Some conditions will require that a statement or block of statements be executed over and over again a specified number of times, or until a condition is met or satisfied. These different ways of handling conditions are called *control structures,* and they are a critical part of almost all Perl programs.

Perl includes the following control structures, which are examined in detail in the sections that follow:

◆   **if/else**
◆   nested **if/else**
◆   **unless**
◆   **while**
◆   **until**
◆   **do...while** and **do...until**
◆   **for**
◆   **foreach**

Finally, three operators are discussed that allow you to break out of a control structure prematurely: *next*, *last*, and *redo*. These operators are necessary because there will be times when a certain condition will require leaving a control structure before it terminates naturally or re-executing the loop due to some condition before the loop ends normally.

The following section examines how Perl statements can be grouped together to form statement blocks. While many (perhaps even most) Perl statements can be executed individually, the Perl programmer will often use a control structure with the express intent of performing some action on a group of statements in sequence. Perl provides a way of syntactically signifying that a set of statements should be acted on as a group through the use of statement blocks.

Statement Blocks

A *statement block* (also called a *code block*) is used to execute a block, or set, of statements after the conditional part of the control structure is tested. A block of statements is made up of one or more programming statements surrounded by matching curly braces. The left or opening curly brace indicates the beginning of a statement block, and the right (closing) curly brace indicates the end of the statement block. A statement block is equivalent to a loop that executes exactly one time.

The syntax of a statement block looks like this:

```
{
    statement 1;
    statement 2;
    statement 3;
    statement n;
}
```

4

The statements in a code block are executed in order, from first to last. The only exception to this is if one of the statements is a *next*, *last*, or *redo* operator. The effect of these operators on the execution of statement blocks will be discussed later.

A code block does not have to have any statements in it to be considered a legal construct in Perl. As we will see in some of the code in this chapter, there are times when you must have to have a statement block, but you don't want there to be any statements to be within the block. To do this, just use the opening and closing curly brace either side-by-side, as in: { }, or on separate lines, like this:

```
{
}
```

Both forms create a legal, though empty, statement block where one is required.

Finally, a statement block can be labeled. This allows other program constructs, like a **goto** or a **last**, to name the block the operator is applied to. A labeled statement block looks like this:

```
MYSTATEMENTBLOCK: {
    statement 1;
    statement 2;
    statement 3;
    statement n;
}
```

Then, somewhere else in the program, you can write a statement like this:

```
goto MYSTATEMENTBLOCK;
```

Now that you have an understanding of how statements can be grouped together to form statement blocks, the control structures that will perform operations on these statement blocks can be discussed.

Branching Structures

The first types of control structures to look at are called *branching* structures. These control structures test a conditional expression and then transfer (branch) control of the program to a different line of the program. We will look at two branching structures: the **if/else** statement (and nested **if/else** statements) and the **unless** statement.

The if/else Statement

Let's start with the basic **if/else** structure. Here is the syntax:

```
if (expression){
   statement block
} else {
      statement block
}
```

This form of the **if/else** structure executes by first evaluating the expression after the **if** keyword. If the expression evaluates to True, then the statement block immediately following the opening curly brace is executed. If the expression evaluates to False, then the **else** keyword is executed, which in turn executes the statement block following the opening curly brace after **else**.

The following small program implements a withdrawal function from the world of banking:

```
$account_balance = 5000;

print "Enter the amount you would like to withdraw: ";
$wd = <STDIN>;
chop($wd);
if ($wd < $account_balance) {
```

```
    $account_balance = $account_balance - $wd;
    print "Please take your money.\n";
    print "Thank you.\n";
} else {
    print "You have insufficient funds for this transaction.\n";
}
```

If the value of $wd is less than the value of $account_balance, the amount of the $wd is subtracted from $account_balance and two messages are printed. If, however, the value of $wd is greater than the value of $account_balance, then the **else** part of the structure is executed and the "insufficient funds" message is printed.

4

The **else** part of the **if/else** structure is optional and can be left out if you don't want any program code executed when the value of the expression is False. Here is an example:

```
print "Enter your password: ";
$passwd = <STDIN>;
chomp($passwd);
if $passwd = $master_passwd {
    print "Welcome to the Master System.\n";

}
```

Nested if/else Statements

An **if/else** statement can be nested inside another **if/else** statement. In fact, you can nest **if/else** statements many layers deep, though more than three or so layers probably means you need to think harder about your program design.

In other programming languages, nested **if/else** statements often get tricky to read and maintain because it is hard to tell which **else** goes with which **if**. In Perl, however, since the curly braces are required for an **if/else** construct, keeping the **if/else** statements straight is easy.

Here is an example of a nested **if/else**:

```
print "Enter the amount you would like to withdraw: ";
$wd = <STDIN>;
chomp($wd);
if ($wd < $account_balance) {
    $account_balance = $account_balance - $wd;
```

```
if ($account_balance < 100) {
    print "Your transaction is approved, \n";

    print "but your account is below the allowed limit. \n";

    print "Please make a deposit soon.\n";
} else {
        print "Your transaction is approved.\n";
}
    print "Please take your money.\n";
    print "Thank you.\n";
} else {
    print "You have insufficient funds for this transaction.\n";
}
```

In the preceding example above, it is easy to see follow the nesting of the **if/else** statements because a logical indentation style is used. Also, as was mentioned earlier, Perl's required use of the opening and closing curly braces in a **for** loop keeps nested **if/else** statements in order. Here is an example of several nested **if/else** statements written without indentation:

```
$a = 2;
$b = 3;
$c = 4;
if $a = 2 {
if $b < 2 {
print "Which if is controlling?\n";
else {
if $c > 4 {
print "Is this if entered?\n";
}
else {
print "Which if does this else go to?\n";
}
}
}
```

Even with the curly braces, this program fragment is hard to make sense of. Indentation, while certainly not required by Perl, makes code a lot easier to read and understand. Here is the previous example indented in a logical style:

```
$a = 2;
$b = 3;
$c = 4;
if $a = 2 {
   if $b < 2 {
       "print "Which if is controlling?\n";
   } else {
         if $c > 4 {
            print "Is this if entered?\n";
         } else {
             print "Which if does this else go to?\n";
         }
    }
}
```

4

if/elsif Statements

For more complex conditional statements, you can use the **elsif** keyword in
an **if/else** structure. Here is the general syntax for **if/else** with **elsif**:

```
if (expression 1) {
   statement 1;
   statement 2;
   statement 3;
   statement n;
} elsif (expression 2) {
   statement 1;
   statement 2;
   statement 3;
   statement n;
} elsif (expression 3) {
   statement 1;
   statement 2;
   statement 3;
   statement n;
} else {
   statement 1;
   statement 2;
   statement 3;
   statement n;
}
```

The **elsif**s are evaluated in turn until one of them evaluates to True, in which
case the statement block is executed, and program control passes to the

statement following the end of the **if/else** structure. As expected, if no **elsif** evaluates to True, then the **else** statement block is executed. There is no limit to the number of **elsif**s in one **if/else** structure, though it is generally accepted that too many **elsif**s will make a program hard to read and maintain.

The unless Statement

There are times in a program when you want to use a control structure that executes when the conditional expression is False. Perl provides a control structure to do this: **unless**. **unless** says, in effect, "As long as the expression is False, do this." Here is the syntax for the **unless** statement:

```
unless (expression) {

    statement block

} else {

        statement block
```

Perl evaluates the expression, and if the expression is False, the first statement block is executed. If the expression evaluates to True, the statement block following **else** is executed.

Here is an example of **unless** using the banking example from the beginning of the chapter:

```
print "Enter the amount you would like to withdraw: ";
$wd = <STDIN>;
chop($wd);
unless ($wd > $account_balance) {
    $account_balance = $account_balance - $wd;
    print "Please take your money.\n";
    print "Thank you.\n";
} else {
        print "You have insufficient funds for this transaction.\n";
}
```

In this example, the statement blocks following **unless** execute if the expression evaluates to False. If the expression evaluates to True, then the statement block following **else** executes.

Branching structures transfer control of a Perl program from one place to another. Often, instead of branching, you will want to repeat a set of statements over and over again until some condition is met. The structures that perform this looping behavior are the subject of the next section.

Looping Structures

The **if/else** and **unless** control structures are examples of what are called branching structures. The control of the program branches, or transfers, either to either the statement block of the **if** keyword if the expression evaluates to True or to the statement block of the **else** keyword if the expression evaluates to False. The next control structures we are going to look at are *looping*, or *iterative*, control structures. They execute a statement block a specified number of times based on either a control variable or until some condition becomes True or False.

4

The while Statement

while is a construct that executes a statement block over and over as long as its conditional expression evaluates to True. Here is the syntax for **while**:

```
while (expression) {
    statement 1;
    statement 2;
    statement 3;
    statement n;
}
```

Here is an example, again from the banking world, of the **while** structure:

```
print "Enter the amount you would like to withdraw: ";
$wd = <STDIN>;

chomp($wd);
while ($wd < $account_balance) {
    $account_balance = $account_balance - $wd;
    print "Please take your money.\n";
    print "Thank you.\n";
    print "Enter the amount you would like to withdraw: ";
    $wd = <STDIN>;
}
```

This example works very similarly to the **if/else** structure introduced earlier, except instead of just executing the statement block once if the conditional expression is True, the statement block is executed over and over until, in this case, $wd becomes greater than $account_balance. Once $wd does become greater than $account_balance, the control of the program transfers to the line after the closing curly brace of the **while** structure.

If the conditional expression is False when the **while** statement is first executed, the statement block will be skipped altogether, and program control will fall to the line following the closing curly brace of the block. You might want to put a line of code after the **while** structure informing the users that the conditional expression that they thought would take them into the statement block loop tested False.

One word of warning: endless loops are all too easy with a **while** structure. This happens when the conditional expression never evaluates to False. For example, in the banking examples above, if the account balance is never decreased by the amount of a withdrawal (which is itself a bug), then the $wd variable will never be greater than the $account_balance variable. There are times when this is exactly what you want to do, but for many situations an endless loop can be generated when it is not really wanted.

Sometimes you do not want a loop to perform "while" a certain condition is true, but instead want the loop to perform "until" a certain conditions becomes false. The next section discusses a Perl construct for this type of loop—the **until** statement.

The until Statement

The looping equivalent of **unless** is **until**. **until** will cause the statement block to loop until the conditional expression becomes true. Here's yet another example from the banking world:

```
print "Enter the amount you would like to withdraw: ";
$wd = <STDIN>;
chop($wd);
until ($wd > $account_balance) {
    $account_balance = $account_balance - $wd;
    print "Please take your money.\n";
    print "Thank you.\n";

    print "Enter the amount you would like to withdraw: ";

    $wd = <STDIN>;
```

```
    chop($wd);
}
```

This example looks very similar to the **unless** example we examined earlier. Of course, we are looping through the statement block instead of just executing it once, as long as the conditional expression evaluates to False. Just as with **while** (except for how we expect the conditional expression to evaluate), if the conditional expression evaluates to True, the entire statement block is skipped, and program control transfers to the line right after the closing curly brace.

The next section discusses a looping structure that will be familiar to those of you who have experience with C or Fortran—the **do** loop.

Using the do Function to Create do...while and do...until

Perl does not actually have either the **do...while** or **do...until** structure built into the language. However, Perl does have a **do** function, which, when combined with the **while** statement or the **until** statement, can be the functional equivalents of **do...while** and **do...until**. You will want to use a **do...while** or a **do...until** when you want the loop to be evaluated at least once before the conditional expression is tested. Putting the **while** or the **until** at the bottom of the loop, instead of the top, guarantees that this will happen.

The syntax of the **do** function is quite simple:

```
Do {
    statement 1;
    statement 2;
    statement 3;
    statement n;
}
```

To make a **do...while** or **do...until** structure, simply add the looping construct (a **while** or **until** statement) to the end of the **do**, after the closing curly brace. Here is an example of **do...while** that prints the numbers 1 through 10 on the same line:

```
$x = 0;
do {
```

```
    $x++;
    print "$x ";
} while ($x < 10);
```

It is important to remember that putting the looping construct at the
bottom of the **do** loop will generate one more execution of the loop than
if the looping construct is at the top of the loop. Here is an attempt to write
the previous example above using a conditional test that really belongs at
the top of the loop:

```
$x = 0;
do {
    $x++;
    print "$x ";
} while ($x <= 10);
```

When this example is run, the following line is printed:

```
1 2 3 4 5 6 7 8 9 10 11
```

This result is one more number than was intended and results from the
conditional test being at the bottom of the loop. The variable $x is assigned
11 and is printed before the expression "11 <= 10" is tested. Changing "less
than or equal to" to "less than" insures that the loop will stop after $x is
assigned 10.

The same example can be written using a **do...until**. All that has to be done
is to change the conditional test from "less than or equal to" to "greater than
or equal to". Here is the code for the **do...until**:

```
$x = 0;
do {
    $x = $x + 1;
    print "$x ";
} until ($x >= 10);
```

Another way to write this code fragment using the **until** statement is to
replace the "less than or equal to" with "equal to", as in:

```
$x = 0;
do {
    $x = $x + 1;
```

```
    print "$x ";
} until ($x eq 10);
```

CAUTION: If you use "=" instead of "eq" for the conditional test in the preceding program fragment, you will not get the results you expect. Remember that Perl stores scalar variables (such aslike $x) and constants (such as 10) as strings, even if a number is assigned to the variable. Perl then makes conversions from string data to numeric data "on the fly" when necessary. You have to use string comparison operators on these data types if you want to get the proper results.

4

The **do...until** loop, like the **until** statement, is used when you want to loop through a statement block until the conditional expression becomes True.

Many programming situations that require a looping structure will also be situations in which the programmer wants to control how many times the statement block inside the loop gets executed. For example, you may want to create a loop that increments a value by another value six times. The Perl control structure used for this type of loop is the **for** loop.

The for Loop

The **for** loop is a more complex looping structure than a **do**-constructed loop because the **for** loop is used when you want to have a lot more control over how the structure loops through the statement block. This will become clear when we look at an example, but first, here is the syntax of the **for** loop:

```
for (InitialExpression; TestExpression; IncrementExpression) {
    statement 1;
    statement 2;
    statement 3;
    statement n;
}
```

The **for** loop uses the InitialExpression to set an initial value for the control variable that will determine how many times the statement block is looped through. TestExpression determines the condition to terminate looping, and IncrementExpression defines an amount to increase or decrease the value of the control variable for each loop. Here is a simple example of a **for** loop used to print the numbers 1 through 100:

```
for ($x = 1; $x <= 100; $x++){
   print "$x ";
}
```

In this example, the control variable is $x, which is given an initial value of 1. The test expression declares that **for** will loop through the statement block as long as $x is less than or equal to 100. When this condition is no longer true, control will be transferred to the line after the closing curly brace. Finally, the increment expression says to increment $x by 1 each time through the loop.

Here is another example with more than one statement in the statement block:

```
for ($x = 1; $x <= 100; $x++) {
   $z = $x * $x;
   print "$x ", "$z ";
}
```

This example squares each value of $x and assigns it to $z as it loops, and prints both $x and $z.

The increment step of a **for** loop does not have have to be an increment, it can be a decrement. For example, the following **for** loop will count down from 100 to 1:

```
for ($x = 100; $x >= 1; $x--){
   print "$x ";
}
```

Finally, the increment/decrement step in a **for** loop can be any value, not just 1, as has been used in the previous examples. Here is a **for** loop that prints only the odd numbers between 1 and 100:

```
for ($x = 1; $x <= 100; ($x += 2)) {
   print "$x ";
}
```

The increment/decrement step can be any legal statement that changes the value of the control variable, so in this example we have $x increase by 2 for each loop through the statement block. This ensures that each value of $x will be odd, since we initially assigned $x the value 1.

The syntax for the **for** loop used in this section is the standard syntax as defined by the creator of Perl. You can, however, vary this syntax for various purposes. The next section shows how to change the syntax of the **for** loop to achieve certain effects.

Variations of the for Loop

4

You can vary the **for** loop several different ways to achieve the results you need for your program. The first variation is to leave out the increment part of the **for** syntax. When there is no increment to a **for** loop, the control variable stays at its initialized value and the loop continually repeats, checking the test expression each time. The **for** loop itself, since it isn't incrementing the control variable, cannot cause the test expression to become true. Usually, you will use this type of **for** loop when you want input from the user to cause the **for** loop to stop. Here is an example of a **for** loop that terminates when the user enters a number outside of a range:

```
for ($x = 1; $x < 125;) {
    print "Enter a number: ";
    $x = <STDIN>;
    print $x;
}
```

There is no increment of $x in the **for** loop. The loop continually asks the user to input a number and then prints the number as long as the number is less than 125. If the user enters 125 or greater, the **for** loop stops, and program control transfers to the line after the closing curly brace.

Another way to vary the structure of the **for** loop is to move the initialization expression out of the body of the loop and to also put the increment expression outside the parentheses of the loop. This is generally done only when the value of the control variable has to be computed by some complex process that should not be done within the body of the **for** loop. Here is a code fragment that shows a **for** loop with the control variable initialization outside the body of the loop:

```perl
$x = 1;
for (; $x <= 10; ) {
    print "$x ";
    $x++;
}
```

This code fragment will print the numbers 1 through 10, but only the test expression is contained in the parenthetic portion of the **for** loop. This code fragment could have been written like this:

```perl
$x = 1;
for (; $x <= 10; $x++) {
    print "$x ";
}
```

Still another variation of the **for** loop is to have more than one initialization expression and increment expression. Here is another example, but this time the **for** loop counts up from 0 to 10 with one variable and counts down from 10 to 0 with another variable:

```perl
for ($x = 0, $y = 10; $x <= 10; $x++, $y--) {
    print "$x " . "$y " . "\n";
}
```

The output of this **for** loop is:

```
0 10
1 9
2 8
3 7
4 6
5 5
6 4
7 3
8 2
9 1
10 0
```

Notice that there is only one test expression. There cannot be more than one test expression in the **for** loop, or the program will simply skip past the loop.

Some variations of the **for** loop are used as timing mechanisms for programs. For example, a **for** loop that has no increment, test, or increment expressions and no statements in its body will create an infinite loop. Here is an example of a **for** loop that can only be stopped by using your computer system's Program Break command:

```
for (;;) {
}
```

4

You will probably never use this form of a **for** loop in your Perl programs, but it is a legal way to use a **for** loop. Even though no initial, test, or increment expressions are used, the semicolons for the initial and test expressions must be written within the parentheses. Also, even though the loop has no statements to operate on, the opening and closing curly braces must be written since the **for** loop expects a statement to be placed within them; in this case the statement just happens to be the empty statement.

A more common way to use a **for** loop as a timer is to have a loop perform nothing for a particular number of steps, effectively pausing your computer program. To do this, you initialize a control variable, a test expression, and an increment expression, but leave out the body of the loop (no statement or statement block). This is a very common program construct and one that all beginning computer programmers learn to write. Here is a program fragment that will cause a program to pause while for the duration of the loop:

```
for ($x = 0; $x <= 5000; $x++) {}
```

Even though there is no statement or statement block for the loop to operate on, the **for** loop is expecting at least one statement, so the opening and closing curly braces must be written, just as was seen in the earlier infinite **for** loop.

Perl programs often contain different types of objects that contain data, such as lists and arrays. Perl has a special **for** loop to loop through each item in an object, the **foreach** loop, which is the subject of the next section.

foreach Loops

foreach loops through a list of values, such as an array, copying each value into a variable, executing the instructions in the statement block on the variable, and then moving on to the next item in the list. Here is the syntax for **foreach**:

```
foreach $x (@list) {
    statement 1;
    statement 2;
    statement 3;
    statement n;
}
```

Theis next simple example will clarify the operation of the **foreach** statement. The following code prints the numbers assigned to the array "@numbers" in the first line:

```
@numbers = (1,2,3,4,5,6,7,8,9,10);
foreach $x (@numbers) {
    print "$x ";
}
```

The line starting the **foreach** loop assigns the first value of @numbers, 1, to $x. Then the statement block is executed, and the value of $x is printed. The program then loops back to the **foreach** statement, and the next element in @numbers is assigned to $x. This continues until the last element in @numbers is printed. The **foreach** loop terminates and transfers control of the program to the line after the closing curly brace.

An important effect of the **foreach** loop is that if you modify the value that is copied into the variable ($x in the previous example above), the corresponding value in the list (@numbers above) is changed also. For example:

```
@numbers = (1,2,3,4,5,6,7,8,9,10);
foreach $x (@numbers) {
    $x = $x + 1;
}
print @numbers;
```

In this example, when @numbers is printed, the items in the array become (2,3,4,5,6,7,8,9,10,11) instead of the numbers 1 through 10 that we initially assigned to @numbers.

foreach loops are common to many Perl programs because so much of Perl programming involves performing operations on lists of data in some form or another.

All of the control structures examined to this point have been allowed to terminate naturally through the normal execution of the construct used. For example, the looping structures have iterated through their statement blocks either until a condition became false or while a condition remained true. There are ways to exit control structures before the construct actually finishes execution, and the operators that perform this function are examined in the next section.

4

The Next, Last, and Redo Operators

There are situations in the use of a control structure when you will need to exit the structure before it is allowed to terminate normally (by the test expression becoming true or false). In the early days of programming languages, a **goto** statement would be used to exit a loop or branching structure, but as any decent programmer knows, using a **goto** creates code that is hard to read and maintain. Perl provides two statements, *next* and *last*, that allow the programmer either to force a looping structure to iterate (*next*) or to jump completely out of the loop and move to the line of program code immediately following the closing curly brace (*last*).

Next

The *next* operator is used to force a looping structure to skip all remaining statements in a statement block and iterate the loop. For example, here is a "superstitious" **for** loop:

```
for ($x = 1; $x <= 100; $x++) {
   if ($x eq 13) {
      next;
   }
   print "$x ";
}
```

This example prints the numbers 1 through 100, skipping 13 when it is encountered in the **for** loop by executing the *next* operator when $x is equal to 13. Keep in mind that **next** is executed in conjunction with the **for** looping structure, not the **if** structure it is part of.

Last

While *next* automatically transfers control to the end of the statement block and starts the next iteration or loop, *last* transfers control of the program out of the loop altogether. The *last* operator is used when a condition arises that necessitates leaving the loop prematurely. If, using the "superstitious" **for** loop from the previous example above, encountering the number 13 is a condition for terminating the loop, the following code will work:

```
for ($x = 1; $x <= 100; $x++) {
    if ($x eq 13) {
        last;
    }
    print "$x ";
}
```

This example will print only the numbers 1 through 12. When the variable $x takes on the value 13, the *last* operator is executed, and control of the program transfers to the line after the closing curly brace, skipping the print statement.

Again, just as with the *next* operator, *last* is only executed in conjunction with the **for** looping structure, not the **if** structure *last* is part of.

Redo

While the *next* and *last* operators transfer program control out of a loop, the *redo* operator forces the program to re-execute the loop structure without testing the conditional expression. The *redo* operator can also be used within a statement block to re-execute the statement block beginning at the first statement in the block.

Here is an example of using *redo* in a statement block to create a looping effect:

```
{
    print "Enter your name (Enter 'end' to exit): ";
    $name = <STDIN>;
    chomp($name);
    if ($name ne "end") {
```

```
        print $name . "\n";
        redo;
    ; else (last;)
}
```

This little program will continue to prompt the user to enter his or her name and print it out until the word "'end'" is entered for input. The *redo* operator creates this looping effect by transferring program control to the beginning of the statement block.

Redo can also be used in a looping structure such as **while** or **until** if some condition requires the program to transfer control back to the beginning of the loop. *Redo* doesn't provide the looping effect; it merely causes the program to begin the loop again without evaluating the conditional expression. Here is an example:

4

```
$name = "";
while ($name ne 'end') {
    print "Enter a name (Type 'end' to exit): ";
    chomp($name = <STDIN>);
    if ($name eq "") {
        redo;
    }
    print "$name " . "\n";
}
```

In this program, the user is constantly prompted to enter a name. If the user enters the word "'end'", the program will exit out of the **while** loop. If the user enters a blank line or presses ENTER, the *redo* operator will cause the program to go back to the beginning of the loop and prompt the user again to enter a name.

The same program can be written using **until** instead of **while**, and *redo* will have the same effect. Here is the code:

```
$name = "";
until ($name eq 'end') {
    print "Enter a name (Type 'end' to exit): ";
    chop($name = <STDIN>);
    if ($name eq "") {
        redo;
    }
    print "$name " . "\n";
}
```

The only difference between using a **while** loop and using an **until** loop in these two examples is that with the **until** loop the word "'end'" will be printed because the loop is always executed one time after the condition becomes true.

Simulating the switch Statement

If you're a C/C++ programmer, you are probably wonderinged why the **switch** statement wasn't discussed after the **if/else** statement. The reason is simple: - Perl doesn't have a built-in **switch** statement, though one can be created using the programming constructs that have been discussed in this chapter.

If you don't know what a **switch** statement is, here's a quick explanation. In C/C++, the **switch** statement provides the programmer with a structured, nested **if/else** construct that is more efficient than a series of nested **if/else** statements and is much easier to read and maintain. Here is the syntax of the **switch** statement in C/C++:

```
switch(expression) {
    case constant 1:
        statement sequence
        break;
    case constant 2:
        statement sequence
        break;
    case constant 3:
        statement sequence

        break;
    case constant n:
        statement sequence
        break;
    default:
        statement sequence
}
```

The expression in the first line of the **switch** statement has to evaluate to either to a character or an integer value. Then, each **case** clause is evaluated to see if the expression equals the constant associated with the **case** clause. If there is a match, the sequence of statements following the **case** clause is executed, followed by a break, which transfers control of the program to the line after the closing curly brace of the **switch** statement. If there is no match, and the **default** clause is present, the statement sequence following **default** is executed. The **default** clause is optional, however, and if it is not present and there is no match in the **switch** statement, the program simply drops out of the **switch**, and the line after the closing curly brace is executed.

Here is a very simple example of the **switch** statement in a C++ program fragment:

```
int ab = 50;
switch(ab) {
   case 50:
      cout << "Please make a deposit to bring your account balance
            up.\n";
   case 100:
      cout << "You're okay but watch out.\n";
   case 1000:
      cout << "Can we borrow some?\n";
   default:
      cout << "Insufficient data. Please call customer service.\n"
}
```

4

One limiting factor of the C/C++ **switch** statement is that the **case** clause only works with constants, not conditional expressions.

Here is the same program fragment written using a simulated **switch** statement written in Perl:

```
$ab = 50;
SWITCH: {
   if ($ab < 100) { print "Please make a deposit.\n"; last SWITCH;
}
   if ($ab < 1000) { print "You're okay but watch out.\n"; last
                     SWITCH; }
   if ($ab > 1000) { print "Can we borrow some?\n"; last SWITCH; }
   print "Insufficient data. Please call customer service.\n";

}
```

This simulation begins by having the first **if** evaluate its test expression. If the expression is true, the program prints out the message and then executes *last*, which transfers control of the program to the line after the statement block. If the expression is false, the next **if** statement is tested. If none of the **if** statements evaluate to true, the last statement in the statement block is executed.

An Example Using Several Program Control Constructs

Here is a longer example program that brings together several of the constructs discussed in this chapter. You should be able to read through this program and understand what it does. Here is the code:

```
$account_balance = 5000;
print "Enter your PIN (Press 'Enter' to exit): ";
chop($id = <STDIN>);
while ($id ne "") {
    print "Enter the amount to withdraw (Type 'end' to exit): ";
    chomp($wd = <STDIN>);
    if ($account_balance <= 0) {
        print "You are currently overdrawn.\n";
        last;
    }
    if ($wd eq "") {
        redo;
    }
    if ($wd > $account_balance) {
        print "Insufficient funds.\n";
        print "Do you wish to withdraw a lesser amount (Y/N)? ";
        chomp($yorn = <STDIN>);
        if ($yorn eq "Y") {
            redo;
        } else {
            last;
        }
    }
    print "Please wait while we process your transaction.\n";
    $account_balance = $account_balance - $wd;
    for ($x = 0; $x <= 10000; $x++) {};
    print "Thank you.\n";
    print "Would you like to make another withdrawal (Y/N)? ";
    chomp($yorn = <STDIN>);
    if ($yorn eq "Y") {
        redo;
    } else {
        last;
    }
}
print "Thank you and come again.\n";
```

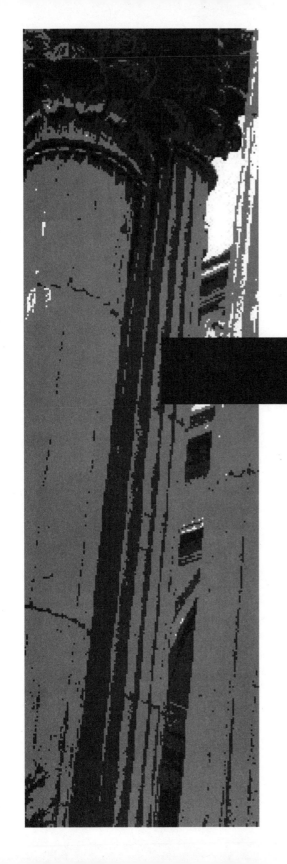

CHAPTER 5

Pattern Matching
and Regular
Expressions

One of the motivations for the creation of Perl was the need for a language that is very good at text processing. Much of what constitutes text processing involves looking for patterns in text in order to process the text in some way. Regular expressions are patterns you create to match against patterns in the text you are processing. Perl will compare your regular expressions with a bunch of text and either return the truth or falsity of the comparison or perform some operation on the text (such as substitution). This chapter will cover in detail the types of regular expressions you can write and how to use them to process text.

Writing Regular Expressions

If you have been working with computers for very long, you are probably already very familiar with pattern matching using regular expressions. When you are looking for a file in your directory using a command such as **dir myfile*.*** (**ls myfile*.*** in Unix), **myfile*.*** is a regular expression the operating system uses to match against the files in the directory.

Simple Regular Expressions

Simple regular expressions in Perl work in much the same way. To create a regular expression in Perl, write a pattern you want to match against some text and surround it in slashes (/), which is Perl's pattern operator and the default pattern delimiter. The following program creates a list of names and then creates a regular expression that tries to match a name or names in the list:

```
@names = qw(Jill Bill Joan Bob John);
foreach (@names) {
    if (/J/) {
        print "$_ ";
    }
}
```

The first line of the program utilizes a handy operator for creating lists, *qw*. *qw* takes a list of elements and surrounds each one with quote marks, which makes creating a quoted list much faster than having to type all the quote marks. Remember that the $_ variable (defined in Chapter 2) is the default variable for most operations.

This program works by matching the regular expression /J/ against each name in the list. If there is a match, the list is printed. The result of this program is the line of text:

```
Jill Joan John
```

You can narrow the scope of the pattern matching by adding to the characters in the regular expression. For example, here is a modification of the program above to search only for names that begin with "Jo":

```
@names = qw(Jill Bill Joan Bob John);
foreach (@names) {
    if (/Jo/) {
        print "$_ ";
    }
}
```

With this program, only the names Joan and John will be printed.

To carry out this example to its natural conclusion, you can search for a whole name by including the name in the regular expression, as in:

```
@names = qw(Jill Bill Joan Bob John);
foreach (@names) {
    if (/Jill/) {
        print "$_ "; # prints Jill
    }
}
```

You can also match multiple characters that are the same in regular expressions. An example of this might be looking for words in a list that contain "oo" in them. Groups of the same characters are matched by including the character and an asterisk in the regular expression. To match words that contain "oo", the regular expression will have to include "o*" in it. This tells Perl to matoch any text that has zero or more of the letter "o" in it.

Here is a program that matches words that contain at least the letters "so" and perhaps more "o"s:

```
@words = qw(soon tune soap baloon);
foreach (@words) {
    if (/so*/) {
        print "$_ ";
    }
}
```

This program will print the following:

```
soon soap
```

5

There are many, many more variations on writing regular expressions than just what you've seen so far. The previous examples are meant to give you a taste for writing regular expressions and pattern-matching programs in Perl. Now it is time to cover pattern matching in depth so you can learn how to write more complicated, and useful, regular expressions.

Pattern Matching

Regular expressions can be written in Perl to match patterns based on one character or multiple characters in a text string. Perl has a full set of operators to handle any of the different types of pattern matching you will want to perform. The next section will cover matching single characters and the following sections will cover matching multiple characters.

Matching Single Characters

The simplest pattern you can write a regular expression to match is the single character pattern. You learned how to write this type of regular expression above, matching the letter "J" against a list of names. You can also write a regular expression that will match any character in a string using the *dot* (.) operator. The *dot* operator simply matches any single character presented to it. Here is an example of using the *dot* operator to match all the words in a list:

```
@words = qw(hello goodbye glass onion birthday warm gun);
foreach (@words) {
    if (/./) {
        print "$_ ";
    }
}
```

This program will print all the words in the list because the *dot* operator matches any character and every word that has at least one character in it.

You can use the *dot* operator in combination with another character to create a more complicated regular expression. For example, to match all the words in a list that contain the letter "g", you can write a regular expression like the one in the following program:

```
@words = qw(hello goodbye glass onion birthday warm gun);
foreach (@words) {
    if (/g./) {
```

```
        print "$_ ";
    }
}
```

This program will print:

```
goodbye glass gun
```

The regular expression matches any word in the list that has a "g" in it, except if the "g" comes at the end of the word.

Another way to match a single character is by using a character class. A *character class* is a set of characters against which Perl will match a text string. A character class is created by defining a set of characters within a left and right square brace. For example, a character class for all the lowercase alphabetic characters is defined as:

5

```
[abcdefghijklmnopqrstuvwxyz]
```

You can write a shortcut for this characters class as:

```
[a-z]
```

Here is a short program that will match all lowercase characters in a text string:

```
@words = qw(hello GOODBYE glass ONION birthday WARM Gun);
foreach (@words) {
    if (/[a-z]/) {
        print "$_ ";
    }
}
```

This program will print:

```
hello glass birthday Gun
```

To match both lowercase and uppercase characters using a character class, you can create the following character class:

```
[a-zA-Z]
```

If you want to match on digits instead of alphabetic characters, you can create a character class of digits:

```
[0123456789]
```

or, in shortcut form:

```
[0-9]
```

Here is a program that will pick out the numbers from a list of words and numbers:

```
@words = qw(hello GOODBYE  9A 909 happiness 9 gun);
foreach (@words) {
    if (/[0-9]/) {
        print "$_ ";
    }
}
```

This program will print:

```
9A 909 9
```

So far, you have seen examples of what can be called *standard* character classes, such as the lowercase letters, the uppercase letters, and the set of whole numbers. You are not, of course, limited to these classes; you can create your own. If you want to match only the strings that have the letters "e" and "s" in them, the following character class will work:

```
[es]
```

Here is a program that will match on strings that contain any of the lowercase vowels in them:

```
@words = qw(hello zzzzz goodbye xxxxx brrrrrr);
foreach (@words) {
    if (/[aeiou]/) {
        print "$_ ";
    }
}
```

This program will print:

```
hello goodbye
```

To make things easier for the programmer, Perl provides abbreviations for the standard character classes for words and digits (and spaces, though we haven't looked at an example of matching on a space yet). The abbreviation for matching on words is \w; for matching on digits, \d; and for matching on spaces, \s, where "\" is the backslash character. Here is an example that matches on digits using the Perl abbreviation for the digit character class:

```
@words = qw(hello zzzzz 909 xxxxx 9 brrrrrr);
foreach (@words) {
    if (/\d/) {
        print "$_ "; # prints 909 9
    }
}
```

The abbreviation for the word character class (\w) is equivalent to the following character class: [a-zA-Z0-9_]. No, the character class you just saw does not contain a typo. The \w class does indeed include the digits 0-9 because, as you'll remember, numbers are treated as strings in Perl unless and until you need to perform a mathematical operation on them. The underscore character is included as part of the word character class abbreviation, making the class equal to the legal characters for Perl variable names.

Here is a program that matches on the words in a list using the \w abbreviation:

```
@words = qw(hello zzzzz 909 xxxxx 9 brrrrrr);
foreach (@words) {
    if (/\w/) {
        print "$_ ";
    }
}
```

This program will print the following:

```
hello zzzzz 909 xxxxx 9 brrrrrr
```

The other character class abbreviation is \s, which is an abbreviation for all the space characters (spaces, carriage returns, linefeeds, tabs, and formfeeds).

You match on a space character in the same way you match on any of the other character classes.

You can also match on the negative of a character class, as in "match all characters that are not alphabetic". To do this, put the caret symbol (^) before the character class you are matching against. If you are using a character class abbreviation, use the uppercase character of the abbreviation instead of the lowercase character. Here are some examples:

[^**a-z**] # matches anything that is not a lowercase alphabetic character

[^**0-9**] # matches anything that is not a number

W # matches anything that is not in the word character class

S # matches anything that is not a space character

Matching on single characters, while important, doesn't reveal the real power of regular expressions. The next section shows how regular expressions can be used for complex text-processing applications by allowing you to match on groups of characters.

Matching Groups of Characters
The real power of regular expressions becomes obvious when you use them to match groups of characters, such as all words with the characters "oo" in them, or all words with "xxxx" at the end of them.

Multipliers   To match on groups of characters, Perl provides special characters for specifying patterns called *multipliers*. The first multiplier is the asterisk (*****), which means match on zero or more of the preceding character. For example, the following pattern matches on zero or more of the letter "a":

```
/a*/
```

Here's an example of matching using the asterisk:

```
@words = qw(bad boy baaaad bear bend);
foreach (@words) {
    if (/ba*/) {
        print "$_ "; # prints bad boy baaaad bear bend
    }
}
```

Using the asterisk is very nonrestrictive, since it will essentially match on anything.

Another multiplier you can use to match groups of characters is the plus sign (+), which matches one or more of the preceding characters. This provides a slightly more restrictive match than the asterisk multiplier since it won't match zero characters. To match one or more of the letter "a" in a string, you can use:

```
/ba+r/
```

which will match one "b", one or more "a"s, and one "r".

Here is an example:

```
@words = qw(bad bark bear baaark bork);
foreach (@words) {
    if (/ba+r/) {
        print "$_ "; # prints bark baaark
    }
}
```

A third multiplier is the question mark (?), which matches zero or one of the preceding characters, and is written like this:

```
/ba?ke/
```

This regular expression will match both "bake" and "bke".

For situations where you want to match a numbered range of a particular character, Perl provides a general multiplier. You can use the general multiplier when you want to match, say, three to five "a"s. To form a general multiplier, you enclose the range in curly braces after the letter you are matching on, like this:

```
/ba{3,5}ke/
```

This regular expression will match "baaake", "baaaake", and "baaaaake", but it will not match "baake" or "bake".

There are several variations of the general multiplier. To match on a certain number or more of a character, leave off the second number, as in /ba{3,}ke/, which will match three or more "a"s. If you want to match a certain number or less of a character, write an expression like **/ba{0,3}ke/**, which will match zero to three "a"s. If you want to match an exact number of a character, write **/ba{3}ke/**, which will match exactly three "a"s.

You have to be very careful using a quantifier in a pattern search, because they will match on anything and everything in the string as long as the match is still successful. This is called "greedy searching." An excellent example of this is the asterisk, which matches on zero or more instances of the pattern. So, when your regular expression looks like this:

```
(/s*/)
```

it will match anything in the string, whether it contains an "s" or not. If you use a quantifier like ".", it will greedily match on anything, even the end-of-string character "\n", if you use the *s* modifier.

Parentheses   Parentheses are used to group patterns that you want to remember for later matching. For example, the following regular expression:

```
/abcd(.)abcd\1/
```

will match "abcdeabcde" but not "abcdeabcdf."

The parentheses go around the pattern you want to remember, and the *backslash* operator followed by a number (\1 in the example above) goes where you want to match on the remembered pattern. The number 1 represents the number of the remembered pattern, so there can be more than one remembered pattern in a regular expression. Here is an example of multiple remembered patterns:

```
/abc(.)def(.)\1ghi\2/
```

In the regular expression above, the \1 matches the character after the "c", and the \2 matches the character after the "f". Of course, the numbers don't have to be in order, so the following regular expression is perfectly legal (though Perl does assign them in the order they're found):

```
/abc(.)def(.)\2ghi\1/
```

Alternation   Another way to group patterns is using alternation, where the match is on, say, an "e" or an "f" or a "g". To say this in Perl, the regular expression is:

```
/e|f|g/
```

using a bar (|) as the *or* operator.

You can, of course, match on alternating multiple characters as well as single characters, as in:

```
/eg|fgh|gghi/
```

For example, the pattern (/bug|bugg/) matches both "bugy" and "buggy".

Pattern Anchors

There are times when you will want the regular expression to match a text string at a particular place in the string, not just at any point as is normal for Perl. To accomplish this, Perl provides pattern anchors to predetermine where a match is allowed to occur.

5

The first pattern anchor (\b) forces a pattern match to occur at a word boundary. Using this anchor, the following regular expression:

```
/heal\b/
```

matches "heal" but not "healed" or "healing".

You can also anchor a pattern on a nonword boundary like this:

```
/heal\B/
```

which will match "healed" and "healing" but not "heal".

Another pattern anchor is the caret symbol (^). A regular expression like:

```
/^h/
```

matches "heal" but not "ahem" or "noah".

Finally, to anchor a pattern at the end of a string, use the dollar sign (**$**). The following regular expression:

```
/h$/
```

matches "noah" but not "heal" or "ahem".

The Substitution Operator

One of the most common uses of regular expressions is to make substitutions in a body of text, say changing all occurences of "ie" to "ei". To do this, you write a regular expression of the form:

```
s/pattern being changed/replacement string/
```

The *substitution* operator has to precede the two patterns. Also, a trailing slash has to be in place to delimit the end of the substitution.

Here is a program that performs a substitution of "ie" to "ei":

```
@words = qw(recieve decieve);
foreach (@words) {
    s/ie/ei/;
    print "$_ ";
}
```

The output of this program will be:

```
receive deceive
```

Substitutions can also be done using multipliers in the regular expression. Here is an example:

```
@words = qw(aaa oooooo bbb);
foreach (@words) {
    s/o+/x/;
    print "$_ ";
}
```

The output of this program is

```
aaa x bbb
```

There are other variations of the *substitution* operator, mostly switch-like operators that can change the behavior of the operator, but they will be discussed later. Next, you need to learn how to match against a variable other than $_.

Matching Against Other Variables

So far, you have learned how to match the text strings held in the $_
variable. There will be times, however, when you need to perform pattern
matching against another variable, such as a scalar. To do this, you need to
use the =~ operator to tell Perl that the pattern you are matching against is
not in $_ and is somewhere else.

The =~ operator works by associating a regular expression on its right side
with whatever is on the left side, which can be any expression that yields a
scalar string value. Here is an example:

```
$string = "Shipshape";
$string =~ /psh/;
```

This program produces no output, but the value of the last expression is true
because the regular expression that is the object of the =~ operator is found
in the scalar variable.

5

You can also perform substitutions using the =~ operator. Here is an example
that changes the spelling of a word:

```
$string = "recieve";
$string =~ s/ie/ei/;
print $string;
```

The output of this program will be:

```
receive
```

Now that you know how to match on variables other than $_, there are some
advanced substitution commands you need to learn.

Advanced Substitution

The substitution examples you have seen so far will make only one
substitution in the target text string. In other words, the following program:

```
$string = "gee gee";
$string =~ s/e/o/;
```

will result in $string being "goe gee". If you want to make a substitution for all occurrences of the regular expression in the target string, you have to append a "g" to the end of the *substitution* operator. Here is the same example as above, using "g" to replace all the "e"s with "o"s:

```
$string = "gee gee";
$string =~ s/e/o/g;
```

Now $string is equal to "goo goo".

You can also put a scalar variable where the replacement string in the *substitution* operator goes, like this:

```
$rep_string = "o";
$string = "gee gee";
$string =~ s/e/$rep_string/g; # same result as above
```

Perl pays close attention to the case of the characters in a string, so that the pattern /e/ will not match "E". If, however, you want Perl to ignore case when doing a substitution or other pattern match, you can append an "i" to the end of the *substitution* operator, putting before or after a "g" if one is there, or in the place where the "g" goes. Here is an example:

```
$string = "geE gEe"
$string =~ s/e/o/gi;
print $string;
```

This program will print "goo goo". If the "i" had been left out, the program would have printed "goE gEo".

Matching Using ?? and reset

So far, you have seen how to match patterns using the // *pattern-matching* operator. Another *pattern-matching* operator is ??, which unlike //, matches a pattern only once. For example, the following script shows how, for a single match, ?? works just like //:

```
$string = "Four score and seven years ago, …."
if $string =~ ?score? {
    print "What's the score?\n"; # this line is executed
}
```

This operator is most often used in a loop where you can use the results of the ?? match to drop out of the loop. Here's an example:

```
while ($input = <STDIN>) {
    print $input;
    if ($input =~ ?\bend\b?) { last; }
    reset;
}
```

This little script will continue to print the value of $input until the word "end" is typed. Each time input other than "end" is typed, the ?? operator is reset by the **reset** keyword. It should be noted that the you can use any of the standard loop-exiting techniques in conjunction with the // operator in order to avoid having to use ?? and **reset**.

The Split Operator

One of the most powerful and useful operators in Perl's repertoire is the *split* operator. *Split* takes a regular expression and a text string as arguments and splits the text string into pieces using the regular expression as a delimiter. For example, given a string:

```
"Mike McMillan, 7200 Walnut Road, North Little Rock, AR, 72216"
```

the *split* operator, with a comma as the regular expression argument, will return the parts of the string that don't match the regular expression (each data item in this example). Here is an example of using *split* in a program:

```
$string = "Mike McMillan,7200 Walnut Road,North Little
        Rock,AR,72216"
@data = split(/,/,$string);
```

@data is now equal to ("Mike McMillan", "7200 Walnut Road", "North Little Rock", "AR", "72116").

Another way to use the *split* operator is to put the result of the operator into individual fields, like so:

```
$string = "Mike McMillan, 7200 Walnut Road, North Little Rock,
        AR, 72116";
($name, $address, $city, $state, $zip) = split(/,/,$string);
```

5

The result of this program is that the variable $name = "Mike McMillan", $address = "7200 Walnut Road", $city = "North Little Rock", $state = "AR", and $zip = "72116".

You can place a limit on how many fields are split. To do this, place an integer value that represents the limit after the data you are splitting, like this:

```
$string = "Mike McMillan,7200 Walnut Road,North Little Rock,
          AR,72116";
($name, $address, $allelse) = split(/,/, $string, 3);
```

When this code fragment is run, $name will contain "Mike McMillan", $address will contain "7200 Walnut Road", and $allelse will contain "North Little Rock,AR,72116".

The *split* operator can work with many different kinds of patterns, not just a specific delimiter. One example that you will see often is splitting a string up into individual words, storing the result in an array. Here's a script that does this:

```
$string = "Four score and seven years ago, blah blah blah";
@gaddress = split /\s+/, $string;
print "@gaddress\n"; # displays "Four score and seven years ago,
                     # blah blah blah
print $gaddress[3]; # displays "seven"
```

In the script above, the pattern that is matched is one or more whitespace characters. So, if the scalar $string had big gaps between the words, only the words themselves would be put into the array. Interestingly, the pattern /\s+/ is actually the default for the *split* operator, so the following script will accomplish the same thing as the script above:

```
$string = "Four score and seven years ago, blah blah blah";
@gaddress = split, $string;
print "@gaddress\n"; # displays "Four score and seven years ago,
                     # blah blah blah
print $gaddress[3]; # displays "seven"
```

The Join Operator
As you may have guessed, the *join* operator is used to glue strings together. Like *split*, *join* takes two arguments, but for *join* the first argument is just the

character you want to join the strings together with and the second argument is a list of strings.

Here is an example of using *join* to glue together a string split using the *split* operator, only with a different delimiter:

```
$string = "Mike McMillan,7200 Walnut Road,North Little
          Rock,AR,72116";
@data = split(/,/, $string);
$new_string = join(":", @data);
print $new_string;
```

This program will print:

```
Mike McMillan: 7200 Walnut Road: North Little Rock: AR: 72116
```

Some Regular Expression Odds and Ends
When you perform a successful pattern match in Perl, each match creates a set of special read-only variables. These variables are named $1, $2, $3, and so on for each match. After a match, these variables are available to you for use later in your programs. Here is an example:

```
$_ = "Four score and seven years ago";
/(\w+)\W+(\w+)\W+(\w+)/;
print "$1 $2 $3";
```

This program will print:

```
Four score and
```

Another read-only variable that gets assigned a value on a successful match is $&. On a successful match, $& is assigned the part of the string that matched the pattern. In the example above, $& is equal to "Four score and".

You can also match the parts of a string before a match with the variable $`, and you can match the parts of a string after a match using the variable $'. Here is a program that demonstrates how these variables work:

```
@words = qw(Four score and seven years ago);
/score/;
print "$`$&$'";
```

This program will print:

```
Four score and seven years ago
```

with $` matching "Four", $& matching "score", and $' matching "and seven years ago".

There are also some regular expression extensions that are quite useful for pattern matching. These extensions are used by surrounding them in parentheses within the regular expression where they are to be used. The first of these is ?=, which is a zero-width, positive lookahead assertion. An example of a pattern that is zero-width is a word boundary, which has a width of zero but, nonetheless, does exist.

An example of how you would use ?= can be seen in the following regular expression:

```
/\w+(?=\s)/
```

This regular expression will match a word followed by a space, but because of the ?= assertion, will not include the space in the $& variable. An example of a string that would match this regular expression is "hello goodbye", where the match is on "hello", but not "hellogoodbye", which is just one word with no space.

Another regular expression extension is ?!, which is a zero-width, negative lookahead assertion. You will use this extension when you want to match a text string that *doesn't* follow the string in the ?! assertion. Here is an example:

```
/\w+(?!\s)/
```

This regular expression will match a word that is not followed by a space. For example, /hello(?!goodbye)/ will match any instance of "hello" not followed by "goodbye".

A final regular expression extension is ?i, which means to use case insensitivity with the particular string you are trying to match, and not in the regular expression itself. This way, if you have some data that needs to be case sensitive and some that needs to be case insensitive, Perl can tune its pattern matching to the data and not have to hard-code case matching into the regular expressions. An example will clear this up. Here is an example of hard-coded case matching:

```
$name = "Abraham Lincoln";
/$name/i;
```

You can alter this program fragment so that the data determines whether Perl's pattern matching should or shouldn't be case sensitive like this:

```
$name = "(?i)Abraham Lincoln";
/$name/;
```

The Translation Operator

Data translation is a special case of pattern matching because it does not use regular expressions. This operator searches a string for a list of characters and replaces them with another list of characters. The syntax for the *tr* operator is:

5

```
tr/SearchList/ReplaceList/cds
```

where SearchList is the list of characters to look for and ReplaceList is the list of characters to replace with. The options c, d, and s are covered in a table at the end of this chapter.

A common use of the *tr* operator is to change the case of a set of characters. Here's an example:

```
$_ = "Now is the time for all good people to come home.";
tr/a-z/A-Z/;
# $_  gets NOW IS THE TIME FOR ALL GOOD PEOPLE TO COME   HOME
```

In this example, $_ is the target of the translation. When $_ isn't the target, you have to use the *binding* operator (=~), like this:

```
$string = "Now is the time for all good people to come home.";
$string =~ tr/a-z/A-Z/;
# $string gets NOW IS THE TIME FOR ALL GOOD PEOPLE TO COME HOME
```

If you don't use the *binding* operator, the *tr* operator will return the number of matches it finds. Of course, you can use this to your advantage if you want to count the occurrences of a character in the target string. For example:

```
$_  = "Now is the time for all good people to come home.";
$num_ohs = tr/o/o/; # $num_ohs gets the value 8
```

When you are doing translations, beware that if the string to be replaced is longer than the string replacing it, the last character of the replacement string is repeated. For example, look at the following script:

```
$_ = "12345678";
tr/5678/123/;
print $_; # 12341233 is displayed
```

In the example above, the string to be replaced is longer than the replacement string. So, the 8 in the string doesn't have a corresponding replacement, which means that the last character of the replacement string, 3, is repeated.

For the final translation example in this section, you can use the d option to delete the specified character in a translation. Here's a script demonstrating how this works:

```
$_ = "now is the time for all good people to come home";
tr/ //d;
print $_; # displays nowisthetimeforallgoodpeopletocomehome
```

In this example, the character to be replaced is the whitespace character, represented by a blank space between the first two slashes. No replacement character is specified, but the deletion option is. The result is that each whitespace character in $_ is deleted, and the string is compressed into just characters.

Options for Pattern Matching

Many of Perl's pattern-matching operators have optional modifiers. The following tables list these modifiers.

Table 5-1 references the options you can provide at the end of a regular expression to control how Perl perfor ms pattern matching. Table 5-2 identifies the different options when performing substitution. Table 5-3 presents the options you can specify when performing translations in Perl, and Table 5-4 lists the different embedded pattern options.

Pattern-matching Codes

Table 5-5 presents the pattern-matching codes you can use in regular expressions.

Option	Description
g	Match all possible patterns
i	Ignore case
m	Handle string as multiple lines
o	Evaluate just once
s	Handle string as single line
x	Ignore white space in pattern

Pattern-
Matching
Options
Table 5-1.

Option	Description
g	Change all occurrences of pattern
i	Ignore case in pattern
e	Evaluate replacement string as expression
m	Handle string as multiple line
o	Evaluate just once
s	Handle string as single line
x	Ignore white space in pattern

Substitution
Operator
Options
Table 5-2.

5

Option	Description
c	Translate all characters not specified
d	Delete all specified characters
s	Replace multiple identical output characters with single character

Translation
Operator
Options
Table 5-3.

Option	Description
i	Ignore case in pattern
m	Handle pattern as multiple lines
s	Handle pattern as single line
x	Ignore white space in pattern

Embedded
Pattern
Options
Table 5-4.

Code	Matches
\a	Alarm
\n	Newline
\r	Carriage return
\t	Tab
\f	Formfeed
\e	Escape
\d	Digit
\D	Nondigit
\w	Word
\W	Nonword
\s	Whitespace character
\S	Non-whitespace character

Pattern-
Matching
Codes
Table 5-5.

Summary

Pattern matching is one of Perl's strongest features and was the major motivation for the creation of the language. This chapter has provided you with an introduction to using regular expressions in Perl to process text through pattern matching. Using the features covered in this chapter, you can (and should) play with creating more complex regular expressions to discover just how powerful pattern matching is in Perl.

CHAPTER 6

Input/Output
in Perl

This chapter introduces you to how Perl handles input and output, both from standard devices (the keyboard and the screen) and from disk files. You have already done some work with Perl output via the *print* operator. To write programs that are interactive, you need to learn how to get input from the keyboard, and in order to save the results of your Perl processing, you need to learn how to read from and write to disk files. All of these topics will be covered in this chapter.

Filehandles

Perl sends data to output devices and receives data from input devices via input/output (I/O) channels. These I/O channels are called *filehandles*. For input from the keyboard and output to the printer, Perl provides two filehandles for you, STDIN and STDOUT, respectively. There is also a prenamed filehandle for I/O errors, STDERR.

For disk I/O, you have to provide a filehandle for the file you are reading from or writing to. For example, if you want to read from a file named "data", you will write a line of Perl code like the following:

```
open(INPUT, "data");
```

This code uses the **open** function to open the disk file for reading data. **open** takes two arguments, a filehandle and a filename, in that order. The filehandle can be any name of your choosing, and it is standard Perl style to put the whole filehandle in capital letters. The filename must be in quotes and has to be the name of an actual file. Because Perl is such an open language, if you try to open a file that doesn't exist, Perl will not report an error, so be careful that you always open a file that does indeed exist.

There is another syntax for writing to a file, which will be covered in the section on file I/O.

Standard Input (STDIN)

When you want to get input from the user in your Perl programs, you will use the STDIN filehandle. (In a different context, STDIN might not mean "keyboard input". This chapter discusses standard input as being input received via the keyboard by the user of the program.) To get input from STDIN, you enclose the filehandle with Perl's operator for reading lines of text, the *angle* operator (<>). Doing this will cause Perl to read the next line of input from STDIN. You will have to do something with the line of input read, and generally you will make an assignment from the *STDIN* operator, either in scalar context or in list context. For example, the following line of code reads the next line of input from STDIN and assigns it to a scalar variable:

```
$line_of_data = <STDIN>;
```

When this line of code is executed, the Perl processor will stop and wait for the user to enter a line of text. When the user hits the ENTER key, the line of input will be terminated.

You need to be aware that the scalar variable that receives data from STDIN will contain the newline character (\n) as well as the data. The following program illustrates this:

```
$line_of_data = <STDIN>; # the user enters "this is a test"
print "true" if ($line_of_data ne "this is a test");
```

6

This program will print "true" because the real value of $line_of_data is "this is a test\n".

Since you normally don't want to keep the newline character, Perl provides a function for getting rid of this character, *chomp*, which you have already seen in use. The *chomp* operator is so widely used when getting input from STDIN that you will normally see the following line of code used for getting input:

```
chomp($line_of_data = <STDIN>);
```

This is a shorter version of the following lines of code:

```
$line_of_data = <STDIN>;
chomp($line_of_data);
```

When an assignment from STDIN is made to a list variable, the input is treated as array elements, each line of data being one array element until the user presses the end-of-file character (see your OS manual for what this character is).

For example, the following line of code:

```
@array_of_data = <STDIN>;
```

combined with the following input from the user:

```
Line 1
Line 2
Line 3
```

creates an array of three elements. The elements of the array can be accessed in the usual way:

```
print $array_of_data[1]; # prints "Line 2" with a newline character
```

While getting one line of input is fine, more often your programs will require that the user enter lots of lines of input. When this situation occurs, the standard way to write the code is to write a loop around STDIN. The following short program accepts input from the user and changes it to lowercase:

```
while (chomp($line_of_data = <STDIN>)) {
    $line_of_data =~ tr/A-Z/a-z/;
}
```

This program will accept user input and translate it to lowercase until there is no more input from the user. When there is no more input, STDIN returns **undef**, which evaluates to false, and the **while** loop terminates.

As with most things in Perl, there is a shorter way to write the loop than described above. The $_ variable can be used to receive input from the angle operator for situations where input is coming from STDIN. With this in mind, the program above can be written like this:

```
while (<STDIN>) {
    chomp;
    tr/A-Z/a-z/;
}
```

A couple of things about this program need to be pointed out. First, the assignment of STDIN to $_ is automatic and the variable is assumed wherever it is needed. So, the **chomp** function above is operating on $_, even though the variable isn't written, as is the case with the next line, where the *tr* operator is working on the $_ variable, even though, again, the variable is not actually written. Also, you can't perform the **chomp** function on the *angle* operator, so a line like:

```
while (chomp(<STDIN>)) {
```

is illegal and will generate an error.

Input from the Angle Operator

Another way to receive input is through the *angle* operator (<>) without putting STDIN within the operator. If you include filenames on the command line when you launch your Perl program, the *angle* operator will open each file and grab input from them. If you don't put any filenames on the command line, Perl will get input from STDIN instead.

When you want to get input from a file or files, you invoke your program in the usual way but you put the filename or names after the program name. For example, if you have a file named file1 that you want to provide input to your program, you will invoke Perl like this:

```
perl myprog.pl file1
```

If you want to get input from more than one file, just add them to the argument list like this:

```
perl myprog.pl file1 file2 file3
```

The *angle* operator simply reads each file line-by-line until there is no more input in the files. The *angle* operator also causes the files to be treated as if they were one big file. Here is a simple example:

```
while (<>) {
    print $_;
}
```

If you have a file named file1 with the following lines:

```
This is line1
This is line2
This is line3
```

6

this program will print each line just as it looks in the file. The program is invoked like this:

```
perl myprog.pl file1
```

If you don't provide the *angle* operator with a filename in the command line, Perl will look to STDIN for input.

When a program gets input using the *angle* operator, the *angle* operator is actually looking at a special variable, @ARGV, for filenames. If you are a C programmer, you already know what @ARGV does, but for those who don't already know C, the @ARGV variable is set by Perl to be an array containing each command-line argument it finds. When you invoke a Perl program like this:

```
perl myprog.pl afile
```

the contents of @ARGV is one element, a file. Since this variable is completely accessible from within a Perl program, you can change the value of the variable within a program. For example, the following program changes the contents of @ARGV to other filenames (the program is invoked like this: perl myprog.pl file1 file2 file3):

```
@ARGV = ("filea", "fileb", "filec");
while (<>) {
    print $_;
}
```

This is not the preferred way to open files for input, but it is an option. Later you will learn how to properly open files for reading and writing.

Standard Output (STDOUT) Using the print Function

For output to the standard output device, the screen, Perl uses the **print** function. **print** takes two arguments, the filehandle of the I/O channel being printed to, and a string or list of comma-separated strings. If you are printing to STDOUT, you can leave off the filehandle, since standard output is the default filehandle for the function. So, if you want to print a string, you can write:

```
print STDOUT "This is a string";
```

though the following works as well and is the accepted way of using the **print** function in Perl:

```
print "This is a string";
```

Since **print** can also print a list of strings, the following also works:

```
print "This ", "is ", "a ", "string";
```

Also, since **print** is a function, you can write the above lines in a more functional style, like this:

```
print("This is a string");
print("This ", "is ", "a ", "string");
```

6

As in C, when you want to print a line of text and a newline character so that the next printed text is on a new line, you can include the newline character in several places. Here are some examples:

```
print "This is a string", "\n";
print "This is a string\n";
print "This ", "is ", "a ", "string", "\n";
print "This is a string" . "\n"; # the dot operator is for
    concatenation
```

You can also leave off the text part of the print function, in which case whatever is in the variable $_ will be printed. Here is an example:

```
while (<STDIN>) {
    print;
}
```

This program will print whatever the user enters as input, since the variable $_ gets all user input without an explicit assignment to another variable.

When you are using the **print** function to print arithmetic expressions, be careful where you place the parentheses, since **print** is looking for parentheses as a way to indicate its argument list. Here is an example of printing an arithmetic expression that gives unintended results:

```
print (2*2) + 2; # prints 4
```

This line of code prints 4 because the argument to the function is contained within the parentheses and everything after the closing parenthesis is ignored. To get the expected output of 6, rewrite the above line of code like this:

```
print ((2*2) + 2); # now prints 6
```

If you come to Perl from a backround in a language such as Basic, you might have a hard time getting used to **print** being a function and not an operator. However, after you track down a few bugs like the one above, you'll get used to the concept fairly quickly.

Formatted Output with printf

You can gain more control over how your output is formatted by using the **printf** function, which is very similar to the function of the same name in C. This function takes two arguments, a format control string and a text string or list of text strings.

The format control string determines how its argument will be printed. Within the format control string are field specifiers that define the type of data to be printed and the size of the field in which it will be printed. The data types that can be specified in the format control string include:

Data Type	Meaning
c	Character
d	Decimal number
e	Exponential floating-point number
f	Fixed-point floating-point number
g	Compact floating-point number
ld	Long decimal number

Data Type	Meaning
lo	Long octal number
lu	Long unsigned decimal number
lx	Long hexadecimal number
o	Octal number
s	String
u	Unsigned decimal number
x	Hexadecimal number
X	Hexadecimal number with uppercase letters

It is easier to explain format control strings by showing some examples of simple ones, so let's look at a few Perl statements that use the **printf** function:

```
printf "%10s", "Hello";
```

This example prints the string "Hello" in a 10-position field, with the string being right-justified in the field, so that the string is printed starting in position 6, like this:

```
     Hello
```

Notice that the field specifier begins with a percent sign (%). This lets Perl know that what is coming is part of the format control string, not the string to be printed.

Here is an example using a decimal number:

```
printf "%10d", 1000;
```

This example prints the number 1000 in a ten-position field, also right-justified. The following code uses a variable as the second argument to the **printf** function and demonstrates how to format floating-point numbers:

```
$pi = 3.14159;
printf "%5.2f", $pi;
```

6

This example prints 3.14 in a five-position field, which means the number is shifted to the right one position, since the number itself takes up four positions. If you specify a field length that is not long enough to hold the number, Perl will automatically adjust the field length so that the number will fit. So, if the format control string above had been "%1.2f", the number 3.14 would still have been printed.

Of course, you can print many strings using one format control string. Here is an example:

```
$pi = 3.14159;
printf "%10s %5d %5.2f\n", "Hello", 123, $pi;
```

This example will print:

```
     Hello   123  3.14
```

When there is more than one format control string in the **printf** function and each string is separated by a space, the space will be printed between each item.

Printing with Here Strings (or Here Documents)

Perl supports the concept (taken from the Unix shell) of *here strings*, or *here documents*. The idea behind here strings is that you tell Perl to print a text string on lines of text until you get to *here*, where *here* is some marker in the text. A few examples will make this immediately clear.

Here is some text to be printed:

```
Now is the time
For all good men
To come to the aid
Of their party.
End
```

You want to print the main body of the text but not the word "End". You can use a *here string*, like this:

```
print <<End;
Now is the time
For all good men
```

```
To come to the aid
Of their party
End
```

This example will print:

```
Now is the time
For all good men
To come to the aid
Of their party
```

The word "End" is not printed because the **print** statement is told to print everything right up to the target of the << operator.

You can also combine here strings in one **print** function, like this:

```
print <<PartI, <<PartII;
Now is the time
For all good men
PartI
To come to the aid
Of their party
PartII
```

6

This example prints the same thing as the example before.

Finally, you can put your here marker in quotes or not and the result remains the same. For example:

```
print <<'End'; # or print <<"End"
Now is the time
For all good men
To come to the aid
Of their party
End
```

File Input/Output

File I/O is very similar to standard I/O in Perl. To perform file I/O, you will have to create a filehandle that serves as the I/O channel for file reading and writing. However, unlike standard I/O, where Perl provides default file-handles that don't have to be specified, you will have to explicitly create a filehandle whenever you want access to a file. The following sections will show you how to open and close files, read from files, write to files, and test for different attributes of files.

Opening and Closing Files

To open a file for reading and/or writing, you first have to give the file a filehandle. The filehandle can be any name you choose to give it, since it is stored in its own namespace and doesn't coexist with variable names, keywords, etc. The only proviso for filehandles is that they be written in all capital letters, so as to avoid any confusion with new keywords, etc., that are defined in the future.

To open a file, you will use the **open** function. The **open** function takes two arguments, a filehandle and an expression, which is the name of the file to be opened. The expression can be a full pathname to a file, or a scalar holding a full pathname to a file. Here is a simple example of opening a file for input:

```
open(FILE, "myfile");
```

Notice that the filename is surrounded by quotes. If the file has an extension, it must be included as part of the filename. You can also precede the filename with a lesser-than sign (<) to indicate the file is to be read from, like this:

```
open(FILE, "<myfile");
```

Next, here's an example of opening a file for output:

```
open(FILE, ">myfile");
```

In this example, the filename is preceded by a greater-than sign (>). This signifies to Perl that the file is being opened for output and to begin writing at the beginning of the file. If the file doesn't exist, Perl will create it. If you want to append data to the end of an existing file, you precede the filename with two greater-than signs, like this:

```
open(FILE, ">>myfile");
```

If you want to open a file for both reading and writing, you can write either of these two lines:

```
open(FILE, "+<myfile");
open(FILE, "+>myfile");
```

Either of these will accomplish the same thing—allow reading and writing to a file—and can be used interchangeably.

To close a file, use the **close** function, with the filehandle as its argument. For example:

```
close(FILE);
```

You won't see the **close** function used in many Perl programs because when a Perl program is exited, all open files are automatically closed. Also, when you reopen a previously opened filehandle, the previously opened file is closed automatically. However, if you do need to close a file before your program is finished because you want to flush out the I/O channel, you can use the **close** function. In fact, for all but the shortest Perl scripts, you should include a **close** function to avoid any messy situations that could arise.

File Input

You've already seen how to open a file for input. Now it's time to learn how to actually read information in from a file. Reading from a file is mostly just like reading from standard input. With that in mind, here's a simple example of opening a file and reading in all the lines of data from the file:

```
open(FILE, "myfile");
while (<FILE>) {
    print;
}
close (FILE);
```

This example will print each line of data from the file followed by a newline character, so that each line of data from the file will be printed on a separate line. The filehandle is placed inside the angle operator, so the **while** loop will continue to read lines from the file as long as there is data in the file. As with standard input, the data is assigned to the special variable $_ , which is what the **print** function uses as its argument.

For many applications, you will not want to keep the newline character as part of the input from the file, so you need to add the **chomp** function like this:

```
open(FILE,"myfile");
while (<FILE>) {
    chomp;
    print;
}
close(FILE);
```

This example deletes the newline character from the value of $_, but with the newline gone, all the data will be printed on the same line. Of course, if you want to print the data on separate lines after you've removed the newline character with **chomp**, you can always rewrite the **print** function like this:

```
print "$_ \n";
```

Handling File-opening Errors

Once in a while, you will try to open a file that doesn't exist. Because Perl tries to be as flexible as possible, it will allow this to happen without telling you there is no such file. The data you write to the file will end up at the bottom of the bit bucket and you will be none the wiser. To keep this from happening, Perl provides two functions, **warn** and **die**, which can notify you that the file you are trying to open doesn't exist.

Both of these functions work by sending a message, of your choosing, to STDERR to be displayed when the file that is being opened can't be opened (often because it doesn't exist, but not exclusively for that reason). The main difference between the two is that **die** will cause your program to exit, while **warn** will allow the program to continue.

Here is an example of the **warn** function:

```
open(FILE,"myfile") or warn "The file cannot be opened.\n";
while (<FILE>) {
    print;
}
print "The program continued executing.";
```

If the file "myfile" cannot be opened, the warning message is printed and the line "The program continued executing". is also printed. If "myfile" can be opened, the contents of the file are printed as is the last line of the program.

Writing this same code using the die function will produce different results. Here is the code:

```
open(FILE,"myfile") or die "The file cannot be opened.\n";
while (<FILE>) {
    print;
}
print "The program continued executing.";
close(FILE);
```

In this example, if the file "myfile" cannot be opened, the message "The file cannot be opened". is printed and the program quits execution. You should use the **die** function when not being able to open a file is a critical enough error to stop the program; and you should use the **warn** function when you can code an alternative to not being able to open a file or when not being able to open the file isn't critical to the program. If you don't use one of these two functions, and you try to open a file that doesn't exist, Perl returns **undef**.

In the examples of **die** above, a newline character was added to the end of the message. If you want to see where in your program the error message was generated, leave the newline character off. Perl will print the program name and the line number where the error was generated. Here is an example:

```
open(FILE,"myfile") or die "File cannot be opened";
while (<FILE>) {
    chomp;
    print;
}
close(FILE);
```

If the name of this program is test.pl, and the file cannot be opened, the following message will be printed:

```
File cannot be opened at test.pl line 1.
```

This technique also works with the **warn** function.

6

File Output

To write data out to a file, you will use the **print** function, with the filehandle of the file you are writing to and the data as its arguments. Here is an example of a simple Perl program that opens a file for output and writes a single line of data to the file:

```
open(FILE,">myfile");
print FILE "This is the first line of data";
```

This example will open a file named "myfile" and write the text string "This is the first line of data" to the file. The **open** function uses the greater-than sign to signify that the file will be written to at the beginning of the file. If there is already data in the file, the data will be deleted and the new data will be written to the file. Here is an example of writing data to a file, only this time the data will be appended to the end of the file:

```
open(FILE,">>myfile");
print FILE "This data is appended to the existing data";
```

As with other uses of the **open** function, if a file is open for output and the file doesn't exist, Perl will create it.

File Tests

As you have just seen, it is possible with the **open** function to overwrite all the data in a file completely by accident. Since Perl is both a responsible and a flexible language, there are tests you can perform to check the existence of a file as well as many other things. There are over 20 file tests, but we will only cover 4 or 5 of them in detail. A table at the end of this section will list all the file tests available in Perl. You can read more about the other tests in the online Perl documentation.

A file test in Perl is written with a dash followed by a letter followed by the filename, with the letter representing a switch for determining which test to perform.

For example, the test to see if a file exists is written:

```
-e "myfile";
```

The test returns true if the file exists, false otherwise. Here is an example of using this test to determine how to write to a file based on whether or not the file exists:

```
if (-e "myfile") {
    open(FILE,">>myfile");
}
else {
    open(FILE,">myfile");
}
```

In this example, if the file exists, it is opened for appending; if it doesn't exist, it is opened for writing using just the single greater-than sign.

Other common tests you may want to perform on files is to check to see if they are readable and/or writeable. To check if a file is readable, you use the **-r** test, as in:

```
$file = "myfile";
if (-r $file) {
    open(FILE,"myfile");
}
```

To check if a file is writable, you use the **-w** test, like this:

```
$file = "myfile";
if (-w $file) {
    open(FILE,">>myfile");
}
```

Another thing you might find occasion to test is whether or not a file is executable. This is done with the **-x** test. Here is an example:

```
$file = "perl.exe";
if (-x $file) {
    print "This file is executable. Don't write to it.\n";
}
```

The following table lists all the file tests in Perl. Be aware that depending on the operating system you are using, some of these tests may not be available.

Test	Result
-r	File is readable
-w	File is writable
-x	File is executable
-o	File is owned by user
-R	File is readable by real user
-W	File is writable by real user
-X	File is executable by real user
-O	File is owned by real user
-e	File exists
-z	File exists but has zero size
-s	File exists and has non-zero size
-f	File is plain file
-d	File is a directory
-l	File is a symlink
-S	File is a socket
-p	File is a named pipe
-b	File is a block-special file
-c	File is a character-special file
-u	File is setuid
-g	File is setgid
-k	File has the sticky bit set
-t	isatty( ) on filehandle is true
-T	File is a text file
-B	File is a binary file
-M	Modification age in days
-A	Access age in days
-C	Inode-modification age in days

Getting More File Information with stat

While the file tests are useful for obtaining individual pieces of information about files, they are not all-inclusive. There is still more information you can obtain about files using the **stat** function. This function returns the following information about the specified file:

◆   Device number of filesystem

◆   Inode number

◆   File mode

◆   Number of links to file

◆   Numeric user ID of file's owner

◆   Numeric group ID of file's owner

◆   The device identifier

◆   Total size of file in bytes

◆   Last access time

◆   Last modify time

◆   Inode change time

◆   Preferred blocksize for file system I/O

◆   Actual number of blocks allocated

Each of these items is returned by the **stat** function as a list. The following program illustrates how to use the **stat** function to collect this information on a file:

```
($dev,$inode,$mode,$nlink,$uid,$gid,$rdev,
 $size,$atime,$mtime,$ctime,$bsize,$blocks)
 = stat "myfile";
```

This program takes the information collected by **stat** and stuffs it into each of the scalar variables. Beware that not all operating systems will have a value for all the elements of the **stat** function, so you will have to experiment to see which elements are supported by your system.

A Final Example

Here is an example that combines a lot of what you have learned in this chapter about standard and file input and output. This program opens a file,

6

allows the user to enter data for the file, and then writes the data to the file. Here is the code:

```
if (-e "myfile") {
    open(FILE,">>myfile") or die "File error - can't open";
    while (<STDIN>) {
        print File $_;
    }
}
else {
    open(FILE,">myfile") or die "File error - can't open";
    while (<STDIN>) {
        print FILE $_;
    }
}
```

This program first checks to see if the file already exists. If it does, it opens the file for appending and then loops through standard input, allowing the user to enter lines of data until they type the end-of-file code. If the file doesn't exist, the file is opened for writing (which also creates the file) and then loops through standard input again. Each **open** function also has a **die** function to handle the error generated if for some reason the file cannot be opened.

Summary

This chapter has shown you how to use Perl's standard input and output operators and functions for getting data into and out of Perl. Most importantly, especially for programmers who don't have a C/C++ background, you learned how to work with Perl's input and output standard filehandles, STDIN and STDOUT, which are used for getting input from the user and printing output to the screen or a printer. You also learned how to read and write data from disk files. These operations are very important because your Perl programs have to communicate with their environment.

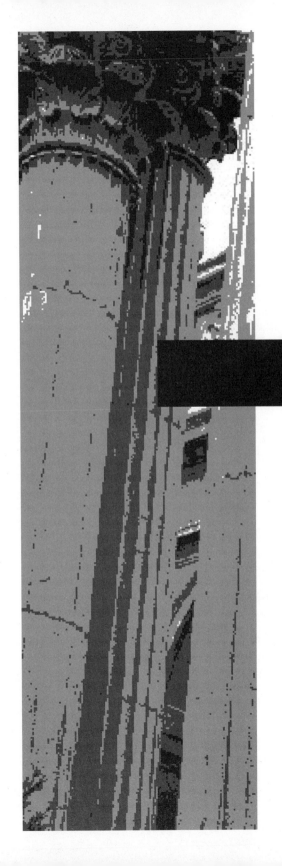

CHAPTER 7

Report Formatting in Perl

As you know, Perl stands for "Practical Extraction and Report Language". The previous chapters have covered many of the extraction aspects of Perl, and this chapter looks at how it can be used to create formatted reports.

The Format Template

Report formatting in Perl involves creating a report template, which consists of the report and parameters for the layout. The report part of the template can include column titles, labels, simple graphics, constant text, and other things, while the parameters part of the template will consist of variable data found in a program or in disk files.

If you are a Basic programmer, you can think of a report template as a fancy sort of **print using** statement, where you tell the program to print its data using a predefined template that forces the data to conform to the rules of the template.

The template you design for a Perl report is called a *format*. A format is like a subroutine in that while it is defined within a Perl program, it is defined in a separate portion of the program and is invoked in a manner similar to a subroutine.

You create a report format by creating a format definition. A format definition consists of the keyword **format**, then the format's name followed by an equal sign (=), followed by the format definition. Here is the syntax for a format definition:

```
format formatname =
FieldLine
Data_value1, Data_value2, Data_valuen
.
```

The format name can be any name you wish to give it, though conventionally the format name is the same as the filehandle name you are using.

Following the format name is an equal sign, which signifies to Perl that the format definition is to follow. On the next line is a *FieldLine*, which will consist of some sort of report template information. After each FieldLine is a line consisting of data values, usually Perl scalar variables or any expression that evaluates to a scalar. Each variable (or expression) must be separated by commas.

After a line of data values can be another FieldLine, followed by a line of data values, and so on until the whole report format is defined. The last line of a report format always consists of a dot. The dot signifies to Perl that the format definition is complete.

The most important part of a report format is the contents of the FieldLine, since this line defines how the data will look. The following section will explain in detail what can go into a FieldLine.

Defining FieldLines

Before the details of the FieldLine are covered, you need to get an overview of what a Perl report format looks like. Here is a very simple format to print a set of name labels:

```
format SIMPLEFORMAT =
Hello, my name is: @<<<<<<<<<<<<<<<<<<<<<<<<<
$name
I work for: @<<<<<<<<<<<<<<<<<<<<<<<<<<<<
$company
```

This example shows two FieldLines and two data lines. The first field line consists of two parts: some constant text ("Hello, my name is:") and a *fieldholder*. The fieldholder tells Perl to plug in a value from the data line below it. A fieldholder begins with an "at" sign (@), followed by a series of formatting symbols, telling Perl how to print the data.

The different formatting symbols will be discussed below. The data line below the first FieldLine consists of a scalar variable, $name, whose value is plugged into the line above. Below the first data line is another FieldLine and another data line. The report format is then completed with a dot.

Fieldholders

There are several types of fieldholders and formatting symbols for different types of data values. However, almost all fieldholders begin the same way, with an "at" sign (@). After the "at" sign comes a formatting symbol that lets Perl know what kind of data is to be placed in the fieldholder. The number of format symbols indicates to Perl how many characters can be placed in the field. So, ten formatting symbols indicates a 10-character field.

The formatting symbols for text fields are the angle brackets (< and >) and the vertical bar (|). A left-pointing angle bracket is used to indicate that the field is to be left-justified in the fieldholder. If the data doesn't use all the space allocated to it, the fieldholder is filled with spaces to the right of the data. A right-pointing angle bracket indicates a right-justified field, with

7

spaces added to the left of the data if the value doesn't use all the space allocated to it. A vertical bar is used to indicate that the data should be centered in the field, filling both sides of the field with spaces if the data value is too short to use the space allocated to it.

The following are sample fieldholders for text fields:

```
@<<<<<<<<< # a ten-character, left-justified text field
@>>>>>>>>>>>>>>>>>>> # a twenty-character, right-justified text field
@||||||||||||||| # a fifteen-character, centered text field
```

Numerical fieldholders begin like text fieldholders, with an "at" sign. The rest of the fieldholder is filled with pound signs (#), with an optional decimal point. There are no other symbols available, like a comma or a dollar sign, but you can add them yourself with some extra programming. Here is an example of a seven-number numerical fieldholder with two decimal places:

```
@######.##
```

The actual field width, of course, is ten if you count the decimal place and the two digits after the decimal.

Normally, when a data value is plugged into a fieldholder, Perl quits putting data into the fieldholder when Perl reaches a newline character.

However, there may be situations where you want a data value with perhaps many newlines to be plugged into one fieldholder. Perl provides a special fieldholder to do this, the multiline field. As usual, the multiline field begins with an "at" sign (@), which is then followed by a single asterisk (*). So, using this fieldholder with this data value:

```
$nameaddinfo = "John Doe\n100 Main Street\n Anytown, US 00000";
```

will result in the following output:

```
John Doe
100 Main Street
Anytown, US 00000
```

The final type of fieldholder to discuss is the *filled field*. A filled field is a field that usually takes up more than one line, so that the data values are filled into the field until there is no more data. A common use of the filled field is to format a long data value that covers more than one line.

Unlike the other fieldholders, the filled field starts with a caret symbol (^), not an "at" sign.

If you have data that will span more than one line, you could write the format like this:

```
format MULTILINE =
Course: @<<<<<<<<<<<<<<<<<  Description: ^<<<<<<<<<<<<<<<<<<<
             $course,
$description


^<<<<<<<<<<<<<<<<<<<

$description

^<<<<<<<<<<<<<<<<<<<

$description
.
```

This sample format creates a filled field for the course description, so that the part of the description variable that doesn't fit on the first line will be put on the second line, and any remaining data will be placed on the third line. This format, however, doesn't take into consideration the fact that the description variable may not have enough data to fill lines 2 and 3. Instead, if only one line of data is needed, the format will print two blank lines. To fix this problem, Perl provides a text-suppression character, the tilde symbol (~). You use this symbol whenever you don't want any blank lines to print in a filled field. Using the suppression character, you can rewrite the format above like this:

```
format MULTILINE =
Course: @<<<<<<<<<<<<<<<< Description: ^<<<<<<<<<<<<<<<<<<<
          $course,                     $description
~                                      ^<<<<<<<<<<<<<<<<<<<
                                       $description
~                                      ^<<<<<<<<<<<<<<<<<<<
                                       $description
.
```

7

Now, if the value of the description variable doesn't need any of the extra lines, no blank lines will be printed.

What if the value of the description variable needs more than the three lines given to it in the format? One answer, of course, is to include as many fieldholders as you think will be necessary to cover the possible maximum length of the variable, but that's a novice programmer's way to solve the problem. Perl provides a neat shortcut by letting you write two tildes side by side before the second fieldholder line, telling the format that it should continue adding fieldholder lines until the full value of the variable is output. This way, the variable value can take up one line or one hundred lines (or more!) and each line will be printed until the whole value has been output. Here is the final format for the filled field example:

```
format MULTILINE =
Course: @<<<<<<<<<<<<<<<<<< Description: ^<<<<<<<<<<<<<<<<<<<
        $course,                         $description
~~                                       ^<<<<<<<<<<<<<<<<<<<
                                         $description
.
```

At the end of this chapter, you will see an example that uses the filled field format to print data.

The write Function

Now that you've seen how to create report a format, it's time to learn how to generate the report defined by the format. A report is generated using the **write** function. The **write** function takes a filehandle and generates the report for it using the current format for the filehandle.

With that in mind, take a look at a simple one line format and the Perl program that generates the report:

```
format ONELINER =
Hello, I'm @<<<<<<<<<<<<<<<<<
$name
.
$name = "John Doe";
open(ONELINER,">labels");
write (ONELINER);
```

This program prints the line of text "Hello, I'm John Doe" to the filehandle ONELINER, which in turn creates a file named "labels", overwriting any existing data in the file.

The filehandle can be any legal filehandle, so you can also create report formats for standard output (the display), as in:

```
format STDOUT =
Hello, my name is @<<<<<<<<<<<<<<<<<<
$name
.

$name = "John Doe";
write;
```

This program prints "Hello, my name is John Doe" on the standard output device.

The two previous examples had their data contained in the program itself. More commonly, the data for a report format will be found in another file. This example prints the same line of text as above, but this time pulling the information from a file called "names":

```
format ONELINER =
Hello, my name is @<<<<<<<<<<<<<<<<<<
$name
.
open(ONELINER,">labels");
open(NAMES,"names");
while (<NAMES>) {
    chomp;
    write(ONELINER);
}
```

This example loops through the "names" input file, generating the report line and writing it to the file "labels" until no more names are found in the input file.

Here is an example that uses numeric fieldholders to print numeric data. This example also demonstrates that you can use an expression in place of a scalar variable in a report format. The input file for this example contains several accounts, with each line consisting of an account number, an old balance,

7

and a current payment amount. The report format prints this information plus a current balance amount. Here is the code:

```
format ACCTLIST =
Account Number       Old Balance    Current Payment    New Balance
@########            @######.##          @###.##        @######.##
$acctnum,            $oldbal,            $cp,            $oldbal - $cp
.
open(ACCTLIST,">acctlist");
open(ACCOUNTS,"accounts");
while (<ACCOUNTS>) {
    chomp;
    ($acctnum, $oldbal,$cp) = split(/,/);
    write(ACCTLIST);
}
```

If the "accounts" file has this data:

```
2312367893,14356.34,234.45
7245294834,23653.23,567.34
8238734922,534.56,75.25
```

the file "acctlist" will contain this report:

```
Account Number              Old Balance         Current Payment
New Balance
2312367893                    14356.34                   234.45
14121.89

Account Number              Old Balance         Current Payment
New Balance
7245294834                    23653.23                   567.34
23085.89

Account Number              Old Balance         Current Payment
New Balance
8238734922                     534.56                     75.25
459.31
```

As an alternative to this report, you may just want to print the report heading one time, followed by the lines of data, so that the report looks like this:

```
Account Number                Old Balance          Current Payment
New Balance

2312367893                      14356.34                 234.45
14121.89
7245294834                      23653.23                 567.34
23085.89
8238734922                        534.56                  75.25
459.31
```

Here is the previous program, altered to create this report:

```
format ACCTLIST =
@########            @######.##              @###.##    @######.##
$acctnum,           $oldbal,               $cp,        $oldbal - $cp
.
open(ACCTLIST,">acctlist");
print ACCTLIST "Account Number     Old Balance   Current Payment
                New Balance\n\n";
open(ACCTLIST,">>acctlist");
open(ACCOUNTS,"accounts");
while (<ACCOUNTS>) {
    chomp;
    ($acctnum, $oldbal,$cp) = split(/,/);
    write(ACCTLIST);
}
```

7

Changing the Filehandle Using select

In the last section, you saw that when you call the **write** function without
specifying a filehandle, the output of **write** goes to STDOUT, which is
the currently defined filehandle if no other filehandle has been specified.
You can change the filehandle before sending output to it using the **select**
function, which takes a filehandle as its arguments and makes it the currently
defined handle. Here is an example:

```
print "This goes to STDOUT because no other filehandle is
      specified\n";
select(NEWFILEHANDLE);
print "This now goes to NEWFILEHANDLE\n";
select(STDOUT);
print "This goes back to STDOUT\n";
```

Being able to change the currently defined filehandle is important when you want to associate a report format of a different name than the filehandle the report is being output to. Remember: normally, a report format and a filehandle have the same name. If, however, you want to use a different report format with a filehandle, you have to be able to change the filehandle using the **select** function.

The first step to take when changing a report format is to store the old filehandle in a scalar variable. While this step is not absolutely necessary, doing so will be helpful if there are problems with the code later. The next step is to select a new report format and save it to a special Perl variable that stores the current report format, $~. Once the report format name is changed, the filehandle needs to be changed using the **select** function. Since the old filehandle has been stored in a variable, just use the variable as the argument to **select**. Translating these steps into Perl code yields the following example:

```
$oldfhandle = select(OLDFH);
$~ = "NEWFORMAT";
select($oldfhandle);
```

This example is quite simple, but the concept behind it, being able to change formats, is important for longer and more complex reports.

Top-of-Page and Other Report Page Adjustments

Since many of your reports in Perl will ultimately be sent to a printer, you will need to be able to adjust your reports for the constraints of the printed page. For example, if you are printing to a laser printer or a printer with a cut-sheet feeder, you will need to be able to know how to tell your report to go to the top of the next page to continue printing (also called pagination). You will also need to be able to do things like change the length of a page for nonstandard print jobs and change the line count of a page for instances when extra lines are sent to output. This section will show you how to accomplish these things.

To perform pagination, Perl provides a top-of-page format. The top-of-page format is defined just like other formats, only the extenstion "_TOP" is added. Here is a sample top-of-page format:

```
format REPORT_TOP =
Heading 1      Heading 2      Heading 3
.
```

When a new page is created in Perl, this format will be printed each time. If you want to add a page number somewhere in the format, Perl provides a special variable that tracks how many times the top-of-page format has been called for a filehandle, $%. You can use this variable as a page number variable like this:

```
format REPORT_TOP =
Heading 1        Heading 2        Heading 3           @<
                                                      $%
.
```

This format will print the page number to the right of the heading line for each page that is generated by the report.

Perl has a special variable that tracks the number of lines left on the current page of the current filehandle, $-. Using this variable can be important because when you mix a **print** function with the **write** function, $- will be incremented after a **print**. You can, however, decrement $- manually if you want the variable to reflect a different number. Here's an example:

```
write(REPORT); # $- is incremented
print REPORT "This is another line of output\n"; # $- is
             incremented
$- --; # $% now reflects the proper number of output lines to the
filehandle
```

You can also change the top-of-page format for a report format just like you can change the format itself. As usual, a Perl special variable tracks the top-of-format name, and this variable is $^. Use a normal assignment statement to change the variable to a new top-of-page format.

Earlier, you saw an example of a Perl report format that printed a heading at the top of the page before invoking the format. Now that top-of-page formats have been covered, the example can be rewritten, using a top-of-page format. Here is the new code:

```
format ACCTLIST =
@########          @######.##           @###.##    @######.##
$acctnum,          $oldbal,             $cp,       $oldbal - $cp
.
format ACCTLIST_TOP =
Account Number     Old Balance     Current Payment     New Balance\n\n
.
```

7

```
open(ACCTLIST,">acctlist");
print ACCTLIST "Account Number      Old Balance     Current Payment
                New Balance\n\n";
open(ACCTLIST,">>acctlist");
open(ACCOUNTS,"accounts");
while (<ACCOUNTS>) {
    chomp;
    ($acctnum, $oldbal,$cp) = split(/,/);
    write(ACCTLIST);
}
```

Summary

Report formatting is one of the main reasons Perl was originally developed. The formatting commands you've learned in this chapter are not found natively in any other programming or scripting language. You have to use some sort of reporting engine with another language to perform reporting like you can with Perl. The only price you have to pay for this feature is the time you will have to spend learning how to properly format your reports. However, once you have learned the ins and outs of formats, you will find them invaluable for reporting the results of your Perl programs.

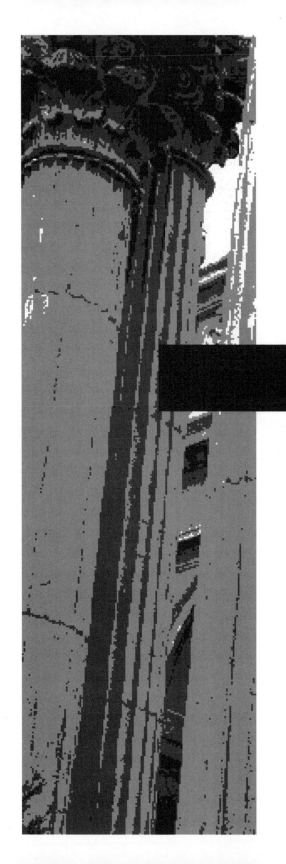

CHAPTER 8

Perl's Built-in Functions

This chapter presents a reference of Perl's built-in functions. You have already seen some of them, such as **write** and **chomp**. There are many, many more that do everything from perform advanced mathematical operations to provide low-level i/o communications.

Perl functions can be run with or without parentheses around the function's arguments, and if you don't use parentheses, you may get strange results from a function due to precedence rules. For example, here is some Perl code that uses the **print** function without parentheses:

```
print 10 + 11 + 12;
```

This example, as expected, prints the number 33. If you rewrite the function using parentheses to group the arithmetic expression, like this:

```
print (10 + 11) + 12;
```

Perl prints 21. Perl thinks that the numbers 10 and 11 are the only arguments to the function, not an expression that should be calculated first. The warning switch, **-w**, will issue a warning if it is used when invoking Perl, letting you know that the remainder of the expression (+ 12) is useless.

Perl Functions

Perl's built-in functions are listed here in alphabetical order. Each function name is followed by a simple example to illustrate its use and its syntax (how it should be called and the arguments it needs).

/Pattern/

/ / or **m/ /** is the *match* operator, as you saw in Chapter 5. The **m** modifier tells Perl to treat the string as multiple lines.

Syntax:

```
/Pattern/
m/Pattern/
```

Example:

```
$_ = "abc";
print "true" if /abc/; # prints "true" because pattern matches $_
```

?Pattern?

?? is a pattern-matching operator also, the difference being that once it performs a successful match, it quits until it is turned back on by **reset**.

Syntax:

```
?Pattern?
```

Example:

```
$_ = "abcabcabc";
print "true" if ?abc?; # prints "true" for the first match of "abc"
```

abs

This function returns the absolute value of its argument. If no argument is present, it will return the value of the $_ variable.

Syntax:

```
abs(Value)
```

Example:

```
print abs(5); # prints 5
print abs(-5); # prints 5
```

accept

This function is used by a socket server to accept a new socket connection.

Syntax:

```
accept(NewSocket, Socket)
```

Example:

```
$conn = accept(newSock, Sock);
```

atan

This function returns the arctangent of Y/X.

8

Syntax:

```
atan2(Y, X)
```

Example:

```
print atan2(2,1); # prints 1.10714871779409
```

bind

This function is used to attach a name to a socket connection.

Syntax:

```
bind Socket, SocketName
```

Example:

```
bind(Socket, $Sock);
```

binmode

This function tells Perl to work with a file in binary mode, for operating systems that distinguish between binary and text files. It is necessary because systems that do distinguish between these modes will translate \r\n sequences to \n on input, and \n is translated to \r\n on output. You also need this function because files are normally opened in text mode.

Syntax:

```
binmode(Filehandle)
```

Example:

```
open(FILE, "myfile.doc");
binmode(FILE);
```

bless

This function takes a reference and makes it an object of the class named as the (optional) second argument. If no class name is given, the current package is used.

Syntax:

```
bless(Ref, Classname)
bless(Ref)
```

Example:

```
Package Graphics;
sub new {
    my $line = {}; reference to an empty hash
    bless $line; makes $line an object of the Graphics class
    return $line;

}
```

caller

This function returns the package name, filename, and line number that the currently executing subroutine was called from. *Expr* tells the function how many stack frames to go back before the current stack frame.

Syntax:

```
caller Expr
caller
```

Example:

```
($packname, $fname, $lnumber) = caller; # gathers caller info into
variables
```

chdir

This function changes the current directory to the one specified in *Expr*, if it exists. If *Expr* is omitted, **chdir** changes the current directory to the home directory.

Syntax:

```
chdir Expr
```

8

Example:

```
$newdir = "c:\apps\data";
chdir($newdir); # working directory is now "c:\apps\data"
```

chmod

This function is used to change the permissions set on a list of files.

Syntax:

```
chmod( List)
```

Example:

```
$chmod = chmod 0777, $file1, $file2. $file3);
```

chomp

This function deletes the trailing newline character (\n) from its argument. The function also returns the number of characters deleted.

Syntax:

```
chomp(Variable)
chomp(List)
chomp
```

Example:

```
$variable = "Hello, world\n";
chomp($variable); # $variable now has the value "hello, world"
```

chop

This function deletes the last character of its argument. Its return value is the character deleted. This function has in the past been used to remove the newline character, but is not as safe as **chomp**, since any last character is deleted.

Syntax:

```
chop(Variable)
chop(List)
chop
```

Example:

```
$variable = "Hello, world\n";
chop($variable); # $variable now has the value "Hello, world"
chop($variable); # $variable now has the value "Hello, worl"
```

chown

This function changes the ownership of the specified list of files.

Syntax:

```
chown(List)
```

Example:

```
$ch = chown($file1, $file2, $file3);
```

8

chr

This function returns the ASCII character represented by *Number*.

Syntax:

```
chr Number
```

Example:

```
print chr(97); # prints the letter "a"
```

chroot

This function, available only to the superuser, changes the root directory of the specified file.

Syntax:

```
chroot(FILE)
```

Example:

```
Chroot($file);
```

close

This function will close any open file, socket, or pipe associated with *Filehandle*.

Syntax:

```
close Filehandle
```

Example:

```
open(FILE,"myfile");
# file processing goes here
close(FILE);
```

closedir

This function closes a directory handle, named by *Dirhandle* and previously opened by the **opendir** function.

Syntax:

```
closedir DirHandle
```

Example:

```
opendir MYDIR "c:\windows\system";
# directory processing statements
closedir MYDIR;
```

connect

This function attempts to initiate a connection with the named socket process.

Syntax:

```
connect SOCKET, SOCKET_NAME
```

Example:

```
connect(Socket, $sock_conn) || die "Can't connect: $!\n";
```

cos

This function returns the cosine of *Expr*. *Expr* is expressed in radians.

Syntax:

```
cos Expr
```

Example:

```
$num = 1;
print cos($num); # prints 0.54030230586814
```

crypt

8

This function encrypts a string just like the Unix function "crypt".

Syntax:

```
crypt PlainText, Salt
```

Example:

```
Crypt($name,  $pass);
```

dbmclose

This function closes the binding between a DBM file and a hash.

Syntax:

```
dbmclose Hash
```

Example:

```
# %db_hash stores DBM records
dbmclose(%db_hash);
```

dbmopen

This function opens a binding between a hash and a DBM file. The specified mode determines the protection provided to the hash.

Syntax:

```
dbmopen Hash, DatabaseName, Mode
```

Example:

```
dbmopen(&db_hash, $dbm_file, 0666);
```

defined

This function returns true if *Expr* has a value and returns **undef** if *Expr* doesn't have a value.

Syntax:

```
defined(Expr)
```

Example:

```
$pi = 3.14159;
print "True" if defined($pi);
```

delete

This function deletes a key and its associated value from a hash.

Syntax:

```
delete(Expr)
```

Example:

```
%courses = ("101","Algorithms","201","Intro to Perl");
$old_course = "101";
delete($courses{$old_course}); # deletes 101 and Algorithms from hash
```

die

This function prints the value of *List* concatenated to STDERR. Use this function to display a meaningful error message to the user.

Syntax:

```
die(List)
```

Example:

```
open(FILE,"testfile") or die("Can't open file"); # prints "can't open file
                                                  # at prog1.pl line 1"
```

do

This function executes the series of commands specified in *Block* and returns the value of the last expression. You can also use **do** with a loop modifier to create a **do**...loop structure (see Chapter 4).

8

Syntax:

```
do Block
until Expression
```

Example:

```
do {
    # code line 1
    # code line 2
    # code line n
} until # conditional expression
```

dump

This function causes an immediate core dump. If you specify a label, the program will restart by executing at the point referenced by the label. If a label isn't specified, the program will restart from the top.

Syntax:

```
dump Label
dump
```

each

This function returns a list consisting of the key and associated value for the next value of a hash. You can use this function to iterate over the data pairs of a hash.

Syntax:

```
each(Hash)
```

Example:

```
%courses = ("101","Data Structures","201","Algorithms");
($key,$value) = each(%courses); # $key gets "101", $value gets "Data
                                # Structures"
```

eof

This function returns true if the next file read on *Filehandle* is the end of file; **eof( )** tests for the last line of a group of files, and **eof** returns the end-of-file status on the last file read.

Syntax:

```
eof Filehandle
eof( )
eof
```

Example:

```
open(FILE,"myfile");
while (<FILE>) {
```

```
    if (!eof(FILE)) {
        # file processing statements
    }
}
```

eval

This function executes the value of *Expr* as if it were a Perl program. The following program prompts the user to enter a line of Perl code and then evaluates it.

Syntax:

```
eval Expr
```

Example:

```
print "Enter a line of code to evaluate:";
chomp($line_of_code = <STDIN>);
eval($line_of_code);
```

exec

This function terminates the Perl script that is currently executing and executes another program instead.

Syntax:

```
exec List
```

Example:

```
if (!$file) { exec 'ls $file }
```

exists

This function returns true if the hash key specified in *Expr* exists in its hash.

Syntax:

```
exists Expr
```

8

Example:

```
%courses = ("101","Data Structures","201","Algorithms");
$key_to_check = "201";
print "true" if exists($courses{$key_to_check}); # prints true
```

exit

This function evaluates *Expr* and aborts the current program with the value of *Expr*. You can also use **exit** without *Expr* and a value of 0 will be returned.

Syntax:

```
exit Expr
```

Example:

```
# some Perl statements go here
exit; # Perl program aborts at this line
```

exp

This function returns *e* to the power *Expr*.

Syntax:

```
exp Expr
```

Example:

```
$exponent = 5;
print exp($exponent); # prints 148.413159102577
```

fcntl

This function calls the Unix "fcntl" (file control) function. To make sure you get the right descriptors for the function, import the Fcntl module first.

Syntax:

```
fcnt Filehandle, Function, Scalar
```

fileno

This function returns the file descriptor for a filehandle.

Syntax:

```
fileno Filehandle
```

Example:

```
$fdesc = fileno($f_handle);
```

flock

This function calls the Unix utility "flock".

Syntax:

```
flock Filehandle, Operation
```

fork

This function, when successful, creates a child process using Unix's "fork" utility.

Syntax:

```
fork
```

8

format

This function creates a report format. See Chapter 7 for all the details.

Syntax:

```
format FormatName =
    picture line
    value list
```

formline

This function formats a list of values based on the value of *Picture*. This function is used internally with Perl formats.

Syntax:

```
formline Picture, List
```

getc

This function returns the next byte from the input file specified by *Filehandle*. If *Filehandle* is left out, **getc** gets its input from STDIN.

Syntax:

```
getc Filehandle
getc
```

Example:

```
print getc; # prints the first byte from STDIN
```

getgrgid

This function looks up a group file entry by a group number. It returns a list containing $name, $passwd, $gid, and $members.

Syntax:

```
getgrgid(GID)
```

getgrnam

This function looks up a group file entry by a group name. It returns a list containing $name, $passwd, $gid, and $members.

Syntax:

```
getgrnam(Name)
```

gethostbyaddr

This function translates a network address to its hostname. It returns a list containing $name, $aliases, $addrtype, $length, and a list of raw addresses, @addrs.

Syntax:

```
gethostbyaddr(Addr, Addrtype)
```

gethostbyname

This function translates a network hostname to its address. It returns a list containing $name, $aliases, $addrtype, $length, and a list of raw addresses, @addrs.

Syntax:

```
gethostbyname(Name)
```

gethostent

This function iterates through the /etc/hosts file and returns each entry one at a time. It returns a list containing $name, $aliases, $addrtype, $length, and a list of raw addresses, @addrs.

Syntax:

```
gethostent
```

8

getlogin

This function returns the current login from /etc/utmp.

Syntax:

```
Getlogin
```

Example:

```
$login = getlogin;
```

getnetbyaddr

This function translates a network address to a network name. It returns a list that consists of $name, $aliases, $addrtype, and $net.

Syntax:

```
getnetbyaddr(Addr, AddrType)
```

getnetbyname

This function translates a network name to a network address. It returns a list that consists of $name, $aliases, $addrtype, and $net.

Syntax:

```
getnetbyname(Name)
```

getnetent

This function iterates through the /etc/networks file, returning a list containing $name, $aliases, $addrtype, and $net for each entry.

Syntax:

```
getnetent
```

getpeername

This function returns the socket address (packed) for a connected socket.

Syntax:

```
getpeername(Socket)
```

Example:

```
$sock_addr = getpeername(Socket);
```

getpgrp

This function returns the process group for the current process ID.

Syntax:

```
getpgrp(PID)
```

getppid

This function returns the parent process's process ID.

Syntax:

```
getppid
```

getpriority

This function returns the current priority for a process.

Syntax:

```
getpriority(Which, Who)
```

Example:

```
$curr_pri = getpriority(0,0); # gets the priority for the current
                              # process
```

getprotobyname

This function translates a protocol name to its number. It returns a list that contains $name, $aliases, and $protocol_number.

Syntax:

```
getprotobyname(Name)
```

getprotobynumber

This function translates a protocol number to its name. It returns a list that contains $name, $aliases, and $protocol_number.

Syntax:

```
getprotobynumber(Number)
```

getpwent

This function iterates through the /etc/passwd file, returning in list context $name, $passwd, $uid, $gid, $quote, $comment, $gcos, $dir, and $shell.

8

Syntax:

```
getpwent
```

getpwnam

This function translates a username to a its *passwd* file entry. If you use it in list context, it returns $passwd, $uid, $gid, $quote, $comment, $gcos, $dir, and $shell. If you use it in scalar context, it returns just the user ID.

Syntax:

```
getpwnam(Name)
```

getpwuid

This function translates a user ID to its passwd file entry. If you use it in list context, it returns $passwd, $uid, $gid, $quote, $comment, $gcos, $dir, and $shell. If you use it in scalar context, it returns just the user name.

Syntax:

```
getpwuid(UID)
```

getservbyname

This function translates a port name into a port number. When this function is used in list context, it returns $name, $aliases, $port_number, and $protocol_name. When this function is used in scalar context, it returns the port number.

Syntax:

```
getservbyname(Name, Proto)
```

getservbyport

This function translates a port number into a port name. When this function is used in list context, it returns $name, $aliases, $port_number, and $protocol_name. When this function is used in scalar context, it returns the port name.

Syntax:

```
getservbyport(Port, Proto)
```

getservent

This function iterates through the /etc/services file, returning in list context $name, $aliases, $port_number, and $protocol_name. In scalar context, the function returns the port name.

Syntax:

```
getservent
```

getsockname

This function returns the name of the named socket.

Syntax:

```
getsockname(Socket)
```

getsockopt

This function returns the socket option specified.

Syntax:

```
getsockopt(Socket, Level, Option)
```

Example:

```
$sock_opt = getsockopt(S, $level, $option);
```

glob

This function returns the value of Expr with filename expansions. *Expr* is optional, and if left out, $_ is used by default.

Syntax:

```
glob Expr
```

8

Example:

```
@filelist = glob($_);
```

gmtime

This function converts the system time to a nine-element time based on Greenwich Mean Time. Each element is numeric, so if you want to convert, say, the day of the week to a string, you will have to provide a function to do that.

Syntax:

```
gmtime Expr
```

Example:

```
($seconds, $minutes, $hours, $monthday, $month, $year, $weekday,
$yearday, $isdst) = gmtime(time);
```

goto

goto transfers control of your Perl script to the argument following it, whether it is a label, an expression, or a named subroutine (**goto &Name**). The most common form of **goto** is shown in the example below.

Syntax:

```
goto Label
goto Expr
goto &Name
```

Example:

```
print "You are here.\n";
goto There;
print "You are between here and there.\n"; # this doesn't print
There: print "You are there.\n";
```

grep

This function looks for instances of *Expr* in *List*. *Expr* can be a regular expression or just a character expression and if a match is found, returns the value of *List*.

Syntax:

```
grep Expr, List
grep Block, List
```

Example:

```
@list = qw(now is the time for all good people to come to the aid
of their
party);
@glist = grep {/oo/} @list;
print @glist; # returns the elements of @list
@glist1 = grep {"ie"} @list;
print @glist1; # returns an empty list because no match was found
```

hex

This function evaluates *Expr* as a hexadecimal string and returns the decimal equivalent.

8

Syntax:

```
hex Expr
```

Example:

```
$num = hex("ffff10"); # $num gets 16776976
```

import

This function, though not built in, is used by modules to export their functions into the calling program.

Syntax:

```
import Classname, List
import Classname
```

index

This function returns the position of *Substr* in *Str*, starting with *Position*, if specified. The **index** function always returns just the first occurrence of *Substr*. The position is zero-based, so if **index** finds the substring at the first position of the string, the value of the function is 0. If *Position* is omitted, the starting position defaults to position 0.

Syntax:

```
index Str, Substr, Position
index Str, Substr
```

Example:

```
$str = "This is a line of text.";
$substr = "line";
$position = index $str, $substr; # $position gets the value 10
```

int

This function returns the integer part of *Expr*.

Syntax:

```
int Expr
```

Example:

```
$int_value = int(123.34); # $int_value gets the value 123
```

join

This function joins the strings that make up *List* into a single string separated by the value of *Expr*.

Syntax:

```
join Expr, List
```

Example:

```
@list = qw(Tom Jane Bob Elise Mary Bill);
@list = join ":", @list; # @list now has the value
                         # (Tom:Jane:Bob:Elise:Mary:Bill)
```

keys

This function returns all the keys for the Hash named.

Syntax:

```
keys Hash
```

Example:

```
%workdays = (
    "Monday" => "1",
    "Tuesday" => "2",
    "Wednesday" => "3",
    "Thursday" => "4",
    "Friday" => "5",
);
print keys %workdays; # prints MondayTuesdayWednesdayThursdayFriday
```

8

kill

This function sends a signal to a list of processes.

Syntax:

```
kill(List)
```

Example:

```
@processes = ($child1, $child2, $child3);
kill 'Stop', @processes;
```

last

This statement exits immediately from the block named *Label,* or if there is no label, exits from the innermost loop.

Syntax:

```
last Label
last
```

Example:

```
for ($x = 1; $x < 100; $x++) {
    print "$x ";
    if ($x == 75) { last; }
}; # this for loop will print 1 through 75 and then exit the loop
```

lc

This function returns the value in *Expr* in lowercase.

Syntax:

```
lc Expr
```

Example:

```
print lc "PERL"; # prints "perl"
```

lcfirst

This function returns the first character in *Expr* in lowercase.

Syntax:

```
lc Expr
```

Example:

```
print lcfirst "PERL"; # prints "pERL"
```

length

This function returns the length in bytes of the value in *Expr*, or of $_, if *Expr* is left out. Use this function only on scalar values.

Syntax:

```
length Expr
length
```

Example:

```
$string = "Four score and seven years ago";
$len = length $string; # $len gets the value 30
```

link

This function creates a new filename linked to the old filename.

Syntax:

```
link(Oldfile, Newfile)
```

listen

This function tells your program to listen for incoming connections to the socket and set up a buffer for them of Queuesize.

Syntax:

```
listen(Socket, Queuesize)
```

local

This function declares one or more variables to be locally scoped.

Syntax:

```
local Expr
```

8

localtime

This function takes the value returned by the **time** function and converts it to the time for the local time zone. Like **gmttime,** this function returns a nine-element list of numeric values.

Syntax:

```
localtime Expr
```

Example:

```
($seconds, $minutes, $hour, $monthday, $month, $year, $weekday, $yearday,

$isdist) =
    localtime(time);
```

log

This function returns the logarithm of *Expr*. If *Expr* is omitted, it returns the logarithm of $_.

Syntax:

```
log Expr
log
```

Example:

```
$value = 100;
$log_value = log($value); # $log_value gets the value 4.60517018598809
```

lstat

This function returns the statistics on a file, except that if the last component of the requested file is a symbolic link, the statistics returned will be those of the symbolic link.

Syntax:

```
lstat(Expr)
```

map

This function evaluates the *Block* or *Expr* for each element in *List* and returns a list with each evaluated element.

Syntax:

```
map Block List
map Expr, List
```

Example:

```
@soldiers = qw(McClellan Grant Lee Custer);
@generals = map { split /,/ } @soldiers;
# @generals gets McClellanGrantLeeCuster
```

mkdir

This function creates a directory named Filename and sets the permissions specified by Mode.

Syntax:

```
mkdir(Filename, Mode)
```

8

my

This function declares one or more variables to be private to the innermost block, subroutine, **eval**, or file. Variables declared by **my** exist only while the environment they were declared in is active.

Syntax:

```
my Expr
```

Example:

```
sub sortproc {
    my $temp_var; # $temp_var exists only while the subprocedure sortproc
is being executed
    …. # lines that sort something
}
```

new

This is not a built-in function, but a constructor method to let you construct new objects of the type *Classname*. See Chapter 11 for an example of the **new** method.

Syntax:

```
new Classname, List
new Classname
```

next

This command causes the next iteration of a loop or *Label*, much like the **continue** statement in C.

Syntax:

```
next Label
next
```

Example:

```
for ($x = 1; $x <= 20; $x++) {
    if ($x eq 13) { next; }
    print "$x ";
}; # this loop prints 1 2 3 4 5 6 7 8 9 10 11 12 14 15 16 17 18 19 20
```

no

This function does the opposite of the *use* operator, which means it doesn't import the modules into the program.

```
no Module, List
```

oct

This function takes an octal value in *Expr* and returns the decimal equivalent.

Syntax:

```
oct Expr
```

Example:

```
$num = oct(10); # $ num gets the value 8
```

open

This function opens the file indicated by *Expr* and associates with the filehandle named in *Filehandle*. See Chapter 6 for a full explanation on using the **open** function.

Syntax:

```
open Filehandle, Expr
```

opendir

This function opens a directory named *Expr*.

Syntax:

```
opendir(DirHandle, Expr)
```

ord

This function returns the ASCII numeric value of the first character in *Expr*.

Syntax:

```
ord Expr
```

Example:

```
$string = "abc";
print ord($string); # prints the value 97
$string = "ABC";
print ord($string); # prints the value 65
```

pack

This function takes a list of values and creates (packs) a binary structure, with the return value of the function being the string that contains the structure. The template is a series of characters that give the order and types of values.

8

See the Perl documentation for a full listing of the different characters and their meanings.

Syntax:

```
pack Template, List
```

Example:

```
$alpha = pack "cccc", 97, 98, 99, 100; $alpha gets "abcd"
```

package

This declaration creates a new namespace. See the discussion of variable scoping in the text.

Syntax:

```
package Namespace
```

Example:

```
Package MyPack;
my $scalar; # $scalar is visible only within package MyPack, not
whole program
```

pipe

This function creates a pair of connected pipes, one for reading and one for writing.

Syntax:

```
pipe(ReadHandle, WriteHandle)
```

pop

This function returns the last value of an array, treating the array like a stack. This is a destructive function, meaning that the array is shortened by the element returned by the function.

Syntax:

```
pop Array
pop
```

Example:

```
@generals = qw(McClellan Grant Lee);
print pop @generals; # Lee is displayed
```

pos

This function returns the offset (position) in *Scalar* where the last **m/ /g** search through *Scalar* stopped.

Syntax:

```
pos Scalar
```

Example:

```
$string = "these the their those";
while ($string =~ m/th/g) {
    print pos $string ","; # prints 2 8 12 18
}
```

8

print

This function prints a string or comma-delimited list of strings to the *Filehandle*, usually STDOUT. STDOUT is the default if *Filehandle* is omitted. This function returns a 1 if successful and a 0 if unsuccessful. If no argument is provided, the value of $_ is printed.

Syntax:

```
print Filehandle List
print List
print
```

Example:

```
print STDOUT "This is a sample print out";
print "This is a sample print out"; # this also goes to STDOUT
```

printf

This function prints a formatted list to the specified filehandle or to the current filehandle.

Syntax:

```
printf(FileHandle, List)
```

printf(List)

push

This function adds the value of *List* to the elements of *Array*, treating *Array* like a stack by adding the value of *List* to the end of *Array*.

Syntax:

```
Push Array, List
```

Example:

```
@soldiers = qw(McClellan Grant Lee);
push @soldiers, qw(Custer Selfridge);
# @soldiers now has the value McClellan, Grant, Lee, Custer, Selfridge,
```

q/String/

This function creates a literal by surrounding the value in *String* with quotes, depending on which version of the function you use.

Syntax:

```
q/String/
qq/String/
```

```
qx/String/
qw/String/
```

Here is a list of the quotes created by **q**:

◆   **q:** ' '
◆   **qq:** " "
◆   **qx:** ` `
◆   **qw:** ( ) or a word list

A common use of the **q** function is to create a list of individual words, like this:

```
@yanks = qw(Grant McClellan Sherman Custer); # same as the line below
@rebs =  ("Lee", "Davis", "Pemberton");
```

rand

This function returns a random fractional number between 0 and the value of *Expr*. If *Expr* is omitted, a random number between 0 and 1 is calculated.

Syntax:

```
rand Expr
rand
```

8

Example:

```
$random = (rand 3) * 100; # $random gets the value 0.3753662109375
```

read

This function reads the specified *Length* of bytes from the file specified by *Filehandle* and stores it in *Scalar*. If *Offset* is given, the data from the function is stored *Offset* bytes from the beginning of *Scalar*.

Syntax:

```
read Filehandle, Scalar, Length
read Filehandle, Scalar, Length, Offset
```

Example:

```
open(OUT,"text.txt");
read OUT, $text, 100; # reads the first 100 bytes from "text.txt" into the
variable $text
```

readdir

This function reads all the files from a directory handle into a list.

Syntax:

```
readdir(DirHandle)
```

Example:

```
opendir Tdir, "c:\perl";
@files = readdir(Tdir);
print "@files"; # prints all files found in c:\perl
```

readlink

This function returns the name of a file pointed to by a symbolic link.

Syntax:

```
readlink(Expr)
```

recv

This function receives messages on a socket.

Syntax:

```
recv(Socket, Scalar, Len, Flags)
```

redo

This function causes the code in *Label* to be executed again, effectively creating a loop for a block of code.

Syntax:

```
redo Label
redo
```

Example:

```
$x = 0;
LOOP: while ($x < 10) {
    $x += 1;
    if ($x = 5) { redo LOOP; }
} # will print 1 through 4 and then print 5s continuously
```

ref

This function returns a true value if *Expr* is a reference. For example, if the reference is to a hash called \%hash, the return value will be HASH.

Syntax:

```
ref(Expr)
```

Example:

```
$ref = \%hash;
print ref($ref); # prints HASH
```

8

rename

This function renames the files specified in *Oldfilename* to the name specified in *Newfilename*.

Syntax:

```
rename Oldfilename, Newfilename
```

Example:

```
$file1 = "sample.txt";
$file2 = "example.txt";
rename $file1, $file2; # sample.txt becomes example.txt
```

require

This function is used to assert a dependency on its argument. If *Expr* is a module, the module is introduced, but none of its symbols are added into the current package.

Syntax:

```
require(Expr)
require
```

return

This function is used in a subroutine to return a value to the calling procedure. If **return** is omitted, the subroutine returns the value of the last expression evaluated.

Syntax:

```
return Expr
```

Example:

```
sub max {
    my $biggest = shift(@_);
    foreach $arg (@_) {
        if ($biggest < $arg) {
            $biggest = $arg;
        }
    }
    return $biggest; # the value of $biggest gets sent to calling
procedure
}
```

reverse

This function takes the elements of *List* and reverses their order.

Syntax:

```
reverse List
```

Example:

```
@soldiers = qw(McClellan, Lee, Grant, Pemberton,);
print reverse @soldiers; # prints Pemberton,Grant,Lee,McClellan
```

rewinddir

This function resets the position of a directory handle to the beginning so that **readdir** can read from the first of the directory.

Syntax:

```
rewinddir(DirHandle)
```

rindex

This function looks for a substring in a string going backwards from the end of the string or backwards from Position.

Syntax:

```
rindex(Str, Substr, Position)
rindex(Str, Substr)
```

8

rmdir

This function removes the specified directory if it is empty.

Syntax:

```
rmdir(DirName)
```

s///

This is the substitution operator. See Chapter 5 for a full discussion of substitution in regular expressions.

Example:

```
$text = "reciept deciet conciet";
$text =~ s/ie/ei/g; # $text becomes "receipt deceit conceit"
```

scalar

This function can be used to force an expression to be evaluated as a scalar.

Syntax:

```
scalar(Expr)
```

seek

This function sets the file pointer within a file by moving the pointer *Offset* bytes into the file specified by *Filehandle*, starting at the position specified by *Whence*. The value of *Whence* can be 0, the beginning of the file; 1, the current position in the file; or 2, the end of the file.

Syntax:

```
seek Filehandle, Offset, Whence
```

Example:

```
open(OUT,"text.txt");
seek OUT, 0, 0; # sets the file pointer to the beginning of
                # "text.txt"
```

seekdir

This function sets the current position on a directory to *Position*.

Syntax:

```
seekdir(DirHandle, Position)
```

select (output filehandle)

This function (not related to the next function of the same name) sets the output filehandle specified or the current filehandle if one isn't specified.

Syntax:

```
select(FileHandle)
select
```

Select (ready file descriptors)

This function (not related to the previous function of the same name) determines what file descriptors are set for reading, writing, or exception reporting.

Syntax:

```
select(Rbits, Wbits, Ebits, Timeout)
```

send

This function sends a message (and flags, if specified) to the specified socket.

Syntax:

```
send(Socket, Message, Flags, To)
send(Socket, Message, Flags)
```

setpgrp

This function sets the current process group for the specified PID.

Syntax:

```
setpgrp(PID, PGRP)
```

8

setpriority

This function sets the current priority for a process.

Syntax:

```
setpriority(Which, Who, Priority)
```

shift

This function shifts the first value of *Array* off the array and returns it. If *Array* isn't specified, the function shifts @ARGV or @_.

Syntax:

```
shift Array
shift
```

Example:

```
@soldiers = ("McClellan", "Lee", "Grant", "Pemberton");
$old_soldier = shift(@soldiers); # $old_soldier gets "McClellan"
```

shutdown

This function tells the Socket to shutdown in the manner specified in *How*.
How can be 0 (further receives are not allowed), 1 (further sends are not
allowed), or 2 (further sends and receives are not allowed).

Syntax:

```
shutdown(Socket, How)
```

sin

This function returns the sine of *Expr* expressed in radians.

Syntax:

```
sin Expr
```

Example:

```
$num = 1;
$num_sine = sin($num); # $num_sine gets the value 0.841470984807897
```

sleep

This function causes a Perl script to pause for *Expr* seconds. If no *Expr* is
specified, the script pauses forever.

Syntax:

```
sleep Expr
sleep
```

Example:

```
sub pause_to_think {
    sleep 60;
```

```
} # a nonsense function that when called will pause the script for 60
seconds
```

socket

This function opens a socket and binds it to the filehandle specified in *Socket*.

Syntax:

```
socket(Socket, Domain, Type, Protocol)
```

socketpair

This function creates an unnamed pair of sockets.

Syntax:

```
socketpair(Socket1, Socket2, Domain, Type, Protocol)
```

sort

This function takes the elements of *List* and returns them in standard string sort order. The second prototype above shows that you can also provide your own sort routine to the function. See Chapter 11 for examples of using your own sort routines.

8

Syntax:

```
sort List
sort named_sort List
```

Example:

```
@soldiers = qw(McClellan Pemberton Lee Grant);
print sort @soldiers; # prints GrantLeeMcClellanPemberton
```

splice

This function removes the elements of *Array* specified by *Offset* and *Length* and replaces them with the elements specified by *List*. If *Length* is omitted, the function removes everything from *Offset* on.

Syntax:

```
splice Array, Offset, Length, List
splice Array, Offset, Length
splice Array, Offset
```

Example:

```
@soldiers = qw(McClellan Lee Grant Pemberton);
@defeated = splice(@soldiers, -1); # @defeated gets the value "Pemberton"
```

split

This function searches the string given in *Expr* for a delimiter given in
/Pattern/, returning a list of substrings created by dividing the string at the
delimiter. If *Limit* is specified, only that many substrings will be created. The
example below is the most common form of the **split** function.

Syntax:

```
split /Pattern/, Expr, Limit
split /Pattern/, Expr
split /Pattern/
split
```

Example:

```
$soldiers = "McClellan,Lee,Grant,Pemberton";
($general1, $general2, $general3, $general4) = split /,/, $soldiers;
# $general1 gets McClellan, $general2 gets Lee, and so forth
```

sqrt

This function returns the square root of *Expr*, and if *Expr* isn't specified,
returns the square root of $_.

Syntax:

```
sqrt Expr
```

Example:

```
$num = sqrt(4); # $num gets the value 2
```

srand

This function sets the random number seed for the *rand* operator.

Syntax:

```
srand(Expr)
```

stat

This function returns various statistics that describe a file, including:

- ◆ *dev*   Device number of the file system
- ◆ *ino*   Inode number
- ◆ *mode*   File mode
- ◆ *nlink*   Number of hard links to the file
- ◆ *uid*   User ID of file's owner
- ◆ *gid*   Group ID of file's owner
- ◆ *rdev*   Device identifier
- ◆ *size*   Size of file in bytes
- ◆ *atime*   Last access time
- ◆ *mtime*   Last modify time
- ◆ *ctime*   Inode change time
- ◆ *blksize*   Preferred block size for filesystem
- ◆ *blocks*   Number of blocks allocated to file

Syntax:

```
stat(FileHandle)
```

8

study

This function forces Perl to create a more detailed data structure of the scalar specified (or $_) in order to perform more efficient pattern matches.

Syntax:

```
study(Scalar)
study
```

substr

This function returns the substring in *Expr* specified by *Offset* and *Length*. If *Length* isn't specified, the function returns everything starting at *Offset*.

Syntax:

```
substr Expr, Offset, Length
substr Expr, Offset
```

Example:

```
$string = "Now is the time for all good people";
$sub1 = substr($string,7,8); # $sub1 gets the value "the time"
$sub2 = substr($string,7); # $sub2 gets the value "the time for all good
                           # people"
```

symlink

This function creates a new filename symbolically linked to the old filename.

Syntax:

```
symlink(Oldfile, Newfile)
```

syscall

This function passes the elements of *List* to the system call specified as the first element of *List*.

Syntax:

```
syscall(List)
```

sysopen

This function opens a filename and associates with a filehandle, giving the file the rights specified in *Mode*, and optionally, the permissions specified in *Permissions*.

Syntax:

```
sysopen(FileHandle, Filename, Mode)
sysopen(FileHandle, Filename, Mode, Permissions)
```

sysread

This function tries to read the specified *Length* of bytes from *FileHandle* into *Scalar*, starting at *Offset*.

Syntax:

```
sysread(FileHandle, Scalar, Length, Offset)
sysread(FileHandle, Scalar, Length)
```

system

This function executes a program on your system specified by *List*.

Syntax:

```
system List
```

8

Example:

```
system("dir"); # performs a directory call on your operating system
```

syswrite

This function tries to write the *Length* number of bytes from *Scalar* into *FileHandle*, starting at *Offset*.

Syntax:

```
syswrite(FileHandle, Scalar, Length, Offset)
syswrite(FileHandle, Scalar, Length)
```

tell

This function returns the current position of the file pointer in *Filehandle*.

Syntax:

```
tell Filehandle
tell
```

Example:

```
open(OUT,"text.txt");
seek OUT,10,0;
$pos = tell OUT; # $pos gets the value 10
```

telldir

This function returns the current position of *readdir* on *DirHandle*.

Syntax:

```
telldir(DirHandle)
```

tie

This function binds a variable to a class. See Chapter 11 for further details.

Syntax:

```
tie(Variable, Classname, List)
```

tied

This function returns a reference to the object the specified variable is tied to.

Syntax:

```
tied(Variable)
```

time

This function returns the number of non-leap seconds since the epoch (January 1, 1970).

Syntax:

```
Time
```

Example:

```
print time; # prints 872184416 (enterprising souls can determine
            # when I wrote this!)
```

times

This function returns a list giving the user and system CPU times for the current process and any child processes.

Syntax:

```
times
```

tr///

This is the *translation* operator, described in detail in Chapter 12.

Syntax:

```
tr///
```

8

truncate

This function truncates the file named by *Filehandle* or *Expr* to *Length*.

Syntax:

```
truncate Filehandle, Length
truncate Expr, Length
```

Example:

```
open(OUT,"text.txt");
truncate OUT, 10; # text.txt is truncated to length of 10
```

uc

This function takes the value of *Expr* and returns it in all uppercase.

Syntax:

```
uc Expr
```

Example:

```
$os = "Unix";
print "Is it $os or ", uc($os),?"; prints "Is it Unix or UNIX?"
```

ucfirst

This function returns the value of *Expr* with the first character capitalized.

Syntax:

```
ucfirst Expr
```

Example:

```
$os = "unix";
print "$os programmers don't like to capitalize the first letter in ",
ucfirst($os);
# the line above prints "unix programmers don't like to capitalize the
first letter in Unix"
```

umask

This function sets the umask (the permission bits to disallow) for the process and returns the old one.

Syntax:

```
umask(Expr)
umask
```

undef

This function undefines the value of *Expr*, freeing up memory. If you use it by itself, it simply returns an undefined value, which can be used to indicate an error.

Syntax:

```
undef Expr
undef
```

Example:

```
$town = "Vicksburg";
undef $town; # undefines the value of $town
```

unlink

This function deletes a list of files.

Syntax:

```
unlink(List)
```

unpack

This function takes the packed data structure in *Expr* and expands it into a list value.

Syntax:

```
unpack(Template, Expr)
```

8

unshift

This function prepends *List* to the front of *Array*, just the opposite of the **shift** function.

Syntax:

```
unshift Array, List
```

Example:

```
@soldiers = qw(Lee Pemberton);
@yanks = qw(McClellan Grant);

unshift @soldiers, @yanks; # @soldiers becomes McClellan, Grant, Lee,
                           # Pemberton,
```

untie

This function deletes the binding between a variable and a package.

Syntax:

```
untie(Variable)
```

utime

This function changes the access and modification times of the file or files named in *List*.

Syntax:

```
utime List
```

Example:

```
$now = time;
utime $now, $now, "text.txt";
# the access and modification time for the file is now system time
```

values

This function returns a list of the values of the hash specified in *Hash*.

Syntax:

```
values Hash
```

Example:

```
%battles = (
    Mississippi => Vicksburg,
    Maryland => Antietam,
    Virginia => Richmond,
    Georgia => Atlanta,
);
@battles = values %battles;
```

wait

This function waits for a child process to terminate and returns the PID of the process.

Syntax:

```
wait
```

waitpid

This function returns true when and if a child process terminates. Valid flag values can be found in wait_h.pm.

Syntax:

```
waitpid(PID, Flags)
```

wantarray

This function determines whether or not the currently executing subroutine is looking for a list value. If so, the function returns true.

Syntax:

```
wantarray
```

8

warn

This function is used to write a message to STDERR like the **die** function, but unlike **die**, **warn** doesn't exit or throw an exception.

Syntax:

```
warn List
```

Example:

```
open(OUT,"text.txt") or warn "Cannot open file";
```

Summary

As you can tell from this chapter, Perl has a great number of functions you can use in your programs. Many of them, however, are based on Unix utilities and may or may not be functional on Windows systems. The best way to find out is to give them a try. Also, as the Windows implementations of Perl become more mature, more and more of the functions that previously worked on Unix now will become available for Perl for Win32.

CHAPTER 9

Custom Functions

Perl provides the programmer with the capability of creating user-defined functions (commonly called *subroutines* in Perl) in much the same way user-defined functions are supported by the C/C++ language. This chapter will provide you with the background you need to create your own sub-routines in Perl. The subjects this chapter will discuss include: a comparison of local, global, and formal variables and the scope rules for variables in Perl; returning values from subroutines; passing command-line arguments to subroutines; passing arrays and hashes to subroutines; and subroutine prototypes.

Declaring and Calling Subroutines in Perl

You declare a subroutine in Perl using the **sub** keyword, followed by a name for the subroutine and a block of code that defines the functionality of the subroutine, as follows:

```
sub NAME BLOCK;
```

You can also declare a subroutine with only its name, saving the definition block of code for later, like this:

```
sub NAME;
```

This type of function declaration is known as a "forward" declaration, meaning the full definition of the function will come later (or forward) in the program.

Finally, if you want to declare a subroutine with a prototype (to be discussed later in the chapter), use this form:

```
sub NAME(PROTO);
```

To call, or execute, a user-defined subroutine, use the following syntax:

```
NAME(LIST);
```

where **name** is the name of the subroutine and LIST is a list of the arguments to the subroutine. If the subroutine has been declared elsewhere in the program, you can leave off the parentheses surrounding the argument list, like this:

```
NAME LIST;
```

Here are some simple examples of declaring and calling Perl subroutines:

```
sub max; # declared with no code block
sub min(@); # declared with a prototype
sub min {
    # code for min goes here - examples with real code shown later
}
```

Now that you know how to declare and call subroutines, the next thing to learn is how to work with the variables that are used by subroutines and the calling program. Perl has three variable types: global variables, local variables, and formal parameters, which are the variables that go in the subroutine argument list. The following section describes these variable types and their use in user-defined subroutines.

Variables and their Scope

Perl is a modern programming language and, as such, it provides for the *lexical scoping* of variables. Lexical scoping means that variables that are defined within a subroutine or block of code are local to that particular subroutine or block. The following sections explain how to use variables with user-defined subroutines.

9

Global Variables

Global variables are declared outside of any subroutine or function and can be accessed by any part of a Perl program, including subroutines. Any variable that just springs into existence, without any sort of declaration, is considered a global variable. For example, the following simple Perl program declares a global variable that a subroutine accesses and returns as its value:

```
$global_var = 100;
sub simple {
    return $global_var;
}
print simple;
```

When this program is run, the value 100 is returned and printed on the screen. As this example shows, global variables can be accessed anywhere in a Perl program.

When a global variable is declared, its value is maintained in memory throughout the lifetime of the program in which it is declared. There are some advantages to using global variables. One advantage is that if a certain value is needed by different parts of your program, that value is probably best stored in a global variable. Also, if a variable needs to maintain its value throughout the execution of a program, it is best declared as a global variable.

Good programming style dictates that global variables should only be used when absolutely necessary. There are three major reasons why:

1. Global variables take up valuable memory even when they are not needed by the program.
2. Using many global variables can become troublesome when they are used in a large program and it becomes hard to track down their values at different times in the program.
3. Using global variables in subroutines when a local variable can be used makes the subroutine less general because the subroutine depends on a value defined outside the subroutine itself.

Local Variables

Local variables are private to the subroutine in which they are declared. This means that a locally declared variable cannot be accessed by any other part of a Perl program. There are two types of locally declared variables in Perl: dynamic variables and lexical variables. A *dynamic variable* is one that is visible to any subroutines called within the subroutine where the dynamic variable is declared. Dynamic variables are declared with the **local** keyword, which has the following syntax:

```
local VAR;
```

Lexical variables, on the other hand, really are private variables because you can only get at their value from inside the actual subroutine in which they are declared. The syntax for declaring lexical variables is:

```
my VAR;
```

Here is an example of how a lexical variable differs from a global variable:

```
$value = 100; # global variable
sub return_value {
```

```
    my $value; # lexical variable
    $value = 50;
    return $value;
}
print return_value; # prints 50
print $value; # prints 100
```

The first **print** function returns 50 because the value of $value within the context of the subroutine is 50. The second **print** function returns 100 because the value of $value within the context of the whole program is 100.

Here is another simple program that demonstrates how lexical variables work:

```
sub simple {
    my $value = 100;
}
print $value; # prints nothing
```

This program prints nothing because the variable $value is only valid within the scope of the subroutine. Outside the subroutine, in the main program, the variable has no value and Perl simply returns an empty string as the value of the **print** function.

Generally, lexical variables are declared at the beginning of a subroutine, but this doesn't have to be the case. A lexical variable can be declared anywhere within the body of a subroutine, even on the last line, and it will still be treated as a lexical variable, as long as it is declared as a lexical variable before it is used.

9

The advantages to using lexical variables are:

◆ Memory for variables is used only when necessary.

◆ Memory used by lexical variables is released when the subroutine is finished executing.

◆ Keeping track of subroutine variables is easier because they are defined within the subroutine and only referenced within it.

Formal Parameters

The third type of variable used by a subroutine is the *formal parameter*, or *subroutine argument*. Many subroutines in Perl will be called with a list of one or more arguments that are passed to the subroutine. These arguments are also called *named formal parameters* (in math-speak). In C/C++, named formal parameters look like this:

```
void display_num (int num)
{
    cout << num;
}
```

where the named formal parameters, or parameter in this case, appear enclosed in parentheses after the name of the function. Unlike C/C++, Perl does not have named formal parameters. However, in a later section you will learn how to take the contents of the @_ special variable and assign it to a list of lexical variables, effectively passing the list of command-line arguments to the subroutine. These variables, being lexical variables, are handled privately within the subroutine and have all the characteristics of standard lexical variables.

Returning Values from Subroutines

Returning a value from a subroutine simply means passing a value calculated in some way by the subroutine back to the calling program or subroutine. Subroutines return a value by calling the **return** function with a value as its argument. Here is a simple subroutine declaration that returns a value:

```
sub display {
    return $_;
}
```

This subroutine, when called, returns the value found in the variable $_. If there is nothing in $_, the subroutine will return the empty string.

If the **return** function is not called in a subroutine, the subroutine will return the value of the last expression in the subroutine. What will be the returning value of the subroutine below?

```
sub calc {
    $pi = 3.14159;
    $r = 12;
    $calc = $pi * ($r * $r);
}
```

If you use this subroutine in a program, like this:

```
sub calc {
    $pi = 3.14159;
    $r = 12;
    $calc = $pi * ($r * $r);
}
 $circumf = calc;
```

the value of $circumf will be the value of the expression $calc = $pi * ($r *
$r), which is also considered to be the value of the subroutine. If a subroutine
doesn't calculate a value, but instead performs some other function, such as
displaying a message, the subroutine will still have a value. If the subroutine
executes successfully, its value is 1; if it cannot execute, its value is 0. Here is
an example where calling a subroutine produces an effect that was probably
not intended:

```
sub greeting {
    print "Hello ";
}
print greeting; # returns "Hello 1"
```

In this example, the subroutine prints its message and then returns the fact
that it ran successfully. A better way to write the subroutine above is like this:

```
sub greeting {
    return "Hello ";
}
print greeting; # prints "Hello " only
```

9

Finally, you can have more than one **return** function in a subroutine.
Whichever return is executed first will be the value of the subroutine. Here is
an example:

```
sub even_odd {
    my $num = shift(@_);
    return "even" if (($num % 2) eq 0); # function terminates when
                   an even number is passed to the function
    return "odd" if (($num % 2) eq 0); # function terminates when
                   an odd number is passed to the function
}
print even_odd(2); # prints "even"
```

Passing Arguments to a Subroutine

As mentioned earlier, Perl does not have named formal parameters. However, you don't really need named formal parameters because any arguments to a subroutine are stored in the special variable @_. Simply access each element of @_ like you would access any element of an array. Here is a subroutine that uses @_ to keep a list of numbers to sum and a program that calls the subroutine:

```
sub sum {
    my $sum = 0;
    foreach $num (@_) {
        $sum += $num;
    }
    return $sum;
}
$total = sum(1,2,3,4); # $total gets the value 10
```

In this example, each number in the argument list is an element of the @_ and is processed in turn by the **foreach** loop.

Another way to access the argument list is to access each element of @_ individually. This method works best (only) if you know in advance the length of the element list. Here is an example:

```
sub sum {
    my($num1, $num2) = ($_[0], $_[1]);
    my $sum = $num1 + $num2;
    return $sum;
}
$total = sum(1,2); # $total gets the value 3
```

Passing Data Structures to Subroutines

It is possible in Perl to pass a whole array or hash to a subroutine using something known as a *typeglob*. A typeglob is a way of referring to all the different data types a variable can have at once by adding an asterisk (*) prefix to the variable name. In other words, if you have an array named @soldiers, a scalar variable named $soldiers, and a hash named %soldiers, you can refer to any of these by the typeglob *soldiers.

When you want to pass a whole structure such as an array or hash to a subroutine, you have to use a typeglob reference to the structure. When you do this, you pass what is, in effect, a global copy of the structure to the subroutine—which means your code can make a permanent change to the structure. When you pass the array by accessing @_ , you are working with a local copy of the array and any changes you make will not be permanent. Here's an example, followed by an explanation:

```
@soldiers = qw(McClellan Lee Grant Pemberton);
sub change_title {
    local(*generals) = @_;
    foreach $name (@generals) {
        $name = $name . "-General";
    }
}
title(*soldiers);
print $soldiers[1]; # prints "Lee-General"
```

This program begins by creating an array called *soldiers* that contains some soldier names. Then a subroutine called **change_title** is defined. This subroutine takes the array coming in from @_ and assigns it to the typeglob *generals. Then each element of the array @generals is accessed, and their name is changed by adding their rank. After the subroutine definition is a call to the subroutine, passing the typeglob *soldiers, which is just the proper way to pass the global array @soldiers. The subroutine does its work, and the last line of the program demonstrates that each element of the array has had a title/rank added to the name. Clearly, you can see that the array passed to the subroutine is treated globally since the elements are actually changed. The same type of processing can occur with a hash as well as an array.

Subroutine Prototypes

Perl versions 5.003 and above allow you to declare a subroutine prototype that tells Perl the number and type of arguments expected to be given to the subroutine. The prototype appears in parentheses after the subroutine name, and it consists of a Perl variable type prefix ($, @, %, &, *) with an optional backslash before the variable prefix. If the backslash is present in the prototype, it means the argument must start with that character. For example, a subroutine prototype like this:

```
sub sum (\@)
```

means that the argument to the subroutine has to be an array name, like @numbers.

9

If a subroutine is called and the argument(s) to the subroutine don't match the prototype, Perl will raise an error. Subroutine prototypes, then, can help enforce good programming practice. Examine the following Perl program:

```
sub sum ($$) {
    my ($num1, $num2) = ($_[0], $_[1]);
    my $sum = $num1 + $num2;
    return $sum;
}
print sum(1);
```

When this program is executed, an error will occur because the subroutine prototype specifies two arguments to be passed to the subroutine, but in actuality only one argument is passed. Had the prototype been left out, Perl would have executed the program without an error, simply assigning the empty string to the second argument.

Another prototype modifier is the semicolon. When a semicolon is placed in an argument list, it means that all the arguments before the semicolon are mandatory and all the arguments after the semicolon are optional. The program above can be rewritten using the semicolon, so that at least one number is passed to the subroutine, but not more than one argument is necessary for the subroutine to execute successfully. Here is the rewritten program:

```
sub sum ($;$) {
    my ($num1, $num2) = ($_[0], $_[1]);
    my $sum = $num1 + $num2;
    return $sum;
}
print sum(1);
```

Subroutine prototypes can also do interesting things when the backslash is left off. The prototypes @ and %, for example, take all the actual arguments and force them into list context. So, if you use one of these prototypes and pass the subroutine scalar arguments, the scalars will actually be passed to the subroutine in list context. The program below shows a simple example of how this works:

```
$stooge1 = "Moe";
$stooge2 = "Larry";
$stooge3 = "Curly";
```

```
sub myrev (@) {

   return reverse (@_);
}
print newrev $stooge1, $stooge2, $stooge3; # prints "CurlyLarryMoe"
```

The program above utilizes a user-written **reverse** subroutine (a useless task in reality) by actually calling the real **reverse** function. Since the **reverse** function wants a list as its argument, using the @ prototype with the **newrev** subroutine guarantees that a list is what the subroutine gets, no matter what the contexts of the actual arguments are. In the program above, scalar variables ($stooge1, $stooge2, $stooge3) are passed to the subroutine, but the prototype gobbles them up into an array (list), which is passed to **reverse**.

Recursive Subroutines

A **recursive** subroutine is a subroutine that calls itself in the execution of the subroutine. Recursion is likened to a circular definition because a recursive subroutine is essentially a subroutine defined in terms of itself. So, a recursive subroutine is a subroutine that calls itself as part of its execution.

The best way to explain a recursive subroutine is to show a clear example, and the best example of recursion is the factorial operation. For those of you who aren't familiar with calculating a factorial, the factorial of an number is the product of all the whole numbers between 1 and that number. In mathematical terms, factorial is expressed like this: N!, where N is the number you want to calculate the factorial of. For example, 5! is equal to 5*4*3*2*1 or 120. Here is a program that calculates factorials, using a recursive subroutine:

9

```
sub factr {
   my $num = $_[0];
   my answer;
   if ($num eq 1) { return 1; }
   $answer = factr($_[0] - 1) * $num;
   return $answer;
}
print factr(5); # prints 120
```

Here is how the recursive subroutine works. The first line of the subroutine gives the variable $num the initial argument, 5. A lexical variable is declared to store the results of the factorial operation. Then $num is checked to see if it is equal to 1. If it is, then the value 1 is returned because 1 factorial is equal to 1. The next line is where the real work is accomplished. Each time this line is called, the subroutine is called recursively with an argument 1 less than the last argument. This happens until $_ is equal to 1, and then the subroutine begins returning each recursive call. Here is a trace of the computations that occur after $_ is equal to 1:

1 * 1 = 1

1 * 2 = 2

2 * 3 = 6

6 * 4 = 24

24 * 5 = 120

Then the final calculation, 120, is stored in the $answer variable, and it is returned to the calling program.

Here's another example of a mathematical problem that can be solved with recursion—exponentiation. The problem of raising a number to a given power can easily be seen as a recursive process, because you continually multiply a number by itself for a number of times that equals the exponent of the equation. Obviously, 2 to the eighth power is equal to 2 times 2 times 2 times 2 times 2 times 2 times 2 time 2, or 256. There are actually two ways to solve this problem. Here is a script that uses a recursive process to solve the exponentiation problem:

```
print expt(2,8);
sub expt {
    my $base = $_[0];
    my $num = $_[1];
    my $answer;
    if ($num eq 0) { return 1; }
    $answer = $base * expt($base, ($num-1));
    return $answer;
}
```

This example is similar to the last example in that the recursive step builds up a base of temporary computations that are finally computed when the base case of the procedure, ($num eq 0), becomes True.

Any subroutine that uses a recursive calculation to obtain a value can also use an iterative calculation to obtain the same value. Recursion is used in those cases where the iterative solution is longer and more complex than the recursive solution. However, keep in mind that if you're not used to thinking recursively, it can be hard to write recursive functions. Coming up with recursive solutions to complex problems takes time and practice.

Finally, one word of warning about using recursive subroutines. If you don't have an **if** statement in the subroutine that forces the subroutine to return without making the recursive call, you will find the subroutine will get endlessly lost in a loop. Every recursive subroutine must look for a condition that ends the recursion, which is often called a *terminating* condition.

Program Design with Functions

Functions play an important part in a style of computer programming called *structured programming*. A structured program is one that is made up of functional (get it?) components, with each component playing a clear role in the overall strategy of the program. The functional components of a structured program will often be custom functions, such as the ones you've learned about in this chapter. This style of programming results in programs that are easy to understand, easy to maintain, and easy to debug.

When you design your programs using structured programming techniques, each program will almost naturally become a set of functions fit together to solve a problem. One way to assure that this happens is to use a top-down approach to designing your program. This approach suggests that you first look at the overall problem you are trying to solve and work from this view of the problem (the "top" view) down to the actual code that makes up the program. You can compare this method to creating an outline before you write an essay. With a program, instead of having topics or chapters, you have functions. For example, here is the top-level view of a simple program that gets input from the user, calculates a result, and displays that result to the user:

```
Get_input();
Calculate_result();
Display_result();
```

Once this skeleton is created, you can begin to fill in the details, usually by creating more functions. Here's an example of filling in the details for the **Get_input( )** function:

```
Display_Gui();
Wait_for_input();
Check_input();  # for accurancy, etc.
Pass_input_to_calculator();
Clear_input();
```

From here, you will fill in more details for each of these functions until you finally get down to writing Perl code. If you are wondering just how far you should go in creating functions for your programs, a common rule of thumb is that if a section of code is longer than a page in length it should be broken up into a function.

Another structured programming technique you can use is bottom-up programming. With this technique, you start with a basic function and work your way up to more functions. This technique is commonly used when the problem you are trying to solve is not well understand or the program's requirements haven't been fully decided on. For example, if you use a bottom-up approach to solving the problem discussed previously, you might first write the **Display_Gui** function, then the **Wait_for_input** function, and so on.

Each of these techniques is useful in creating structured programs, and in reality, most programming efforts involve using both techniques. Pick the technique or mix of techniques you are most comfortable with and try to use it consistently. Whichever technique or mix you choose, using structured programming techniques will improve both the quality of your programs and the efficiency of your programming.

Problems with Functions

Generally, programming with functions solves more problems then it creates, but there are always a few wisenheimers out there who complain about structured programming. Their most common complaint is that calling too many functions unnecessarily slows down a program. This complaint has been rendered practically moot in this day of 200+MHz processors. While improvements in hardware have led to some misuses in software (feature bloat), these improvements have also made it possible to write slower, yet more structured programs that still run at acceptable speeds.

Another common complaint about structured programming is that it forces someone with less organized thought processes into a rigid, by-the-book software formula that leaves no room for creativity. Of course, this complaint merely reveals the narrow-mindedness of the programmer. You can be just as creative trying to divide a program up into functional components as you can in creating a spaghetti bowl of code.

Finally, some programmers complain that structured programs are actually harder to debug because, when reading through the code, you are constantly having to move back and forth from one function to another, rarely following a linear course through the code. For large programs, this complaint does have some validity, but improvements in debuggers have made it easier to follow a program trace in and out of different functions. Also, if a program has adequate documentation within the program (using comments liberally), it will be easier for another programmer to follow the functional flow of the program.

Summary

The use of custom-built functions, or subroutines, in Perl make it a very powerful, problem-solving language. Being able to create user-designed functions increases the expressiveness of a language, allowing it to be used to solve a wider range of problems. The use of functions also enables the programmer to make a program easier to read, maintain, and debug. Programming with functions also makes it easier to create programs that have fewer bugs in the first place.

9

CHAPTER 10

References and Anonymous Data Structures

One of the features that separates Perl from other scripting languages is its ability to work with references. *References* are like pointers in C/C++; they contain the address of another variable. Like pointers, references play an important role in advanced programming in Perl. They allow the passing of whole data structures to functions, the creation of complex data structures such as arrays of arrays and hashes of hashes (not to mention arrays of hashes and hashes of arrays), and the building of anonymous data structures that let you use Perl to solve powerful, dynamic programming problems. This chapter will introduce you to how Perl uses references and how to create complex and anonymous data structures using references.

What Is a Reference?

Like pointers in other languages, references are somewhat hard to explain to beginning programmers. A classic analogy is the mailbox. Most companies have a mailroom where mail for employees is deposited. Each employee has a mail slot that has his or her name on it. When the mail is distributed, the mail clerk matches the name on the envelope with the name on the slot. The name on the slot is a reference for the clerk to use when distributing mail.

A Perl reference is a variable that contains, or holds, the address of another variable. You can think of a Perl reference like the employee name on the mail slot. All that the reference holds is a memory address. You can say that just as the name on a mail slot points to the place to put that person's mail, a Perl reference points to an address where a variable's data (holding data) is stored.

Hard and Symbolic References

Perl has two types of references: hard and symbolic. A *hard* reference simply points to the data that is stored in the variable being referenced. If you create a reference to a variable named $data, a hard reference will refer directly to the data stored in that variable. Using the mailroom analogy, a hard reference points to the mail stored in the mail slot.

A *symbolic* reference points not to the data stored in a variable, but to the variable name. So, if you create a symbolic reference to the variable $data, the reference will point to the variable itself, not to the data stored in the variable. Using the mailroom analogy again, a symbolic reference points to the name on the mail slot, not the mail in the slot.

Although both types of references are used, hard references are more straightforward and will be discussed in more depth in this chapter than symbolic references.

Creating References

You can create references to scalars, arrays, and hashes. The following sections describe how to create each kind of these references.

Creating References to Scalars

You create a reference to a scalar by using the *backslash* (\) operator. This operator precedes the name of the variable you want to create a reference to on the right-hand side of an **assignment** statement. On the left-hand side will be a standard scalar variable. Here is an example:

```
$string_data = "Some string value";
$a_hard_reference = \$string_data;
```

The first line of the example simply assigns a string to the variable $string_data. The second line assigns a reference to $string_data. The *backslash* operator precedes the variable name, telling Perl to store the address of $string_data to the variable $a_hard_reference.

The creation of a reference to a numeric scalar is done in the same way. For example:

```
$numeric_data = 3.14159;
$another_hard_reference = \$numeric_data;
```

10

Creating References to Arrays

A reference to an array is created just like a reference to a scalar, using the *backslash* operator. Here is an example:

```
@generals = ("McClellan", "Grant", "Lee", "Pemberton");
$hard_ref_to_array = \@generals;
```

The second line of the script assigns the address of the array @generals to the variable $hard_ref_to_array.

Creating References to Hashes

Finally, a reference to a hash is created just like scalars and arrays. For example:

```
%generals = ( "Yank_General",  "Grant",
              "Yank_Officer", "Custer",
              "Reb_General", "Lee",
              "Reb_Officer", "Stuart");
$hard_ref_to_hash = \%generals;
```

As with the other examples, the *backslash* operator is used to assign the address of the hash to the variable $hard_ref_to_hash.

Dereferencing References

To get at the value that a reference is pointing to, you have to dereference the reference. If you don't dereference a reference before obtaining its value, the value you get will be the memory address of the data being referenced. Here's a script that displays the value held by a reference without dereferencing first:

```
$data = "Some text goes here";
$hard_ref = \$data;
print $hard_ref; # displays SCALAR(0xb75de4)
```

The following sections will show you how to properly dereference references to scalars, arrays, and hashes.

Dereferencing a Reference to a Scalar Using $

You dereference a reference to a scalar by adding an extra dollar sign ($) to the reference variable. For example, here's the proper way to write the script above to dereference the variable $hard_ref:

```
$data = "Some text goes here";
$hard_ref = \$data;
print $$hard_ref; # displays Some text goes here
```

Adding the extra dollar sign before the reference variable tells Perl to dereference the reference and get at the value being pointed to.

As you can probably guess, references to numeric data are dereferenced in the same way. Here's an example:

```
$number = 561;
$hard_ref = \$number;
print $$hard_ref; # displays 561
```

You can change the value of a scalar reference by dereferencing the reference. Here is a simple example of changing the value of a numeric scalar:

```
$number = 561;
$hard_ref = \$number;
$$hard_ref += 3;
print $number; # $number now has the value 564
```

The value of $number changes to 564 because when the reference is incremented, the value it points to is what is actually incremented. In other words, both $$hard_ref and $number point to the same physical memory location.

Dereferencing a Reference to an Array Using $

Array references are dereferenced in the same manner as you dereferenced a scalar reference. Simply add an extra dollar sign to the array reference variable. Here is a simple script that creates a reference to an array and displays the array elements by dereferencing the array reference:

```
@names = ("Jay", "Meredith", "Steven", "Allison", "Mason", "Rachel");
$hard_ref = \@names;
foreach (@names) {
    print "$$hard_ref[$i++]\n";
}
```

When this script is run, each name is listed separately on a line, using the *foreach* construct to loop through the array, like this:

```
Jay
Meredith
Steven
Allison
Mason
Rachel
```

If you try to access the reference variable without dereferencing it, you get a value like this: ARRAY(0xb75df0).

10

If you want to get at the whole array reference at once, you must dereference the array reference using the at sign (@) instead of the extra dollar sign. The following script, for example, prints all the names of the array by accessing the array reference as a whole:

```
@names = ("Jay", "Meredith", "Steven", "Allison", "Mason", "Rachel");
$hard_ref = \@names;
print @$hard_refl; # displays JayMeredithStevenAllisonMasonRachel
```

If you perform an operation on an array reference that is destructive (or constructive), the array that is being referenced changes. Here is an example of the results of using the **pop** function on an array reference:

```
@names = ("Jay", "Meredith", "Steven", "Allison", "Mason", "Rachel");
$hard_ref = \@names;
$gone = pop(@$hard_ref) # $gone gets the value "Rachel"
print @names; # displays JayMeredithStevenAllisonMason
```

In this example, the **pop** function permanently removes the last item from the array, despite the fact that it was performed on an array reference. The array contents still change because the reference points at the actual contents of the array.

Dereferencing a Reference to a Hash Using $

As you may have guessed, you dereference a reference to a hash just like you dereference references to scalars and arrays. Here's an example:

```
%comp_lang_dev = ("Perl", "Larry Wall",
                  "Java", "James Gosling",
                  "C", "Dennis Ritchie",
                  "C++", "Bjarne Stroustrup",);
$hard_ref = \%comp_lang_dev;
$lang = "Perl";
print "Perl was originally developed by $$hard_ref{$lang}.\n";
```

When this script is run, it will display:

```
Perl was originally developed by Larry Wall.
```

As with arrays, if you want to dereference the whole hash, you must preface the reference variable with a percent sign (%), as in %$hard_ref.

Dereferencing Using { }

Another way to dereference a reference is using the curly braces. Here are some examples:

```
$number = 561;
$hard_ref = \$number;
print ${$hard_ref}; # displays 561
@names = ("Punch", "Judy");
$array_ref = \@names;
print ${$array_ref}[0]; displays Punch
```

Using curly braces in this way isn't necessary and only makes the precedence of the code easier to understand for the programmer. Perl, of course, already knows the proper precedence.

Dereferencing Using ->

The -> operator can also be used to dereference references, and it has the added advantage of being easier to read than using curly braces or using double dollar signs. Here is an example of using -> to dereference a reference to an array:

```
@generals = ("McClellan", "Pemberton", "Grant", "Lee");
$hard_ref = \@generals;
print $hard_ref->[2]; # displays Grant
```

The -> operator has the added advantage of suggesting to the person reading the code, using the example above, that the reference points to the array element that has an index value of 2.

10

You can also use the -> operator with references to hashes. Here is an example:

```
%comp_lang_dev = ("Perl", "Larry Wall",
                  "Java", "James Gosling",
                  "C", "Dennis Ritchie",
                  "C++", "Bjarne Stoustrup");
$hard_ref = \%comp_lang_dev;
$lang = "Perl";
print $hard_ref->{$lang}; # displays Larry Wall
```

The -> operator is the "preferred" way to dereference array and hash references, if for no other reason than just because it is easier to read. When you have to look at a lot of curvy, or bracketed, symbols all jumbled together, you tend to lose track of what's what. Also, having to type all those symbols in sequence can lead to carpal tunnel syndrome.

Creating and Using References to Filehandles

Filehandles can have references point to them just like scalars, arrays, and hashes. To create a reference to a filehandle, use the *backslash* operator as usual and follow that with an asterisk, the typeglob indicator. (If you need a refresher on the typeglob data type, see Chapter 2.) Here is a simple script that creates a reference to a filehandle:

```
$ref_to_fh = \*STDOUT;
```

This line of code creates a reference to the default output filehandle, STDOUT.

So how would you use this in a program? One scenario might be to have a subroutine that prints a value or set of values to a particular filehandle, depending on which filehandle is passed to the subroutine. Another scenario might be to have a subroutine gather input from some input source, with the input filehandle being passed to the subroutine.

The following listing presents one of the canonical "Beginning Programming" examples—the gradebook. This script either opens a file and calculates the class grade average for a test if a nondefault input filehandle is specified, or, if the default input filehandle is specified, the user will be prompted to enter a grade for each student and the class average is then calculated. The filehandle is passed as a reference to the proper subroutine, one for STDIN and a different subroutine if a file is to be read.

```
$ref_to_fhin = \*{shift(@ARGV)};
if ($$ref_to_fhin eq "*main::STDIN") {
    gather_input($ref_to_fhin);
} else
    {
        input_from_file($ref_to_fhin);
}

sub gather_input {
    @names = ("Jay", "Meredith", "Steven", "Allison", "Mason", "Judy");
```

```
        foreach (@names) {
            print "Enter the grade for $_: ";
            $grade = <>;
            $class_total += $grade;
        }
    }

sub input_from_file {
    my $fhref = shift(@_);
    open($fhref,"test.txt") || die "Cannot open file\n";
    $class_total = 0;
    $num = 0;
    while (<$fhref>) {
        chomp;
        ($name, $grade) = split /,/;
        if ($grade eq "") {
            last;
        }
        $class_total += $grade;
    }
}
print "\nThe class grade total is $class_total.\n";
$avg = $class_total/6;
print "The class average is $avg.\n";
```

Here is one sample output from this program:

```
c:\perl\bin>perl grades.pl STDIN
Enter a grade for Jay: 92
Enter a grade for Meredith: 94
Enter a grade for Steven: 96
Enter a grade for Allison: 98
Enter a grade for Mason: 100
Enter a grade for Judy: 91
The class grade total is 571.
The class grade average is 95.1666666666667 (Must be a graduate
                Statistics class!)
```

10

Here is another sample output from this script:

```
C:\perl\bin>perl grades.pl FILE
The class grade total is 564.
The class grade average is 94.
```

Passing the filehandle as a reference to the subroutines is very straightforward, and you should be able to follow the code in this example without any trouble. The only tricky part of this script is the test of the filehandle when it is dereferenced, in the second line of the listing. The test checks to see if the dereferenced variable is equal to "*main::STDIN" instead of just "STDIN". This is because the typeglob that is passed to the reference variable is actually named "*main::STDIN". Remember that every Perl program is running in package Main, and STDIN is an object of this package.

Building Complex and Anonymous Data Structures

While Perl is a very powerful language, with most of the features you will ever need in a language, it does not contain any built-in complex data structures. The common Perl data structures (scalars, arrays, and hashes) are all flat, linear structures. Perl does not have the equivalent of a multidimensional array or hash built into the language. You can build multidimensional data structures using references, however, and the following sections will show you how to build arrays of arrays, arrays of hashes, hashes of hashes, and hashes of arrays.

Perl also allows the creation of anonymous data structures. An anonymous data structure is a data structure that is not explicitly assigned a variable name. For example, the following line of code creates a named array:

```
@names = ("Hunter", "Meredith", "Bryce", "Allison", "Carmen", "Mason");
```

An anonymous data structure is created by associating the data structure with just a reference, not a variable name. This technique allows you to create data structures dynamically and not be tied down to a variable. The techniques for creating anonymous data structures will be shown in the following sections also.

Arrays of Arrays (Multidimensional Arrays)

Since Perl only has one-dimensional arrays, to build a multidimensional array you have to create an array of arrays. Again, this material was covered in Chapter 3, but it's a good idea to review this material again here, since an array of arrays is the most fundamental of the complex data structures.

As you will recall, an array of arrays is created using square brackets to create the arrays within an array. Here's an example, continuing to use the gradebook example you have been working with:

```
@grades = (
    ["Jay", 92],
    ["Meredith", 94],
    ["Steven", 96],
    ["Allison", 98],
    ["Mason", 100],
    ["Judy", 91],
);
$array_ref = \@grades;
print "$array_ref->[0][0]'s grade is $array_ref->[0][1].\n";
```

When this script is run, the following output is displayed:

```
Jay's grade is 92.
```

You can imagine each array as the rows of a matrix. The $0,0^{th}$ element of the matrix is "Jay". The $0,1^{st}$ element of the matrix is 92. Using this scheme, it is easy to pull out any of the information you want from the data structure.

Another way to work with this data structure is to build it as an anonymous array. To do this, you will still create an array of arrays, but instead of assigning it to an array variable, you will assign it to a reference. Here is the example above, rewritten as an anonymous data structure:

```
$array_ref = [
    ["Jay", 92],
    ["Meredith", 94],
    ["Steven", 96],
    ["Allison", 98],
    ["Mason", 100],
    ["Judy", 91],
];
print "$array_ref->[0][0]'s grade is $array_ref->[0][1].\n";
```

10

This script produces the same output as the script above, but there are a few differences between these two examples. Notice how the array of arrays is built in the second example. Instead of surrounding the individual bracketed lists in parentheses to indicate an array structure, the arrays are surrounded by square brackets. These square brackets are used to create an anonymous array. Also, since the anonymous array is already assigned to a reference, no other assignment statement is necessary. In the first example, after the array of arrays was created, the array variable had to be assigned to a reference.

Dereferencing an anonymous array happens in the same way as dereferencing a named array.

Transposing a Matrix

In matrix arithmetic, one common function is to transpose a matrix. A matrix transpose takes the rows of the matrix and makes them columns, and takes the columns of the matrix and makes them rows. The code to do this is very easy to understand—you simply create an outer loop and an inner loop, using the loops to exchange column and row elements of the old matrix into the corresponding row and column elements of the new matrix. The following listing presents the code.

```perl
$mat_ref = [
            [100, 200, 300],
            [400, 500, 600],
            [700, 800, 900],
          ];
for ($i = 0; $i < 3; $i++) {
    for ($j = 0; $j < 3; $j++) {
        $mat_ref1->[$j][$i] = $mat_ref->[$i][$j];
    }
}
for ($i = 0; $i < 3; $i++) {
    for ($j = 0; $j < 3; $j++) {
        print $mat_ref1->[$i][$j];
    }
    print "\n";
}
```

Here is the output when this script is run:

```
C:\perl\bin>perl matrix.pl
100 200 300
400 500 600
700 800 900
100 400 700
200 500 800
300 600 900
```

Arrays of Hashes

Another way to organize a gradebook is with an array of hashes. Each student name is a key into a list of grade values. Here is a script that creates an array of hashes assigned to an array variable:

```
@gradebook = (
    {"Jay" => "92,95"},
    {"Meredith" => "94,96"},
    {"Steven" => "96,91"},
    {"Allison" => "98,100"},
    {"Mason" => "100,92"},
    {"Judy" => "91,98"},
);
$array_ref = \@gradebook;
print $array_ref->[0]{"Jay"};
```

When this script is executed, the output will be:

```
92,95
```

Notice that on the last line, where the array of hashes is dereferenced, the second subscript is bordered with curly braces. This is because, of course, the second element of the data structure is a hash and a hash key is always presented within curly braces.

You can also create an anonymous array of hashes. This next script takes the example above and makes the array of hashes data structure anonymous:

```
$array_ref = [
    {"Jay" => "92,95"},
    {"Meredith" => "94,96"},
    {"Steven" => "96,91"},
    {"Allison" => "98,100"},
    {"Mason" => "100,92"},
    {"Judy" => "91,98"},
];
print $array_ref->[0]{"Mason"};
```

10

This script, when executed, will produce the following output:

```
100, 92
```

The difference between the two scripts is, of course, that the array of hashes is created as an anonymous data structure. When the data structure is created, it is surrounded by square brackets, in the same way that the anonymous array of arrays above was created.

Hashes of Arrays

You can create a hash of arrays in much the same way you create an array of arrays. Here is a small script that creates a class roll that a busy teacher can use:

```
%classes = (
    data_structures => [
        'Allison',
        'Mason',
        'Kristin',
        'Jake'
    ],
    algorithms => [
        'Meredith',
        'Hunter',
        'Rachel',
        'Stephanie',
        'Lauren'
    ],
);
$hash_ref = \%classes;
print $hash_ref->{algorithms}[1];
```

When this script is run, the following output is displayed:

```
Hunter
```

You can create a hash of arrays directly by assigning the structure anonymously to a reference. Here is the script to do this:

```
$hash_ref = {
    data_structures => [
        'Allison',
        'Mason',
        'Kristin',
        'Jake'
    ],
    algorithms => [
```

```
                'Meredith',
                'Hunter',
                'Rachel',
                'Stephanie',
                'Lauren'
        ],
};
print $hash_ref->{algorithms}[1];
```

When you create an anonymous hash of arrays, the whole structure is surrounded with curly braces, not with parentheses as in the previous example. When this script is executed, you will get the same output as the script created with a hash variable.

Hashes of Hashes

In the last section you saw how to associate a hash with an array so that when you present a key, a list is returned. A hash of hashes lets you associate one key with another key, so that when you present two keys, a value is returned. Here's an example of how you could implement a gradebook with a hash of hashes representation:

```
%classes = (
    data_structures => {
        Allison => '93',
        Mason   => '94',
        Kristin => '91',
        Jake    => '95',
    },
    algorithms => {
        Meredith  => '92',
        Hunter    => '100',
        Rachel    => '91',
        Stephanie => '95',
        Lauren    => '93',
    },
);
$hash_ref = \%classes;
print $hash_ref->{algorithms}{Meredith};
```

10

When this script is executed, the following output is displayed:

92

The script above creates a named hash of hashes. As with our other examples, you can implement this gradebook example using an anonymous representation instead. Here is the script:

```
$hash_ref = {
    data_structures => {
        Allison => '93',
        Mason   => '94',
        Kristin => '91',
        Jake    => '95',
    },
    algorithms => {
        Meredith  => '92',
        Hunter    => '100',
        Rachel    => '91',
        Stephanie => '95',
        Lauren    => '93',
    },
);
print $hash_ref->{algorithms}{Meredith};
```

When this script is run, you will get the same output as the example above. The key difference between the two scripts is how the data structure is passed to the reference variable. In the first, named variable example, the data structure is passed to the variable through parentheses. This means that, as with the other named data structure examples in this section, the data structure is surrounded with parentheses. In the second, anonymous hash of hashes representations, the data structure is passed to the reference variable with curly braces, as you can see in the script.

Creating Anonymous Data Structures on the Fly

Because Perl is a semi-interpreted, weakly typed language, data types can simply appear and be used; they don't have to be declared as you do with more strongly typed languages. For example, when you want to use a variable for some reason in the middle of your script, you simply assign it a value and start using it. You don't have to declare its data type at the beginning of the script.

More complex data structures, like the ones you've learned about in this chapter, can also be created "on the fly". In the previous section, you saw how to create a hash of hashes by assigning it to a reference variable. Another way to do the same thing is to simply reference two hash keys and assign them a value. The following script shows a standard hash of hashes implementation (from the previous section, but commented out) and an "on the fly" partial implementation of the same data structure:

```
#%classes = (
#    data_structures => {
#         Allison => '93',
#         Mason   => '94',
#         Kristin => '91',
#         Jake    => '95',
#    },
#    algorithms => {
#         Meredith  => '92',
#         Hunter    => '100',
#         Rachel    => '91',
#         Stephanie => '95',
#         Lauren    => '93',
#    },
#);
#$hash_ref = \%classes;
#print $hash_ref->{algorithms}{Meredith};
$gradebook{data_structures}{Allison} = 93;
$gradebook{data_structures}{Mason} = 94;
$gradebook{algorithms}{Meredith} = 92;
$gradebook{algorithms}{Stephanie} = 95;
print $gradebook{data_structures}{Mason};
```

This script will output Mason's score:

```
94
```

10

In the above script, you can see how easy it is to quickly create an anonymous data structure such as a hash of hashes. It is just as easy to create other data structures. Here is a script that creates an "on the fly" hash of arrays:

```
$gradebook{algorithms}[0] = "Allison";
$gradebook{algorithms}[1] = "Mason";
$gradebook{data_structures}[0] = "Meredith";
$gradebook{data_structures}[1] = "Terri";
print $gradebook{algorithms}->[0];
```

When this script is executed, the output displayed is

```
Allison
```

Notice in this example how the arrow is used to associate an array index with the hash key. You could have written this statement like this:

```
print $gradebook{algorithms}[0];
```

As was mentioned earlier in this chapter, the arrow simply makes the statement easier to read for humans; Perl has no preference for how you write statements of this kind.

All of the data structures presented in the chapter can be created using this "on the fly" technique, and you are encouraged to experiment with creating your own complex data structures in this manner.

References to Subroutines

Variables and data structures aren't the only objects that can be referenced in Perl; you can also create references to subroutines. Also, as with the other data structures you've examined in this chapter, subroutines can be either named or anonymous. This section will discuss how to create references to both named and anonymous subroutines and how to dereference both types.

Creating a reference to a named subroutine is quite simple. Here is a script that creates a reference to a simple subroutine and then calls that subroutine through the reference:

```
sub display_greeting {
    print "Welcome to the world of Perl programming!\n";
}
$ref_to_sub = \&display_greeting;
&$ref_to_sub;
```

The subroutine **display_greeting** is assigned to a reference by adding the *backslash* operator to the subroutine name, just like with other objects. The subroutine is executed by appending the subroutine prefix (&) to the reference variable, as seen in the last line of the script. When this script is executed, the line "Welcome to the world of Perl programming!" is displayed.

You can create and work with a reference to an anonymous subroutine in much the same way. Here is a script that executes just like the script above, only this time the subroutine is anonymous:

```
$ref_to_sub = sub {
    print "Welcome to the world of Perl programming!\n";
};
&$ref_to_sub();
```

When you create an anonymous subroutine like this, be sure to include the semicolon at the end of the assignment statement because, as was just said, this statement is ultimately an assignment statement, not a subroutine declaration.

A common use for subroutine references is in callback functions, where an array of subroutines is set up in a table and a Perl script calls on one or more of the subroutines. The example below sets up a table of three types of greetings—a Central, Eastern, and Western greeting for, respectively, the people from the central, eastern, and western United States. The script prompts the user to tell it where they are from, and then the proper subroutine is called. Here's the script:

```
sub central_greeting {
    print "Hello!";
}
sub eastern_greeting {
    print "Yo!";
}
sub western_greeting {
    print "Howdy!";
}
%greetings = (
    "Central"    => \&central_greeting,
    "Eastern"    => \&eastern_greeting,
    "Western"    => \&western_greeting,
);
print "Are you from the (Central, Eastern, Western) US? ";
$where = <>;
$hash_ref = \%greetings;
$sub_ref = $hash_ref->{$where};
&$sub_ref();
```

10

The subroutines that are used in this script are very simple and don't require any additional explanation. The hash %greetings is made up of keys that identify the three parts of the United States and their values, which are references to the appropriate subroutine for that key. After the user is prompted to enter where they are from, a reference to the %greetings hash is assigned. Then a reference to the proper subroutine is assigned, followed by a line that executes the proper subroutine.

Symbolic References

Take a look at the following script:

```
$num = 20;
$ref = "num";
$$ref += 5;
print $num; # displays 25
```

What the heck is going on here? What is going on is the use of a symbolic reference.

Remember that a hard reference is a reference to a memory location. When you create a hard reference to a variable and then change the value of the reference, you change the value that is stored in the memory location being referenced. If you try to dereference a variable that is not a hard reference, after Perl decides the variable is not a reference, it treats the variable's contents as a variable identifier. So, the contents of the variable ("num" in the example above) get a dollar sign attached to them. When evaluating the line:

```
$$ref += 5;
```

Perl first substitutes $num for $ref, and then it attaches the other dollar sign, making the left-hand side of the statement become $$num. Now you have a regular reference, and the right-hand side of the statement is evaluated. The end result of all this is that the value of $num becomes 25.

Symbolic references have less use than hard references in Perl and can actually cause trouble if you accidentally reference a symbolic reference when you're trying to reference a hard reference. Perl has a module you can use to restrict the use of symbolic references, strict.pm. You use this module to control the use of symbolic references like this:

```
use strict 'refs';
$num = 20;
$ref = "num";
$$ref += 5;
```

When this script is run, you get the following error message:

```
Can't use string ("num") as a SCALAR ref while "strict ref" in use
at chap10.pl line 4
```

strict stays in effect until the end of the block of code it was declared in. If you want to turn it off, you can do so by adding the statement no strict 'refs'.

Summary

References are an important determinant of whether or not a language can be considered a powerful programming language or just a toy language. Perl's use of references places it in the first category. Through the use of references, you can create complex data structures that are necessary for solving complex programming problems. This chapter discussed how Perl implements references and how to use them to create complex data structures such as arrays of hashes and hashes of arrays. This chapter also introduced you to anonymous data structures, another important feature of a truly powerful programming language.

10

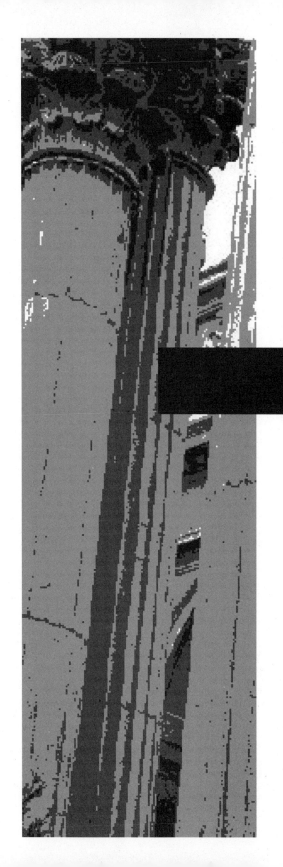

CHAPTER 11

Object-oriented Programming in Perl

Perl has achieved popularity primarily because as a language, it provides considerable functionality with a minimum of coding. Another reason is that the same application can run, virtually with little or no changes, between different machines and different operating systems.

Object-oriented programming has achieved popularity primarily because it promotes code reusability, which in turn maximizes the use of any coding effort. Instead of creating the same bit of code over and over again, you create it once and reuse it many times. An additional advantage of using an object instead of creating the same bit of code and including it within a library is that you can inherit from an object, extend its methods, override them where needed, and generally provide the most flexible as well as efficient use of any coding effort.

So it seems that object-oriented techniques using Perl makes a lot of sense.

This chapter provides an overview of the object-oriented capabilities of Perl. The following is a list of capabilities:

◆ **Encapsulation**   Being able to create a complex data structure, and package it in order to encapsulate the data.

◆ **Inheritance**   Being able to inherit from this object and provide new methods.

◆ **Polymorphism**   Being able to inherit from this object and create altered methods, with binding to the correct method occurring at run time.

These capabilities use OO-based terminology. Object-oriented applications can also include the use of *delegation*, which is a form of message passing, and *persistence*, which is the preservation of the value of a variable or data item beyond the termination of a function or application.

 WEB LINK: There are several good Web sites that contain information about object-oriented programming. Once such site is the OO SoapBox, located at **http://www.progsoc.uts.edu.au/~geldridg/cpp/**, which contains links to various sites, papers, and examples demonstrating OO technologies. The site has links specifically for Perl and other languages in addition to the more general OO-based information.

Several different Perl technologies are necessary to create and work with objects, such as Perl references, packages and modules, and tied variables. Appendix B contains the Perl modules with additional information on these subjects (perlref, perlmod, perltie, respectively). These technologies will also be demonstrated in this chapter as they are used to create Perl objects, beginning with the next section, which covers creating an object class using packaging.

Encapsulation—Creating a Perl Object Class Module

When working with Perl to create an object, you will instead create a Perl module, a package containing a class with the same name as the module file. This file in turn contains a definition for a simple or complex data structure such as an instance variable, anonymous hash, or array, and returns a reference to the new data structure. Then, instead of accessing the data components directly, an application accesses them through a set of methods, defined as subroutines within the class module file.

A Perl package is really an alternative namespace, and an effective technique for isolating data, to prevent other namespaces from impacting on that data. Once the package is included within a file, as demonstrated a little later in this section, the symbol table for that package is the one the Perl compiler accesses from that point on. The symbol table contains references to all variables declared within the package namespace, as discussed in Chapter 3. To access symbols from another package/namespace, you then have to preface the symbol with the package name and double colon, with syntax such as:

```
$Someobject::someelement
```

11

A Perl module is a file with the same name as the package, and which exports symbols (such as variables or functions) or contains the definition of a Perl class, or both. The main point of a module, a file with a mandatory extension of .pm, is that the module is meant to be used and reused, so the contents must be accessible externally.

With exporting, a module that exports symbols includes the Exporter module, which provides a default **import** method the importing module can inherit from. This import method is invoked when the module is included in an application by the *use* operator. The new module creator can choose which symbols to export by default, defined by the use of @EXPORT, and which to export by request only, with the use of @EXPORT_OK, as the following code block demonstrates:

```
package Somemodule;
use Exporter;
@ISA = qw(Exporter);

@EXPORT = qw(VAR1 VAR2 VAR3);
@EXPORT_OK qw(VAR4 VAR5);
```

In this example, the symbols VAR1, VAR2, and VAR3 would be loaded by default, and the symbols VAR4 and VAR5 would only be loaded if they were requested in the including application. The @ISA shown in the code is an array that tells Perl to look for a specific method if a method of that name can't be found in the package.

The Perl manual stresses not to export methods or anything that doesn't need to be exported. Exporting a symbol by default clutters the namespace where the module is included, and increases the risk of name clashing if one of the symbols you are exporting by default is also included within the namespace of the package including the exporting module.

T IP: Read more on the Exporter module by accessing the Exporter manpage, included with the standard Perl documentation.

A better approach to ensure reusability of a module is to take the time to define the module as a class and create methods to access or alter class object data.

Creating a Scalar Instance

Creating an object class is actually fairly simple, requiring the creation of the package with the same name as the module, creating a constructor and possibly a destructor method, and defining the data structure of the object. At a minimum, this is all you need to create a Perl object class.

As an example, an object is created, called "Photo", that provides a photo identifier when the object is created, as shown here:

```
package Photo;
use strict;
# create the simplest type of
# object, which is scalar instance
sub new {
    # Get the name of the class, always passed as first parent
    my $class = shift;

    # Get photo identifier
    my $self = shift;

    # bless object and return
    bless \$self, $class;
    return \$self;
}
```

The backslash shown in the example creates a reference to the variable, which is what is returned from the object constructor. This object example is about the simplest type of Perl object you can have, which is a scalar instance. However, it also demonstrates the major components of an object class.

First, the object name is given as the package name, shown in the listing as "Photo". Additionally, the filename must be the same as that given to both the package and object name. In this case, the file would be named Photo.pm. After the package name is the **use strict** statement to prevent unsafe constructs, followed by the *object* constructor. Most often, the object constructor is named *new*, though there is no standard defining this and another name would work as well, as long as it is documented.

The *object* constructor is nothing more than a method that creates the instance of the *new* object, in this case a scalar variable, and then uses the special **bless** function, which maps the constructed item to the specified class, if one is given. The second parameter to the function is the class type. Not providing the class maps the object to the current package. **bless** returns the object reference and is usually positioned as the last line of the function, as the following line of code demonstrates:

```
return bless \$self, $class;
```

11

However, you can also return the reference on a separate line, as demonstrated previously.

NOTE: The **bless** function can take two parameters: the object and the object class. If you want others to inherit from your class, you must use the two-parameter approach, so that the object is mapped to the correct class.

Once the module for the object has been created, it can be used in any Perl application. As an example, the following creates a new instance of Photo, passing in a photo id of "13", and then accessing this same value from the newly created object instance:

```
package main;
use Photo;
my $photo = new Photo(13);
print "photo=$$photo\n";
```

What happens with this code is that the Photo package is incorporated into the application with the *use* operator, a shortcut technique for the following:

```
BEGIN {
require Photo;
import Photo->import();
}
```

Begin in this last code block is actually the package constructor, the *require* loads subroutine definitions from the other package at run time, and the *import* imports these subroutines into the namespace of the application. If no import list is specified, the import routine (in the package or inherited by default from the Exporter module) determines which subroutines get loaded into the namespace. The advantage of the *use* operator is that the *require* and *import* happen at compile rather than run time.

In addition to implementing methods for the object, you can also export functionality using the Exporter module, discussed earlier, or using *Autoload*, which is used with delegation, a more advanced object-oriented topic not covered in this chapter. You can use the Exporter module with an object class as long as you don't export the methods, which would defeat the purpose of creating a class.

What made this package a class? A Perl class is, by definition, a module with methods used to set and access class data, or to perform a set of behaviors defined for that specific class. A module is just a package with a name equivalent to the class name, followed by the extension .pm.

Creating an Object Using an Anonymous Hash

The object class shown previously is technically a correct object class, but not a very useful one. Normally objects have more than one piece of useful information, information that can be defined at the time the object is created or later. Based on this, a superior data structure to use would be an array, or better yet, an anonymous hash. Both of these data structures allow for multiple data fields, and the anonymous hash allows for named access of the fields, which gives it an edge for use with Perl objects.

Taking the first example, it is extended to create a Photo object that has a photo identifier, photographer name, date, and title. An anonymous hash is used to create the new object, as shown here:

```perl
package Photo;
use strict;

# create object using anonymous hash
sub new {

    # Get the name of the class, always passed as first paren
    my $class = shift;

    # Get object reference
    my $self = {};

    # define photo properties
    $self->{ID} = undef;
    $self->{TITLE} = undef;
    $self->{PHOTOGRAPHER} = undef;
    $self->{PHOTODATE} = undef;
```

11

```
    # Get photo properties
    my ($id, $title, $photographer, $photodate) = @_;
    $self->{ID} = $id;
    $self->{TITLE} = $title;
    $self->{PHOTOGRAPHER} = $photographer;
    $self->{PHOTODATE} = $photodate;

    # bless object and return
    return bless $self, ref($class) || $class;
}

sub return_title {
    my $self = shift;
    print " Photo title is $self->{TITLE}\n";
}
1;
```

In this implementation of the *Photo* object, instead of a scalar reference the object is created as an anonymous hash. As this allows access of individual items based on name, in this case property name, it makes an ideal data structure for use with objects.

Once the hash is created, four properties are added to it and set to be undefined: ID, Title, Photographer, and Photodate. These values are then accessed from the passed-in parameters when the object's **new** function is called, as shown in the following code block:

```
package main;
use Photo;
my $photo = new Photo(13, "Vermont Fall Foliage","Joe Brown",
"Oct. 1, 1997");
```

In addition to using an anonymous hash, an access method is created to print out the photo title. Using this method is as simple as invoking the method from the object, as shown next:

```
$photo->return_title();
```

This prints out a message with "Photo title is Vermont Fall Foliage".

Also notice from the previous listing that the class variable is not passed as is to the **bless** function, but instead the **ref** function is used to pull out the class reference if an object is passed instead of the class. This is because a new object can be created by direct access to the class, or by invoking the new function from an object instance that was originally created from the class, as the following code block demonstrates:

```
use Photo;

my $photo = new Photo(13, "Vermont Fall Foliage","Joe Brown", "Oct. 1,
1997" );
my $newphoto = $photo->new(131,"Vermont Fall Foliage A","Joe Brown",
"Oct.1, 1997");
$newphoto->return_title();
```

Instead of printing out "Photo title is Vermont Fall Foliage", this code would print out "Photo title is Vermont Fall Foliage A". With the use of the **ref** function, the class is derived when the **new** function is called from the object rather than the class, and the object is subsequently mapped to the appropriate class.

Creating an Array-based Object

In addition to creating the class using an anonymous hash, an array could be used, and the constructor would then look similar to that shown here:

```
my $ID = 0;
my $TITLE = 1;
my $PHOTOGRAPHER = 2;
my $PHOTODATE = 3;

# create the simplest type of
# object, which is scalar instance
sub new {
    # Get the name of the class, always passed as first paren
    my $class = shift;
    # Get photo identifier
    my $self = [];

    # Get photo properties
    my ($id, $title, $photographer, $photodate) = @_;

    $self->[$ID] = $id;
    $self->[$TITLE] = $title;
    $self->[$PHOTOGRAPHER] = $photographer;
    $self->[$PHOTODATE] = $photodate;
```

11

```
    return bless $self, $class;
}
```

In this case, four variables are defined to represent the index associated with the item, and then assigned the item to the appropriate array element.

There are advantages to using arrays versus using an anonymous hash. An array can be a little faster, and can use a little less memory by not having to maintain the key-value pair reference. However, it is more efficient to use the anonymous hash with its ability to access a value by name. To add or remove a property, you simply add or remove the named reference.

NOTE: Another technique to use is closures as objects, something not demonstrated in this chapter. There is an excellent tutorial on object-oriented programming for Perl written by Tom Christiansen and is located on the Web at **http://www.perl.com/CPAN-local/doc/FMTEYEWTK/ perltoot.html**. This tutorial provides additional details of creating objects using the different data structures, including closures.

The Object Destructor

Programs including the use of objects maintain references to the object. When these references go away, because of movement out of scope or program termination, the object is destroyed and any memory allocated for it is freed up.

However, there may be times when you want to receive notification that the object is being destroyed, capture the program control momentarily, and perform some functionality. This occurs in the object's *destructor*.

The destructor, unlike the constructor, has a specific name, including case, which you should use: the **destroy** function. This function is included in the object module, and encloses the code to run when the object is destroyed. If your object is, in turn, an inherited object that has used the **bless** function to re-bless the base class reference, you will need to include the **destroy** function in your derived class and call the base class **destroy** method from the derived class.

Why would you want to use a **destructor** method? Two primary reasons are to update some global that might be keeping track of object references, and to free up resources or do other cleanup.

A simple, humorous destructor is added to the Photo class that does nothing more than protest its own destruction, shown in the following code block:

```
sub DESTROY {
    print " no, no, noooooooo\n";
}
```

It sometimes feels as if objects have a life of their own, and now it can be demonstrated. Seriously, though, just including this function within the Photo module will ensure that it is called before the object is destroyed. In a more realistic object implementation, the **destroy** method would likely contain object cleanup code. No other event mapping or effort is required.

Inheriting from an Object

Once you've created an object, you can use it, as is, in any of your applications. However, there might be times when the object's methods and data aren't exactly what you need. You could alter them using code within your applications, but this technique will get tiresome if you need to use the same modified data and methods in several different programs. That's where the concept of *inheritance* comes in.

Inheritance is the ability to include all definitions and methods of a base object, but also to extend this object with your own data and/or methods. You then have all the advantages of the original object, as well as your new functionality. If the original object changes its implementation of any of the objects, this will have little or no impact on your new object implementation because you are using the original object's interfaces to inherit the original object's functionality.

11

The most important thing to remember about creating an object class that can be inherited, becoming a parent class, is to use the two-argument form of the **bless** function:

```
return bless $self, $class;
```

Without the second argument, the object would not be blessed into the appropriate class.

To create an inherited class, you need to include the class within your module and use @ISA to state that the new class is a form of the original class. Applying this to the Photo class created earlier, a new object class is created called PhotoNegative, with the code shown here:

```
package PhotoNegative;

use Photo;
@ISA = ("Photo");
```

Using this new class in the previous application would mean just changing the name of the package and the object, as shown next:

```
package main;
use PhotoNegative;

my $photo = new PhotoNegative(13, "Vermont Fall Foliage","Joe Brown",
"Oct. 1, 1997" );
my $newphoto = $photo->new(131,"Vermont Fall Foliage A","Joe Brown",
"Oct.1, 1997");

$newphoto->return_title();
```

The behavior for the new class is absolutely the same as for the previous class. The object class just created is referred to in the Perl documentation as an "empty subclass test", because it tests whether the original class was set up correctly.

It's nice to know our base or *superclass* object was created correctly, but the new class isn't very helpful. However, adding some new data or functionality to the new object can alter it. So, two new methods are created that print out the values of the photographer's name based on a call to the method **return_photographer**, and print out all the photo's properties based on a call to the method **return_all**. The previous listing contains the new version of the *PhotoNegative* object with these two new methods.

```
package PhotoNegative;

use Photo;
@ISA = qw(Photo);
```

```perl
sub return_photographer {
    my $self = shift;
    print " Photographer is $self->{PHOTOGRAPHER}\n";
}

sub return_all {
    my $self = shift;
    print " Photo ID is $self->{ID}\t";
    print "Photo Title is $self->{TITLE}\n";
    print " Photographer is $self->{PHOTOGRAPHER}\t";
    print "Photo date is $self->{PHOTODATE}\n";
}
```

There is no change to any of the base object's methods or data, only the addition of the two new methods. Using the base object's and derived object's methods would occur without any concern on the part of the developer about which object implemented which method, as shown here:

```perl
package main;
use PhotoNegative;

my $photo = new PhotoNegative(13, "Vermont Fall Foliage","Joe Brown",
"Oct. 1, 1997" );
my $newphoto = $photo->new(131,"Vermont Fall Foliage A","Joe Brown",
"Oct.1, 1997");

$photo->return_title();
$photo->return_photographer();
$newphoto->return_all();
```

The output of running the Perl application that creates the object is:

```
Photo title is Vermont Fall Foliage
 Photographer is Joe Brown
 Photo ID is 131    Photo Title is Vermont Fall Foliage A
 Photographer is Joe Brown    Photo date is Oct.1, 1997
```

If the base object was created without specifying the second class parameter for the blessed reference, an error would occur during the run to the effect that the compiler could not find the **return_photographer** or **return_all** methods in the class PhotoNegative.

11

NOTE: It made no difference whether the two objects were created directly from the derived class or from an instance of the derived class. Again, the use of the **ref** function pulled out the class reference from the object specified.

If the base object did not contain the type of data needed for the derived object, a reference can be added to the new data by overriding the new method, calling the base object's new method with the parameters it needs, and creating the derived object's new data fields. The following listing shows the redefined derived object.

NOTE: Not calling the new method of the parent can result in unpredictable results, and implies a knowledge of the underlying implementation that abrogates the usefulness of object-oriented programming.

```perl
package PhotoNegative;
use Photo;
@ISA = qw(Photo);

# override base object's new method
# create base object, and extend with new properties
sub new {
    my ($class, $ID, $TITLE, $PHOTOGRAPHER, $PHOTODATE, $NEG, $PRINTS) = @_;
    my $self = Photo->new($ID, $TITLE, $PHOTOGRAPHER, $PHOTODATE);

    $self->{NEGNUMBER} = undef;
    $self->{PRNTSAVAIL} = undef;

    $self->{NEGNUMBER} = $NEG;
    $self->{PRNTSAVAIL} = $PRINTS;
    return bless $self, ref($class) || $class;
}

# print out photographer property
sub return_photographer {
    my $self = shift;
    print " Photographer is $self->{PHOTOGRAPHER}\n";
}
```

```perl
# print out all of the inherited object's data properties
sub return_all {
    my $self = shift;
    print " Photo ID is $self->{ID}\t";
    print "Photo Title is $self->{TITLE}\n";
    print " Photographer is $self->{PHOTOGRAPHER}\t";
    print "Photo date is $self->{PHOTODATE}\n";
    print " Negative number is $self->{NEGNUMBER}\t";
    print "Prints Available is $self->{PRNTSAVAIL}\n";
}
```

T IP: To create a successful object, keep it small in the beginning. It's easy to add to an object but not to remove methods, as removing methods will break any applications that are using any one of the deleted methods. A successful object is one that always grows and never shrinks.

Object Overriding

Overriding a base object's methods is actually fairly simple, and you can use two different techniques to accomplish this. The first totally overrides the base object's method; the second overrides the method, performs whatever functionality it was created to perform, and then calls the base object's method.

To demonstrate totally overriding a function, a new version is created of **return_title** in the derived class PhotoNegative that returns both the negative number and title for the object:

```perl
sub return_title {
    my $self = shift;
    print "For Negative Number $self->{NEGNUMBER}\t";
    print "The Title is $self->{TITLE}\n";
}
```

11

The original **return_title** method only printed out the title. Running an application that calls the new **return_title** for the derived object returns the following instead of just the title as the original method did:

```
For Negative Number 1     The Title is Vermont Fall Foliage
```

However, if it is decided that the function is a bit redundant in that it is, in part, duplicating the code in the original base class by printing out the title, the original method can be overridden but the base object's original **return_title** can be called, as shown next:

```
sub return_title {
    my $self = shift;
    print "For Negative Number $self->{NEGNUMBER}\t";

    $self->SUPER::return_title();
}
```

This results in the following output:

```
For Negative Number 1      Photo title is Vermont Fall Foliage
```

The *super* reference refers to the parent class, without having to specify the parent class name. To determine which overriding method you want to use, ask yourself whether you want to extend the base object functionality or replace it. Whenever possible you want to avoid replacing object functionality, particularly for objects you access from sources external to your own development effort. If you replace an existing object's functionality, you have to then re-examine your overriding function each time your base object's source code is upgraded. Extending the underlying method is more likely to ensure, but not guarantee, that your extended method is compatible with future generations of the base object's source code.

Multiple Inheritance

Multiple inheritance (MI) is a supported OO concept in Perl, though its use should be restricted. The primary reason to restrict the use of MI is the possibility of inheriting from two objects, both of which share the same ancestor, and which can cause an object recursion problem with name clashing and the inability to resolve object method calls. However, it can also be a handy technique to include methods from more than one object, if used with caution, and if no other approach, such as straight inheritance, works as well.

Multiple inheritance is when one object inherits from two different base classes, with data and methods of both classes accessible by the newly derived object class. To demonstrate multiple inheritance with Perl, a new base object is created, *Book*, which has the following data fields: AUTHOR,

BOOKTITLE, NEGNUMBER, and PHOTOGRAPHER. The NEGNUMBER field is exactly equivalent to the one created for the PhotoNegative class, which inherits from both Book and the original base class, Photo. Because of this, the NEGNUMBER property is removed from PhotoNegative. Additionally, the PHOTOGRAPHER field for both Book and Photo are the same, so referencing the value of one is equivalent to referencing the value of the other. The field AUTHOR and BOOKTITLE are specific to the Book class. The following listing shows the new Book class:

```perl
package Book;
use strict;

# Book constructor
sub new {
    # Get the name of the class, always passed as first paren
    my $class = shift;
    my $self = {};

    # define book properties
    $self->{AUTHOR} = undef;
    $self->{TITLE} = undef;
    $self->{NEGNUMBER} = undef;
    $self->{PHOTOGRAPHER} = undef;

    # bless object and return
    bless $self, ref($class) || $class;
    # set data values
    $self;
}

# set data values from passed in values
sub _setvalues {
    my $self = shift;
    my ($author, $title, $neg, $photographer) = @_;

    # Get book properties
    $self->{AUTHOR} = $author;
    $self->{BOOKTITLE} = $title;
    $self->{NEGNUMBER} = $neg;
    $self->{PHOTOGRAPHER} = $photographer;
    print "created book object with title $self->{BOOKTITLE}\n\n";
}

# return book title
```

11

```
sub return_book_title {
    my $self = shift;
    print " Book title is $self->{BOOKTITLE}\n";
}
```

The main difference between this class definition and the one for Photo is that Book has a separate method to set its data values.

The only change made to the original *Photo* object was to add a new method **return_id** that prints out the photo identifier. The management of creating and setting the data for the two base objects falls on the *PhotoNegative* object class, which inherits from both classes. This class must now list both classes in **use** and **ISA** statements, to signal that *PhotoNegative* is inheriting from both classes. It must also split out the *Photo* data properties from the *Book* properties and ensure each base's class properties are set correctly. To do this, *PhotoNegative* overrides the **new** method for *Photo*, the primary class object; splits out *Photo*'s data; and then calls *Photo*'s new method. Additionally, *PhotoNegative* splits out *Book*'s data, and sets it using *Book*'s "setvalues" method. Also, the **return_all** method for *PhotoNegative* is altered to reflect the data properties now inherited from both base objects. The following listing shows the altered PhotoNegative class.

```
package PhotoNegative;

use strict;
use Photo;
use Book;
@PhotoNegative::ISA = qw(Photo Book);

# PhotoNegative class constructor

# that calls parent new() method, and

# calls _setvalues method of second inherited class
sub new {
    my $class = shift;
    my ($id, $phototitle, $photographer, $photodate, $neg, $prints,
        $author, $booktitle) = @_;

    my $self = Photo->new($id, $phototitle, $photographer,
                $photodate);

    bless $self, ref($class) || $class;
```

```perl
        $self->_setvalues($photographer, $neg, $author, $booktitle, $prints);
        $self;
}


# sets object properties
sub _setvalues {
    my $self = shift;
    my ($photographer, $neg, $author, $booktitle, $prints) = @_;

    $self->Book::_setvalues($author, $booktitle, $neg, $photographer);
    $self->{PRNTSAVAIL} = undef;
    $self->{PRNTSAVAIL} = $prints;
}

sub return_photographer {

    my $self = shift;
    print " Photographer is $self->{PHOTOGRAPHER}\n";
}

sub return_all {
    my $self = shift;
    print " Photo ID is $self->{ID}\t";

    # call Photo's return title
    $self->SUPER::return_title();

    # call Book's return title
    $self->return_book_title();

    print " Photographer is $self->{PHOTOGRAPHER}\t";
    print "Author is $self->{AUTHOR}\n";

    print "Photo date is $self->{PHOTODATE}\t";
    print "Negative number is $self->{NEGNUMBER}\n";
    print "Prints Available is $self->{PRNTSAVAIL}\n";
}

sub return_title {
    my $self = shift;
    print "For Negative Number $self->{NEGNUMBER}\t";
    $self->SUPER::return_title();
}
```

11

By default, the first base class listed in ISA is the one that becomes the Super class for the derived object. If the class that inherits does not have its own constructor, the first base class constructor is the one invoked. Based on this, when *super* is used in the method **return_all** and **return_title**, this references the *Photo* object, not the *Book* object. Additionally, a new *Photo* is created, but not a new *Book*. Further, the derived object package name must be provided with ISA when using the "strict" module, and including two package names. Normally, the package name is not required with single inheritance.

The application that uses the *PhotoNegative* object must also be changed to add the new parameters when the new object is created. In addition, method calls are added that are specific to the Photo class, the PhotoNegative class, and the Book class. The altered application is shown here:

```
package main;

use PhotoNegative;

my $photo = new PhotoNegative(13, "Vermont Fall Foliage","Joe Brown",
          "Oct. 1, 1997",8,10,"Joe Brown", "Fall in Vermont" );

#call Photo method return_id
$photo->return_id();

# call overridden photo method
$photo->return_title();

# call book method return_book_title
$photo->return_book_title();

# call PhotoNegative method return_all
$photo->return_all();
```

The results of running this application show that the multiple inheritance is working as planned. The output starts with a printout when the *Book* object's values are set, a printout of the *book* id because of the method call to **return_id,** and the return from the **PhotoNegative return_title** method call, which in turn calls the base **Photo return_title** method. The results, shown next, also show the printout from **Book's return_book_title** method, and **PhotoNegative's return_all** method:

```
created book object with title Fall in Vermont.

    Photo ID is 13
    For Negative Number 8     Photo title is Vermont Fall Foliage
```

```
Book title is Fall in Vermont
Photo ID is 13      Photo title is Vermont Fall Foliage
Book title is Fall in Vermont
Photographer is Joe Brown      Author is Joe Brown
Photo date is Oct. 1, 1997     Negative number is 8
Prints Available is 10
```

The use of multiple inheritance seems to have no problems, except if you make one change: Rename the BOOKTITLE data field name in *Book* to TITLE, which is equivalent to a data field in *Photo*. What happens then, since the data field names are the same, is when the internal function **_setvalues** is called for *Book*, it sets the TITLE data field that is accessed by *PhotoNegative*. It also sets the TITLE data field that will be accessed when *PhotoNegative* accesses any **Photo** methods. The results of running the application shown here:

```
created book object with title Fall in Vermont

Photo ID is 13
For Negative Number 8     Photo title is Fall in Vermont
 Book title is Fall in Vermont
 Photo ID is 13     Photo title is Fall in Vermont
 Book title is Fall in Vermont
 Photographer is Joe Brown     Author is Joe Brown
Photo date is Oct. 1, 1997     Negative number is 8
Prints Available is 10
```

As you can see from this output, once the TITLE field is set for the *Book* title, it also overwrites the *Photo* title.

T IP: Try out multiple inheritance yourself, but use it rarely and only when single inheritance just won't work for your needs.

11

Polymorphism

Polymorphism, also known as "late-binding", is the capability of a language to support different implementations of the same method, and having the language compiler know which implementation to invoke based on context or method parameters. There are several different types of polymorphism, differentiated primarily by what happens when it is applied. One type of polymorphism, which is common in object-oriented based Perl applications, has to do with the same method being invoked in a parent class and in any classes that inherit from the parent class. This latter type of polymorphism has already been demonstrated throughout this chapter. When one class inherits from another, calling a method on the child class will call the method on the base class if the child class does not implement the method. If the child class does, then this method is called rather than the base class method.

With the second type of polymorphism, a function with the same name works with different types of parameters. A third type is when a function of the same name behaves differently when passed parameters of different types.

The different types of polymorphism are covered in detail in many books on object-oriented programming. Osborne's *C++ from the Ground Up*, by Herb Schildt (Osborne/McGraw-Hill), provides an excellent discussion on polymorphism.

Summary

This chapter covered some of the basic object-oriented techniques available for your use with Perl. Once you've had a chance to work through the examples in this chapter, you will want to go through the *perlobj*, *perbot*, and *perltoot* modules accessible at **http://www.perl.com**. These cover other Perl object-oriented capabilities, in addition to presenting more examples of each of the basic techniques covered in this chapter.

CHAPTER 12

Advanced Data Manipulation

Whether you are a systems administrator, a database manager, or a scientific programmer, a good portion of your job is likely spent doing some sort of data transformation. This might include extracting summary information out of system log files, taking data exported from a spreadsheet program and converting it for use by some other program, or generating code to write data in a prescribed binary format. It is in the arena of data transformation that Perl truly surpasses other programming languages, especially when it comes to text-based data. Perl's strength in this area is due to the combination of a full suite of I/O functions with numerous text manipulating functions and a powerful regular expression engine.

The process of data transformation as addressed in this chapter can be thought of as occurring in three phases. First, data is somehow loaded into Perl. This may be as easy as reading simple lines of text from a file, or as complicated as unpacking platform-dependent binary data. The middle phase begins when the data of interest has been stored in Perl structures (arrays and hashes) and comprises the "data processing" step. The third and final phase involves the process of formatting the processed data for output. Although convenient for the purposes of discussion, you should keep in mind that these three phases need not be distinct. For instance, the act of parsing a data file for input may be all of the processing of the data that is done. Similarly, the process of writing formatted output may be the extent of the data manipulation.

In this chapter, we will look at examples of the ways in which Perl can help you transform data, concentrating on text data. We begin with two examples of loading data into Perl, each of which highlights different techniques for parsing text. Next we will take a detailed look at sorting data in Perl, since sorting is a common step in most forms of data processing. Then we will review some of the methods you have learned for formatting data for output. Finally, we will take a brief look at the functions Perl provides for the manipulation of binary data. You should already be familiar with most of the functions used in the following examples. The goal of the chapter is really to get you thinking about how you might apply Perl in your particular environment.

Parsing Text Data

The first step of any data processing is to parse the data into a form that is easily manipulated. Whether the data of interest is in text log files or binary database files, you must first get it into Perl before you can do anything with it. When working with text files, the first step, before you write any code at all, is to examine the data in the files carefully to determine what patterns are present and then to decide how best to craft your code to make use of those patterns. Indeed, it is in the act of analyzing the data to be parsed that you can really bring your savvy to bear on a problem.

Finding Strings in Strings

If your task is system administration, much of the data you are likely to deal with will be in text format, also referred to as *ASCII*. This is true of many system configuration files and log files, and since ASCII provides a platform-independent exchange format, it is a common way to pass data between computers. Just because a file is human-readable, however, does not necessarily mean that the data is in a useful format. Often you will want to extract, or digest, or summarize, or otherwise manipulate information in text files, and Perl is just the tool for that.

Much of text data processing can be reduced to the process of finding strings within other strings, and this task can generally be characterized in one of two ways: finding strings that match a desired pattern in a loosely formatted file, or finding "substrings" in strings that are more rigidly formatted.

Strings Matching Patterns: Regular Expressions Revisited

Chapter 5 introduced you to regular expressions in Perl, and you may already have had some occasion to use them. Regular expressions are without question the most powerful tool Perl has to offer when it comes to processing text data; though more than any other tool, they demand careful implementation to be effective.

A Real (Unix) World Example   As an example of using regular expressions in the real world, let's write a Perl script that will work somewhat like the **from** program available on most Unix systems. That is, we want a program that will scan the spool file containing our incoming e-mail messages, and report for each message who sent it and what it's about.

For this effort, we assume that we are working on a system that is running the **sendmail** program to receive mail, but you don't really have to know anything about **sendmail** to understand what we're doing. The important point is the process by which patterns in the data is exploited in the code we create to parse the data. We'll start by reviewing the pertinent features of the

12

format in which the e-mail is stored in the spool file. Here's an example of an e-mail header along with the first few lines of the message text:

From janed@ocean.washington.edu Tue Jun 10 14:30:55 1997
Received: by dune.media.mit.edu; id AA17932; Tue, 10 Jun 1997 14:30:53 –0400
Received: from killer.ocean.washington.edu (killer.ocean.washington.edu
[128.95.250.186]) by media.mit.edu (8.7.5/ML961206) with SMTP id OAA10303
for <matter@media.mit.edu>; Tue, 10 Jun 1997 14:30:50 -0400 (EDT)
Received: by killer.ocean.washington.edu
(951211.SGI.8.6.12.PATCH1042/COFS Revision: 2.30) id LAA08552; Tue, 10 Jun
1997 11:21:59–0700
From: "Jane Doe" janed@killer.ocean.washington.edu
Message-Id: 9706101121.ZM8550@killer.ocean.washington.edu
Date: Tue, 10 Jun 1997 11:21:59–0700
In-Reply-To: Matthew Trunnell Ec-2 matter@media.mit.edu
"What news?" (Jun 4, 3:04pm)
References: Pine.OSF.3.96.970604150109.22988H-100000@dune.media.mit.edu
X-Mailer: Z-Mail (3.2.2 10apr95 MediaMail)
To: Matthew Trunnell Ec-2 matter@media.mit.edu
Subject: Re: What news?
Mime-Version: 1.0
Content-Type: text/plain; charset=us-ascii
Status: RO
X-Status: A
Hey matter,
Long time, no e-mail...good to hear (briefly) from you! Life is pretty good…

The first thing that concerns us is that an e-mail message consists of two parts, a header and the message body, and that the mail spool file contains any number of messages concatenated together and stored in ASCII format. The header contains, among other things, a line beginning "From:" that identifies the sender, and possibly a line beginning "Subject:" containing the subject of the message as specified by the sender, which may precede or follow the "From:" line. For the task at hand, we can completely ignore the message body since the header contains both the sender and the subject of the message. Other significant features of the file format are that the first line of the header begins "From" (no colon), and that there is always a blank line separating the header from the body. To complicate matters, the format of the "From:" line varies a bit depending on the program that sent the mail. We will consider three general formats:

1. From: user@host.domain
2. From: User Name <user@host.domain>
3. From: user@host.domain (User Name)

If available, we want the sender's name; otherwise, we'll settle for the
e-mail address.

Extracting information out of the e-mail header is a perfect task for regular
expressions: there are recognizable patterns in the data, but the format is not
so rigidly fixed that we can find the data we want simply by counting lines or
characters. Here is one approach to the problem:

```perl
my $spooldir = "/usr/spool/mail";              # Location of mail spool
my $user = $ENV{LOGNAME} || getpwuid($<);      # Get username either
                                               # from environment or UID
die "unable to determine username" unless $user;
open (MAIL, "<$spooldir/$user") or die "open: $!";
my($from,$subject);
my $header = 1;
while (<MAIL>) {
    chomp;
    if (/^$/) {                   # blank line; this is not the header
        undef $header;
        next;                     # Skip to next line of input
    }
    if (/^From /) {               # Beginning of header (no colon)
        $header = 1;
        printFrom($from,$subject) if $from;
        $from = $subject = undef;
        next;                     # Skip to next line of input
    }
    next unless $header;
    if (/^From: ([^<|(]*)[<|(]?([^^>|)]*)[>|)]?/) {    # Parse From:
        my $s1 = $1;         # $1 and $2 are is set when the regular
        my $s2 = $2;         # expressions in parentheses are matched.
        $from = $s1=~/@/ ? $s2 : $s1;
        $from = $s1 unless $from;
        next;
    }
    if (/^Subject: (.*)$/) {                    # Parse Subject:
        $subject = $1;
        next;
    }
```

12

```
}
printFrom($from,$subject) if $from;
close MAIL;
sub printFrom {
    my $from    = shift;
    my $subject = shift || "(no subject)";
    printf "%-20s   %s\n",$from,$subject;
}
```

We are careful in the code to keep track of when we are looking at the header. There is no reason the body of a message can't contain a line starting "Subject:", and we wouldn't want to confuse this with the real subject line.

Look closely at the use of regular expressions in the previous example. You should notice that we are using regular expression matching not only to identify the header lines of interest, but also to parse those lines and extract the strings we care about. Careful construction of your regular expressions can save you time and effort later.

Let's examine in detail the intimidating regular expression in the previous example:

```
/^From:  ([^<|(]*)[<|(]?([^>|)]*)[>|)]?/
```

The first part of the expression is obvious: match only lines that begin with "From:" (recall that "^" is the beginning-of-line anchor). Next, there is a subexpression in parentheses which says "match everything up to a "<" or a "(" (or end-of-line)". Anything that is matched by this expression will be stored in the special variable $1 because of the parentheses surrounding the expression. Looking at the three possible formats for the "From:" line, you'll see that we will always match something with that expression. The next part of the regular expression matches anything contained within a pair of angle brackets (<>) or parentheses and stores the match in $2 (without the angles or parentheses). $2 will contain nothing for format 1, the sender's e-mail address for format 2, and the sender's name for format 3. Note that the entire match will succeed if the "^From:" matches regardless of whether anything is found for $2 (or $1 for that matter). Once we have the information, is it a simple matter to determine which of $1 or $2 contains the sender's name, if present, and assign that to the $from variable.

The regular expressions can be made to do even more in the previous example. For instance, some mailers put the sender's name in quotes in the "From:" line (as in the sample header shown). Consider as an exercise how you would modify the regular expression to match the quotes in such a way that they are not stored in $1 or $2.

Data with Regular Delimiters: split Revisited

If data of interest is stored in a file with regular delimiters, such as tabs or commas, then the **split** function is likely the first tool you should reach for. Examples of delimited data include values exported from a spreadsheet program (often the delimiter can be specified when you export); the password file on Unix systems (delimited by colons); and .INI files on Win32 systems (which tend to use "=" as a delimiter). In each of these cases, use of the **split** function can make manipulating the data much easier.

As a more concrete example, here is a fragment of a log file from a Xylogics Annex dialup server:

```
18.85.114.10:1a0e36f0:#01:970819:102103:cli hook:login:bob
18.85.114.10:1a0e36f1:#01:970819:102105:telnet:login:18.85.2.171:25:bob
18.85.114.10:1a0e36f2:#01:970819:102109:telnet:logout:18.85.2.171:bob
18.85.114.10:1a0e36f3:#01:970819:102123:cli hook:logout:bob
18.85.114.10:1a0e36f3:#01:970819:102123:cli hook:acct:0:0:907:804:bob
18.85.114.10:1a0e36f4:#02:970819:102615:cli hook:login:sam
18.85.114.10:1a0e36f5:#02:970819:102618:telnet:login:18.85.13.107:110:sam
18.85.114.10:1a0e36f6:#02:970819:102627:telnet:logout:18.85.13.107:sam
18.85.114.10:1a0e36f7:#02:970819:102638:cli hook:logout:sam
18.85.114.10:1a0e36f7:#02:970819:102638:cli hook:acct:0:0:103:12681:sam
```

The dialup server creates a log entry when someone connects, when they initiate or terminate a telnet session, and when they disconnect. The information recorded includes the IP address of the server, a sequence number, a port number, the time of the message, the type of the message, and other data depending on the message type. As you can see, all of the fields are separated by colons, and the number of fields depends on the message. Notice too that the time is stored in two fields in YYMMDD and HHMMSS format.

12

As an exercise, let's write some code to process a log file in this format to determine how many times each user connected to the dialup server, what the total connect time was for each for the period covered by the log, and which users accessed which machines. This would provide a useful summary of a log file that might easily be hundreds or thousands of megabytes in size. To begin, consider how we would approach the first step of the data transformation, namely, reading and parsing the log file in such a way as to extract the useful pieces of data. Given the regular delimiter, an obvious approach is to open the log file for reading, and then use the **split** function to separate the data fields in each line:

```
while (<LOG>) {
    ($hostip,$seq,$port,$ymd,$hms,$type,$msg,@other) = split /:/;
#
#   (Rest of code here)
#
}
```

The total number of fields in the line depends on the message, but we recognize that the first seven fields are consistent for each message type. We assign those first seven values directly to named variables in one step; additional fields are stored in the @other array. The **split** function has done half our work for us.

Parsing Strings of Fixed Width: substr and unpack

Continuing with the previous example, we want to determine the total duration of each dialup session by comparing the time the user connected ("cli hook:login") to the time the user disconnected ("cli hook:logout"). The time of each message is stored in two fields, which we have assigned via split to the variables $ymd, and $hms. Unfortunately, the format of the time data makes the values very difficult to work with. We need to transform the time values into some more usable format. If we split out the year, month, day, hour, minute and second into separate variables, we can use Perl's **timelocal( )** function to convert the time into Perl's internal time format (seconds since 1 January 1970) which can be easily manipulated. (The **timelocal( )** function is part of the standard Time::Local module.)

Noting that the strings in $ymd and $hms always have fixed length, we might choose to use Perl's substr function to parse them:

```
$year = substr($ymd,0,2);
$mon = substr($ymd,2,2);
$day = substr($ymd,4,2);
Ö
```

In this particular case, however, since we need to parse the entire string, we would do better to use the **unpack** function:

```
($year,$mon,$day) = unpack("a2a2a2",$ymd);
($hour,$min,$sec) = unpack("a2a2a2",$hms);
```

We can actually do this in one step taking advantage of variable interpolation inside of double-quoted strings:

```
($year,$mon,$day,$hour,$min,$sec) = unpack("a2a2a2a2a2a2","$ymd$hms");
```

We will learn more about the **unpack** function later in the section on binary data. Now we can write a subroutine to generate a usable time value:

```
sub parseTime {
    my $timestring = shift;
    my ($year,$mon,$day,$hour,$min,$sec);
    ($year,$mon,$day,$hour,$min,$sec) = unpack("a2a2a2a2a2a2",$timestring);
    # Perl months run from 0-11, so subtract 1 from $mon
return timelocal($sec,$min,$hour,$day,$mon-1,$year,0,0,0);
}
```

Storing the Parsed Data

Finally, we can put the pieces together to build the core of our log processing program:

```
use Time::Local;     # Needed for timelocal() function in parseTime
my $file = "acplog"; # The name of the file containing the log data
open(LOG,"<$file") or die "could not open $file: $!";
my (%logins,%ontime,%hosts,%start);
my ($host,$seq,$port,$ymd,$hms,$type,$msg,$user, @other);
while (<LOG>) {
    chomp;
    ($host,$seq,$port,$ymd,$hms,$type,$msg,@other) = split /:/;
    $user = pop @other;     # The user name is always the last field;
    if ($type eq 'telnet' and $msg eq 'login') {
        # $other[0] is IP address of target machine for this message type.
        # Store IP address and increment access count for $user in
        # %host structure.
    $host{$other[0]}->{$user} ++;     # A "hash of hashes"
    next;
    }
    next unless $type eq 'cli hook';     # Skip unless a "cli hook" message
    if ($msg eq 'login') {
        $logins{$user}++;                # $user has logged on
        $start{$user} = parseTime("$ymd$hms");     # Record start time
    } elsif ($msg eq 'logout') {
        next unless $start{$user};     # $user has logged out
        # Calculate connect time
```

12

```
        $ontime{$user} += parseTime("$ymd$hms") - $start{$user};
        undef $start{$user};        # Reset start time for $user
    }
}
close LOG;
```

As the **while** loop executes, the data of interest is extracted from the lines of the log file and stored in Perl hashes. Look closely at the construction of %hosts. This structure is actually a "hash of hashes": the keys of the hash are IP addresses; the values of the hash are references to another hash whose keys are usernames and whose values are the number of times the users have accessed the given IP address. We'll see how to get data out of this structure later in the section on data formatting.

After the **while** loop has terminated, all of the data we care about is stored in the three hashes, %logins, %ontime, and %hosts. Now we want to think about how to report the data we have culled from the log file. We have a number of options: we can summarize dialup usage by login name, or by full name, or perhaps in order of decreasing usage. Each of these options requires that we sort the data in a particular way, so it's time to take a look at the support Perl provides for sorting.

Sorting

Much of the work in making data more useful involves some sort of sorting. If you are examining error messages in a log file, for example, you may choose to sort the messages by time, or perhaps by severity. If you are preparing an accounting report of some kind, you may want to sort it numerically, or by department name, or by some combination.

Perl provides a general **sort** function that you can augment with sorting rules of your own. In its default form, the **sort** function takes an array as an argument and returns the elements of the array in standard sort order. In this default sorting, all values are treated as strings, so digits sort before capital letters, which sort before lowercase letters.

Thus the code:

```
my @array = ('1to1','one2one','onetoone','OneToOne','121');
my @sorted = sort @array;
print "@sorted\n";
```

will print out:

```
121 1to1 OneToOne one2one onetoone
```

Be aware that sorting by digits is not really the same as sorting numerically. If you use the default sort on an array of simple decimal numbers, the results of a standard sort may or may not be what you expect, depending on the context in which the elements of the array are interpreted. Compare the two lines of output produced by the following code:

```perl
my @sort1 = sort(1.23e-2, 0.123, .123, .0123);
my @sort2 = sort qw(1.23e-2 0.123 .123 .0123);
print "@sort1\n";      # prints: 0.0123 0.0123 0.123 0.123
print "@sort2\n";      # prints: .0123 .123 0.123 1.23e-2
```

In the first call to **sort**, Perl interprets the unquoted numbers as numbers and converts them to a standard internal format before passing them to the **sort** function, where they are interpreted as strings. In the second call, the array of quoted strings (numbers) is not pre-interpreted by Perl, and the resulting sorted array is not in ascending numerical order, though it is in standard sort order. The bottom line is that if you want to sort numerically, use an explicit sort routine as described in the next section.

Creating Your Own Sort Routine

If you need anything other than the default sort—for instance, the ability to sort numerically—you will have to provide the sorting rules explicitly, either in a block of commands enclosed by curly braces ({}) or in a subroutine. The way it works is that the Perl **sort** function executes your commands for each comparison it does; the values being compared are available in the special variables $a and $b. Your code should return a positive integer if the value of $a sorts before $b; 0 if they sort the same; and a negative integer if $b sorts before $a. To facilitate the comparison, Perl provides two special operators, one for strings and another for numbers, both of which return –1, 0 or 1 as appropriate. These are *cmp* and <=>, respectively.

The default sort command can be expressed explicitly as

```perl
my @sorted = sort { $a cmp $b; } @array;
```

12

The simplest way to sort any array of numbers in increasing numerical order is:

```
my @sorted_numbers = sort { $a <=> $b; } @numbers;
```

To do the same sort using a subroutine:

```
my @sorted_numbers = sort numericalsort @numbers;
sub numericalsort {
    $a <=> $b;
}
```

The variables $a and $b must not be declared local to the subroutine (with local or my); they are special variables in the scope of the package containing the sort routine.

Some Examples

If you have an array of well-behaved strings, meaning strings of all one case or with only the leading character capitalized, then Perl's default sort is all you need to arrange them alphabetically. If you have an array of strings of mixed case, you can make your sort case-insensitive as follows:

```
my @sorted = sort { lc($a) cmp lc($b); } @array;
```

This differs from:

```
my @sorted = sort lc (@array);
```

In the former example, the elements of the @sorted array retain their original case.

If you want an array sorted in reverse alphabetical order, you can either use Perl's **reverse** function, as so:

```
my @sorted = reverse sort @array;
```

or you can simply use the *cmp* operator to explicitly swap $a and $b (which is generally more efficient):

```
my @sorted = sort { $b cmp $a; } @array.
```

Similarly, the following command sorts in decreasing numerical order:

```
my @sorted_numbers = sort { $b <=> $a; } @numbers;
```

A More Complicated Example

By providing your own rules, you can create custom sort orders to handle most any data. Consider, for example, the task of sorting an array of IP network addresses. In standard notation, IP addresses are specified as four numbers separated by dots, for instance, 132.239.114.101. A useful sort routine would sort each group of numbers individually, such that networks and subnetworks would be sorted in numerical order, and within each subnetwork, hosts would be sorted in numerical order. Here's how you might do it:

```
my @sorted_addresses = sort IPsort @addresses;
sub IPsort {
    my @a = split /\./, $a;
    my @b = split /\./, $b;
    $a[0] <=> $b[0] || $a[1] <=> $b[1] ||
    $a[2] <=> $b[2] || $a[3] <=> $b[3];
}
```

In this example, local variables are declared (using *my*) to hold the elements of each address being compared, and each corresponding element is compared in turn, if necessary. If the first two elements ($a[0] and $b[0]) differ, the <=> operator gives a positive or negative number as appropriate and the subroutine returns. Only if the first two elements are the same do the next elements get compared, and so on. This same technique of comparing multiple elements can be used to sort heterogeneous data structures.

Formatting Text Data

The final step in data transformation is to reformat processed data for output. This step may be as trivial as printing a few lines of text, as in the e-mail "from" example, or as complicated as writing a binary database file. Often what we seek as output is a report in which the processed data, perhaps sorted, is formatted in a clear and useful way.

12

Creating Output Using the Format Declaration

Let's return to the dialup log processing script and add code to generate a nicely formatted report. What we want is a summary of the total number of connections and average connection length for each user. Here is some code that will produce the desired output, sorted by login name, which makes use of the **format** declaration introduced in Chapter 7:

```
for $user (sort keys %logins) {
    $numCalls = $logins{$user};
    $averageTime = $ontime{$user}/$totalCalls/60;    # convert to minutes
$totalTime = $ontime{$user}/3600                # convert to hours
    write;
}
format STDOUT_TOP =
                        Dialup Usage

USERNAME       CALLS       AVG(m)      TOTAL(h)
---------------------------------------------
.
format STDOUT =
@<<<<<<<<      @####      @###.##     @###.##
$user, $numCalls, $averageTime, $totalTime
.
```

If we want, we can define our own sort routine to sort based on, say, total connect time:

```
sub mySort {
    $ontime{$b} <=> $ontime{$a};    # sort in decreasing numerical order
```

Then we just replace the beginning of the **for** loop with:

```
for $user (sort mySort keys(%logins)) {
```

This way our output will be in terms of the biggest users.

Working with Complex Data Structures
Now let's play with that hash of hashes containing the list of IP addresses mentioned in the log and the users who connected to them.

```
for $addr (sort IPsort keys %hosts) {
    print "The host $host was accessed by\n";
    for $user (sort keys %{$hosts{$addr}}) {
```

```
        print "\t$user ($hosts{$addr}->{$user} times)\n";
    }
}
```

The first step is to sort based on the IP address of each host, which we do in the argument of the first **for** statement. Then, for each host, we sort alphabetically the list of users who connected to that host: sort keys %{$hosts{$addr}}. Recall that the value of each element $hosts{$addr} is actually a reference to another hash. The syntax of the argument in the second call to keys dereferences the value, providing access to the hash it references. The second **print** statement demonstrates how to access the value of a particular element of the referenced hash, which in our example contains the number of times a given user accessed a given host.

The output from the preceding code looks like:

```
The machine 18.85.13.107 was accessed by
    bjp (2 times)
    meg (2 times)
    sam (1 times)
The machine 18.85.2.171 was accessed by
    bob (4 times)
```

Other Text Formatting Tools

Using **format** declarations is not the only way to create nicely formatted text output. One of the other tools you have seen already is the **printf** function. Indeed, we could have opted to use **printf** in our previous example, with a command like:

```
printf "%-8s    %4d    %3.2f    %3.2f\n",
$user, $numCalls, $averageTime, $totalTime;
```

The **printf** approach is certainly simpler when dealing with individual lines of output. The use of **format**, on the other hand, offers the advantage that Perl keeps track of the number of lines on the page and prints headers when appropriate and so forth. Your particular need should determine which tool is best.

12

A brother to **printf** is the **sprintf** function, which builds a formatted string according to your specifications, but does not send the string to output. The format is specified exactly as for **printf**. For example:

```
my $string = sprintf "%-8s    %4d    %3.2f   %3.2f\n",
$user, $numCalls, $averageTime, $totalTime;
print $string;
```

The **sprintf** function will come in handy not so much for output as for converting numerical data to formatted strings that may be used as arguments for other functions.

Working with Binary Data

Not all of the data you will need to handle will be in simple ASCII, human-readable format. If you are working with data collected from scientific instruments, for instance, or perhaps with video or audio data, you'll have to be ready to deal with binary data. Binary data is less friendly than ASCII data for several reasons. The first is that pattern recognition becomes largely impossible; you cannot tell by looking at a string of eight bytes if it should be interpreted as a long integer, or floating-point number, or perhaps two shorts. Generally you'll have to have an explicit description of the format of the binary data before you can parse it. Second, the format of binary data varies from machine to machine. Floating-point numbers, for example, may have a different binary representation on one computer than on another. Also, the byte-ordering of a computer, whether it is "big-endian" (most significant byte first) or "little-endian" (least significant byte first), will affect how binary data is stored.

Reading Binary Data

The basic Perl input facility we have been working with so far, namely the angle operator, is not appropriate for use with binary data. Instead, Perl provides a more basic function that should be familiar to C programmers. This is the **read** function.

To read binary data from a file, first open the file in the normal way with the **open** function. For operating systems that distinguish between binary and text data, you may need to make a call to the **binmode** function to force the file to be treated as a binary file. The **read** function takes as arguments the filehandle from the **open** call, a variable to hold the data, and a number specifying how many bytes are to be read. The return value is the number of bytes actually read. For example:

```
my ($data, $cnt)
open (FILE, "< file.bin") or die "could not open file: $!";
binmode (FILE);
```

```
$cnt = read(FILE, $data, 1024);
print "Only read $cnt (of 1024) bytes\n" unless $cnt = 1024;
```

If the call to read is successful, the variable $data will contain1024 bytes of data. The data is not likely to be useful, however, unless it is parsed into more meaningful pieces.

Parsing Binary Data

The primary tools for parsing and creating binary data in Perl are the **unpack** and **pack** functions. Both of these functions require that you carefully specify the format of the binary data that you are working with. The format is specified as a string of symbolic values representing the structure of the data. We have already seen an example of the use of **unpack**, albeit in an ASCII context:

```
($year,$mon,$day,$hour,$min,$sec) = unpack("a2a2a2a2a2a2",$timestring);
```

In this example, the format specifier instructs unpack to interpret the byte sequence in the variable $timestring as a sequence of six two-character ASCII strings. The value "a" in the format specifier refers to an ASCII value; the trailing "2" is a multiplier.

The following table details the format specifiers for use with **pack** and **unpack**.

a	An ASCII string; pad with nulls if needed (**pack**)
A	An ASCII string; pad with spaces if needed (**pack**); strip trailing nulls and spaces (**unpack**)
b	A bit string with least significant bit first
B	A bit string with most significant bit first
c	A signed char
C	An unsigned char
d	A double-precision float
f	A single-precision float
h	A hexadecimal string, least significant nybble first
H	A hexadecimal string, most significant nybble first
i	A signed integer

12

I	An unsigned integer
l	A signed long
L	An unsigned long
n	A short in big-endian format ("network order")
N	A long in big-endian format ("network order")
p	A pointer to a string
P	A pointer to a structure
s	A signed short
S	An unsigned short
v	A short in little-endian order
V	A long in little-endian order
u	A uuencoded string
x	A null byte
X	Back up a byte
@	Fill with nulls to specified position in string (**pack**)

Most of these specifiers can take a trailing multiplier value. When used with hexadecimal values, the multiplier refers to nybbles; when used with bit strings, the multiplier refers to bits. Keep in mind that a number packed on one machine may not be the same as what you get unpacking the data on another machine. This is particularly true for floating-point values, but applies to any data sensitive to byte-ordering.

An examination of the table of format specifiers should give an indication of the broad range of data to which you can apply the **pack** and **unpack** functions. Indeed, these functions should be all you need to parse any binary data whose format is well defined, or to create any desired binary data structures.

Examples
Here is a little code fragment to determine the byte-ordering of your machine:

```
print "big endian\n" if pack("s",1) eq pack("n",1);
print "little endian\n" if pack("s",1) eq pack("v",1);
```

This example compares the binary representation of a short integer on your system to big-endian and little-endian values.

Now let's consider a more useful example. Suppose you have a C program that generates a binary database of items in your warehouse. The database consists of a series of binary structures defined in C as:

```
typedef struct {
    char    name[32];       /* Name of item: 32 bytes */
    float   price;          /* Price of item: 4 bytes */
    short   part_number;    /* Part number: 2 bytes */
    long    quantity;       /* Quantity in stock: 4 bytes */
} stock_item;
```

Note that the size of the structure as specified is 42 bytes, although it is dependent on the size of shorts, longs, and floats on the host system. Let's start with a Perl script to read and display the items in the database:

```
#     # show_stock.pl:   display items in stock     #     my $length = 42;
# Length of one entry in bytes     my $file = "stock.dat";     # Database
file    open (FILE, "<$file") or die "could not open file: $!";
binmode(FILE);              # For operating systems that care     my
($data,$item);      while(($cnt = read(FILE,$data,$length)==$length) {
$item++;                # Update item count
($name,$price,$part_no,$quantity) = unpack("A32fsl",$data);         print
"Item $item: $name\n";         printf "\tPrice:            $%.2f\n",$price;
# Format price nicely    print "\tPart number:        $part_no\n"    print
"\tQuantity in stock: $quantity\n\n";    }     close(FILE);
```

Depending on the contents of $file, This might generate output similar to:

```
% display.pl
Item 1: widget
    Price:              $19.95
    Part number:        501
    Quantity in stock: 42
Item 2: gizmo (deluxe)
    Price:              $199.99
    Part number:        9724
    Quantity in stock: 1004
```

Observe how carefully we had to specify the format of the input data in the file, both in the format argument to **unpack** and in the length argument to

12

read. The criterion for the **while** loop makes certain that we actually read as many bytes as we need for a complete entry. If we lose track of how many bytes we've read, we're likely to end up with garbage when we try to unpack $data. Also, note the use of **printf** with the price. The price is stored on disk as a floating-point number, and without specifying the output format, **print** would display it as something like 19.949996948242, since that's the floating-point representation (at least on some systems). You always have to be careful with binary data.

To round out the example, let's construct a program to append a new entry to our database.

```
#
#  add_entry.pl:    Add a new item to stock list
#
my $file = "stock.dat";          # Database file
#
#  Could modify code to accept values from command line,
#  but for now, we'll just hard-code a single entry.
#
my $name = "Super Sprocket";
my $price = 42.50;               # A bargain!
my $part_no = 3012;
my $quantity = 300;
my $data = pack("A32fls",$name,$price,$part_no,$quantity);
# Open $file for appending
open(FILE, ">>$file") or die "could not open $file: $!";
print FILE $data;
close FILE;
```

In the preceding code, we used exactly the same format specifier for **pack** as we did in the previous code for **unpack**. This is clearly important if you want to get out what you put in. Since $data is 42 bytes by construction, however, we don't have to specify the length when we write to the file. Indeed, we could not specify a length using **print**, and there is no write equivalent of read. (Recall that **write** is used to print a formatted (text) record; see Chapter 7). Actually, that's not quite true. Perl has two functions for doing low-level I/O, **sysread** and **syswrite** (see your Perl documentation), but by building your binary data structures carefully, you should never need these.

Summary

The examples in this chapter have been created to give a feel for using Perl to solve problems that require some form of data transformation. While this is certainly not the only task to which Perl is well suited, it is one in which Perl shines. Using the techniques and tools you have learned so far, you should be able to apply Perl to a wide range of tasks on your system.

12

CHAPTER 13

Debugging in Perl

It's probably not news to you that many of your Perl programs are not going to run perfectly the first time you run the code. For some errors, such as those run-time errors that happen when the user tries to save a file to disk without a disk in the drive, you will need to write error-handling code, using techniques such as the || operator and the die statement to let the user know why things go wrong. Other errors occur because there is a bug somewhere in the code that prevents it from running. Tracking down and fixing bugs is the process known as *debugging*. Perl contains a multifunction debugger that allows you to use several techniques to find and fix bugs in your Perl code. This chapter shows you how to use the debugger to do things such as list parts of your program, set breakpoints, trace your program's execution, and execute your program one statement at a time.

Loading and Leaving the Perl Debugger

You load the Perl debugger by specifying the -d switch when you run your Perl script. For example, if you have a program named matrix.pl, you can run it through the debugger by typing this at the command prompt (along with any other switches you want):

```
perl -d matrix.pl
```

First, here's the code for the matrix.pl script, which you can use for a reference as you work through this chapter:

```perl
$mat_ref = [
            [100, 200, 300],
            [400, 500, 600],
            [700, 800, 900],
          ];
for ($i = 0; $i < 3; $i++) {
    for ($j = 0; $j < 3; $j++) {
        $mat_ref1->[$j][$i] = $mat_ref->[$i][$j];
    }
}
for ($i = 0; $i < 3; $i++) {
    for ($j = 0; $j < 3; $j++) {
        print $mat_ref1->[$i][$j];
    }
    print "\n";
}
```

When this command is issued, the Perl debugger loads immediately and displays a message telling you a few things about the debugger. The message you receive will look similar to this:

```
Stack dump during die enabled outside of evals.
Loading DB routines from perl5db.pl patch level 0.95
Emacs support available.
Enter h or `h h' for help.
```

main::(matrix.pl:2):	[100, 200, 300],
main::(matrix.pl:3):	[400, 500, 600],
main::(matrix.pl:4):	[700, 800, 900],
main::(matrix.pl:5):	];

DB<1>

The first three lines the debugger displays are system messages. The fourth line says that if you type the letter "h", you can get help on using the debugger. The debugger's help system will be covered later in this chapter.

The next line displays the first executable line of the program loaded with the debugger. When the debugger finds an executable line, it displays the following information about the line:

♦ The package the line is part of (in this case package Main)

♦ The name of the program it is executing (in this case matrix.pl)

♦ The line number of the program statement

After these lines are displayed, the debugger's command prompt is displayed and the debugger is waiting for you to enter a command. The number in brackets is the command number of the debugging session. Each command you enter is numbered so that if you need to, you can reference the command by number later in the debugging session. You will learn how to do this later in the chapter.

Once a debugging session is over, you can exit the debugger by simply entering the command *q* at the debugger command prompt. Entering the exit command returns you to your operating system's command prompt.

Listing Your Program Code

One of the most basic debugging techniques is listing your program. The Perl debugger provides several ways to list your program. The following sections cover the debugger's listing commands.

Using the l command

The **l** (el) command lists the next several lines of your code. When you type the **l** command, the next ten program statements from the current listing point will be printed on the screen.

Here is an example of issuing the **l** command on the matrix.pl program:

```
2==>            [100, 200, 300],
3:          [400, 500, 600],
4:          [700, 800, 900],
5:                      ];
6:      for ($i = 0; $i < 3; $i++) {
7:          for ($j = 0; $j < 3; $j++) {
8:              print $mat_ref->[$i][$j];
9:          }
10:         print "\n";
11:     }
```

Entering the **l** command again will result in the next 10 statements being listed:

```
12:
13:     for ($i = 0; $i < 3; $i++) {
14:         for ($j = 0; $j < 3; $j++) {
15:             $mat_ref1->[$j][$i] = $mat_ref->[$i][$j];
16:         }
17:     }
18:     for ($i = 0; $i < 3; $i++) {
19:         for ($j = 0; $j < 3; $j++) {
20:             print $mat_ref->[$i][$j];
21:         }
  DB<1>
```

You can continue listing your code in this manner until the last line. If you want to specify that the debugger list just one line of code, you can do so by specifying the line number after the **l** command. The following example lists just line 10 of the matrix.pl program:

```
DB<1> l 10
10:                     print "\n";
   DB<2>
```

You can also specify a range of line numbers to list by including the range after the **l** command. Here is an example that lists the lines 8–13 of matrix.pl:

```
DB<2> l 8-13
8:                      print $mat_ref->[$i][$j];
9:              }
10:          print "\n";
11:    }
12:
13:    for ($i = 0; $i < 3; $i++) {
```

If you want to list a certain line number and a specified number of lines after it, you can do so by specifying the line number you want listed, a plus sign (+), and the number of lines you want listed following the specified line number. Here's an example:

```
DB<3> l 5+5
5:              ];
6:    for ($i = 0; $i < 3; $i++) {
7:        for ($j = 0; $j < 3; $j++) {
8:            print $mat_ref->[$i][$j];
9:        }
10:      print "\n";
```

Finally, if your Perl script contains a subroutine, you can list just that subroutine by specifying the subroutine name after the **l** command. For example, if matrix.pl contains a subroutine named **mat_add**, you can list just that subroutine in the debugger using the following command:

```
DB<1> l mat_add
1:    sub mat_add(%mat1 %mat2) {
2:        for ($m = 0; $m < 3; $m++) {
3:            for ($n = 0; $n < 3; $n++) {
4:                $new_mat[$m][$n] = $mat1[$m][$n] + $mat2[$m][$n];
5:            }
```

13

```
6:              }
7:        }
DB<2>
```

The whole subroutine will be listed as long as it can all fit in the debugger window. If it's too large, only part of it will be listed and you can list the rest of it using the **l** command.

Using the w Command

You can display a window of lines that surround a specific line by using the **w** command. For example, if you want to display line 5 and some lines surrounding it, you can enter the following debugger command:

```
DB<1> w 5
2==>                      [100, 200, 300],
3:                          [400, 500, 600],
4:                          [700, 800, 900],
5:                        ];
6:      for ($i = 0; $i < 3; $i++) {
7:          for ($j = 0; $j < 3; $j++) {
8:              print $mat_ref->[$i][$j];
9:          }
10:     print "\n";
11:     }
```

The **w** command displays the line specified, three lines preceding it, and several lines after it, filling up the rest of the debugger window.

Using the // Command

You can use the debugger to search for a pattern in your code by surrounding the pattern in slashes. To search for the keyword **print** in the matrix.pl program, you can issue the following command:

```
DB<1> /print/
8:              print $mat_ref->[$i][$j];
```

Issuing this command will display the first instance of **print**, if the pattern can be found. If a pattern can't be found, the debugger will let you know.

```
DB<2> /foobar/
/foobar/: not found
```

When you are searching for a pattern, you can leave off the final slash, so that your commands can look like this:

```
DB<1> /print
```

If you search for the same pattern a second time, the debugger will look for the next instance of the pattern. Also, when a pattern is found, subsequent searches will search from the line number of the found pattern toward the end of the file. The command discussed next, ??, allows you to search backward through a program.

Using the ?? Command

To search a program backwards to find a pattern, surround the pattern with question marks. If, for example, you've searched through the matrix.pl file for **print** and you want to look for a previous instance of the keyword, use the following command:

```
DB<6> ?print?
20:                print $mat_ref1->[$i][$j];
```

Like the // command, if you search for a pattern with ?? and the debugger can't find it, the debugger will display the pattern and a "not found" message. You can also leave off the trailing question mark when searching for a pattern.

If you search continually backwards through a file for the same pattern and find the first instance of the pattern, a subsequent search for the same pattern will match the last instance of the pattern at the end of the file.

Using the S Command

The **S** command lists all the subroutine names found in the current file. This command displays not only the subroutines you've defined in your program, but also subroutines used by Perl. Here's an example:

```
DB<1> S
Term::ReadLine::Stub::Features
Term::ReadLine::Stub::IN
```

13

```
Term::ReadLine::Stub::MinLine
Term::ReadLine::Stub::OUT
Term::ReadLine::Stub::ReadLine
Term::ReadLine::Stub::addhistory
Term::ReadLine::Stub::findConsole
Term::ReadLine::Stub::new
Term::ReadLine::Stub::readline
main::BEGIN
main::mat_add
DB<1>
```

Of these subroutines listed, only the last, **mat_add,** is a custom subroutine. The rest are subroutines used by Perl internally.

Using the Debugger to Step Through a Program

A commonly used debugging technique is to step through a program line-by-line in order to understand what is happening in the program as each line is executed. The Perl debugger has several commands that allow you to do this, and they are discussed in the following sections.

Using the s Command

The **s** command (notice this is a lowercase "s") is used to execute the current statement of your program. When you issue this command, the current line is executed and the next line to be executed is displayed. Any input or output operations are performed before the next line is displayed, so if your program is looking for input from the user, the debugger will pause until the input is entered before displaying the next line. If the execution of a statement causes output (say to STDOUT), the debugger will display the output before displaying the next line of code. The following example executes the first several lines of matrix.pl:

```
DB<1> s
main::(matrix.pl:11):        }
  DB<1> s
main::(matrix.pl:6):            for ($i = 0; $i < 3; $i++) {
  DB<1> s
main::(matrix.pl:9):            }
  DB<1> s
main::(matrix.pl:7):                for ($j = 0; $j < 3; $j++) {
  DB<1> s
```

```
main::(matrix.pl:8):                        print $mat_ref->[$i][$j];
  DB<1> s
100main::(matrix.pl:8):                     print $mat_ref->[$i][$j];
  DB<1> s
200main::(matrix.pl:8):                     print $mat_ref->[$i][$j];
  DB<1> s
300main::(matrix.pl:10):                        print "\n";
  DB<1>
```

When a subroutine is encountered using the *s* command, the debugger treats it just like the other parts of the program and assumes you want to debug the subroutine also. However, the debugger won't execute the first statement in the subroutine. Instead, it waits for you to issue an **s** command and then proceeds to execute the first statement in the subroutine. The next section discusses how to step through your programs without also stepping through each subroutine.

Using the n Command

The **n** command works similarly to the **s** command in that it executes a statement and displays the next statement to be executed. It differs from the **s** command because it will not step through a subroutine. Instead, it will execute the whole subroutine and then display the first statement after the call to the subroutine.

For example, if the current line as displayed by the debugger is:

```
main::(matrix.pl:22):               &mat_add (\%mat_ref \%mat_ref1);
```

When the **n** command is executed, the subroutine will be executed and the next line of the program is displayed. None of the subroutine lines are displayed, and you cannot debug them using the **n** command.

 T IP: You can mix **s** commands with **n** commands in the same debugging session so that you debug only the subroutines that you need to.

13

Using the r Command

You use the **r** command when you are stepping through a subroutine and you decide that you don't really need to execute the subroutine line-by-line anymore. Issuing the *r* command executes the remainder of the subroutine and displays the first line of code following the subroutine.

Pressing *ENTER* with the *s* and *n* Commands

When you are using the debugger with the **s** or **n** command, you can simply press the ENTER key to execute whichever **s** or **n** command was last entered. This works just like typing either an **s** or an **n**.

Using the Debugger to View Variable Values

When you are debugging a program, you will often want to check the value of different variables while the program is executing. This is a critical aspect of debugging. The Perl debugger offers two commands you can use to view variable values. These commands are discussed in the following sections.

Using the X Command

The **X** command displays the value of any variable that is part of the current package. If you haven't specified another package, the **X** command will grab the values of variables from package Main.

The **X** command can either be issued by itself, in which case every variable of the current package and its value will be displayed, or you can issue it with a variable name, which will display the value of just the variable specified. Let's look at an example:

```
  DB<1> s
main::(matrix.pl:11):      }
  DB<1> s
main::(matrix.pl:6):      for ($m = 0; $m < 3; $m++) {
  DB<1> s
main::(matrix.pl:9):          }
  DB<1> s
main::(matrix.pl:7):          for ($n = 0; $n < 3; $n++) {
  DB<1> X m n mat_ref
$m = 0
$n = 3
$mat_ref = ARRAY(0xb8bd0c)
   0   ARRAY(0xb7a058)
        0   100
        1   200
        2   300
```

```
1    ARRAY(0xb8bf04)
     0    400
     1    500
     2    600
2    ARRAY(0xb8be80)
     0    700
     1    800
     2    900
DB<2>
```

In this example, the first few statements in matrix.pl were executed so that the variables of the program could obtain a value. Once these variables obtained values, the **X** command was issued with the variables $m and $n and the array variable $mat_ref. Notice that these variables were entered without an identifying prefix ($). Had the variables been entered as $m, $n, and $mat_ref, no values would have been displayed because the debugger assumes the prefix.

However, when the values of the variables are displayed, the scalar prefix is displayed along with the variable name and its value, as you can see in the output from the example above.

Issuing the **X** command without an argument displays every variable value pertinent to the current program environment, which includes values for all the environment variables, the special variables, and Perl's internal variables. Obviously, you will be better off specifying just the variables of your program, but if you don't, at least your program's variables will be the last displayed in the long list of Perl variables.

NOTE: If you have two or more variable types that share the same name, you only have to list the variable name once. The debugger will display the value for each variable with that name.

Using the v Command

To display the value of variables in a package other than Main, use the **v** command. For example, if you have a package titled "Secure" in the program matrix.pl, you can display the values of variables in the package like this (assuming the variables have values within the package):

13

```
DB<3> V secure my_var1 my_var2
$my_var1 = "Some value"
$my_var2 = "Some other value"
```

Setting and Working with Breakpoints

Another common and powerful debugging technique is the setting of breakpoints. A *breakpoint* is a place in a program where execution stops. Normally, you will set breakpoints at certain key spots in your program where you will want to examine the value of variables or check to see if the logic of the program is working as you thought it would. The sections that follow will show you how to set and work with breakpoints in the Perl debugger.

Using the b Command

The **b** command is used to set a breakpoint in a Perl program. If you want your program to execute up to line 10, for example, you will issue the following command in the debugger:

```
DB<4> b 10
```

By issuing this command, the program will execute all the statements in the program up to but not including line 10.

You can also use the **b** command with a conditional expression, so that program execution will halt only if the expression evaluates to True. For example, using matrix.pl, if you don't want the program to print the matrix if the 0,0th element is 0, you can issue a command like this:

```
DB<4> b 8 ($mat_ref[0][0]  = 0)
```

TIP: If you try to set a breakpoint on a line that is not breakable, the debugger will display the message "Line x is not breakable", where *x* is the line number specified.

You can also set a breakpoint at a subroutine. When you do this, the debugger will break the program before the first statement of the subroutine is executed.

Finally, once a breakpoint is set, it remains set until you remove it (which is discussed below), and you can set as many breakpoints in your program as you have lines that are breakable.

Using the c Command

Once you have set breakpoints in your program, you can use the **c** command to execute the program until it reaches a breakpoint or the end of the program. The following example shows how this works:

```
DB<11> b 8
  DB<12> c
100main::(matrix.pl:8):          print $mat_ref[$m][$n];
```

In this example, a breakpoint was set at line 8. Then the program was executed using the **c** command, and execution of the program was stopped at line 8, the breakpoint set.

You can also use the **c** command to set temporary breakpoints. Temporary breakpoints are convenient because once the program is executed and the breakpoint is reached, it is deleted automatically by the debugger. Here's an example:

```
DB<13> c 10
200300main::(matrix.pl:10):          print "\n";
```

If you issue another **c** command next, the program will not break at line 10 because the temporary breakpoint is deleted as soon as it is reached.

Using the L Command

In the course of a debugging session, you might set many breakpoints and forget just exactly where they are. You can list all your breakpoints using the **L** command. This command lists the line number and the statement itself, along with a message to let you know that the program will break at this line. Here's an example of listing the breakpoints of matrix.pl (which have been set at lines 8 and 13):

13

```
DB<18> L
8:           print $mat_ref->[$m][$n];
   break if (1)
```

```
13:     for ($m = 0; $m < 3; $m++) {
   break if (1)
```

The statement "break if (1)" simply means that a break will always occur at this line, since (1) evaluates to True.

Using the d and D Commands

In a previous section, you learned that breakpoints can be deleted if they are no longer wanted. The **d** command, along with the line number of the breakpoint you want to delete, is the command to use for deleting single breakpoints. In the next example, the breakpoint at line 8 of matrix.pl is deleted:

```
DB<19> d 8
DB<20>
```

There is no confirming message; the breakpoint is simply deleted. If you want to delete all the breakpoints previously set, use the **D** command. Again, no confirming message is displayed, but all the breakpoints you have previously set are deleted.

Debugging by Program Tracing

Program tracing is a debugging technique in which each line of a program is displayed as it is executed. This technique is particularly useful when trying to debug loops and conditional expressions. This section discusses how to use program tracing to help debug your programs.

Program tracing is "turned on" by issuing the *t* command. When this command is issued, the debugger is said to be in "trace mode". The command is issued by itself, like this:

```
DB<1> t
Trace = on
```

You can use the **trace** command with other debugging commands to effectively debug your programs. For example, here is an example that uses trace mode with a breakpoint to display the execution of a program up to a temporary breakpoint:

```
  DB<1> t
Trace = on
  DB<1> C 10
main::(matrix.pl:11):      }
main::(matrix.pl:6):     for ($m = 0; $m < 3; $m++) {
main::(matrix.pl:9):         }
main::(matrix.pl:7):       for ($n = 0; $n < 3; $n++) {
main::(matrix.pl:8):          print $mat_ref->[$m][$n];
100main::(matrix.pl:8):       print $mat_ref->[$m][$n];
200main::(matrix.pl:8):       print $mat_ref->[$m][$n];
300main::(matrix.pl:10):         print "\n";
  DB<2>
```

Each statement of the program is displayed as it is executed, up to line 10, which is displayed but not executed.

To turn off the trace mode, simply reissue the *t* command. This turns off program tracing automatically.

Debugging with Line Actions

During a debugging session, as the lines of your program are displayed (for instance when you're in trace mode), you will probably want to do things such as display or even change the value of a variable. The Perl debugger provides several commands for performing such *line actions*. The following sections will cover these commands.

Using the a and A Commands

When you want to perform a particular action before a line of code executes, use the **a** command. The **a** command takes a line number and an action as its arguments. Here is an example:

```
DB<1> a 8 print "the 0,0th element is $mat_ref[0][0]"
DB<2>
```

In this example, the **a** command is used to tell the debugger to print the statement in quotes before line 8 is executed. When the program is executed, the following statement appears after the current line is displayed, but before the next debugger command:

13

```
the 0,0th element is 100
```

If you want to perform more than one action, simply separate your Perl statements just as you would a regular Perl statement. Here is an example that displays a message and resets the value of the first element of the matrix:

```
DB<1> a 8 print "the 0,0th element is $mat_ref->[0][0]"; \
cont: $mat_ref->[0][0] = 1000;
DB<2>
```

This example shows both how you can have more than one action per command and how to continue a line when the first line is too long. When you need to break up a line, enter a backslash (\) and press ENTER. The debugger will then display **cont:** and you can continue typing on this line. Also, be sure to notice that the first statement is ended with a semicolon. The second line also has a semicolon, but it is not required.

When you are finished with the line actions for a debugging session, issue the **A** command, which deletes all the line actions currently defined. You cannot selectively delete line actions using the **A** command.

Using the < and > Commands

These commands are used to perform line actions at certain times in your debugging session. The > command is used to perform an action before any other statements are executed, and the < command is used to perform an action after all the other statements have executed. These commands are useful when you know that a variable has a bad value but you can't determine which statement in the code is assigning the value to the variable. For example, when you want to print the value of a variable before a line executes, issue the > command like this:

```
DB<1> > print "the 0,0th element is $mat_ref->[0][0]"
```

If you want the value of the variable to be displayed after a line of code executes, issue the < command like this:

```
DB<1> < print "the 0,0th element is $mat_ref->[0][0]"
```

If during your debugging session you want to see which lines have **a**, <, or > commands associated with them, use the **L** command to display this information (you used it earlier in this chapter to display breakpoints).

Miscellaneous Debugging Commands

The following commands don't fit neatly into any of the earlier headings, so they are discussed here.

Using the R Command

The **R** command is used to restart the debugger without actually quitting it. If you issue the **R** command, you may have to set new breakpoints, line actions, etc., because the old ones are often lost during restart.

Using the H Command

The **H** command is used to display the previous debugging commands you have entered during the current debugging session. Here is an example:

```
 DB<5> H
4: b 13
3: b 12
2: a 8 print "the 0,0th element is $mat_ref->[0][0]"
1: > print "the 0,0th element is $mat_ref->[0][0]"
  DB<5>
```

As you can tell, the previous debugger commands are listed from most recent to least recent. Being able to list them is useful if you want to repeat a particular command, which is the subject of the next section.

Using the ! Command

The ! command is used to repeat a previously issued debugger command. The command's only argument is the line number of the debugger command, which you can find by issuing the **H** command, as shown above.

One use of this command might be if you accidentally delete all your breakpoints and want to set them back, but can't remember where they were set. You can use the **H** command and the ! command to reset them. Here's an example of how this works:

```
 DB<5> H
4: b 13
3: b 12
2: a 8 print "the 0,0th element is $mat_ref->[0][0]"
1: > print "the 0,0th element is $mat_ref->[0][0]"
```

13

```
  DB<5> D
Deleting all breakpoints…..
  DB<5> !4
b 13
  DB<5> !3
Line 12 not breakable
```

As you can see from the last sample input, the ! command simply reissues the command, even if it's one that doesn't work. This command is very handy if you have long debugging commands that are inconvenient to retype.

Using the p Command

Many times in a debugging session you will want to do a quick calculation, perhaps to determine what the value of a variable should be. Perl's debugger provides the **p** command for evaluating the value of an expression while in the debugger. Here's an example:

```
  DB<5> p (95+90+87)/3
90.6666666666667
  DB<5> p $mat_ref->[0][0] + 1
101
```

Using the T Command

The **T** command is used to do a stack trace, which is useful for determining which subroutines are in progress and where they were called from. The following is a sample stack trace that shows how several subroutines are called in a program:

```
  DB<7> T
$ = &main::cube($num) from file calc line 12
$ = &main::square($num) from file calc line 11
```

This stack trace is working with a program called calc.pl. The first line that is displayed after the **T** command is issued shows that the subroutine **cube**, which is within package Main, has been called with a scalar argument ($num) and it is supposed to return a scalar (which is what the beginning $ = means). The second line of the stack trace shows that the subroutine **cube** was called from another subroutine, **square**. This subroutine was also called with a scalar argument and it too is supposed to return a scalar.

Summary

Debugging your programs is as necessary a process as writing the code in the first place. If your programs don't have bugs in them, then you probably aren't writing very sophisticated programs. A good programming language, therefore, should provide good debugging support for the programmer. As you have seen, Perl's debugger provides many tools for debugging and provides a debugging environment that is easy to work with.

13

CHAPTER 14

Working with Directories

In previous chapters, we have examined the ways in which Perl can manipulate files. In this chapter, we will consider the other components of file systems, namely directories. Perl provides a suite of functions that allow the programmer to create and remove directories, to read the contents of and navigate directories, and to change permissions on files and directories. In the following sections, we introduce directory handles to show how to use Perl's built-in functions to manipulate directories. We will also review the concept of file permissions, and show how Perl can be used to manage file and directory security.

Directory Handles

The concept of a directory handle is entirely analogous to that of the filehandles you met in Chapter 6 (except that convention has "filehandle" as a single word). Look at the following simple program that reads all of the entries in the directory specified on the command line, displaying to standard output the contents of the directories and their file types:

```perl
my $dir;
($dir = $ARGV[0]) or die "usage: $0 <directory>";
opendir(DIR,"$dir") or die "could not open $dir: $!";
print "$dir contains: \n";
while ($_ = readdir(DIR)) {
    my $type = fileType("$dir/$_");
    print "\t$_ ($type)\n";
}
closedir DIR;
exit;
```

You can run this example from the command prompt by typing the name of the script followed by a directory name.

You will recognize DIR as the directory handle. It is convention to designate the directory handle in all capital letters, as with filehandles. The function **opendir** is the analogue to **open** for files; **closedir** is the analogue to **close**. From the previous example, you should have guessed that the **readdir** function works for directory handles just like the *angle* operator (<>) works for filehandles, except that we have to assign output to the $_ variable explicitly (if we want it there). We use **die** to catch any errors in the **opendir** statement, exactly as when opening files, and the Perl special variable $! will contain any error message generated by our attempt to open $dir. And, as you may have surmised from the *while* construct, **readdir** returns the undefined value when it has read all of the entries in a directory (as does the angle operator for filehandles).

Here's the code for the previous **fileType** subroutine:

```
sub fileType {
    my $file = shift;
    return "symlink"           if -l $file;
    return "directory"         if -d _;
    return "unreadable"   unless -r _;
    return "fifo"              if -p _;
    return "character special" if -c _;
    return "block special"     if -b _;
    return "socket"            if -S _;
    return "text"              if -T _;
    return "binary"            if -B _;
    return "unknown";
}
```

The subroutine makes use of some of the file tests introduced in Chapter 6. The filename passed to the subroutine has to have a complete path, either relative or absolute, so the file tests can find it. Since **readdir** returns on the filenames themselves, we have to add on the directory path contained in $dir when we pass the filenames to the subroutine, which was done during argument construction.

It should be noted as well that the order of the tests in the subroutine is important, at least under Unix where all of the file types mentioned are supported. (If you want to experiment, try changing the order of the tests and running the program on a directory with interesting file types like /dev, for instance.)

Here is some sample output from the program running on a Unix system:

```
% dir.pl /tmp
/tmp contains:
    . (directory)
    .. (directory)
    .X11-unix (directory)
    .TTX_127.0.0.1_0 (socket)
    .cdaudio (directory)
    krb5cc_423 (binary)
    .e3cd.2b01 (text)
```

14

And the following listing is part of the output from the command on a Windows95 system.

NOTE: We specify the top-level directory using ".".

```
C:\Perl\scripts>perl dir.pl c:\.
c:\. contains:
IO.SYS (binary)
COMMAND.COM (binary)
MSDOS.SYS (text)
CONFIG.SYS (text)
Program Files (directory)
CDROM (directory)
MOUSE (directory)
MSDOS.--- (text)
WINDOWS (directory)
win95 (directory)
My Documents (directory)
Perl (directory)
```

You will note that this program lists all the files in a directory, including hidden files. In particular, the output of this program almost always includes the two special directory entries ".", which refers back to $dir itself, and ".." which refers to the parent of $dir, if there is one, or to $dir if not. These entries will be present in any healthy directory (except for the top-level directory on a disk under Win32, like C:\., but that's another story).

Continuing the analogy to filehandles, we see that, like the angle operator, the **readdir** function can be used in an array context as well as a scalar context; in the former case it returns all of the directory entries at once. We can rewrite our sample program as:

```
my($dir,$file,@files);
($dir = $ARGV[0]) or die "usage: $0 <directory>";
opendir(DIR,"$dir") or die "could not open $dir: $!";
@files = readdir DIR;          # Read all directory entries at once
closedir DIR;
```

```
print "$dir contains: \n";
for $file (@files) {
    my $type = fileType("$dir/$file");
    print "\t$file ($type)\n";
}
```

Reading all of the directory entries in a single step can offer some advantages. For instance, let's exclude the "." and ".." entries from our listing, since we know that they will always be present. To accomplish this, we can simply replace the *readdir* line in the preceding code with

```
@files = grep !/^\.\.?$/, readdir DIR;
```

It is worth pointing out that unlike filehandles, directory handles are always read-only. It doesn't make sense to write directly to a directory; the operating system takes care of modifying the appropriate directory entries when you create or remove files. One final note about directory handles: they actually have a separate namespace from filehandles. This means that if you *really* want to, you can do something like:

```
my ($dir, $file);
($dir = shift) or die "usage: $0 <directory>";
opendir (HANDLE, "$dir") or die "could not open $dir: $!";
while ($file = readdir(HANDLE)) {
    next unless $file =~ /.pl$/;
    open (HANDLE, "<$file") or die "could not open $file: !$";
    print "Here is the Perl script $file:\n";
    while (<HANDLE>) {
        print;
    }
    close HANDLE;
}
closedir HANDLE;
```

Perl will happily keep track of which *handle* is which, even if it's not so easy for a reader of your code to do so.

The DirHandle Module

The Perl standard library provides a module that offers an object-oriented interface to the functions described in this chapter. This is the DirHandle

14

module. It doesn't really offer any additional functionality, but it does give you an alternate interface to deal with directories, if you like that sort of thing. Here is the first example above rewritten to make use of the DirHandle module:

```
use DirHandle;
my ($dir,$dh);
($dir = $ARGV[0]) or die "usage: $0 <directory>";
($dh = new DirHandle ("$dir")) or die "could not create
          DirHandle object: $!";
while ($_ = $dh->read) {
    my $type = fileType("$dir/$_");
    print "\t$_ ($type)\n";
}
exit;
```

In this example, the scalar $dh is defined as a directory handle object. The **read** method is then performed on that object to display the contents of the directory. The *arrow* operator (->) is used to specify the method of the object that is to be executed.

Moving Around Directories

Just as in a command shell, a running Perl script knows the location of a current working directory. The working directory is the location where Perl will look for files that are not specified with a path. By default, the working directory is the one from which you run the Perl script, which may be different from the one in which the Perl script is located. Try the following exercise. First, create a file called "testfile" that contains some lines of text. Next, create a Perl script in the same directory that looks like this:

```
open (FILE, "<testfile") or die "could not open testfile: $!";
while (<FILE>) {
    print;
}
close FILE;
```

Call the Perl script dtest.pl and run it:

```
% ./dtest.pl
```

You should see the contents of the test file. Now **cd** to another directory, for instance,

```
% cd ..
```

and run the Perl script from there:

```
% perlsrc/dtest.pl    ← "perlsrc" is the directory containing the script.
```

You should see that the script fails. Even though the script is located in the same directory as "testfile", the working directory for the running script—and thus the one where the script looks for unqualified filenames—is the directory from which the script was run. This is particularly important to keep in mind if your script is run automatically, perhaps as a **cron** job.

T IP: Because of the potential confusion about working directories, it is good general practice in a Perl script to specify full pathnames for files and directories where appropriate, or to set the working directory explicitly as described in this section.

As you may recall from the example in the opening chapter, Perl allows you to change the working directory from within a script exactly as you would in a command shell. The command is **chdir**. For example:

```
chdir('..') or die "cannot change directory :$!";
```

You may also recall from the first chapter that we introduced the Cwd module, which provides functions to determine the current working directory.

```
use Cwd;
my $dir = cwd();  # gets the current working directory and stores it
in $dir
print "$dir\n";   # Prints the directory from which the script was run
chdir ("..");
$dir = cwd();

print "$dir\n";      # Prints the parent of the starting directory
```

14

The Cwd module also provides an alternate **chdir** function that offers the added feature of automatically updating the PWD entry in the special hash %ENV. This is probably only useful under Unix where the %ENV hash contains a starting value for PWD.

```
use Cwd qw(chdir);          # Use the chdir function in the Cwd module
print "$ENV{PWD}\n";        # The directory from which the script was run
chdir "..";
print "$ENV{PWD}\n";        # The parent of the starting directory
```

File and Directory Security

In this section, we make a brief digression to discuss file and directory security. Perl provides functions to modify the permissions on files and directories, and, under operating systems that support the concept of ownership, to modify user and group ownership of files and directories. Even if you make no effort to specify permissions explicitly when you create files, Perl assigns default permissions that depend in part on settings in your command shell. We'll start with a brief review of file permissions under Unix, since this is where Perl learned them, and then move on to see how Perl allows you to manage them.

File Permissions Under Unix

Under Unix-like operating systems, a file (or directory) may have any combination of three permissions: read, write, and execute. (A file or directory may also have perhaps one or two special permissions as well.) For a directory, execute permission means permission to search (list) the directory; this is different from having read permission in the directory. In addition to file permissions, Unix also supports the concept of file ownership, and allows permissions to be set independently for the owner of the file, the group to which the file belongs, and everyone else. File permissions can be specified numerically as a sum of modes in octal notation as summarized in the following table:

4000	Set user ID on execution (the "setuid" bit)
2000	Set group ID on execution (the "setgid" bit)
1000	"Sticky" bit; varies by operating system
0400	Allow reading by owner

0200	Allow writing by owner
0100	Allow execution by owner
0040	Allow reading by group
0020	Allow writing by group
0010	Allow execution by group
0004	Allow reading by others
0002	Allow writing by others
0001	Allow execution by others

Thus a script that is to be read or executed by anyone, but only modified by the owner, should have mode 0755 (0400+0200+0100+0040+0010+0004+ 0001). If a file has mode 0660, the file's owner and members of the group to which it belongs will be allowed to read and modify the file, but no one else will be granted any access at all. The **setuid** and **setgid** bits allow a program to run with the effective UID and/or GID of the file owner rather than the file user. Because of potential security risks, we recommend not using these at all unless you are quite certain of what you're doing. The meaning of the "sticky" bit varies depending on context and operating system. For instance, under Digital Unix, if the sticky bit is set on a directory which has world write permission, anyone will be able to create files in the directory, but only the owner of a given file (or the owner of the directory) can remove it. (Normally, if you have write permission in a directory, you can remove any files in that directory, whether you own them or not). Check the man page for **chmod(2)** to find out what the sticky bit does on your system.

Default Permissions: umask

When you create a file or directory under Unix, it is assigned default permissions that are determined based on the file mode creation mask, or **umask**, of the shell in which you (or the process creating the file) are running. The **umask** can be thought of as a list of permissions to disallow on newly created files, and is generally specified as a sum of the modes listed previously. A typical **umask** for a command shell is 022. This value means that write permission for the group (020) and others (002) will be unset when a new file is created. That is, the default mode for a file created with a **umask** of 022 is 644; the default mode for a directory will be 755. If the **umask** is 007, files created will be writable by the group but unreadable by

14

others (660); directories will also be unreadable and unsearchable by others (770). Get it?

There is a command called **umask** that is probably built into your command shell that you can use to examine or modify the value of the **umask**. There may also be a separate **umask** program somewhere on your system. Here's how to look at the **umask** of your shell using Perl:

```
% perl -e 'printf "%#o",umask'
```

File Attributes Under Win32

The only file attribute, or permission, that can be managed directly from Perl's built-in functions is the read-only attribute. Perl does allow you greater control over your files' attributes under Win32, but you have to do it a different way. The next chapter shows, for instance, how you can access the **attrib** command directly from within Perl to manage your files.

Managing File Permissions in Perl

Now that we've reviewed the general idea of file permissions, we can move on to see how Perl allows the programmer to manage the permissions of files and directories. In Chapter 6, we saw several examples of how to create files from within Perl. So here's a question you should be able to answer now: What is the default permission on a file created from within Perl? The correct answer, of course, is that it depends on the value of the umask in the shell from which you started Perl.

The umask Function: Changing Default Permissions

To change the default permissions of files (and directories) created in Perl, use Perl's built-in **umask** command. Earlier, we saw an example demonstrating that if you call **umask** with no arguments, it simply returns the current value of **umask**. When called with a numeric argument, the function changes the effective **umask** of the running process. Here's an example using **umask** to control the default permissions on files:

```
umask 0000;    # Allow all permissions on new files
open (FILE, ">file1") or die "could not open file1: $!";
print FILE "Anyone can read or modify this file.\n";
close FILE;
umask 0026;    # Disallow writing by group, and all access by others
open (FILE, ">file2") or die "could not open file2: $!";
```

```
print FILE "This file can be read by the group, but not by others.\n";
close FILE;
umask 0222;     # Disallow writing by anyone (including me)
open (FILE, ">file3") or die "could not open file3: $!";
print FILE "I don't even have write permission to this file.\n";
```

This example creates three files, each with different permissions. Of particular interest is the last file created, file3, which is created read-only. Under Win32, file1 and file2 will be created with normal attributes, while file3 will have the read-only attribute set. If any of the three write-permission bits (user, group, or other) is specified in the file mode, Win32 will not set the read-only attribute. One other thing to note about the example is that we have specified all four digits in the argument to **umask**; **perl –w** will complain if you don't. The **umask** command built into your command shell is probably not so picky.

The chmod Function: Changing Permissions Explicitly

Perl also allows for explicit control of file permissions through the **chmod** function. Here's an example:

```
my $file = "file4";
umask 0222; # sets permissions before the file is created
open (FILE, ">$file") or die "could not open $file: $!";
print FILE "This file is created read-only\n";
close FILE;
open (FILE, ">>$file") or warn "trying to open $file for
            appending:$!\nContinuing...";
chmod 0644, $file; # changes permissions on created file
open (FILE, ">>$file) or die "could not reopen $file for
            appending: $!";
print FILE "This line added to read-only file\n";
close FILE;
chmod 0444, $file;
```

A read-only file is created (because of the value of the **umask**), **chmod** is called to enable write permission on the file, the file is modified, and **chmod** is called again to restore the file's read-only status. This example works as advertised under Win32; the read-only attribute of the file will be set because none of the write bits are specified in the mode argument to **chmod**.

The chown Command: changing Owner and Group

The Perl function **chown** can be used to modify the owner and group of a file or directory explicitly. The file or directory must already exist. The

14

chown function requires the numerical user ID and group ID as arguments. Thus

```
chown 423, 20, "myfile";
```

changes the owner "myfile" to the user with GID 423, and changes the file's group to that group with GID 20. To change the owner but leave the group unmodified, specify –1 for the GID. Using numerical IDs is clearly not very convenient. Fortunately, if you are working on a Unix system, you can probably find the mapping between UID's and usernames in the password file. (And if you're working on a Win32 system, **chown** isn't supported anyway.) Perl even provides a handy function to read a specific user's password entry, and another to look up a GID given a group name. Thus, we can do something similar to:

```
my $user = "matter";
my $group = "users";
my $UID = getpwnam($user); # $UID gets the numeric user ID
my $GID = getgrent($group); # $GID gets the group name
chown $UID, $GID "myfile";
```

To change the owner of a file requires root privileges. Changing the group of a file requires that you either own the file or have root privileges.

Creating and Removing Directories

To create and remove directories, Perl provides a pair of functions that should be familiar to users of either Unix or Win32 (or, more correctly, DOS). These are **mkdir** and **rmdir**. The **mkdir** function in Perl requires that you explicitly specify the mode of the directory to be created:

```
mkdir("testdir", 0775)or die "could not create directory: $!";
```

Bear in mind, though, that the actual mode of the resulting directory will be modified by the current value of the **umask**. Thus, the following code creates a directory with mode 755:

```
umask 022;
mkdir("testdir", 0777)or die "could not create directory: $!";
```

The **rmdir** function behaves exactly like its operating system counterparts. In particular, the function requires that a directory be empty before it will remove it. Here's a simple example:

```
umask 022;
mkdir("testdir", 0755)or die "could not make testdir: $!";
open (FILE,">testdir/testfile") or die "could not open testfile: $!";

print FILE "Here's a line of text.\n";
close FILE;
print "Trying to remove testdir\n";
rmdir "testdir" or warn "could not remove testdir: $!";

unlink "testdir/testfile";    # remove file in testdir
print "Trying again\n";
rmdir "testdir" or die "could not remove testdir: $!";
print "testdir removed\n";
```

Summary

Perl's real strengths come into play when it is used to aid in system administration tasks. One aspect of working with operating systems that systems administrators always hate is the file system. This chapter demonstrated Perl's built-in functions that can help you work with files and directories. After writing a few scripts using these functions you will find that working with a file system, be it Unix or Windows, isn't as odious as it used to be.

14

CHAPTER 15

Managing System Processes

Although the arsenal of Perl's built-in functions is quite substantial, there will be tasks that require you to reach beyond Perl and enlist the help of other programs. Perl provides for this occasion. In this chapter, we will examine the different methods Perl makes available to the programmer for executing programs outside of Perl from within a Perl script.

For the purposes of this chapter, the discussion assumes a Unix-like operating system. This is not intended as a show of operating system favoritism, but rather that many of the functions discussed in this chapter will likely not be implemented by Perl on non-Unix systems. Additionally, some of the programs used in the examples may or may not be available on every system. Where appropriate, direct reference will be made to Windows 95 and Windows NT (referred to collectively as Win32), under which Perl supports a subset of the functions described.

NOTE: Perl was developed in a Unix environment. While there are several different groups who have ported Perl to the 32-bit Windows operating systems, these efforts remain independent of the primary development path and tend to lag behind somewhat. For the purposes of this book, we have used Perl for Win32 build 307 from ActiveWare. As the effort to maintain Perl under Windows matures, expect some of the limitations mentioned in this chapter to be removed.

Launching Processes with the Backtick Operator

The simplest method for running processes from within a Perl script is to use the *backtick* operator. The *backtick* operator is the reverse single quote (`` ` ``), located with the tilde on your keyboard.

This operator will seem familiar to those who have done programming in more traditional Unix shells, from which its syntax is derived. Let's say we want to see who's currently logged onto our computer, using the Unix command "who". We can write:

```
#!/usr/local/bin/perl -w
my @users = `who`;
my ($line,$user,$lastuser,$junk);
@users = sort @users;
```

```
print "The following users are logged in:\n";
for $line (@users) {
    ($user,$junk) = split ' ',$line,2;
    print "\$user\n" unless $user eq $lastuser;
    $lastuser = $user;
}
```

The backticks direct Perl to run the command "who". The output from the command is returned and stored in the array @users; each entry in the array corresponds to a single line of output from the command, including the newline character. We use the **split** function to extract the first word, the username, from each line of output (the rest of the line contains information about which terminal the user is logged into, and how long the user has been on) and take care to print each username only once.

We can also make use of other external programs in conjunction with "who" to provide exactly the information we want via the *backtick* operator. In the following examples we use the Unix commands "awk", "sort", and "uniq" to make certain we report each user only once:

```
#!/usr/local/bin/perl -w
my @users = `who | awk '{print $1}' | sort | uniq`;
my $user;
print "The following users are logged in:\n";
for $user (@users) {
    print "\$user\n";
}
```

Note that we can also assign the output of the *backtick* operator to a scalar, as

```
$userlist = `who | awk '{print $1}' | sort | uniq`;
```

in which case the output from the command would be returned as a single string with embedded newline characters separating the lines of output. In the example, assigning the output of the *backtick* operator in this way would simplify output formatting:

```
#!/usr/local/bin/perl -w
my @users;
my $userlist = `who | awk '{print $1}' | sort | uniq`;
print "The following users are logged in:\n$userlist";
```

15

Using Variables with the Backtick Operator

Any Perl variable contained within backticks will be expanded before the command is passed to the shell for execution. Thus, the code:

```
#!/usr/local/bin/perl -w
my $passwd = "/etc/passwd";
my $npw = `wc -l $pwfile`;
print "There are $npw entries in $pwfile\n";
```

will display the number of lines in the password file. ("wc" is a Unix program that counts characters, lines, and/or paragraphs in a text file.) Of course, the same result could be obtained without resorting to using the "wc" command:

```
#!/usr/local/bin/perl -w
my $passwd = "/etc/passwd";
open (PW, "<$pwfile") or die "couldn't open $pwfile: $!";
my $npw = 0;
while (<PW>) {
    $npw++;
}
close PW;
print "There are $npw entries in $pwfile\n";
```

Or, if we weren't concerned with memory usage, we could say:

```
my (@lines,$npw);
open (PW, "<$pwfile") or die "couldn't open $pwfile: $!";
@lines = <PW>; #gobble up the whole file
$npw = @lines;
close PW;
print "There are $npw entries in $pwfile\n";
```

This last example requires that Perl hold the entire file in memory, which is likely not a problem in this example, but is something to bear in mind. The last example takes advantage of the fact that if you access an array variable in a scalar context, as in the line "$npw = @lines", the value you end up with is the number of array elements (contrast this with the expression "$#lines", which returns the index of the last element in the array).

The Backtick Operator as a Shortcut

In many cases using the *backtick* operator together with external commands provides a shortcut for doing something that could otherwise be done within

Perl. For instance, compare the two following code fragments that read the contents of a file ($file) into an array (@lines):

```
#
#  Using filehandles
#
open (FILE, "< $file") or die "could not open $file: $!";
@lines = <FILE>;
close FILE;


#
#  Using the backtick operator
#
@lines = `cat $file`;
```

Similarly, here are two different methods you can use to list all of the files in a given directory using directory handles and the *backtick* operator ($dir):

```
#
#  Using directory handles
#
opendir(DIR, "$dir") or die "could not open $dir: $!";
@myfiles = map "$dir/$_",readdir(DIR);
closedir DIR;


#
#  Using the backtick operator
#
chomp(@myfiles = `ls -a $dir`);      # Strip trailing newline from output.
```

A Note about Performance

Be advised that you take a performance hit when you use the *backtick* operator. In almost every case, using backticks will be slower than doing the same thing using Perl's built-in functions, sometimes much slower. This is because there is a lot going on behind the scenes with the *backtick* operator. We'll return to this later in the section on the **system** function.

The Backtick Operator Under Win32

The *backtick* operator is available in Perl under Win32 and behaves as described earlier. For instance, the following code fragment will read the names of all the .INI files in the WinNT directory:

```
my @ini_files;
chomp(@ini_files = `dir /b c:\\winnt\\*.ini`);
```

Recall that the backslash (\) is a special character in Perl that is used to escape other special characters, so the backslashes in the directory path must be escaped as shown. The "/b" flag to the **dir** command ensures that we only get filenames in our listing, and not any ancillary header information.

For Commands with no Output:
The system Function

Sometimes we may want to launch an external program that produces no useful output. As a simple example, let's assume we have a script that generates a large text file as output, and that we want to compress the text file using the GNU **gzip** utility so that it takes up less room on the disk.

The **gzip** program by default reports nothing to standard output. While we could do this with the *backtick* operator, the task is more appropriately handled by Perl's **system** function. This function takes as an argument a list of strings that are passed directly to the operating system as if you had typed them into a command shell. From our Perl script:

```
print "compressing $fname\n" if $verbose;
system "gzip $fname";
print "$fname compressed\n" if $verbose;
```

 NOTE: The **gzip** program is not standard on most Unix systems, but is freely available from the GNU archives. If it is not present on your system, you should download it from the Internet. Not only is it very useful in general, but you will find that most Perl source code is distributed in gzipped format (see Appendix F).

In the previous code fragment, the **gzip** program was called and control returned to the Perl script when the command had completed. As with the *backtick* operator, variables are interpolated by **system** before the command is executed. Thus, if we wanted to compress a number of different files whose names were stored in the array @fnames, we could use

```
system "gzip", @fnames;
```

The **system** function actually does provide a return value, though it is not the output from the command being run; rather it is the value returned by the "wait" system command (multiplied by 256). This will make more sense later in the section that discusses the **system** command.

Another Note about Performance

As mentioned before, we could use backticks to invoke **gzip** even though the program returns no output:

```
`gzip $fname`;
```

In general, though, this will not be as efficient as using the **system** function. The reason is that for processes launched via the *backtick* operator, Perl invokes a command shell to run the process. With the **system** function, on the other hand, Perl attempts to launch the process directly, avoiding the overhead of starting the command shell. Note, however, that if the argument to the **system** function (after variable interpolation) contains shell metacharacters (such as "*"), Perl invokes a command shell as with the *backtick* operator. The details of behind-the-scenes work will be described later. The bottom line is that if you are not interested in the output of a command, use **system**, otherwise use backticks to run the command.

Programmers who are new to Perl may tend to make excessive use of the **system** function and backticks either for convenience or because they are not yet familiar with the full suite of functions available in the standard Perl library (not to mention the myriad available in other libraries and modules available via CPAN). For instance, we have seen Perl novices use "system "rm $file"" because they looked in a Perl manual and could not find a "remove" command (the Perl command to remove files is **unlink**).

T..

IP: In general, you should try to make use of the built-in functions in Perl rather than relying too heavily on **system** and its friends. Not only will your code run faster and be more portable, but you'll also have the personal satisfaction of doing things the Perl Way.

The system Function Under Win32

Perl does support the **system** function under Win32. Although the underlying implementation is quite different from that on a Unix system,

15

the behavior is the same. Here is a fragment of code that will make a backup copy of the Autoexec.bat file called Autoexec.bat.

```
my($oldfile,$newfile);
$oldfile="AUTOEXEC.BAT";
# This line replaces the suffix with ".BAK"
($newfile = $oldfile) =~ s/\.\w{3}$/\.BAK/;
system "copy $oldfile $newfile";
```

Here we've used a regular expression to build the name of the backup file simply for demonstration. It would be both easier and more efficient to assign the name to $newfile directly in this case, but the use of the regular expression substitution would allow us to modify the program to accept any 8dot3-style filename and create an appropriately named backup copy.

Launching Programs Without Waiting: The exec Function

The **exec** function is similar to the **system** function except that Perl doesn't wait around for the specified command to end. Returning to the previous example, we could use **exec** to run **gzip** if there is nothing else for Perl to do:

```
open(FILE, ">$fname") or die "could not open $file: $!";
<write data to file>
close FILE;
#
#  Now compress the file with gzip, which may take some time.
#  No need to have Perl wait around.
#
print "compressing $fname\n";
exec "gzip $fname" or die "could not exec: $!";
```

If the **exec** is successful, Perl simply exits while the command passed to **exec** runs in its place. Control is only returned to Perl if the call to **exec** fails, in which case there's probably nothing better for Perl to do than **die** gracefully and informatively.

The exec Function Under Win32

While **exec** is supported by Perl in Win32, its behavior can be a little surprising. With the **system** call, Perl basically passes the arguments to command.com to be executed. With the **exec** call, on the other hand, Perl looks for the specified program to launch it itself. This means you cannot simply exec a command such as "copy", which is built into the command shell, because Perl will not be able to find a program of that name. The workaround for this is to call command.com explicitly:

```
# This call fails: "File not found"
exec("copy $oldfile $newfile") or die "could not exec: $!";

# This call succeeds
exec("command /c copy $oldfile $newfile");
```

NOTE: Earlier ports of Perl to Win32 ran into trouble with **exec** under Windows 95 because of its 16-bit command.com.

Another Approach: Launching Programs Using Filehandles

Assume that we want to write a Perl script that will read the data contained in a text file that has been compressed with the GNU **gzip**. This might be the case, for instance, if our system is running the INN news server (which gzips each day's worth of log files) and we want to parse the data in the logs. One possible approach using the tools we have seen already is simply to make a call to **system** to uncompress the file before we access it and another call to **system** to compress it again when we're done:

```
system "gzip -d $fname";
open FILE "<$fname" or die "couldn't open $fname: $!";
<process data>
close FILE;
system "gzip $fname";
```

This approach has several disadvantages. First, if the file is of substantial size, the system calls to **gunzip** and **gzip** might require a fair bit of time. Second, this method requires that there be enough disk space to accommodate the uncompressed file, and if we bothered to compress the file in the first place, it may well be that we don't have disk space to spare. Now, **gzip** can decompress a file on the fly, leaving the file compressed on disk and writing the uncompressed data to standard output; the command is "gzip –dc". How can we make use of this?

The trick is to employ filehandles in a special way that the Perl **open** function allows. Consider the following expression:

```
open (FILE, "gzip -dc $fname |") or die "could not run gzip: $"!;
```

This command creates a filehandle, FILE, as we saw in Chapter 8, but unlike ordinary filehandles that are connected to files, this one is connected to the output of a command pipeline. When we read from the filehandle FILE, we get the output of the gzip –dc command, which is exactly the data we want. C programmers may recognize that this is performing something similar to a **popen( )** rather than a plain old **open( )**, but we can let Perl worry about that. The important point is that we now have access to the data in the compressed file without having to uncompress the file on the disk. The **gzip** command pipes us the contents of the file as we are ready for it. We access the data exactly as if we were reading from a normal filehandle:

```
open (FILE, "gzip -dc $fname |") or die "could not run gzip: $"!;
while (<FILE>) {
<process data here>
}
close FILE;
```

It should be noted that the filehandle created with the **open** command in the previous code is read-only. It is possible to create a command filehandle to which we can write. Let's say we want our Perl program to send a message via electronic mail. This might be useful if, for example, we want a Perl program to extract information from some log files at scheduled intervals and mail the information to the system administrator. (Programmers mention this example specifically because this is one way we make heavy use of Perl.) Here's how we might do it:

```
my $user = "root";
open (LOG, "<$logfile") or die "could not open $logfile: $!";
open (MAIL, "| /usr/bin/mailx -s \"Log report\" $user")
or die "could not run mailx: $!";
while (<LOG>) {
    print MAIL;
}
close MAIL;
close LOG;
```

It should be noted, too, that the two **close** statements at the end of this example are actually different. One is closing a file, the other terminating a command pipeline. After the first **close**, the Perl special variable $? contains the exit status of the command associated with the filehandle, mailx in this case. Also, the first **close** will not return until the command on the other side of the pipe has terminated.

Is it possible using filehandles to create a pipe to which we can both read and write? That is, can we do something such as

```
open (FILE, "| sort |") …
```

where we print to FILE, which is the standard input of the Unix command sort, and read from the standard output of sort? The short answer is no. The **open** function will not allow both reading and writing to a process associated with a single filehandle. That shouldn't be too much of a limitation, though, as there are other ways to accomplish the same thing if you really want to. In the next section we'll see an example of one method to establish bidirectional communication with another process.

Launching commands with filehandles under Win32 is available to Perl programmers under Win32.

Creating Child Processes Directly: The fork Command

With **system**, we can start a process and wait around for it to exit. With **exec,** we can start a process in place of Perl, and let Perl exit. But what if we want to start a process that runs alongside of Perl? Launching processes via filehandles, as we saw earlier, is one option, assuming that one-directional communication via a command pipeline is what we are looking for. What if we want to start a process and let it run on its own while Perl continues to execute? For this and other more sophisticated needs, we must turn to the **fork** function.

fork is not easy to understand, but it is well worth the effort to learn what it does. Even if you never have occasion to call the **fork** function explicitly, Perl runs something like it implicitly when you use the *backtick* operator or the system function, or when you launch processes using filehandles. Indeed, **fork** provides direct access to the process going on behind the scenes with these other functions. We will start by stating what **fork** does in words, and then we'll spend some time looking at some code.

15

When **fork** is called, the operating system makes a copy of the running process— namely, Perl. This copy is referred to as a child process (and the calling process is then the parent). The child comes into existence executing the Perl script at the location where the **fork** call returns. If successful, **fork** returns to the parent process the process ID (PID) of the child process; to the child process, **fork** returns 0. It's up to the programmer to differentiate between the child and the parent within the code. Let's consider an example in which we start a **gzip** process using **fork**:

```
my $pid;
if ($pid==fork()) {
    #
    # This is the code the parent will execute.
    #
    print "The PID of the child process is $pid\n";
} elsif (defined $pid) {
    #
    #  This is the code that the child will execute.
    #
    exec "gzip $fname";
    exit();
} else {
    #
    #  $pid is undefined, indicating that the call to fork() failed.
    #
    die "could not fork: $!";
}
#
#  Code down here will be run by the parent, but not the child
#
```

This certainly appears more complicated than our previous examples and merits close examination. First, let's contrast the behavior of this code with the previous examples using **gzip**. When called via the **system** function, **gzip** goes to work compressing the file, and further execution of the Perl script is put on hold until the **gzip** process is finished. When **gzip** is called via a simple **exec** function, Perl exits and the **gzip** process takes its place. Now look at the previous code. Assuming the **fork** call succeeds (and if it fails, your system is probably not very healthy), there will be two instances of the Perl program when the call returns. To the parent process, **fork** returns a non-zero value (the PID of the child), and hence the first case in the **if** statement holds true. The parent will execute the **print** statement, and then continue processing the code that follows the **if** block. To the child, **fork** returns zero, and thus in the child process, it will be the second case of the **if** block that evaluates to true. The child then exec's **gzip** exactly as in the example before. Now the parent process, which is the Perl program we started in the first place, is running at the same time as **gzip** (now the child process) is compressing our file.

In the previous example, the child's call to **exit** will only be executed if the call to **exec** fails. If the **exec** call were to fail, and we had forgotten to include the exit in the child portion of the code, the child process would drop out of the **if** block and start executing portions of the script intended for the parent.

TIP: Even though **fork** is most often used with an **exec** as in the prior example, in which case no statements in the Perl script beyond the **exec** should be executed, it's good programming to put the **exit** there just in case (even though 'perl –w' might complain), to keep the child out of the parent code.

Being a Good Parent

The parent-child process relationship implies a certain level of responsibility. In particular, it is important to have the parent acknowledge the completion of the child process (often referred to as the "death" of the child). Otherwise, it is possible for the child process to enter a state of limbo, not running but not terminating; it becomes a "zombie". To prevent this, the parent should execute a call to the **wait** function, which, as its name implies, waits for a child process to die. (This is called "reaping" the child in Unix lingo.) But wait. Wasn't the point of calling **fork** rather than **system** to allow Perl to continue running, rather than waiting? Yes, and there is still a way to do this and be a good parent. When a child process terminates, the operating system sends a specific signal (SIGCHLD) to the running parent process. The trick, then, is to set up a handler in the parent to respond to the signal by issuing a **wait** call.

Here is one way to do it using an anonymous subroutine:

```
$SIG{CHLD} = sub { wait };
```

%SIG is a special associative array in Perl that allows you to specify signal handlers to deal with particular signals. The name of the array element is the signal we want to catch; the value to which the array element is set is either an anonymous subroutine, as in the example, or a reference to a named subroutine.

Here's how we would use a named subroutine:

```
sub reap {
    my $pid = wait(); # The wait call actually returns the PID of the child
}
$SIG{CHLD} = \&reap; # We could also use: $SIG{CHLD} = "reap"
```

When the parent process receives a signal indicating that the child process has completed, it will make the call to **wait** (which is mostly a formality at this point since we know the child process has terminated), so that it can acknowledge the death of the child to the operating system.

Behind the Scenes of the system Function

At this point, you should not be surprised to learn that the **system** function is really a combination of a **fork** and an **exec** and a **wait** (or, more precisely, the corresponding operating system calls). Perl forks a child process, execs the command specified in the argument list to the system function in the child process, and waits for the child process to terminate. The value returned by **system** is the return value of the wait system call (multiplied by 256; the low 8 bits of the return are used if the child process died from a signal). Similarly, to implement the *backtick* operator, Perl forks and execs a shell process to run the desired command. Since both **fork** and **exec** (the operating system calls) incur a fair bit of overhead, the system and *backtick* operators tend to be slow.

The **fork** function is not available at all under Win32, because there is no corresponding **fork** system call. Likewise, there is no **wait** function.

Communicating with Your Children: An Example Using fork

As we have seen in the discussions so far, Perl is not very interactive with its children by default. With the *backtick* operator and command filehandles there is one-way communication. With **system** and **exec**, there is no direct communication. Using **fork**, it is possible to create a pathway for direct two-way communication between Perl and a child process, though it requires a bit of work. The example that follows is on the one hand trivial, in the sense that the child process is chosen to be as simple as possible. On the other hand, the example introduces a very sophisticated method of interprocess communication, namely sockets, and some techniques that we have not seen before. We end the section on **fork** with this example not only because it illustrates the full power of Perl's ability to interact with other processes, but also because it gives a sense of what is going on behind the scenes with the other functions described in this chapter (at least on a Unix system).

A Simple Child Process

This is the child process we will invoke. It is a simple Perl script that prints a line of output, listens for a line of input, and then prints out a second line reporting what it heard. You'll note that the script simply writes to STDOUT and reads from STDIN. All of the details of the sockets are dealt with by the parent.

```
#!/usr/local/bin/perl -w
#
#   child.pl: Simple program to demonstrate communication via
#             sockets.
#
#   Force unbuffered output, since we will be writing to a socket
#
select STDOUT;
$| = 1;
print STDOUT "Hello from your child\n";
my $line = <STDIN>;
chomp($line);
print STDOUT "I heard \"$line\"\n";
exit;
```

The child script can be run by itself. The output it produces might look similar to this:

```
% ./child.pl
Hello from your child
Testing. Testing.          ←This is user input.
I heard "Testing. Testing."
```

A Simple Parent

Following is the parent code. Much of it is taken up with the process of forking and **exec**'ing a child as we have seen before. The one new feature here is the call to *socketpair*. This function creates a pair of sockets, parent

15

and child in this example, that will be used for two-way communication. The other arguments to socketpair specify that we want our sockets in the Unix domain. After the fork, each process takes one socket and closes the other. The child process redirects standard output and standard input to the socket before it execs the script. This way when child.pl is run, it reads from and writes to the socket.

```perl
#!/usr/local/bin/perl -w
#
#  parent.pl: demonstrate the use of sockets for two-
#             way communication.
#
use Socket;

#  Install a signal handler to deal with child
$SIG{CHLD} = sub { wait };

socketpair(PARENT,CHILD,PF_UNIX,SOCK_STREAM,0) or die "socketpair: $!";

if ($pid=fork()) {
    # This is the parent process
    close PARENT;
    select CHILD;
    $| = 1;
    select STDOUT;
} elsif (defined $pid) {
    # This is the child process
    open(STDIN,  ">&PARENT");
    open(STDOUT, ">&PARENT");
    close PARENT;
    select STDOUT;
    $| = 1;
    exec("child.pl");
    exit;
} else {
    die "fork error: $!\n";
}

$line = <CHILD>;
print "My child says: $line\n";
print CHILD "Hello from your parent\n";
$line = <CHILD>;
print "My child says: $line\n";
```

The socket module is used to get the symbolic names used in the call to socketpair (PF_INET and SOCK_STREM).

When parent.pl is run, it generates output similar to the following:

```
% ./parent.pl
My child says: Hello from your child
My child says: I heard "Hello from your parent"
```

Keep in mind that the child here is a simple Perl script for demonstration only. This method can be used to invoke virtually any program that communicates through standard input and output and whose responses can be predicted well enough to code for in the parent.

Communicating with Processes on Other Systems

So far in this chapter we have looked at methods to communicate with processes on the same system that is running Perl. In some cases this communication is limited to starting a process with specified arguments; in others, there is more explicit communication to the standard input or output (or both) of another process we have started. In this section, we examine a method of communicating with a process on a completely different machine that is accessible to our machine over a network. The examples in this section assume a familiarity with TCP/IP programming.

A Simple TCP/IP Client Program: finger

As an introduction to socket-level programming in Perl, we present here an implementation of the **finger** client program written in Perl. This program accepts an argument of the form "user@host" and queries the finger daemon on the specified host for information about the user.

```
#!/usr/local/bin/perl -w#
#   finger.pl: a finger client
#
require 5.002;
use strict;
use Socket;
```

```
die "usage: $0 <user\@host>" if $#ARGV;
my ($user,$host);
($user,$host) = split /@/,$ARGV[0];
$host = 'localhost' unless $host;
my($port,$iaddr,$paddr,$proto);
$port = getservbyname 'finger', 'tcp';
$proto = getprotobyname 'tcp';
$iaddr = inet_aton $remote;
$paddr = sockaddr_in $port, $iaddr;
socket(SOCK, PF_INET, SOCK_STREAM, $proto) or die "socket: $!";
connect(SOCK, $paddr)                       or die "connect: $!";
select SOCK; $| = 1; select STDOUT;    # Force unbuffered output
my @response;      # The response will be an array of lines
@line = <SOCK>;
print "@line";
close SOCK;
```

A Simple TCP/IP Server: rsysd

Next is an example of a TCP/IP server program and corresponding client. The
server process runs on a host computer, listening for requests on
a specified port. When a request comes in (i.e., when a client connects) the
server runs **df**, **ps**, or **uptime** and returns the output to the client along with
the local time on the host. You will have to set $DF, $PS, and
$UP as appropriate for your system.

```
#!/usr/local/bin/perl -w

require 5.002;
use strict;
use Socket;


#
#   Variables for socket connection
#
my ($port, $proto, $iaddr, $paddr);


#
#   Variables pointing to local system commands
#
$ENV{PATH} = "";          # Make certain we have a safe PATH
#my $DF = "/bin/bdf";      # HP-UX
#my $PS = "/bin/ps -ef";   # HP-UX
#my $UP = "/bin/uptime";   # HP-UX
```

```
my $DF = "/usr/ucb/df -k";      # Digital UNIX
my $PS = "/usr/ucb/ps aux";     # Digital UNIX
my $UP = "/usr/ucb/uptime";     # Digital UNIX

$port = 7797;    # "RSYS"
$proto = getprotobyname('tcp');

socket(SOCK, PF_INET, SOCK_STREAM, $proto) or die "socket: $!";
setsockopt(SOCK, SOL_SOCKET, SO_REUSEADDR, pack("l",1))
                                        or die "setsockopt: $!";
bind(SOCK, sockaddr_in($port, INADDR_ANY)) or die "bind: $!";
listen(SOCK, SOMAXCONN)                    or die "listen: $!";

for (; $paddr = accept(CLIENT, SOCK); close CLIENT) {
    ($port, $iaddr) = sockaddr_in($paddr);
    my $name = gethostbyaddr($iaddr, AF_INET);
    my ($cmd, $now, $result);
    chomp($cmd = <CLIENT>);
    $cmd =~ s/\s//g;            # remove any leading or trailing whitespace
    $now = localtime(time);
    print CLIENT "Local time is $now\n";
    ($cmd eq "DF") && do {
        $result = `$DF`;
        print CLIENT "$result\n";
        next;
    };
    ($cmd eq "PS") and do {
        $result = `$PS`;
        print CLIENT $result;
        next;
    };
    ($cmd eq "UP") and do {
        $result = `$UP`;
        print CLIENT $result;
        next;
    };
    print CLIENT "ERR: unknown command $cmd\n";
}
```

The server process runs on a specified port ($port), the numerical value of
which is unimportant as long as the server and client agree on it (and as long
as it's not in use by another process). Once the server is bound to the port, it
enters an infinite loop waiting for client connections. As written, this server
can handle up to SOMAXCONN connections at once (typically about five,

but check your system). If you want your server to be able to handle more client connections simultaneously, you can use the techniques of the previous section to have the server fork a child process to deal with each client request.

The server will run in the foreground unless specifically launched as a background process using a command like (**csh**):

```
% ./rsysd.pl &
```

You can modify the code so that it puts itself in the background (like most daemons do) by adding a simple fork command before the call to socket:

```
if (fork()) {
    exit;
}
```

If the **fork** call succeeds, the parent exits, leaving the child, which is not attached to the terminal, to do the work.

A Client Program: rsys.pl
Here is a sample client program to access the server in the previous example.

```
#!/usr/local/bin/perl -w

require 5.002;
use strict;
use Socket;
use Getopt::Long;     # This is a module to parse command-line arguments

#
#  Variables for socket connection
#
my ($port, $proto, $iaddr, $paddr);

#
#  Variables for command-line arguments
#
my ($do_df, $do_ps, $do_up, $host);
$do_df = $do_ps = $do_up = 0;
GetOptions(
            "d|df" => \$do_df,
            "p|ps" => \$do_ps,
```

```
                    "u|up" => \$do_up,
                    "--"
              ) or usage();
($host = shift) or usage();
($do_df + $do_ps + $do_up) == 1 or usage();

$port = 7797;     # "RSYS"
$proto = getprotobyname('tcp');
$iaddr = inet_aton($host);
$paddr = sockaddr_in($port,$iaddr);

socket(SOCK, PF_INET, SOCK_STREAM, $proto) or die "socket: $!";
connect(SOCK, $paddr)                       or die "connect: $!";

my @result;
select SOCK; $| = 1; select STDOUT;    # force unbuffered output
print SOCK "DF\n" if $do_df;
print SOCK "PS\n" if $do_ps;
print SOCK "UP\n" if $do_up;
@result = <SOCK>;
print @result;
close SOCK;
exit

sub usage {
    print STDERR "usage: $0 [-df|-ps|-up] host\n";
    exit 1;
}
```

The client program takes as arguments a single flag denoting which process we want to run on the server, and the name of the host that is running the server. This example makes use of the **Getopt** module, part of the standard Perl library, to simplify handling of command-line arguments. The subroutine **usage** is called if **GetOptions** fails, or if the user enters the wrong number of arguments. Once the connection is made to the server, the client issues a single command and waits for the response, which it simply prints to standard output with no reformatting.

TCP/IP Programming Under Win32

Happily, most all of the routines to handle socket-layer are supported in Perl under Win32. In particular, the client program in the previous example will run just as happily under Win32 as under Unix. You can also have server

15

processes under Win32, although keep in mind that the **fork** function will be unavailable.

Summary

In this chapter we have explored a range of methods for interacting with other processes from Perl, from simple techniques to launch external programs, to more sophisticated methods of interprocess communication. Using the features in this chapter, you should be able to develop Perl scripts to communicate with virtually any process, either on your local machine, or across the network. Bear in mind, though, that if you want to do something with wide applications, someone may already have written a Perl module to do it for you. At the time of this writing, there are Perl modules that provide interfaces to Telnet, FTP, NIS, NIS+, NNTP, DNS, SMTP (mail), and SNMP, to name some of the networking functionality available. There is also a module to interface to the RPC library, one for OSF's DCE, and a general interprocess communication module, IPC, that is part of the Perl library. Before you set off on any major programming undertaking, have a look at what's available on CPAN (see Appendix E).

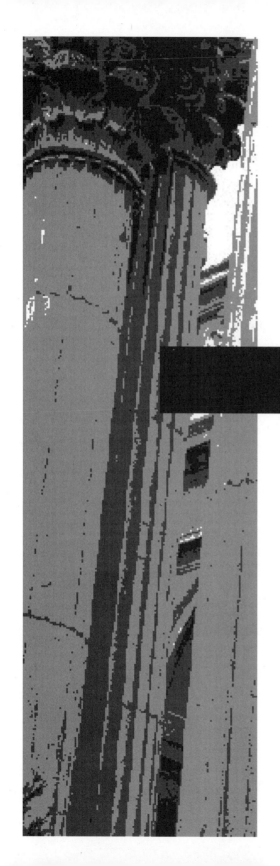

CHAPTER 16

Managing Users in the Windows NT Environment

This chapter deviates from the previous chapters because it discusses using Perl in a specific environment, the 32-bit Windows NT environment. In particular, this chapter will teach you how to use a Perl module, **NetAdmin**, to manage users and groups of users in Windows NT. The first section will discuss what Perl modules are and how to invoke them in your programs. The rest of the chapter will look at the various functions that make up the **NetAdmin** module. Please note that this module will not work in Windows 95; in fact, it won't even load on a Win95 machine.

Perl Modules

A *module* is a library of Perl code that you can import into your program with the **use** directive. A module is recognized by the extension of its filename, which must be .pm. There are many modules that are part of the Perl base and are found with each distribution of Perl. There are others that are specific to particular distributions of Perl, such as the Win32 modules, which are also called *extensions*. They are so called because they *extend* the use of Perl to areas that are not addressed by the Perl base code.

To import a module and its functions into your code, you will call the **use** directive, which is similar to C's **include**. For example, to call a module called **math**, you will write the following line:

```
use math;
```

Now, any of the functions found in the **math** module can be called as if they were defined in the code that called the module. The Win32 modules are called a little bit differently because they are stored in a separate directory. To call a Win32 module, such as **NetAdmin**, use the following code:

```
use Win32::NetAdmin;
```

This form is used because the Win32 modules are installed in a subdirectory called Win32, which is how the ActiveState distribution sets up Perl.

As was mentioned, each module contains a set of functions that can be used for a specific purpose. Most of the Win32 modules also contain examples of how the functions should be used, as in what each function's parameters are, how to call them, etc. Here is a section of the code from the **NetAdmin** module, showing how to call its functions:

```
=item GetDomainController(server, domain, returnedName)
    Return the name of the domain controller for server
```

16

```
=item GetAnyDomainController(server, domain, returnedName)
    Return the name of any domain controller for a domain that is
directly trusted by the server name.
=item UserCreate(server, userName, password, passwordAge,
    privilege, homeDir, comment, flags, scriptPath)
    Creates a user on server with password, passwordAge, privilege,
homeDir, comment, flags, and scriptPath
```

Each module function is prefaced by the identifier "=item". The function name is listed, followed by its arguments and a brief explanation of what the function does. For many of the modules, this documentation should be enough to get you started with using the module. However, there is additional documentation on the Win32 modules in the perl\docs\Perl-Win32 subdirectory that comes with the ActiveState distribution.

To call a function that is imported from a module, you have to use the fully qualified pathname for the function. For example, to use the **UsersExit** function from the module, you will have to call the function like this:

```
n32::NetAdmin;
Win32::NetAdmin::UsersExist('', $a_user);
```

If you try to call the function just using the function name, you will generate an error message.

Now that you understand how to use modules in your Perl code, we can move on to using the **NetAdmin** module to manage users and groups.

Using the NetAdmin Module to Manage Users

The **NetAdmin** module functions are broken up into three groups. The first group focuses on working with user accounts:

◆ **UserCreate** Creates a new user

◆ **UserDelete** Deletes a user

◆ **UserGetAttributes** Gets information on a user (username, password, privileges, etc.)

◆ **UserSetAttributes** Sets attributes on a user (username, password, privileges, etc.)

♦ **UserChangePassword**   Changes a user's password

♦ **UsersExist**   Checks to see if a user exists

♦ **GetUsers**   Gets a list of users from a server

The next group of functions are for working with user groups:

♦ **GroupCreate**   Creates a group

♦ **GroupDelete**   Deletes a group

♦ **GroupGetAttributes**   Gets the comment attribute of a group

♦ **GroupSetAttributes**   Sets the comment attribute of a group

♦ **GroupDelUsers**   Deletes users from a group

♦ **GroupIsMember**   Returns True if user is member of group

♦ **GroupGetMembers**   Returns a list of members of a group

The last group of functions work with local groups:

♦ **LocalGroupCreate**   Creates a local group

♦ **LocalGroupDelete**   Deletes a local group

♦ **LocalGroupGetAttributes**   Gets the comment attribute of a local group

♦ **LocalGroupSetAttributes**   Sets the comment attribute of a local group

♦ **LocalGroupIsMember**   Returns True if user is member of local group

♦ **LocalGroupGetMembers**   Returns a list of members of local group

♦ **LocalGroupAddUsers**   Adds users to local group

♦ **LocalGroupDelUsers**   Deletes a user from local group

Working with Users

The simplest function in the NetAdmin module is **UsersExist**. This function returns True if the user specified exists on the server, and returns **undef** if the user doesn't have an account on the server. The function takes two arguments: the server name (which can be the empty string if you are checking locally) and the username. Here is an example of the **UsersExist** function:

```
use Win32::NetAdmin;
$user = 'Administrator';
if (Win32::NetAdmin::UsersExist('', $user)) { print "$user exists."; }
```

Since the Administrator account is set up by default on Windows NT systems, this code will output "Adminstrator exists". on an NT system.

Another simple **NetAdmin** function is **GetUsers**, which returns the list of all registered users on the specified server. Here is an example:

```
use Win32::NetAdmin;
Win32::NetAdmin::GetUsers('',FILTER_NORMAL_ACCOUNT,\@users);
foreach(@users) {
    print "$_ \n";
}
```

The first line of this script imports the NetAdmin module. The next line actually calls the function. This function takes three arguments: the server name (which is defaulted to the local machine in this example), a filter for the account type (in this example the normal account constant provided by the module), and a reference to an array or list that will hold the user list. This array name can be anything you want. The last section of the code simply loops through the array, printing the usernames one to a line.

The next administrative function of working with users to look at is adding new users, probably the most common administration function in NT. The function in NetAdmin for adding users is called **UserCreate** and takes the following arguments:

◆ **username**   Name of the new user

◆ **password**   User's password

◆ **passwordAge**   Time before password expires

◆ **privilege**   A Perl constant for user privileges

◆ **homeDir**   The user's home directory

◆ **comment**   Comment about the user

◆ **flags**   A Perl constant for user flag

◆ **scriptPath**   Path of the user's login script

As with the constant used in the **GetUsers** function, the constants you need for the **UserCreate** function can be found in NetAdmin.pm file. The constant we will use for the privilege argument is USER_PRIV_USER (standard user privileges), and the constant we will use for the flags argument is UF_NORMAL_ACCOUNT (which stands for User Flag—Normal Account).

These constants are also listed in the win32mod documentation that is part of the Perl for Win32 distribution from ActiveState.

Here is an example script for adding a new user to an NT machine:

```
use Win32::NetAdmin;
$userName = "TestUser";
$password = '';
$passwordAge = 0;
$privilege = USER_PRIV_USER;
$homeDir = "c:\\";
$comment = "This is a test user";
$flags = UF_NORMAL_ACCOUNT;
$scriptPath = "c:\\";
Win32::NetAdmin::UserCreate('', $userName,$password,
                                    $passwordAge,
                                    $privilege,
                                    $homeDir,
                                    $comment,
                                    $flags,
                                    $scriptPath)
                                    or print "Could not
                                    create user.";
```

You will notice that when a pathname is referenced in this code, it is written with two backslashes, as in "c:\\" instead of "c:\". This is necessary because a single backslash has the value of the "escape" character in Perl and has to be "doubled" so that Perl will recognize it as part of a string and not as the "escape" character.

While the Perl program above for adding one user is instructive and somewhat useful, the real power of Perl is evident when you can write a script to add many users during the same session. This is powerful because using Microsoft's graphical tools to add several users at once is slow and repetitive, and can waste the administrator's time when a script can be run once and be finished with the task.

Adding Multiple Users at Once

One way to add many users at once using a Perl script is to create a text file with the user information in it. You might even use Perl to create the text file. Here is a text file that has the information necessary to add users to an NT server:

```
TestUser1,,0,USER_PRIV_USER,c:\,This is test user 1,UF_SCRIPT,c:\
TestUser2,,0,USER_PRIV_USER,c:\,This is test user 2,UF_SCRIPT,c:\
```

The file can contain as many users as you need to add.

With a data file with users in it, a Perl script to add users simply has to open the file, read a line of data into a list of variables for the **UserCreate** function, call the function to create a user, and then move to the next line of data, repeating this process until the data file is empty. Here's a Perl script to accomplish this task:

```
use Win32::NetAdmin;
open(USERFILE,"users.txt");
while (chomp($userline = <USERFILE>)) {
    ($userName, $password, $passwordAge, $privilege,
     $homeDir, $comment, $flags, $scriptPath) = split(/,/,
               $userline);
    Win32::NetAdmin::UserCreate(' ', $userName,
                                        $password,
                                        $passwordAge,
                                        $privilege,
                                        $homeDir,
                                        $comment,
                                        $flags,
                                        $scriptPath)
                                        or print "Could
                                        not create user.";
```

This code will loop through the file of user data, creating a new user for each line of data in the file.

Changing User Passwords

Another very common user management task is changing user passwords. Using Microsoft's User Manager tool to change passwords is easy enough, but you have to navigate through several screens just to get to the password screen. Using Perl, you can write a script that lets you change passwords at the command prompt, saving you valuable time and trouble.

The **NetAdmin** function for changing passwords is **UserChangePassword**. This function takes four arguments:

◆ A domain name

◆ The username

◆ The user's old password

◆ The user's new password

A script to change passwords will have to accept the arguments at the command prompt, when the script is invoked. To do this, you will have to access the special Perl array, @ARGV. This array is filled with the arguments to a script called at the command prompt. Each element in this array will be one of the four arguments to the **UserChangePassword** function. Here's the code for a Perl script to change a user's password:

```
use Win32::NetAdmin;
Win32::NetAdmin::UserChangePassword($ARGV[0], $ARGV[1],
                                    $ARGV[2], $ARGV[3]) or
                          print "Could not change password.";
```

To use this script, call it like this from the command prompt (the script name is chpass.pl):

```
perl chpass MyDomain TestUser1 password drowssap
```

Deleting Users

Another easy task you can perform from the command prompt using **NetAdmin** is deleting users. The **NetAdmin** function for deleting users is **UserDelete**. This function takes two arguments: the server name (which is optional, as always), and the username. Here is the code for a Perl script to delete a user:

```
use Win32::NetAdmin;
Win32::NetAdmin::UserDelete($ARGV[0], $ARGV[1])) or
    print "Could not delete user.";
```

Given a script name of dluser.pl, call the script like this:

```
perl dluser.pl MyServer TestUser1
```

Managing Groups of Users

NT system administrators are often involved with a set of tasks related to group management. As with users, the NetAdmin module provides a full set of functions for managing groups, whether a group is set up locally or within a domain. You can add groups, delete groups, and retrieve members of groups using the functions of NetAdmin. Let's look at retrieving the members of a group first.

Retrieving Members of a Group

The function for retrieving the members of a group is **GroupGetMembers** (**LocalGroupGetMembers** for a local group). This function takes three arguments: the server name, the name of the group you are retrieving members from, and an array to store the member list. The Perl code to retrieve the members of group is similar to the code written earlier to retrieve a list of users on a server. Here's the code for retrieving and printing a list of members of the Administrators group:

```
use Win32::NetAdmin;
$group = "Administrators";
Win32::NetAdmin::GroupGetMembers('', $group, \@grouplist) or
    print "Could not get member list.";
foreach (@grouplist) {
    print "$_ \n";
}
```

To get the list of members of a local group, just change the function name to **LocalGroupGetMembers**.

Creating a New Group of Users

To create a new group, use the **GroupCreate** function. This function takes three arguments: the server name, the group name, and a comment or description. This is another excellent function to implement as a command prompt script. Here is some sample code for creating a new group:

```
use Win32::NetAdmin;
Win32::NetAdmin::CreateGroup($ARGV[0], $ARGV[1], $ARGV[2]) or
    print "Could not create group.";
```

Call this script (named crgrp.pl) like this:

```
perl crgrp.pl WebServer CGIUsers "Create cgi scripts"
```

Deleting Groups

You can delete groups using the **GroupDelete** function, which takes two arguments: the server name and the group name, as in the following script:

```
use Win32::NetAdmin;
Win32::NetAdmin::GroupDelete($ARGV[0], $ARGV[1] or
    print "Could not delete group.\n";
```

To add users to a group, use the **GroupAddUsers** function. This function takes three arguments: the server name, the group name, and a list of users to add. Here is a sample script:

```
use Win32::NetAdmin;
$group = "Users";
@newusers = qw(Adminstrator Guest);
Win32::NetAdmin::GroupAddUsers('', $group, \@newusers);
```

This code adds two users (Administrator and Guest) to the Users group on the local server.

A final example of managing groups is checking to see if a user is already a member of a group using the **GroupIsMember** function. You can use this function to check if a user is already a member of a group before adding them to the group. This function takes three arguments: the server name, the group name, and the username. Here is a script that checks to see if a user is a member of a group before adding them to the group:

```
use Win32::NetAdmin;
$user = "Bill";
$group = "Users";
if (! (Win32::NetAdmin::GroupIsMember('', $group, $user))) {
    Win32::NetAdmin::GroupAddUsers('', $group, $user) or
        print "Could not add user.";
}
```

Summary

This chapter explained how to use the Perl module NetAdmin in the Windows NT environment to work with users and groups. Perl is still an undiscovered secret to many NT administrators who use NT's built-in tools for system administration. Perl offers better performance for NT tasks because writing a script makes it possible to automate much of the work that is currently being done with mouse clicks and typing.

16

CHAPTER 17

Database
Programming
with Perl

The Perl language and the Perl modules provide many avenues for database programming. On many Unix systems, there is a system database feature called DBM. This database lets you store information in key-value pairs into a pair of disk files. Perl provides access to this database through a hash that is associated with the DBM database. Via a hash, you can add data to the DBM database and edit and delete data in the DBM. If you are programming in the Windows world, most Perl distributions provide a similar database function, called SDDM, which you can use just like you would use DBM in Unix.

If you want to read and write record-oriented data, you can create random-access files using Perl. Perl provides functions such as **read**, **seek**, **pack**, **unpack**, and **print** to facilitate working with fixed-length, random-access files.

Perl programmers working in the Windows environment can work with Microsoft Access files by using the Active Data Objects model, which utilizes ActiveX technology. Also available for the Windows environment is the Win32::ODBC module, which allows you to access any ODBC-compliant relational database.

The DBM Database

Working with the DBM database, as was mentioned above, involves associating a hash created in Perl with the DBM database. Once the hash is associated with the DBM, all data processing is carried out through the hash, which acts as a kind of proxy for the DBM. For very simple database needs, the DBM is an easy-to-use solution.

Opening and Closing a DBM

To open a DBM, use Perl's **dbmopen** function, like this:

```
dbmopen(%hash, "dbm", $mode);
```

The first argument to the function, *%hash*, is the name of the hash that will be associated with the DBM. The second argument, *dbm*, is the name given to the database. The final argument, *$mode*, is a number that controls the permission bits of the files to be opened, if the DBM hasn't already been created. On Unix systems, this number, in octal, is 0644. On Windows systems, use 0666. These numbers provide read-write access to the DBM files.

Closing a DBM simply consists of calling the **dbmclose** function, with the hash that is associated with the DBM as the argument. Here is an example:

```
dbmclose(%hash);
```

A DBM database and the association with a hash are also closed when the Perl program that calls them terminates.

Retrieving and Editing Data from a DBM

Once a DBM is open, operations on the associated hash are mapped to the DBM. This means that programming the DBM simply involves performing Perl hash operations. Here are some examples, using a DBM database called Employees that, at the beginning, contains no data. First, you have to open the DBM:

```
dbmopen(%EMP, "Employees", 0666); # use 0644 in Unix
```

Next, you need to add some data:

```
$EMP{"CEO"} = "Bill Smith";
$EMP{"CFO"} = "Mary Jones";
$EMP{"CIO"} = "John Doe";
```

Now that there is some data in the DBM, here's a way to list all of it:

```
foreach $key (keys %EMP) {
    print "the $key is $EMP{$key}.";
}
```

This code produces the following output:

```
The CEO is Bill Smith.
The CFO is Mary Jones.
The CIO is John Doe.
```

If the company decides to downsize (or is it "rightsize" in today's parlance?), the CIO is always the first to get the axe, as in:

```
delete $EMP{"CIO"};
```

Changing a value in the DBM simply involves changing the value of a hash key, like this:

```
$EMP{"CFO"} = "Sally Brown";
```

As you can see, using the DBM database works only when you want to store key-value pairs, which occurs often, but is not very complex. For those situations where you need to store more complex data, but don't want to or can't use a relational database, you can create random-access files using Perl. This is the subject of the next section.

Random-access Files

A way to perform more complex database programming in Perl is through the reading and writing of fixed-length, random-access disk files. The data in a random-access file is structured as records, with each record having the same length. Using the **seek** function, you can access a record in a random-access file directly, without having to read the file sequentially, as you would with a standard text file.

Performing operations on a random-access file involves opening the file, placing the record pointer at the record you want, and either retrieving the record in that position or writing a record to that position. The Perl functions you will use for random-access files include:

Function	Purpose
open	Opening a file
binmode	Set the filehandle to binary mode
seek	Move the record pointer through the file
pack	Make data right length for read/write
unpack	Break data into constituent parts
print	Write data to file
read	Retrieve data from file

Working with Random-access Files

Using the functions listed above, it is relatively easy to work with random-access files in Perl. To see how easy it really is, you will be taken through an example of working with a random-access file called employee.dat, which currently has just one record in it:

John Smith   CEO09/09/90

17

The structure of this record is broken down into a name (15 characters), a title (3 characters), and a hire date (8 characters).

To open this file for read/write access, you write the following line of code:

```
open(EMP, "+>>employee.dat");
```

In the code above, the first argument to the **open** function is the filehandle. The second argument is the file to be opened, prefaced by a plus sign and two greater-than signs. These signs indicate to open the file for read/write access, creating the file if it doesn't already exist. You can also use these signs "+>" to open the file for read/write access (but don't create it if it doesn't exist), or these signs "+<", telling Perl to open the file for read/write access and display an error message if the file doesn't exist.

Once the file is opened, the next step is to put the filehandle in binary mode if this step is warranted by your operating system. The following line of code does this:

```
binmode(EMP);
```

To read data from the file, you must next position the record pointer using the **seek** function. This function takes three arguments—the filehandle; an offset to start reading data from; and the third argument is usually 0, meaning that the second argument will choose an absolute position for the next read/write. Here's an example:

```
seek(EMP, 0*26, 0);
```

The second argument in the example above could have been just 0, but the way to calculate the offset involves multiplying the record number you are looking for in the file by the length in bytes of a record. "0*26" positions the record pointer at the first record in the file.

Now that the record pointer is positioned, you are ready to read a record from the file using the **read** function. This function takes three arguments and returns the number of bytes read by the function. The first argument is the filehandle. The second argument is a scalar that holds the data being read. The third argument is the number of bytes you are going to "read" with the function. Here is a **read** function to "read" the data in this example:

```
read(EMP, $buffer, 26);
```

The next step to accessing the file is unpacking the data from the $buffer variable using the **unpack** function. This function takes two arguments: a template that holds information concerning the information that is to be unpacked, and the name of the scalar used in the **read** function to store the data.

The template specifies the order and the type of data being "unpacked". In this example, the file consists of a name totaling 15 characters, a title totaling 3 characters, and a hiring data totaling 8 characters. The template argument to **unpack** for this structure will be "A15 A3 A8".

The **unpack** function then stores the resulting data into a list of scalars for each piece of the data, like this:

```
($name, $title, $hdate) = unpack("A15 A3 A8", $buffer);
```

So, if you are reading in data from the single record in employee.dat, the following assignments would be made:

```
$name = "John Smith"
$title = "CEO"
$hdate = "09/09/90"
```

Now that the data is read in from the disk, it can be used in some way. To simply print it out, this code will do the trick:

```
print "$name has the title of $title and was hired on $hdate.";
```

Finally, if you are finished with the file, close it using the **close** function, like this:

```
close(EMP);
```

Perl will automatically close disk files when a program terminates, but it is Good Programming Practice to close disk files via program code when you are finished with them.

Writing a record to a random-access disk file involves many of the same operations used in reading data. Of course, instead of reading data from the filehandle, you are going to print data to the filehandle. Also, just as in reading a record, you will have to use the **seek** function to find a place to write the data to the file. Here is an example:

```
$name = "Mary Jones";
$title = "CFO";
$hdate = "03/12/88";
open(EMP, "+<employee.dat"); # open for read/write, display an er-
ror if no file
binmode(EMP); # only if operating system needs it
seek(EMP, 3*26,0);
print EMP pack("A15 A3 A8", $name, $title, $hdate);
close(EMP);
```

17

Database Programming in the Windows Environment

In this section you will learn how to use Perl to access relational databases using Microsoft's ActiveX Data Objects (ADO) and ODBC (Open Database Connectivity). ADO is an OLE interface that exposes a set of objects that provide access to an external data source, such as Microsoft Access or SQL Server. ODBC is a popular data access method that is implemented in Perl using the Win32::ODBC module. Using this module, you can connect to any ODBC-compliant relational database.

ActiveX Data Objects

ActiveX Data Objects (ADO) is an OLE automation interface that provides the programmer with an easy-to-use database access layer that can be used by Perl (and just about any other modern programming language). ADO takes the complexity of the ODBC API (application programming interface) and simplifies it by condensing it into a compact object model and a relatively small number of properties and methods to control the objects. Using these objects, properties, and methods, it is extremely easy to use Perl as a database front-end for many different types of databases.

The ADO Model

The ADO Model is a hierarchical model that defines the objects necessary to connect to an external data source, issue commands (SQL statements) to retrieve data from the database, and collect the returned data into a set of records that can be accessed through program code. These objects, as defined by the ADO Model, are called *Connection*, *Command*, and *Recordset*.

Below these three objects are other objects that are necessary for manipulating a database. The most important of these is the *Fields* object.

Fields is a collection object that holds all the fields defined in a database table. Other objects in this layer of the ADO Model include *Properties*, *Parameters*, and *Errors*.

Next, below the second object layer, is the last layer that holds the individual objects collected in the layer above. This means that the *property* object holds an individual item from the Properties collection; the *parameter* object holds an individual item from the Parameters collection; and the *error* object holds an individual item from the Errors collection. Figure 17-1 shows a graphical view of the ADO Model.

Each object also comes with a set of properties and methods, as was mentioned above. Table 17-1 provides a list of some of the properties and methods used commonly in database programming.

Table 17-1 isn't exhaustive. Please consult the ADO documentation for a list of all the properties and methods included in ADO.

Setting Up Your System to Use ADO

To use ADO, you need to have the OLE-DB SDK loaded on your system. If you have version 3 of Microsoft's Internet Information Server, this SDK is already loaded on your system. If not, you need to download and install the SDK before you can write any Perl code that utilizes ADO. The Microsoft Web site that contains OLE-DB is **http://www.microsoft.com/ado**.

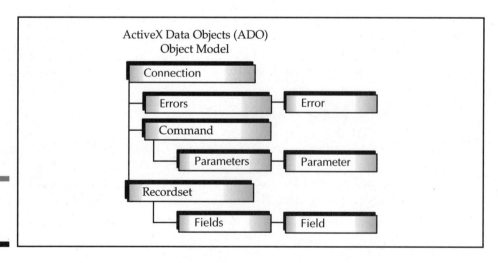

The ADO Model

Figure 17-1.

Property/Method	Function
Open	Creates access to a data source
Close	Closes connection and recordset objects
Execute	Runs a SQL statement
EOF( )	Indicates end-of-file
MoveNext( )	Moves to the next record in the recordset
Value	Retrieves the data within a field object

Properties/
Methods of the
ADO Model
Table 17-1.

17

Once OLE-DB is installed, you need to use the ODBC Data Source Administrator (located in the Control Panel) to create a data source to connect to. When you open the Data Source Administrator, press the Add button to create a new data source. Then choose from one of the drivers listed in the box, depending on the type of database you want to connect to. For the examples in this chapter, you are going to be connecting to a Microsoft Access database, so select the Microsoft Access Driver.

You are then presented with the ODBC Microsoft Access Setup dialog box (see Figure 17-2). You are asked for a Data Source Name (DSN) and a description of the DSN. You must then select a database by clicking the Select button. The Select Database dialog box appears and you use this dialog box to either enter a database name or browse your system to find the database you want. When you make your selection, the pathname for your selection is displayed above the command buttons, as shown in Figure 17-3. There are other selections you can make here, but for this example you are going to use the standard settings, so click the OK button.

The DSN is added to the User DSN tab, and your data source connection is now ready to use. Click OK again to close the Data Source Administrator. Now you're ready to write Perl code using ADO.

Accessing Data with Perl and ADO

To write Perl code using ADO, you first have to load the OLE module. This is necessary because you have to use this module's **CreateObject** function to create an *Automation* object (also called a *Connection* object when you are

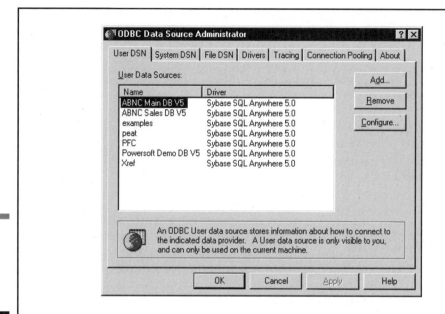

The ODBC
Microsoft
Access Setup
dialog box
Figure 17-2.

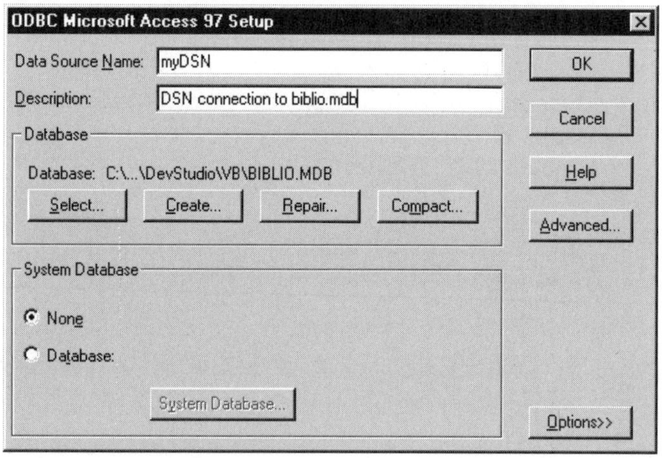

Displaying
the DSN
pathname
Figure 17-3.

using OLE to connect to a database). This is done with the following lines of code:

```
use OLE;
$cnBiblio = CreateObject OLE "ADODB.Connection" or die
        "CreateObject: $!";
```

Note that the variable name used in the code above is $cnBiblio. This variable naming scheme (where the "cn" prefix denotes a connection object) is taken from a scheme Visual Basic programmers use and is helpful when your code has many different connection (or other types) objects. Also note that the second argument to the **CreateObject** function, "ADODB. Connection", must be included exactly as it is, or Perl will generate an error.

After the connection object is created, the next step is to open the data source to allow access to the database. To do this, use the **Open** method of the *Connection* object, like this:

```
$cnBiblio->Open('OLE_Biblio');
```

Here the only argument to the **Open** method is the DSN created earlier.

The next step is to create a SQL statement to access a set of records from a table in the database. You do this by creating a SQL statement and assigning it to a variable. Here is the code for creating a SQL statement:

```
$sql = "Select * from Titles";
```

Any legal SQL statement can be used, not just a simple **Select** statement as shown in this example.

After the SQL statement is created, you have to create a recordset object to store the results of the SQL statement. To do this, the SQL variable is executed using the *Connection* object's **Execute** method. The result is stored in a variable that becomes a recordset object. Here is the code:

```
$rsTitles = $cnBiblio->Execute($sql); # variable is prefaced with
"rs" for                recordset
```

To get at the data stored in $rsTitles, you will use the *Value* property of the Fields object. Each field in the database has to be retrieved individually. The following code loops through the recordset, storing each field of a record in a variable and then displaying the data on the screen:

```
while (!$rsTitles->EOF()) {
    $booktitle = $rsTitles->Fields('Title')->Value;
    $yearpub = $rsTitles->Fields('Year Published')->Value;
    $isbn = $rsTitles->Fields('ISBN')->Value;
    print "Book title: $booktitle\n";
    print "Year published: $yearpub\n";
    print "ISBN: $isbn\n";
    print "\n";
    $rsTitles->MoveNext();
}
```

The first line of the code above sets up the conditional for the loop. In this case, the **while** loop will continue while the end-of-file condition of the recordset object is not true.

The next three lines access some of the Biblio table's fields by using the *Value* property of the Fields object, as explained above. In these lines of code, the field to be accessed is the argument to the *Fields* object.

The next four lines print the data in the field variables and a blank line, respectively.

The last line uses the **MoveNext( )** method to move to the next record in the recordset. This method must be called or the internal data "pointer" will remain on the first record in the recordset.

Finally, you need to close up your connections by issuing the **Close** method, like this:

```
$rsTitles->Close();
$cnBiblio->Close();
```

That's all there is to accessing a database using Perl. Here's all the code from above presented in one listing:

```
use OLE;
$cnBiblio = CreateObject OLE "ADODB.Connection" or die
            "CreateObject: $!";
$cnBiblio->Open('OLE_Biblio');
$sql = "Select * from Titles";
$rsTitles = $cnBiblio->Execute($sql);
```

```
    # variable is prefaced with "rs" for recordset
while (!$rsTitles->EOF()) {
    $booktitle = $rsTitles->Fields('Title')->Value;
    $yearpub = $rsTitles->Fields('Year Published')->Value;
    $isbn = $rsTitles->Fields('ISBN')->Value;
    print "Book title: $booktitle\n";
    print "Year published: $yearpub\n";
    print "ISBN: $isbn\n";
    print "\n";
    $rsTitles->MoveNext();
}
$rsTitles->Close();
$cnBiblio->Close();
```

17

Inserting Data into a Database Using ADO

Adding new data to a database using ADO is as easy as, if not easier than, it is to retrieve data. All you have to do is change the SQL statement to an "Insert Into" statement and make sure you have variables defined with the new data to insert. Here's an example, using a simplified database table called Employee that has three fields—Social Security Number (SSN), LastName, and Department:

```
use OLE;
$cnBiblio = CreateObject OLE "ADODB.Connection" or die
            "CreateObject: $!";
$cnBiblio->Open('OLE_EmpData');
$ssn = '123-45-6789';
$lastname = 'Smith';
$dept = 'Information Systems';
$sql = "insert into Employee (SSN, LastName, Department) ";
$sql .= "values ('$ssn', '$lastname', '$dept');
$cnBiblio-> Execute($sql);
$cnBiblio->Close();
```

You might notice that there isn't an error message for a situation in which the data can't be inserted into the database for some reason other than a syntax error. This is because SQL won't generate an error and there won't be anything for Perl to complain about. So if you want to make sure the data was inserted into the database, you will have to write more code to check the condition for yourself.

The Win32::ODBC Module

The Win32::ODBC provides the Perl programmer with a different, though similar, data access layer for database programming. Like ADO, Win32::ODBC tries to simplify database programming by providing a smaller yet powerful set of functions for database manipulation. This module differs from ADO primarily in the names of the functions and in offering a larger number of functions for more control over a database.

Win32::ODBC can be found at Dave Roth's Web site (**http://www.roth.net**). When you download the module, check to make sure you have a version of Perl that will work with the module. As I write this, the most current version of Win32::ODBC does not work with the most current version of Perl for Win32.

Using Win32::ODBC

As with ADO, the first thing you have to do to use Win32::ODBC is create a DSN. Once a DSN is created, you can begin programming with the module. Creating a *Connection* object is different than with ADO. Here is an example:

```
Use Win32::ODBC;
$cnBiblio = new Win32::ODBC("OLE_Biblio");
```

The Perl keyword **new** creates a new object, in this case a *Connection* object.

The next thing you will do is create a SQL statement for creating a recordset. Here is the code:

```
$cnBiblio->SQL("select * from Titles");
```

To retrieve the data from a field, you write a statement like this:

```
$cnBiblio->Data('Title');
```

When you want to move to the next record in the table, you use a function called **FetchRow**, like this:

```
$cnBiblio->FetchRow();
```

Finally, when you are finished, you close the connection like this:

```
$cnBiblio->Close();
```

Here is a complete listing, using Win32::ODBC, of the first example from the section on ADO:

```
use Win32::ODBC;
$cnBiblio = new Win32::ODBC("OLE_Biblio");
$sql = "select * from titles";
$cnBiblio->Sql($sql);
while (!$cnBiblio->Eof()) {
    $booktitle = $cnBiblio->Data('Title');
    $yearpub = $cnBiblio->Data('Year Published');
    $isbn = $cnBiblio->Data('ISBD');
    print "Book Title: $booktitle\n";
    print "Published in $yearpub\n";
    print "ISBN: $isbn\n";
    $cnBiblio->FetchRow();
}
$cnBiblio->Close();
```

The most commonly used functions from the Win32::ODBC module are listed in Table 17-2.

Function	Purpose
ConfigDSN	Configures a DSN
Connection	Returns the connection number of the ODBC connection
Close	Closes the ODBC connection
Data	Returns the contents of field name or whole row
DataHash	Returns contents of fields as associative array
DataSources	Returns a hash of data sources and remarks
Error	Returns the last encountered error
FetchRow	Returns the next record from the recordset
FieldNames	Returns an array of field names from the data set
GetConnections	Returns array showing which connections are open

ODBC
Functions
Table 17-2.

Function	Purpose
GetDSN	Returns configuration for specified DSN
new	Creates a new ODBC connection
RowCount	Returns the number of rows affected by SQL statement
Run	Executes the current SQL statement
SetCursorName	Sets the name of the current cursor
SetPos	Moves the cursor to the specified row in the recordset
ShutDown	Closes the ODBC connection
Sql	Executes the specified SQL statement
Transact	Forces connection to perform either Commit or Rollback

ODBC
Functions
(*continued*)
Table 17-2.

Remember that Win32::ODBC can be used with any ODBC-compliant database, making this module indispensable for situations where the database you want to use doesn't have an ADO-type driver available for it.

Summary

Database programming in Perl can be performed in several different ways. For small applications, you might decide to use Perl's built-in functions for creating different types of files for storing data. For larger applications, you will probably want to use either the ODBC functions or some other tool such as ADO for database programming. Using ODBC, you can connect Perl to any ODBC-compliant relational database, which today means most of the relational databases you will come across in a commercial environment.

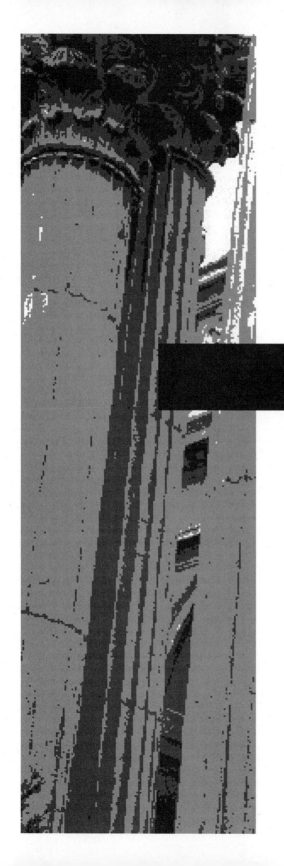

CHAPTER 18

Perl CGI
Programming

One of the applications for which Perl has seen extensive use is in writing CGI programs for the World Wide Web. CGI programs are used to process online transactions, to provide animation and other dynamic elements to otherwise static Web pages, to simplify system administration tasks, and for a myriad other applications. The feature that all CGI programs share in common is the manner in which they exchange data with client Web browsers. Given that CGI data exchange involves nothing more than parsing text input and outputting formatted text (HTML code), it should not come as a surprise that Perl has become a preferred language for the task.

We begin this chapter with a brief review of the primary features of the Common Gateway Interface (CGI). Specifically, we will examine how data is passed from a Web browser into a CGI program, and how the program is expected to produce output. Then we will move on to look at some examples of CGI programs that demonstrate how Perl makes short work of dealing with CGI data. Next, we'll introduce the Perl CGI module, now part of the standard Perl distribution, which makes the task of writing CGI programs simpler and more elegant. We'll end the chapter with a few words on the topic of security in CGI programming.

The following discussion assumes a working knowledge of HTML, the language used to create Web documents. If you are at the stage of writing CGI code, then you must have already had some exposure to HTML. If you have never had the occasion to write or read any HTML code, you would do well to refer to *HTML: The Complete Reference* (Osborne/McGraw-Hill) before delving into the realm of CGI programming.

A Brief Review of CGI

Before we begin, please note that this section is not intended to provide a full CGI tutorial, but to highlight the features of CGI that we will use in subsequent discussion. As we work through this section, you should be thinking about how you would use Perl to parse the input data in its various formats. To that end, the presentation here is intentionally brief. Examples will be presented in the following section.

The Common Gateway Interface, or CGI, defines a method that can be used to pass data between Web clients (browsers) and programs run by the Web server, called CGI programs. CGI programs are used to extend the capabilities of static HTML pages, both on a small scale, by adding simple features such as animation or dynamic page creation to documents, and on a larger scale by providing an interface to other non-Web services available on the host system. The fact that a CGI program runs on the server machine and not the client machine distinguishes it from other types of Web programs (such as Java applets), and makes it more appropriate for any tasks that involve interacting with the server.

Passing Data to the CGI Program

The way CGI works is basically that the Web browser accepts input data from an HTML document (generally a form), or from special text appended to an URL. The browser encodes the data into a text string, and passes this data string (the "query string") to the Web server, which in turn runs the CGI program. The server makes the data in the query string available to the CGI program in one of two ways depending on how the CGI program was invoked by the browser. The CGI program then does whatever it does, and generates some HTML code that the server passes back to the browser.

For the purpose of this discussion, assume a simple HTML form that requests two pieces of data—a user's login name and the user's full name—and passes them to a CGI program called add_name.cgi. The relevant HTML code might look like the following:

```
<FORM ACTION="/cgi-bin/add_name.pl">
Enter your login name: <INPUT TYPE="text" NAME="login">
Enter your full name:   <INPUT TYPE="text" NAME="name">
<INPUT TYPE="submit">
</FORM>
```

Once the user of the Web browser has input the requested data into the form and clicked on the Submit button, the browser combines the input data into a query string to be passed to the server. In general, a query string is composed of a series of data element pairs in the form **key=value**. Multiple data pairs are separated by an ampersand (&). In this particular example, there are two named data elements, "login" and "name". Before the browser passes the query data on to the Web server, it may have to encode certain characters in the string so they will not be incorrectly interpreted by the Web server.

HTML Encoding

Although CGI input data will always be text, certain characters may have special meaning depending on how the data is passed from client to server. These characters include those that have special meaning in HTML, including spaces, forward slashes (/), and others that are potentially dangerous in that they may have special meaning to a command shell on the server. To prevent such characters from being incorrectly interpreted by the Web server or the CGI program itself, the browser encodes the characters as follows: each questionable character is replaced by the hexadecimal number representing the character's position in the ASCII character set, prefixed with a percent sign (%). For instance, a question mark (?) has ASCII code 0x3F (63 in decimal). In HTML-encoded form, this character would be expressed as %3F. One exception to the general encoding scheme is that spaces can be encoded as plus signs (+).

In our example form, if the user enters "tomo" for the login name and "Tom O'Brien" for the full name, the query string generated by the browser would be:

```
login=tomo&name=Tom+O%27Brien
```

Notice that both the space and the apostrophe have been encoded. It's up to the CGI program to decode these characters; the Web server does not do the decoding for you. For a list of the characters that will be, or should be, encoded by the client, see any reference on HTML. Be aware, though, that any ASCII character may be encoded, even regular alphabetic characters. Your CGI program must be prepared to decode any properly encoded data.

The manner in which the encoded query string is passed to the CGI program depends on which of two methods is specified in the form tag of the HTML code. The two methods are **get** and **post**. The Web server sets the environment variable request_method to one of these two values to let the CGI program know how it was invoked.

Query Data Passed Using Get

Get is the default method to pass form data to CGI programs. In this method the query string is appended to the URL of the CGI, separated by a question mark. In the previous example, since no method is specified in the form tag, the **get** method is assumed. The URL passed to the server would look something similar to the following: **http://server.company.com/cgi-in/ add_name.pl?login=tomo&name=Tom+O%27Brien**.

The Web server makes the input data available to the CGI program in the environment variable query_string. If a CGI program is invoked from an HREF tag (as opposed to an HTML FORM), or by a user entering the URL of the program directly in the browser, a query string may be explicitly appended to the URL. In this case, the user or HTML programmer must take care to encode the query string properly.

Query Data Passed Using POST

When a CGI program is invoked by a form using the **post** method, the query string is made available by the server to the program's standard input. Further, the number of characters in the (encoded) input string is specified in the environment variable content_length. To use the **post** method in the example form, the FORM tag would be rewritten as:

```
<FORM ACTION="/cgi-bin/add_name.pl" METHOD=POST>
```

18

Using Extra Path Data with CGI Programs

Another method by which data can be passed to CGI programs is in the form of extra path information appended to the CGI URL. This method relies on the Web server's ability to recognize when the actual path information stops, so that the CGI program can be executed. The extra data is made available to the CGI program in the environment variable path_data. For example, we might arrange to invoke the add_name.cgi script using the URL: **http://server.company.com/cgi-bin/add_name.cgi/update?login=tomo&name=Tom+O%27Brien**.

In this case, the Web server runs add_name.cgi with the environment variable path_data containing the value "/update" and the query_string variable containing the encoded query string as before.

CGI Environment Variables

As already indicated, the Web server makes certain information available to the CGI program via environment variables. We have seen that the server passes the request method, and the query string or query length as appropriate. In fact, the Web server supplies a good bit more information through environment variables, including data about the client browser, the address of the client machine, and some details about the server itself. In the following section, a CGI program will be presented to display the full set of environment variables.

Outputting HTML Data

The far end of a CGI program is concerned with the generation of HTML to be displayed on the client browser. As far as the CGI program itself is concerned, it is just writing text to standard output; the Web server passes the HTML code to the browser. Recall that an HTML document consists of a header and a body; the two are separated by a blank line. When writing static HTML code, you worry only about the body; the server provides all of the header information when the document is sent to the browser. A CGI program, on the other hand, must generate some header information, generally a "Content-type" line at least, which the server will augment with more information if necessary.

Basic CGI Programming in Perl

Now we are prepared to focus on the central issue of the chapter—namely, why Perl is so well suited to CGI programming. We are not so much concerned here with what you can do with CGI as with how Perl can help you do it. Since we already have good reason to choose Perl for general system programming tasks, the discussion in this section will highlight the features of Perl that make it a good choice for CGI programming in particular.

Some Basic Examples

Let's begin by looking at a very simple CGI script written in Perl. This program takes no input from the browser. When invoked, it simply runs the Unix command **who** on the server and sends the output to the browser in the form of an HTML document. (The **who** command lists the users who are logged into the computer.)

```
#
#   showwho.cgi: show who's logged on the server
#
print "Content-type: text/html\n\n";
my $who_cmd = '/bin/who';
my $who = `$who_cmd`;
print <<EOM;
<HTML>
<HEAD><TITLE>Who is on the server</TITLE></HEAD>
<BODY>
<H1>Who is on the server</H1>
<PRE>
<TT>
$who
</TT>
</PRE>
</BODY>
</HTML>
EOM
exit;
```

The program begins by generating a "Content-type" line, followed by a blank line to separate it from the body of the document. Together these form a partial header, which will be completed by the server before the document is sent to the browser. The bulk of the code is taken up by the business of generating the HTML code, for which purpose we use a *here* document construct. We have also saved some time by specifying that the output of the **who** command is preformatted (using the <PRE></PRE> tags), and storing the output of the *backtick* operator in a scalar variable. Sample output from this program is displayed in the context of another example in Figure 18-3.

18

Here is another little program that displays all of the variables set in the CGI program's environment:

```
#
#  showenv.cgi:    Display all environment variables
#
print "Content-type: text/html\n\n";
print <<EOM;
<HTML>
<HEAD><TITLE>The CGI environment</TITLE></HEAD>
<BODY>
<H1>The CGI environment</H1>
<TABLE>
EOM
for $key (sort keys %ENV) {
    print "<TR><TH ALIGN=RIGHT>$key<TD>$ENV{$key}</TR>\n";
}
print <<EOM;
</TABLE>
</BODY>
</HTML>
EOM
exit;
```

It is instructive to invoke this program in different ways to see exactly how data is passed to the CGI program in the environment variables. For instance, try running this program as "/showenv.cgi?up=up&down=down", or write a simple form to POST some data to the program. Figure 18-1 shows the output of this CGI program invoked as:

```
/cgi-bin/showenv.cgi/extra/path/info?name=this+tune
```

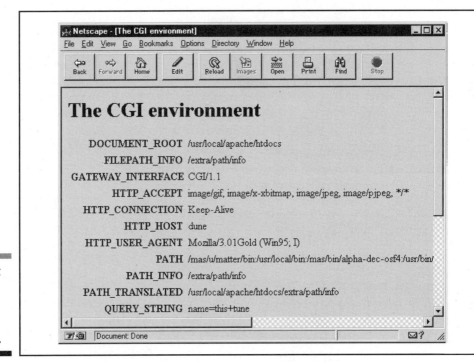

Parsing Input Data

As you read through the review of CGI, armed as you are now with a working
knowledge of Perl, you were no doubt formulating Perl code in your mind to
parse the CGI input. Since the task of handling input data is common to
most CGI programs, it is beneficial to develop a set of reusable functions to
handle the job. Following is a pair of routines to acquire the query data,
regardless of which method was used to invoke the program, and to parse the
data into a handy Perl structure.

```
sub getQuery {
my $query = undef;
if ($ENV{'REQUEST_METHOD'} eq 'GET') {
        $query = ENV{'QUERY_STRING'};
elsif ($ENV{'REQUEST_METHOD'} eq 'POST') {
        read(STDIN, $query, $ENV{'CONTENT_LENGTH'});
}
$query;
}
sub parseQuery {
```

```
my $query = shift;
my (%input, @elements, $element, $key, $value);
@elements = split /&/, $query;
for $element (@elements) {
    $element =~ tr/+/ /;                        # decode +'s to spaces
    ($key, $value) = split /=/, $element;
    $key =~ s/%([\dA-Fa-f]{2})/pack("C",hex($1))/ge;     # decode key
    $value =~ s/%(\dA-Fa-f]{2})/pack("C",hex($1))/ge;    # decode value
    if (defined $input{$key}) {
        $input{$key} .= "\0$value";
    } else {
        $input{$key} = $value;
    }
}
\%input;
}
```

The **split** function handles the task of extracting the elements of the various data pairs in the query string, and the keys and values are then decoded with a clever regular expression. The regular expression searches for pairs of hexadecimal digits following a percent sign. If any such two-digit hexadecimal number is found the **hex** function converts it to a decimal value that is used as the argument to the **pack** function. The output of **pack** is then substituted back into the string in place of the encoded character. The facility with which Perl handles the encoded query data, especially the elegant use of regular expression to decode any HTML-encoded characters, is one of the many reasons for Perl's popularity as a CGI programming language.

The **parseQuery** function returns a reference to a hash containing the key/value pairs passed in the query string. Note that the routine handles multiple values for a single key by joining the values together using a null character (\0). Here is a little program that makes use of the routines presented above. This example does nothing more than display a nicely formatted list of the query data passed to it. This can be useful for testing HTML forms, and will be used in another example.

```
#
#   testparse.CGI: Display parsed input data
#
my $query = getQuery();
my $input = parseQuery($query);    # $input is a reference to a hash
print "Content-type: text/html\n\n";
print <<EOF;
<HTML>
```

```
<HEAD><TITLE>Query Example</TITLE></HEAD>
<BODY>
<CENTER>
<H3>Here are the key/value pairs passed to the CGI program:</H3>
<TABLE>
<TR><TH ALIGN=RIGHT>Key<TD ALIGN=LEFT><Value(s)<\TR>
EOF
for $key (sort keys %{$input}) {
    print "<TR><TD ALIGN=RIGHT>$key<TD ALIGN=LEFT>";
    print join ", ", split /\0/, $input->{$key};
    print "<\TR>";
}
print <<EOF
</TABLE>
</CENTER>
</BODY>
</HTML>
EOF
exit;
```

Sample output from the testparse.cgi script is shown in Figure 18-2.

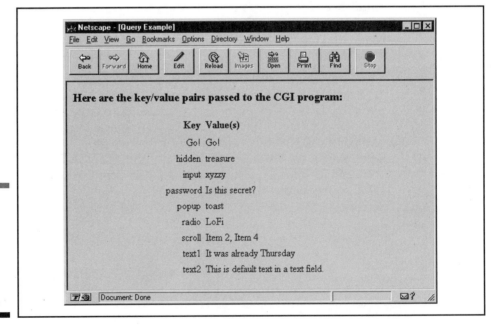

Output from the testparse.cgi program (*See Figure 18-6 also*)

Figure 18-2.

Outputting HTML

The business of generating HTML code from the CGI program is quite straightforward, as you have no doubt gathered from the preceding examples. The technique of employing a *here document* allows the programmer to embed HTML code directly in the source of the CGI program, while **print** statements can be used for shorter pieces of code.

The details of creating HTML headers merit further attention. In the examples presented so far, the extent of the header produced by the CGI program is a line specifying the content type, which in many cases is sufficient. In addition to satisfying the Web server's need for a header, this keeps your program from being dependent on the server's choice of a default content type. There are, however, other elements you may choose to include in your CGI header, such as a "Status" line. For instance, you can specify "Status: 204 No Response" to tell the browser that the program has run but is not going to generate any output. You may also add handlers to your CGI code to generate meaningful status codes in the event of any errors during the execution of the program, such as "Status: 500 Internal Server Error". You should be able to find a full listing of HTML status codes in your favorite HTML documentation.

Two other useful header lines to keep in mind are "Expires", which tells the browser that the data on the page expires after the specified time and should be reloaded, and "Location", which instructs the server to serve up a different document. For example, the following trivial CGI program redirects the server to the document "under-construction.html":

```
print "Location:  under-construction.html\n\n";
exit;
```

When using a "Location" line in a header, no "Content-type" should be specified.

Outputting other Content Types

Do not assume from the few examples presented previously that your CGI program is limited to outputting text data. For instance, it is perfectly valid to have your CGI program send binary image data (assuming the client browser will accept it), as in the following code:

```
my $file ="picture.jpg";
my $length = (stat($file))[6];
```

```
open(FILE,"<$file") or die "could not open $file: $!";
@data = <FILE>;
print "Content-type: image/jpeg\n";
print "Content-length: $length\n\n";    # extra line to end header
print @data;
```

The environment variable http_accept offers some clue to the CGI program
as to what data types the browser is prepared to deal with.

A Frames Example

One popular extension to basic HTML is the concept of frames, and CGI
programs are well suited to generating documents with frames. The technique
of using frames in a document involves two steps. First, the frameset is defined,
and, second, the frames are filled with documents or CGI output as specified in
the frameset definition. Using extra path information is a convenient way to
have a single CGI program both generate a frameset and populate the frames.
Consider the following CGI code that takes as input (via **get**) the name of
another CGI program (the target) and displays the output of that CGI program
in one frame and its source code in another. The program expects that its name
will be prepended to the query string of the target CGI, and looks for the target
in the same directory containing the original script. A sample usage is:

```
/cgi-bin/showcgi.cgi?testparse.cgi/extra/path/info?up=up
```

Here is the code:

```
#
#  showcgi.cgi: Display the output of a CGI program along with its source
#
my $query = getQuery();
my($cgi,$args);
if ($ENV{'PATH_INFO'}) {

    $cgi = $query;

    showCGI();
} else {
```

```
        $query =~ /([^\?\/]*)(.*)/;      # Separate my name from query string
        $cgi = $1;
        $args = $2;
        buildFrames();
    }
exit;
sub showCGI {
    print "Content-type: text/plain\n\n";
    open(CGI,"<$cgi");
    while (<CGI>) {
        print "$_";
    }
    close CGI;
    exit;
}
sub buildFrames {
    print "Content-type: text/html\n\n";
    print <<EOF;
<HTML>
<HEAD><TITLE>ShowCGI: $cgi</TITLE></HEAD>
<FRAMESET rows="50,50">
<FRAME SRC="$cgi$args" NAME="cgi">
<FRAME SRC="$ENV{'SCRIPT_NAME'}/display?$cgi" NAME="source">
</FRAMESET>
</HTML>
EOF
    exit;
}
```

Figure 18-3 shows the output of this program when used on the showwho.cgi script presented earlier. The program is actually invoked twice, once at the request of the browser, when the **buildFrames** function is executed, and again at its own request, when **showCGI** is called to fill the bottom frame with the text of the target script. The presence of extra path data, appended to the URL when the program invokes itself, is what distinguishes the instances of the program.

Some other notes about the example: observe how the target CGI script and its query string (and extra path info if present) are separated from the primary CGI script in its query string by a single regular expression match: Perl shines again. Also, note how the **showCGI** function specifies a content

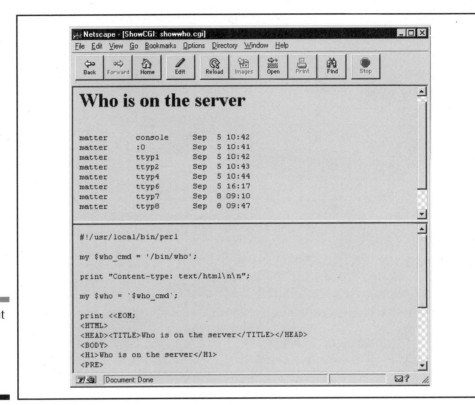

type of "text/plain" so the browser won't interpret any HTML code that might
be present in the source of the target CGI. An interesting aside: what do you
suppose happens when you invoke the showcgi.cgi script on itself, as
"/cgi-bin/showcgi.cgi?showcgi.cgi"?

The Perl CGI Module

Given that the CGI programming community has embraced Perl, it should
not come as a surprise that a Perl module has been developed specifically for
creating CGI code. Written by Lincoln Stein, the module is called simply
CGI.pm and, as of Perl version 5.004, is part of the standard Perl library. (It is
also available by itself from CPAN.) The CGI module offers a number of

features that can greatly simplify writing CGI code. These include automatic parsing of query data, a suite of functions providing shorthand for sequences of HTML code, and error-handling routines that generate useful information to the browser.

A Simple Example

Let's begin with a short CGI program making use of the CGI.pm module. Similar in some respects to the showwho.cgi script presented earlier, this program runs the **traceroute** command from the server. It uses as a destination either an IP address supplied in a query string, or, if none is specified, the IP address of the client machine.

18

NOTE: Traceroute is a program that makes clever use of the "time to live" field in ICMP packets to reveal the gateways that network packets must pass through en route to a specified host. The program is available under many versions of Unix, and under Windows NT, where it is called tracert.

Before we present the CGI traceroute program, here's a little HTML form to invoke it:

```
<HTML>
<HEAD><TITLE>Traceroute demo</TITLE><HEAD>
<BODY>
<FORM ACTION="nph-trace.cgi" METHOD=GET>
<H1>Traceroute demo</H1>
<CENTER>
Traceroute from server to
<INPUT TYPE=TEXT NAME=HOST SIZE=30>
(default is client host)
<P>
<INPUT TYPE=SUBMIT VALUE="Go!">
</CENTER>
</FORM>
</BODY>
</HTML>
```

Figure 18-4 shows the input form as it appears in a browser.

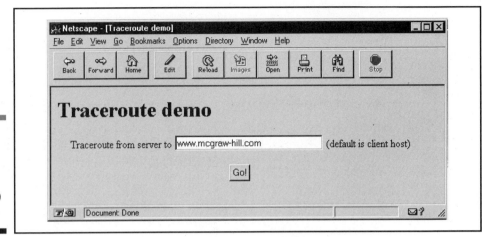

A form to
launch the
traceroute
demo
(nph-trace.cgi)

Figure 18-4.

And this is the CGI program itself (nph-trace.cgi):

```
#
#   nph-trace.cgi
#
use CGI;
use CGI::Carp qw(fatalsToBrowser);
$| = 1;          # we require unbuffered output
my $query = new CGI;
my $host_addr = $query->server_name;
my $dest_addr = $query->param('host') ? $query->param('host')
                                      : $query->remote_addr;
die "Bad character ($1) in hostname" if $dest_addr =~
/([\\;*><`|])/;
die "no destination address" unless $dest_addr;
print $query->header(-type=>'text/html',
            -status=>'200 OK',
            -nph=>1,
            );
print $query->start_html('Traceroute demo');
print $query->h1('Traceroute demo');
print $query->h2('From',$host_addr,'to',$dest_addr);
print $query->hr;
print "<PRE><TT>\n";
open (TRACE,"/usr/sbin/traceroute $dest_addr |");
while (<TRACE>) {
    print;
```

```
}
print "</PRE></TT>\n";
print $query->hr;
print $query->end_html;
exit;
```

The output generated by the CGI program is shown in Figure 18-5.

In the beginning of the code, $query is declared as a new CGI object and already Perl has taken care of parsing all of the input data, regardless of the request method. The input data is available to the programmer via the **param** method in the $query object. In general, named input data can be retrieved as:

```
$value = $query->param('name');
```

The names of the parameters themselves are available as:

```
@names = $query->param;
```

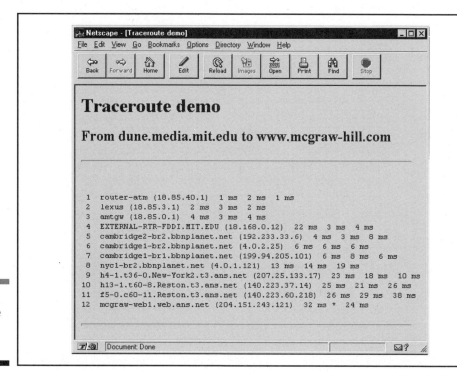

Output from
the traceroute
demo
Figure 18-5.

In addition, the server environment variables are directly available through methods in the CGI object. Two examples appear in the code above: remote_addr and server_name. Other useful methods include path_info, query_string, request_method, accept, and user_agent. Given the output of the showenv.cgi script, you can probably guess the rest.

Look at the **print** statements in the code and you will see how the CGI module can save the programmer a good bit of typing when it comes to generating HTML. The **header** function with no arguments creates the "Content type: text/html" line and the blank line separating the header from the body of the page. With additional arguments it will create a "Status" line, as in the example code, or an "Expire" line, or anything else you care to have in the header. The **start_html** function returns the <HTML> and <HEAD> tags, as well as the <TITLE></TITLE> tags and the opening <BODY> tag. The **h1** function joins its arguments with spaces and wraps the resulting string in <H1> and </H1> tags. As you might expect, there are similar functions for generating headers of other levels (**h2->h6**), as well as a handful of others that take no arguments, such as the "hr" in the previous code (which creates a <HR> tag).

There is one other unusual feature about the previous example—it is written as a "no-parse-header", or NPH program. Normally, the Web server waits for a CGI program to finish running before it passes the output on to the browser. With an NPH CGI program, on the other hand, the output of the CGI program is sent to the browser as it is generated. In the case of the traceroute example, this is desirable because it is possible that the **traceroute** command will take as much as a minute to finish, and in some cases might never exit. By displaying the output to the browser as it is generated, the user has the option of interrupting the script if desired. We set the autoflush variable ($|) to true in the code to ensure that the output of traceroute is passed along as it is generated. The manner in which a CGI program is designated as NPH depends on the server. Some, like NCSA and Apache, require that the name of the program begin with "nph-"; others look for certain information in the header, which is provided in the previous example by setting nph to true in the call to the **header** function.

Error Handling and Debugging with CGI.pm

In the CGI.pm program above, you may have noted that we make use of a second module, CGI::Carp. This module defines alternate functions for **warn** and **die**, the basic error-reporting routines, as well as for **croak**, **confess**, and **carp**, the module-friendly error routines defined in the Carp module. These replacement functions add extra information to the error message they create, such as a timestamp, so that the resulting entry in the error log of the Web server will be more useful. The use of qw(fatalsToBrowser) tells the module to send any fatal errors messages (those generated by **die**, **croak**, or **confess**) both to the normal server log and to the browser. This can greatly simplify the process of debugging code.

Another technique for debugging code that uses CGI.pm is to run the code by hand offline. The CGI module accepts input in the form **key=value** pairs, either specified on the command line to the program or entered interactively to the program's standard input. The input data is formatted into an appropriate query string and made available to the program in the normal way (via the **param** method). This is a convenient way to clean up code, and is in general much more efficient that wading through server log files to trace problems.

18

A Form Example

The functions used in the nph-trace.cgi code are only a small subset of those available in CGI.pm. It is in the creation of HTML forms that the benefits to the programmer of using the CGI module become fully apparent. Consider the following example, which creates the form shown in Figure 18-6:

```
use CGI qw(:standard);
my $query = new CGI;
print header, start_html('CGI.pm Form Demonstration');
print h1('CGI.pm Form Demonstration');
print start_form(-action=>'testparse.cgi',
                 -method=>'post');
print hidden(-name=>hidden, -value=>'find this');
print "<TABLE>\n";
print "<TR><TH>Text input:<TD>",textfield(-name=>'input'),"</TR>";
print "<TR><TH>Password input:<TD>",password_field(-name=>'password'),
      "</TR>";
my @radioValues = ('LoFi','HiFi');
my %radioLabels = ('LoFi' => 'AM','HiFi' => 'FM');
print "<TR><TH>Radio buttons:<TD>",radio_group(-name=>'radio',
                                              -value=>\@radioValues,
                                              -labels=>\%radioLabels),
      "</TR>";
my @popupList = ('toast','jack-in-the-box','fly ball');
print "<TR><TH>Popup list:<TD>",popup_menu(-name=>'popup',
                                          -value=>\@popupList),"</TR>";
my @scrollList = map "Item $_",(1..10);
print "<TR><TH>Scrolling list:<TD>",scrolling_list(-name=>'scroll',
```

Perl from the Ground Up

```
                                                  -value=>\@scrollList,
                                                  -multiple=>'true',
                                        -size=>3),"</TR>";
print "<TR><TH>Text field:<TD>",textarea(-name=>'text1',
                                          -rows=>2,-cols=>20),</TR>;
my $default = "This is default\ntext in a text field";
print "<TR><TH>Text field (with default text):<TD>",textarea(-name=>
      'text2',
                                                  -rows=>2,
                                                  -cols=>20,
                                                  -value=>$de
                                                  fault),

      </TR>;
print "</TABLE>\n";
print submit('Go!');
print end_html;
exit;
```

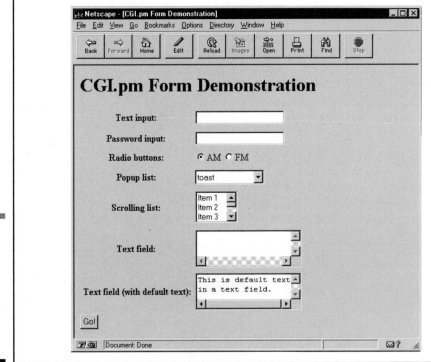

Output of
the CGI
module form
demonstration
—this form
sets a number
of data items

Figure 18-6.

18

We'll spend a bit of time looking at this example because it shows off a number of the features of the CGI module. To begin, in the first line of the code, when we **use** the CGI module, we take advantage of the :standard tag, which imports most of the useful symbols into the namespace of the main program. This means we can simply write **print start_html** instead of having to qualify the function name as in previous examples: **print $query->start_html**. In a short program like this, we don't really need to worry about cluttering up the namespace. The CGI module defines several such tags to allow more control over your namespace, including :form, :html2, :html3, and :netscape. See the CGI.pm code for a full listing of the tags and their associated symbols.

There are several other noteworthy features in the previous example. First, observe that we can freely mix calls to the **CGI.pm** functions that output HTML with straight HTML code. In the sample code, we define an HTML table to handle the formatting, and place explicit HTML table row and table data tags around the calls to the **CGI.pm** functions in the **print** statements. Second, observe the usage of the **radio_group**, **popup_list**, and **scrolling_list** functions—in particular, the fact that they can take as arguments a reference to an array, for the list item values, and a reference to a hash, for the list item labels (as in the call to radio_buttons). Note that it is also acceptable to pass explicit array data, as in the following code:

```
print popup_list(-name=>'fish',
-value=>['one','two','red','blue']);
```

These particular functions exemplify the way in which a CGI module can shield the programmer from much of the verbosity of HTML. For example, the single call to popup_list in the line above generates the following HTML code:

```
<SELECT NAME="fish">
<OPTION VALUE="one">one
<OPTION VALUE="two">two
<OPTION VALUE="red">red
<OPTION VALUE="blue">blue
</SELECT>
```

NOTE: You should be well aware of the fact that the password type input field, used in the previous example, is not at all secure. While the characters entered may not appear on the browser as they are typed, they still travel as unencrypted text over the network. If the data is submitted using the GET method, the "password" actually appears in the URL. The bottom line here is that you should use password type entry fields if you are seeking security. If you want to exchange data safely with CGI programs over the network, look into setting up a secure server, a topic well beyond the scope of this chapter.

To learn the full suite of functions available in CGI.pm and their various options, run **perldocCGI** on your system, or look at the documentation inside the code for the module itself.

A Final Note: CGI Security

No discussion of CGI programming can be complete without a few words about the potential dangers of CGI. Indeed, the importance of dealing with security issues when it comes to CGI programs cannot be overemphasized when you consider that CGI is a method by which almost anyone on the Internet can execute a program on your machine. If the CGI program is not carefully constructed, a malicious user may find other uses for it than those for which it was originally intended. This is not say that you should avoid writing CGI programs; if you are aware of the potential difficulties, they can be avoided.

The first rule of safety when writing CGI code is not to execute any command on your system with arguments that come from the query string. If you must, be very careful to check the string for potentially dangerous characters, that is, characters that may have special significance to the command shell. The nph-trace.cgi example demonstrates how you might screen your query data. You should also be careful to specify full paths for system commands executed from your CGI program. Perl offers a special command line flag, -T, that requests that the Perl compiler check certain basic security features of the program's environment. For instance, the compiler will generate a fatal error if you attempt to execute a system command without specifying a full path, unless you have carefully set the path in the %ENV hash. The use of the –T flag is referred to as "taint checking". The –T flag can be specified on the first line of the script (the "shebang" line), for instance:

```
#!/usr/local/bin/perl -T
```

You should enable taint checking during the development of any CGI program that runs system commands or writes to local files.

Another thing to keep in mind is that a CGI program is executed with the permissions of the effective user running the Web server. These permissions are typically rather limited, which may make it difficult for your CGI program to do everything you want it to. For instance, you may run into trouble if you want your CGI program to access a database on the server that has restricted permissions. This may in turn tempt you into making your CGI program **setuid**, or configuring the Web server to run with greater permissions. Both of these options should be viewed with great trepidation. There is usually a safer way to accomplish what you want to do. Fortunately, many Web servers will not allow you to run CGI programs that have the setuid bit set, at least not without special configuration. You should only run setuid CGI programs if you are certain of what you are doing.

18

One last thing that should be pointed out is that you can implement a certain measure of access control within the CGI program itself. That is, using such information as the client machine's IP address (in the environment variable remote_addr), and the remote user's identification (in the environment variable remote_user, if available), your CGI program can decide whether to allow access to certain data or functionality. Even so, you should probably not trust the information about the client machine too far unless you are running a secure Web server, as there are ways to falsify such data. As with other aspects of computer security, the more you understand about how things work, the more secure you can make your environment. And the converse is even truer: Unless you have a thorough understanding of how things work, it is best to be very cautious.

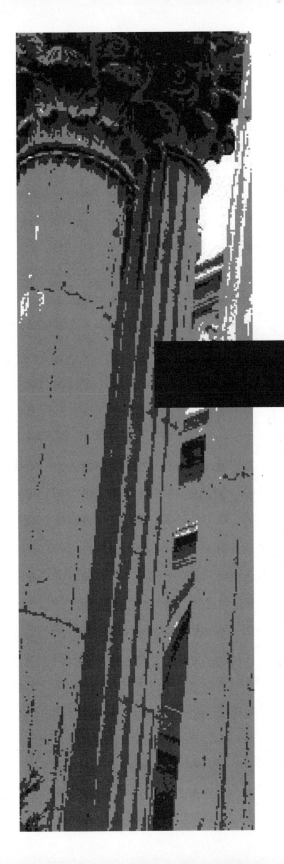

CHAPTER 19

Internet-related Libraries, Modules, and Utilities for Perl

The most common server-based applications, in spite of all the new innovations, are still CGI based. You had a chance to work with CGI (Common Gateway Interface), in Chapter 18. The module used for the examples in that chapter was CGI.pm by Lincoln Stein, unarguably the most popular CGI module in use today. This chapter goes into depth on the functionality CGI.pm provides, including an overview of the different module methods. Another popular source of Internet functionality is covered, the cgi-lib.pl, a Perl library rather than a module. The cgi-lib.pl library is probably second only to CGI.pm in use in Perl Internet CGI applications.

Both CGI.pm and lib-cgi were created for CGI applications only. The lib-www Perl modules, also known as LWP and as the WWW Protocol library for Perl, contain modules for handling Web robots; file shipping, through proxies or not; Web server technology; handling FTP requests; handling MIME types; and dealing with other Web-related technologies. The modules are so extensive that this chapter mainly covers the major module types, but not each module's methods in detail.

Chances are that most of your Internet application needs will be met by CGI.pm, LWP, or lib-cgi.pl. However, there are also several other Internet-based modules available to cover functionality such as accessing a Netscape history database, extending the Apache Web server, and FastCGI. These modules and their functionality are also discussed.

There are several utilities already written that you can use without modification at your Web site. Some of the more popular of these utilities, along with the Web sites that include them, are covered at the end of the chapter.

Refresher: Libraries, Modules, and Utilities

Before getting into reviewing some of the more popular Internet-based Perl libraries and modules, this section provides a short refresher on the difference between a Perl library and a Perl module. First, libraries were the only available technique to package reusable code before Perl version 5. However with Perl version 5, you can now create object modules in addition to libraries. Second, libraries contain reusable functions that are incorporated into the calling application and called directly. Modules, on the other hand, usually contain object classes, and, instead of accessing a specific function, you create an object and then invoke that object's method.

Both techniques are widely used with Internet applications. In fact, the two most popular reusable code sources in use are cgi-lib.pl, a library; and

CGI.pm, a module. As you will see later in this chapter, the reason both are so popular is that they are easy to install and use in your applications.

Libraries and modules differ from utilities, or applications. A *utility* is basically a Perl application that requires little or no modification to incorporate for your own use. Perl developers have been a remarkably generous group of people, creating utilities such as mail form handlers, visitor counters, shopping carts, and other handy applications that you can copy, modify, and use. Not only will this save you coding time, but it's also a terrific technique to begin your next level of Perl education—after this book, of course.

The lib-cgi.pl Library

19

The lib-cgi.pl library is a Perl version 4 implementation that isn't as common as it has been, but is still in fairly widespread use. Most Perl developers consider CGI.pm from Lincoln Stein to be a Perl version 5 replacement. However, lib-cgi.pl is a simple-to-use, easy-to-implement alternative if you find Perl version 5 modules and objects difficult.

WEB LINK: The cgi-lib library can be downloaded from the cgi-lib home page, which can be accessed at **http://www.bio.cam.ac.uk/ cgi-lib**. Access the link for cgi-lib, which then displays the library in your browser window. Then use the browser Save As feature to save cgi-lib.pl to your own machine.

Though originally created for Perl version 4, lib-cgi.pl will work equally well with Perl version 5. The library contains several functions that you can call directly in your CGI application. The **ReadParse** function processes the input passed to the CGI application, either from directly appending name-value pairs to the hypertext link that calls the application, or from an HTML form. The input is then *unescaped* and parsed out into name-value pairs. To move these name-value pairs into a list, you can use the function SplitParam, passing to it the variable generated by the **ReadParse** function.

The **PrintHeader** function creates the HTTP request line that informs the server that the data being returned to the client is in HTML format. If you return any form of a result page to your Web page reader, you must precede the HTML with the HTTP request line. The function prints out a line equivalent to the following:

```
Content-type: text/html\n\n
```

NOTE: Double linefeeds at the end of the line are required.

The **HtmlTop** and **HtmlBot** functions print out the opening and closing HTML statements. The opening HTML statements are the beginning and ending HEAD tags, the TITLE tags, and the beginning BODY tag. The Web page title is passed into the **HtmlTop** function call. The ending HTML statements are the closing BODY and HTML tags.

The **MethGet** and **MethPost** functions return true if the form **get** method or form **post** method is used, respectively. The **MyBaseUrl** function returns the base URL of the application minus any query or path strings. The **FullUrl** function returns the base URL and the query and path strings.

The two functions **PrintVariables** and **PrintEnv** return the input variables and the CGI environmental variables respectively, formatted nicely to make them easier to view. The variable generated with the call to **ReadParse** is passed to **PrintVariables**, but no parameter is used with **PrintEnv**. As an example of using these two functions, the following code shows an HTML document that contains two text fields, two radio buttons, a hidden field, and a submit button. The form posting method is **get**, which is the default, and which means that the form contents are concatenated onto the application URL as name-value pairs. The application the form sends its data to is called "form.cgi".

```
<html>
<head>
<title>Form to CGI Example</title>
</head>
<body>

<TABLE border=0 width=80% align=center>
<tr><td>
<form action="http://unix.yasd.com/book-bin/form.cgi">
What is your name: <input name="name"><P>
What is your email: <input name="email"><P>
<input type="hidden" name="hidden_field" value="CGIAPP">
Which color do you prefer: <input type="radio" name="color"
value="red" checked> red or
<input type="radio" name="color" value="blue"> blue
<P>
```

```
<input type=submit value="Submit Form">
</form>
</td></tr></table>
</body>
</html>
```

The CGI application used to process the form's results uses the **PrintVariables** and **PrintEnv** functions to print out the form fields and their associated values, and to print out the environmental variables that can be accessed by the CGI script. The Perl script for form.cgi is shown in the next code block.

```
#!/usr/local/bin/perl

require "cgi-lib.pl";

MAIN:
{
   # Read in all the variables set by the form
   &ReadParse(*input); # variables are stored in a hash referenced
                       by *input

   # Print the header
   print &PrintHeader;
print &HtmlTop ("Demonstration of cgi-lib");

# print out the form variables
   print "<HR><p>These are the name-value pairs submitted to this
         Application</p><HR>";
   print &PrintVariables(*input);
   # print out the environment variables
   print "<HR><p>These are the values of the CGI Environmental
     Variables</p><HR>";
   print &PrintEnv();

   # finish HTML page
   print &HtmlBot;
}
```

The cgi-lib.pl library is included into the application. The first library function call is to **ReadParse** to read in the form fields and parse them into name-value pairs and store these pairs into a local variable. Passed into **ReadParse** is a typeglob, a reference to a nontyped variable, which the

ReadParse method then uses to load information passed from the external CGI variables, including the form data. Next, the **PrintHeader** function is called to print out the HTTP request line, and the **HtmlTop** function is called to print out the document head section, and begin the document body.

The next call prints out the form field names and associated value using **PrintVariables**. The input to this function is the typeglob variable reference generated by the **ReadParse** function.

All of the form fields are listed with their respective values, including the hidden field. If no value were supplied for a field, the field would not be included in the printout. The **PrintVariables** function outputs the variables and applies a bold font to the label, and an italic font to the value.

TIP: Hidden fields are a popular technique to use with CGI to maintain an association between a multiple page form application and the Web page reader working through the different pages. An identifier for the reader is generated and then stored in a hidden field with each page.

The next function call in the CGI application is to the cgi-lib function **PrintEnv**, which prints out the CGI environment variables. These variables include the query string that contains the form fields and values, the user agent used to access the form and generate the CGI function call, the location of the form, the remote host, the server port, and a host of information.

The last of the cgi-lib functions are used for error handling. The first is **CgiError** which generates a Web page with an error message, either one passed in as a parameter, or a default one. The second error function is **CgiDie**, which prints out the error message and then terminates the CGI application.

Again, cgi-lib.pl works well with Perl version 5, and is a very simple set of functionality to use when you begin CGI development. Another powerful but simple-to-use tool is CGI.pm, discussed next.

The CGI.pm Object and Methods

Many Internet developers use the CGI.pm module for many of their CGI applications. It is powerful; relatively easy to use, especially if you have had a chance to work with Perl objects; and it simplifies CGI application development. Lincoln Stein wrote and maintains CGI.pm, and the module is now included as part of the standard Perl modules, beginning with version 5.004.

W **EB LINK:** The CGI.pm home page can be seen at **http://www. genome.wi.mit.edu/ftp/pub/software/WWW/cgi_docs.html**. The module is now included as part of the Perl installation, but this site has beta releases, important information, and tips.

19

Chapter 18 provides an excellent introduction to CGI.pm in addition to general CGI and Perl programming. If you haven't had a chance to read this chapter first, you should do so now as the rest of this section assumes you have had the CGI.pm introduction. Reading Chapter 11 Perl is also recommended before working with CGI.pm.

This section will provide an overview of the CGI object methods, and give some examples of how these methods work. To start, you need to create a CGI *query* object. This object can be created using a couple of different techniques. First, creating the object with no parameters will parse input values from a form posting (using either **get** or **post**), and return an object reference, as shown in the following code:

```
$queryObject = new CGI;
```

Another technique creates a query object using an input file:

```
$queryObject = new CGI(FILENAME);
```

Yet another technique creates a query object by passing in name-value pairs, or passing in your own string using URL escape syntax. This technique might be used to create a CGI object with some data after you have formatted it in some way. Creating an empty query object can be accomplished by passing in an empty string or hash. However, for the most part you will use the first technique described, which is passing no parameters so that the CGI object parses the form posting data.

Once you have created the CGI query object, you can process the parsed-in data, add to the data or alter it in some way, and output the results to a new, generated HTML document. To demonstrate some of the methods you can use with CGI.pm, the form used earlier in the chapter that called a CGI application named form.cgi is used for this new example. The cgi-lib application is replaced with one written using CGI.pm. Instead of printing out the CGI environment variables and the form parameters, an HTML header and paragraph are printed, incorporating the form data. The new CGI application is shown in the following code block.

```
use CGI;
my $queryObject = new CGI;

MAIN:
{
  # print HTTP header
  print $queryObject->header;

  # create HTML document header, title
print $queryObject->start_html(-title=>'Example of using CGI',
                     -author=>'Shelley',
                     -BGCOLOR=>'white');
  # print out header with name
  print $queryObject->h1("Hello ", $queryObject->param('name'));

  # print out paragraph
  print $queryObject->p("I hear you like the color ",
                   $queryObject->param('color'));

  # finish document
  print $queryObject->end_html;
}
```

This CGI application used six different CGI methods. The first was to create the query object:

```
My $queryObject = new CGI;
```

The CGI constructor is used that parsed the form data into name-value pairs. Notice that the CGI module is included without importing any symbols into the application's namespace. It could have imported the standard symbols using the "standard" format, as follows:

```
use CGI qw(:standard);
```

Then instead of having to write **print $queryObject->header**, accessing the method through the object, **print header** could be used directly. The reason is that the most commonly used methods are imported into the namespace. However, since this chapter is demonstrating the CGI methods, it is clearer to prefix the method with the object name and the "standard" import technique won't be used.

After creating the CGI query object, the HTTP header line is printed using the method **header**. Next, the HTML head section is created. Unlike with cgi-lib, you have several options you can specify with the method to create the header. You can specify any of the following parameters when calling the HTML starting method, **start_html**:

```
-title=>'some title string'
-author=>'Web page author email'
-base=>'true if base document'
-xbase=>'URL of alternate base document
-meta=>{'copyright'=>'copyright 1997, shelleyp'...}
-style=>{'src'=>'some style sheet'}
-target=>{'main'}
```

Notice that some of the parameters such as the meta parameter can itself contain other parameters. If you specify any other parameter besides the standard ones, as in the example with the -bgcolor parameter specification, this is added to the HTML **body** statement, as is, with no other alteration.

You can also specify scripting blocks using the -script parameter, and using attributes such as -language to specify scripting language, and -src to specify a scripting source file. You could also pass in an entire scripting block by using the -code parameter. However, this could get clumsy and the src attribute is a better option.

Once you have created the HTML head section, you can now use one of several methods to fill in the body of the document. In the very simple example, an H1 header element is created and included a welcome message incorporating the value from the name field passed in from the form. A paragraph element is also created and includes a mention of which color the Web page reader had chosen as their preferred color. Notice that in both methods calls—"h1" for the header and "p" for the paragraph—multiple parameters are passed in:

```
print $queryObject->h1("Hello ", $queryObject->param('name'));
print $queryObject->p("I hear you like the color ",
                    $queryObject->param('color'));
```

The CGI query object will concatenate all parameters passed into the method for these functions. The form-posted data is accessed by passing the form field name into the **param** method, which then returns the associated value for that name. Again, when including the CGI module, the example could also have included an HTML element shortcut that could print out the header and paragraph using the following:

```
print h1("Hello ", $queryObject->param('name'));
print p("I hear you like the color ",
                    $queryObject->param('color'));
```

To use these HTML element shortcuts in the application, you need to use the following line of code:

```
use CGI shortcuts;
```

At the end of the CGI application, the HTML document is closed using the method **end_html**, which prints out the closing BODY and HTML tags.

Incorporating Style into a CGI Application

One attribute not used with the **start_html** statement is the use of the -style attribute. With this a Cascading Style Sheet (CSS1) style-sheet definition can be linked in, which applies automatically to all the specified HTML elements. Style sheets are the W3C recommended technique to apply presentation characteristics to HTML document elements.

WEB LINK: The specification for CSS1 can be read at the W3C home page at **http://www.w3.org/**. Other specifications such as that for HTML can also be found at this site.

Styles can be included using several different technique. A sample application is created next that demonstrates all of them. This CGI application is shown in the following code block.

```
use CGI qw/:standard :html3/;

my $queryObject = new CGI;
```

```
MAIN:
{
  $instyle<<STYLEEND;
  <!--
  H1.header { color: red;
      background.color: black;
      font-style: sans-serif }
  -->
  STYLEEND

  # print HTTP header
  print $queryObject->header;

  # create HTML document header, with linked
  # style sheet, and incode style sheet
  print $queryObject->start_html(-title=>'Example of using CGI',
                  -author=>'Shelley',
                  -style=>{-src=>'http://www.company.com/css/co.css',
                  -code=>$instyle});
  # use styles to alter element presentation
  print $queryObject->h1({class=>'header1'},"Welcome ",
$queryObject->param('name'));

  print $queryObject->p({-style=>'background-color: red'},
                  "Example of using inline "),
      $queryObject->span({-style=>'color:yellow'},"style");

# finish document
  print $queryObject->end_html;
}
```

The -style parameter is added to the **start_html** method. The first technique demonstrated in the code creates a variable to hold a style-sheet definition that is then added in using the -code attribute of the style heading parameter. This forms a style-sheet block in the header of the HTML document:

```
<STYLE type="text/css">
<!--
    H1.header { color: red;
                background.color: black;
                font-style: sans-serif }
-->
</STYLE>
```

The second technique is to use a linked-in external style sheet file, which is specified using the -src- attribute of the style heading parameter:

```
<LINK REL=STYLESHEET TYPE="text/css"
HREF="http://www.company.com/css/co.css">
```

The third technique is to use a style-sheet class name for one of the HTML elements, in this case an H1 header. The style used is the style-sheet definition added to the document with the -code attribute:

```
<H1 class='header1'>Welcome ...</H1>
```

Next, an inline style sheet is used with two elements, a paragraph element, and a span element. To support the span HTML element, an import is also added to the **include** statement for the module. The style sheet for the paragraph sets the background color to red, and the span element with its associated style sets the one word enclosed with the span element to a yellow color font.

The CGI module includes support for most, if not all, standard HTML elements. You can find out which elements are supported by performing a search for the element tag name in the module code.

Adding Form Elements

The elements demonstrated at this time have been nonform elements such as paragraphs and headers. The CGI module also has several methods defined specifically to create HTML form elements such as a text field, button, password field, radio buttons, and the other elements.

What better way to demonstrate the use of the form elements than to re-create the form used earlier in the chapter that called the original versions of form.cgi. The example includes the CGI application that re-creates this form in the following block of code. The application can then be accessed directly from the browser location field.

```
use CGI;

my $queryObject = new CGI;

MAIN:
{
```

```
# print HTTP header
print $queryObject->header;

# create HTML document header, with linked
# style sheet, and incode style sheet
print $queryObject->start_html(-title=>'Example of using CGI',
                               -author=>'Shelley');

# start form
print $queryObject->startform(-method=>"GET",
                              -action=>"http://www.yasd.com/book
bin/form.cgi");
print "What is your name:";
print $queryObject->textfield(-name=>'name');
print $queryObject->p();

print "What is your email:";
print $queryObject->textfield(-name=>'email');

print $queryObject->hidden(-name=>'hidden_field',
                  -default=>'CGIAPP');
print $queryObject->p();

print $queryObject->radio_group(-name=>'color',
      -values=>['blue','red']);
print $queryObject->p();

print $queryObject->submit(-value=>"Submit Form");

# finish document
print $queryObject->end_html;
}
```

19

In the code, the first method called is **startform**, which takes parameters of form data encoding type, form posting method type, and form action. The defaults are accepted for encoding, which is **application/x-www-form-urlencoded**, and the defaults for posting method, which is **get**, so the form did not pass in these two parameters After the form is started, the code adds two text fields to input the Web page reader's name and email. These fields are created using the **textfield** method, and passing in the field name. Parameters could also be used to define the visible field length and the allowed number of characters, as well as a default value. However, to match the original HTML form, none of the textfield attributes were used. In the code, each textfield is preceded with a label and followed with an empty parameter method call, adding white space between the form input elements.

After the textfield form elements, the code creates the hidden field. Again, this type of form element won't show visually, but the value of the field will be passed with the other form data. The example uses the CGI method **hidden** to create this field, and passes in the name and default value parameters.

The next form element is the radio button group, and this is created with the use of the **radio_group** method. For this method, the example passed is the group name and a list of values, each of which becomes a separate button. No default button is specified for the group, so the first radio button will be selected. Also, the example doesn't pass in an associative array of labels, and the labels then become identical to the button values. In this case the two values are "red" and "blue" and the labels show as the same.

This section quickly demonstrated some of the methods you can use with CGI.pm. There are other methods, such as those that support frames. However, this section demonstrated how important CGI.pm is for any form of CGI development. The next section discusses the use of the LWP modules.

An Overview of the LWP objects

LWP is the lib-www Perl module (or modules), written by Gisle Aas, and which has objects to handle most Web-based protocols and activities. Its primary focus seems to be on handling Web client activities, such as HTTP, FTP, news, mail, file transfer, and other client-based services.

WEB LINK: The home site for the LWP modules can be found at **http://www.linpro.no/lwp**. This site maintains information about the most recent release of the modules, any known problems, and a listing of applications that have been created using LWP.

Based on the HTTP protocol, the LWP modules are request-response based, with a request being sent to a Web server and a response being returned from a Web server. As with other Web clients, such as browsers, there is no state maintained between the requests, or between the responses. To maintain this state, Netscape or HTTP style cookies need to be maintained, or information needs to be embedded within the request data that ties it into other requests.

An example of this is the use of hidden fields with Web page forms, discussed in the section on CGI.pm.

The LWP is made up of several objects, and the documentation included with the LWP module provides an overview of each of the objects. This is a help in understanding which object relates to what other object, considering that LWP is not one module but many, with some of them dependent on others. When you are finished reading this chapter and want to do some work with LWP, you should consider reading the LWP documentation (in a file called LWP.html), included with the installation. This not only provides a more in-depth overview of the different LWP classes, but also shows the class inheritance more clearly than is possible here.

How the LWP modules work can be relatively uncomplicated. To begin most client-based transactions, you can create a Request object using the class HTTP::Request. Attributes sent to the object constructor include the HTTP method, such as **post** or **get**, the URL of the document being accessed, headers with key-value pairs containing information to pass during the request, and a content attribute to include any data, no specified format. To create a Request object, use syntax similar to the following:

```
use LWP::UserAgent;

my $req = new HTTP::Request 'GET','http://www.yasd.com/index.htm';
```

This example also includes incorporating the UserAgent class code with the *use* operator. The UserAgent class is discussed further on.

The example creates a Request object using the **post** method and passes in the URL of the document being requested. After the object is created, methods such as **content** and **content_type** can be used to alter object properties, such as the type of document being transmitted for **content_type** and the form data for content.

In order to access the response to the request, you will also need to create a *UserAgent* object. This object handles the actual communication between the client and the server, in addition to any error handling. The *UserAgent* object has several different attributes such as "agent", which is how the *UserAgent* identifies itself; a "timeout" property to specify a timeout if no response is returned within a specified time period; and a "from" attribute that can include an email address of the person creating the request.

To actually get a response from the server, you send the Request object as a parameter to the **request** method for the *UserAgent* object. The **request** method then returns a new *Response* object. To demonstrate this, the following code block creates and uses these three objects to create a request and listen for a response.

```
use LWP::UserAgent;
$useragnt = new LWP::UserAgent;

my $reqst = new HTTP::Request POST => 'http://www.yasd.com/index.htm';
$reqst->content_type('application/x-www-form-urlencoded');

my $reslt = $useragnt->request($reqst);
```

Once the result is obtained, it can be checked to see if the request was successful, using the method **is_success**. Then the application can process the returned content, accessible by the "content" property of the *Response* object.

One possible way to parse the content is to parse the HTML using the HTML::Parser class, another module that is included with the full bundle LWP set. The parsed results can then be used by other classes, such as the HTML::TreeBuilder class.

The HTML::TreeBuilder class can actually build an HTML syntax tree out of the returned result. Once the syntax tree is built, you can access specific elements, or nodes as it were, or you can print a formatted output of the tree using HTML::Formatter class. An object created with the Formatter class can in turn print out the tree in either text format, using the class HTML::FormatText, or postscript format, using the class HTML::FormatPS.

If you aren't requesting an HTML document, you can post or access an article from a newsgroup by using the same Request object, but using the **get** method to access an article and the **post** method to post one. Be careful with your newsgroup URL, or you might have messages popping up where you don't want them, or in too many places.

To perform a simple document retrieval, you might want to use the LWP::Simple module, and the **get** method to retrieve the document. This type of document retrieval reduces this portion of your script to just a few lines of code:

```
use LWP::Simple;
my $doc = get 'http://www.yasd.com/index.htm';
```

Another use of LWP is the situation where you need to work through a proxy. The *UserAgent* object has the **proxy** method, to which you can pass the URL of the proxy server:

```
$useragnt->proxy(ftp => 'http://proxy.yourcom.com/');
```

Additionally, you can access a socket directly using the Socket object, or construct a Uniform Resource Locator with the *URI::URL* object.

One of the first original uses of LWP was to create the well-known MOMSpider. A spider, or robot, is an autonomous agent that traverses the Internet collecting and returning certain information. Commercial search engines such as WebCrawler use a robot to find the links that you access when you use the WebCrawler service to find Web sites based on a query with specified keywords.

19

Some other Internet Libraries and Modules

From any CPAN site you can access the modules subdirectory, and from there access the by-category subdirectory. This contains a listing of subdirectories for modules by category, such as "Networking Devices" and the "World_ Wide_Web_HTML_HTTP_CGI", both of which will interest you if you want to use Perl for Internet and Web applications. The second category just mentioned contains the modules and libraries discussed in this chapter, and others.

WEB LINK: You can access the closest CPAN Web site to you by using the "Nearest CPAN Site" application available at the Perl home page at **http://www.perl.com**.

Among the modules found is one that contains an object, Netscape::History, that allows you access to the history file that Netscape creates. You can go through the URLS of the history list and even delete entries. Another Netscape-specific module does the same with Netscape cache, with an object appropriately named *History::Cache*.

If your Web is run with an Apache Web server, as many are, you will be interested in the Apache modules. One of particular interest is

HTML::Embperl, which allows you to embed Perl into an HTML document as server-side script, and have that script processed by the server before the document is sent to the client. With this you can access a database on the server and send database data back directly within the Web page. The script can be accessed as a CGI application or as mod_perl, or Perl module directly off the server.

The mod_perl is the Apache/Perl Integration project, and you can access information about this effort, and what modules support the integration, from the most recent mod_perl readme.

WEB LINK: At this time, the most recent perl_mod module and readme can be accessed at **http://www.perl.com/CPAN-local/ modules/by-category/15_World_Wide_Web_HTML_HTTP_CGI/ Apache**.

The advantage of having a Perl application run directly as an extension of a Web server is that there is no overhead to wait for the CGI startup process, and there is no need to begin a thread for each CGI request. The module processes are already running, a savings in both time and resources. However, the disadvantage is that a poorly written perl_mod application can have adverse impact on your server's performance.

Server-side scripting with Perl is also supported with other Web servers such as Microsoft's Internet Information Server. You should check the documentation with your server to see what forms of server-side scripting it supports, or if it supports server extensions created in Perl.

As mentioned in the last section about Web robots, the category subtitled "WWW" contains a module with a class called WWW:Search that provides an API for search engines. If you are interested in any in-depth search engine development for your Web site, you should take a look at this module.

The category labeled "FCGI" is for FastCGI module FCGI. FastCGI is CGI extensions that enable CGI applications to run faster and perform more efficiently. One downside to CGI applications is that there is concern about the drag CGI applications have on a Web server machine. FastCGI hopes to begin eliminating some of the problems associated with CGI applications.

WEB LINK: To learn more about FastCGI, visit the FastCGI Web site at **http://www.fastcgi.com/**.

There are other terrific modules you can access directly from CPAN; you should check them out after you have had a chance to work with some of the modules and libraries covered in this chapter and the rest of this book.

Internet-based Utilities and Web Sites   19

If you are new to Perl and just starting to explore its uses for your Web site, spend some time looking at the many freeware and shareware Perl applications you can copy, and in most cases modify, for your own needs. Not only will this save you time by providing the application you need, it's also a great way to learn how to use some of the modules and libraries discussed in this chapter.

Utility and Application Types

One popular script is a password or authentication script. This type of script checks a password against the name in a special password file, and only permits the person who submitted the information to the script to enter the Web page being accessed if the name and password match.

Search engines are other popular utilities, and most sites now have some form of search capability on their documents.

Probably one of the most common Perl/CGI applications is the guestbook, whereby the person accessing the site signs the virtual guestbook, which the site Web master and others can then read at a later time. The information from the guestbook application is usually stored in some persistent manner.

Another very popular utility is the visitor counter. This result of this application is usually included in a Web page using Server Side Includes (SSI). SSI is a technique to include a separate HTML document or CGI application directly into an HTML document. The document is given a special extension, usually .shtml or .stm, that acts as a signal to the Web server to open the document and parse it for commands before sending the document to the client. An example of including a CGI application could be:

```
<!--#include file="book-bin/counter.cgi" -->
```

 TIP: The visitor counter was popular for a time, but is rarely used with new sites. Most people just aren't interested in how many people have been to the page before. However, if you want to track your visitor count to a page, you can include a nonprinting version of the counter that maintains a persistent count of the visitors that you can then access from a file or a password-protected Web page.

A banner generator is an application that can alter the ad images that show in a banner in a page. However, you can use it anytime you want to add an animated image to your page without using the newer dynamic HTML technologies. This type of application uses what is known as "server-push" technology. A connection is made between the page and the server, and the server literally "pushes" new content to the page at specified times.

Mailforms, or mailers, or mailto applications, are also popular. With these the Web page visitor fills in a form, which is then sent to a CGI application, which pulls out the form information and emails the information to the e-mail recipient.

Online shopping, shopping cart, or Web store applications are probably the most common method for online shopping still used, regardless of all the new commerce technologies. Shopping applications use a combination of static and CGI-generated forms to "follow" shoppers as they peruse online store Web pages.

The Utility and Application Web Sites

To find and download these Perl utilities and applications, you should check out some of the many sites that provide them.

A favorite CGI site is the Selena Sol's Public Domain CGI Script Archive, located at **http://selena.mcp.com/Scripts/**. This site has scripts Selena Sol and Gunther Birzniek have been creating over the years, plus scripts and utilities donated by other CGI developers. Though some of the scripts are in other programming languages such as C or C++, most are in Perl. There is also a page with links to other helpful sites.

Another excellent resource site is CGI Scripts to Go, located at **http://www.virtualville.com/library/scripts.html**. This site has an excellent classification system, and it's easy to find more than one script of the type you are looking for. All the scripts at this site are in Perl.

Probably the best-known script site is Matt's Script Archive. You cannot work with Perl and the Internet for very long without coming across a reference to this Web site, which offers scripts to handle HTTP cookies, guestbooks, form mail, counters, animation, and almost any topic of interest. The scripts are nicely and attractively organized and are probably the most "tested" scripts in the world. Why? Because they are used at so many sites. Matt's site can be found at **http://www.worldwidemart.com/scripts/**.

19

The CGI Resource doesn't necessarily have scripts to download. It only has links to about 180 sites on CGI and Perl. If you can't find what you are looking for at the other sites mentioned in this section, check out the links from this site. It can be reached at **http://www.cgi-resources.com/**.

Summary

Even though Perl has been around since long before the World Wide Web was first spun, Perl's reputation is based in large part on its role in Internet and World Wide Web programming. This chapter has introduced to you to ways you can use Perl for creating interactive Web content. However, CGI programming in Perl has been criticized as slow and inefficient. As this book goes to press, the ActiveState company is working on ways to more closely tie Perl to the Web server in order to speed up CGI processes. If they can achieve this, critics of Perl and CGI will have to reevaluate their arguments.

CHAPTER 20

An Introduction to Web Programming with PerlScript

There is little doubt that Perl is the favorite scripting language for server-side Web programming. An estimated 80 to 90 percent of all dynamic Web pages are generated by Perl. But what about scripting on the client side, for those Web pages that need to display dynamic content without the back-end processing of writing to a file or accessing data in a database?

For client-side Web programming, the Perl solution is a scripting variation of the language called PerlScript. PerlScript is an ActiveX scripting engine that allows you to write code for both Web servers and Web browsers. PerlScript is a product of ActiveState, the developers of a popular Win32 version of Perl. You can download the current version of PerlScript for Windows NT or Windows 95 from their Web site at **http://www.activestate.com**.

Why Use PerlScript?

Using a language such as PerlScript makes it possible to programmatically control the content of your Web pages. It is also possible to use PerlScript to access the Web browser itself. The following sections describe how PerlScript can be used to enhance your Web pages and their content. It needs to be noted here that as of this writing PerlScript only works with the Microsoft Internet Explorer family of Web browsers, so the examples in this chapter will probably not work with Netscape or other browsers.

Working with HTML Objects

An HMTL object is just the typical display object (such as an input box) found in many Web pages. A common use of HTML objects is the input form, with the guestbook being the most frequently seen use of the input form. These types of forms can be easily created using strictly HTML tags, but if you want to display information in a form using HTML, it will have to be hard-coded into the form.

PerlScript, on the other hand, can be used to display real-time data in an HTML object. You sometimes see Web sites that can display your IP address on their form. PerlScript can be used to do this by having it grab the user's Environment Address variable that holds their IP address. Of course, an example like this can also be coded on the server side, but handing off some of the processing to the client side helps distribute the load and can give a hit-heavy Web server a break.

Working with the Browser Object

Using PerlScript, the *Browser* object and its many properties are exposed for access by your scripts. This means that most of the browser's features, such as the title bar and the history list, can be controlled by PerlScript. You can change the look of the browser window by controlling the handling of window features such as frames.

The MSIE Scripting Object Hierarchy

The browser, as an object, is also made up of several objects that you need to be aware of when you write your own PerlScript scripts. The following sections will outline the major objects found in PerlScript.

The Window Object

The *Window* object is the main object of the Web browser, and the one from which all other objects are derived. This object has one event, *OnLoad*, that allows you to run a script when the Web page containing the script is loaded into the browser.

The *Window* object has three methods you can call:

◆ **Alert**   Displays a message box with one OK button

◆ **Status**   Displays a text string in the status area at the bottom of the browser

◆ **Open**   Opens a new *Window* object

In the following example, the *window* object is identified by the variable called $window. This example shows you how the **alert** method is called:

```
<html>
<head>
<script language = "PerlScript">
$window->alert("Danger Will Robinson!");
</script>
</head>
</html>
```

This code creates the Web page shown in Figure 20-1.

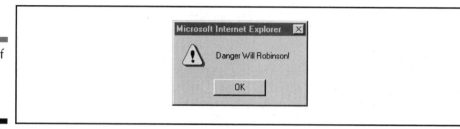

The Frame Object

The *Frame* object allows you to work with frames within a window. Because there can be more than one frame in a window, the *Frame* object is actually an object array. Frames can be referenced in your scripts using either the frame name or its array reference from the *Frame* object. For example, if you have two frames named topFrame and botFrame, they can be referenced either by those names or by *Frames(0)* and *Frames(1)*, depending on the order in which the frames were defined.

The Document Object

The *Document* object refers to the actual Web page you are working with. When you are displaying text on a Web page from within a script, you will reference the *Document* object. For example, the line of PerlScript that prints a greeting on a Web page looks like this (this example is explored in more detail below):

```
$window->document->write("Hello, world!");
```

You can use the *Document* object to create new Web pages from the script embedded in an existing Web page.

The Form Object

The *Form* object is also an object array, since you can have more than one form on a Web page. As with the *Frames* object, the *Form* object array starts at element 0. The *Form* object is what you will use to create user input forms and scripts that can automatically validate the forms before they are submitted to the server.

The Element Object

This object is actually a collection of the different controls, or widgets, that are placed on a form on a Web page. These controls include text boxes, command buttons, combo boxes, etc. The *Element* object is also an object array.

It is possible to reference every control on a form by simply referencing its place in the element array. However, as you will see later, each control also has a name, and it is much easier to reference a control by its name.

Working with Multiple Documents

PerlScript can be used to reference values from one loaded document in another currently loaded document. This scenario can occur when you have a Web page that contains two frames, with Document A loaded into the first frame and Document B loaded into the other frame. You can use PerlScript to take data from Document A and put it in Document B, or you can place controls on Document A that will be used to control the objects of Document B.

20

Creating New Web Pages at Run Time

One of the biggest advantages of using PerlScript is the ability to create a new Web page at run time, while the user is interacting with the Web site. For example, if a user provides the necessary input, you can create a Web page customized for that person using only PerlScript to create the content.

Processing User Input

Like a regular programming language, PerlScript allows you to create variables and store data gathered interactively from the user in those variables. A common use of this feature is to check user input on a form to be sure it meets certain criteria. In addition to simply validating user input, PerlScript can also perform a full range of mathematical operations and functions on data entered by the user. This cannot be done with HTML.

Working with ActiveX Controls

Since PerlScript is an ActiveX scripting engine, you can use it to both create ActiveX controls for Web pages and interact with other ActiveX controls place on a Web page. Using this feature, you can create Web pages that have the look and feel of Windows.

A Short Client-side Scripting Lesson

Before you dive into some PerlScript examples, you might need to brush up on how a client-side script is embedded in a Web page. When you are creating server-side scripts in Perl, a tag from the Web page calls a Perl program residing on the Web server; when you want to create dynamic Web content from the client side, you have to embed the script in the Web pages' HTML code.

The following example creating a Web page that displays the classic "Hello, world!" message will make this clear. Here is the code followed by a description of how it works:

```
<html>
<head>
<title> PerlScript "Hello, world!" Example</title>
<script language = "PerlScript">
sub DisplayMessage {
    $window->document->write("Hello, world!");
}
</script>
</head>
<body>
<script>
DisplayMessage();
</script>
<p>Generated by PerlScript.
<p>
</body>
</html>
```

The first three lines of the script are standard HTML. The fourth line tells the browser that the scripting language being used is PerlScript. The next three lines are a PerlScript function definition called **DisplayMessage**. The middle line of the function does all the work, calling the **write** method of the *Window-Document* object and telling the method to display the line "Hello, world". The next two lines after the function definition close the SCRIPT and HEAD tags.

After the HEAD tag is closed, the BODY tag is called. All PerlScript functions are declared in the heading section of a Web page and they are called in the body section. The tag <SCRIPT> tells the browser that it is to process the code that follows. The function is called next, just as you would call any Perl function. Since there is only one function used in this example, </SCRIPT> is called next to close the script. Finally, a simple line of HTML is displayed ("Generated by PerlScript") and the Web page is closed by calling </BODY> and </HTML>.

The Web page that results from this example is shown in Figure 20-2.

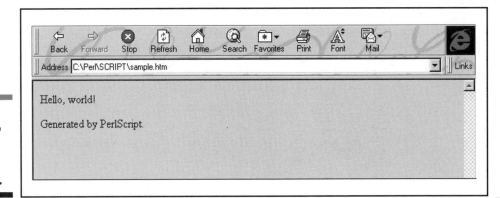

A "Hello,
World!" Web
page created
by PerlScript
Figure 20-2.

Getting a Little More Complex

Just generating text, even if it is by calling a PerlScript function, isn't exactly
"rocket science" client-side scripting. However, you can't just launch into an
online order form, so the following example will show you how to add buttons
and text boxes to a Web page.

Adding a Text Box and an Input Button to a Web Page

Adding screen widgets such as text boxes and input buttons to a Web page
is done using standard HTML and doesn't require the use of any scripting
language. For those of you who don't know HTML, here's how to create
widgets using HTML.

First, widgets and other Web page objects can't just be added to a Web page.
You must designate the area they are to be placed in on the Web page as a
form. You do this by using the form HTML tag. This tag will contain all the
widgets you use on a Web page. The FORM tag looks like this:

```
<form action = " " name = "Widgets">
```

The *action* property is usually set as an empty string because no real action is
being performed by the form. The *name* property is set because our scripts
will need to reference the form name to use its properties.

Widgets, whether they are text boxes or input buttons, are considered
"input" objects in HTML. This is because these objects are normally placed on

a Web page to collect input from the user. When a widget is placed on a Web page, you have to identify its type, its name, and other properties depending on the type of widget it is. The following line of code defines a text box widget:

```
<input type = "text" size = "70" name = "InputString">
```

This line of HTML is called an input tag. The first property that is set is the *type*, which is set to "text", to designate a text box. The second property, *size*, is set to "70", which determines the length of the text box.

The last property, *name*, gives the input box a name, which you will need to reference in a script. Adding this line to the other HTML necessary to create a Web page gives you the following, which adds a text box to a blank Web page:

```
<html>
<head>
<title>Creating text boxes and input buttons</title>
<body>
<form action = " " name = "Widgets">
<input type = "text" size = "70" name = "InputString">
<p>Text box for gathering user input<p>
</form>
</body>
</html>
```

The text box generated by this code is displayed in Figure 20-3.

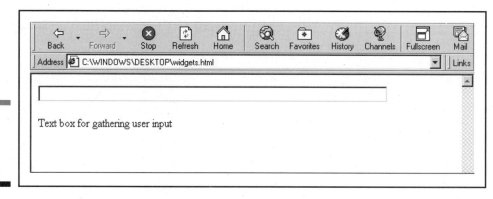

A text box
created with
HTML

Figure 20-3.

The next thing to create is an input button. The same type of HTML tag is used, you just need to change the object type from "text" to "button" and add a caption for the button. Here is the HTML tag to create an input button:

```
<input type = "button" name = "DisplayText" value = "Display Text Below">
```

You can add this tag to the code above to position an input button below the text box, like this:

```
<html>
<head>
<title>Creating text boxes and input buttons</title>
<body>
<form action = " " name = "Widgets">
<input type = "text" size = "70" name = "InputString">
<p>
<input type = "button" name = "DisplayText" value = "Display Text Below">
</form>
</body>
</html>
```

The Web page generated from this code is shown in Figure 20-4.

Connecting the Widgets with a Script

Now that you understand how to put widgets on a Web page to create a user input form, you need to know how to make the form do something. A simple task to start with is to program the input button to display the text typed into the text box.

Widgets on a Web page react to events initiated by the user. For example, to get an input button to do something, you have to write a script that is run

Including an
input button
with the text
box

Figure 20-4.

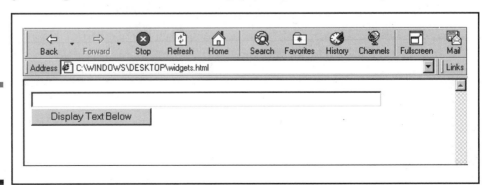

when the button's *onClick* event occurs. Each widget has a set of events you can write code within. The last section of this chapter lists the different events you can program in PerlScript.

To get the input button in our little example to display text entered by the user, you have to create a function that performs the task when the input button is clicked. The function simply takes the text in the text box and displays it below the input button in another text box. Here is the PerlScript function to do this:

```
sub Widgets::DisplayText_onClick() {
    $text = $Widgets->InputString->{'Value'};
    $Widgets->OutputString->{'Value'} = $text;
}
```

The first line of the function defines the function by naming it using the name of the button being programmed and the event being programmed for.

The next line takes the value of the first text box, named InputString, and assigns it to the scalar $text. The last line then takes the scalar and assigns it as the value of the other text box, which causes the contents of the scalar to be displayed in the text box.

The function is then added to the HTML code already created to result in the following:

```
<html>
<head>
<title>Creating text boxes and input buttons</title>
<script language = "PerlScript">
sub Widgets::DisplayText_onClick() {
    $text = $Widgets->InputString->{'Value'};
    $Widgets->OutputString->{'Value'} = $text;
}
</script>
<body>
<form action = " " name = "Widgets">
<input type = "text" size = "70" name = "InputString">
<p>
<input type = "button" name = "DisplayText" value = "Display Text Below">
<p>
<input type = "text" size = "70" name = "OutputString">
</form>
</body>
</html>
```

The Web page this script generates is shown in Figure 20-5.

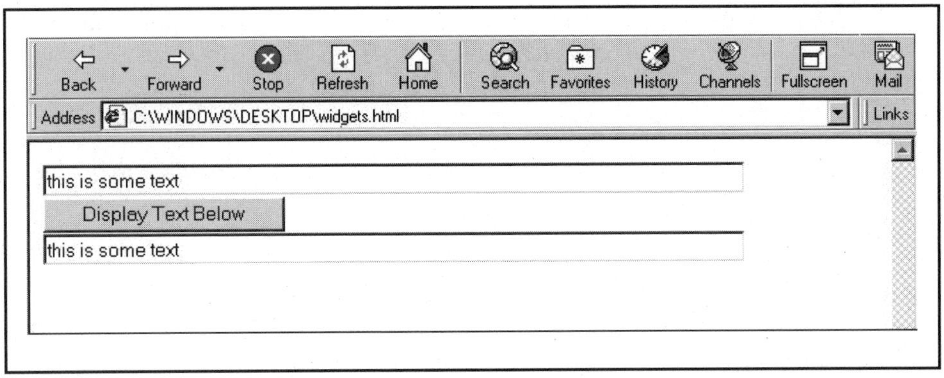

Displaying text in another text box

Figure 20-5.

Adding More Tricks and Controls

You can, of course, use almost all of Perl's functionality with PerlScript. Here is a sample script that, building on the examples above, translates all the text entered by the user in the first text box to uppercase and displays it in the second text:

```
<html>
<head>
<title>Creating text boxes and input buttons</title>
<script language = "PerlScript">
sub Widgets::DisplayText_onClick() {
    $text = $Widgets->InputString->{'Value'};
    $text =~ tr/[a-z]/[A-Z]/;
    $Widgets->OutputString->{'Value'} = $text;
}
</script>
<body>
<form action = " " name = "Widgets">
<input type = "text" size = "70" name = "InputString">
<p>
<input type = "button" name = "DisplayText" value = "Display Text Below">
<p>
<input type = "text" size = "70" name = "OutputString">
</form>
</body>
</html>
```

Figure 20-6 displays the Web page resulting from this script.

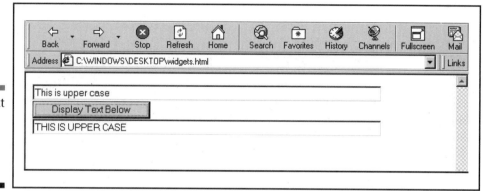

Translating text
from
lowercase to
uppercase

Figure 20-6.

Another common control you find on input forms is a combo box, or
pop-up menu.

Combo boxes can be created in HTML using the Select tag. This tag lets you
create the combo box and provide a list of selections to choose from in the
box. Here's how the HTML for the SELECT tag looks:

```
<select name = "select_option">
    <option selected> Item 1
    <option> Item 2
    <option> Item 3
    <option> Item 4
</select>
```

Now you can look at a simple script that lets you pick from a group of
famous CEOs and prepare their email addresses for a message. Here is
the script followed by an explanation:

```
<html>
<head>
<script language = "PerlScript">
sub Mailer::Convert_onClick() {
    $email = $Mailer->ceo_name->options(0)->{'Text'};
    $email =~ tr/ //d;
    $Mailer->Address->{'Value'} = $email;
}
</script>
</head>
<body>
<h1>Send Email To a Famous CEO</h1>
```

```
<form action = " " name = "Mailer">
<p><strong> Pick a CEO to send email to: </strong>
<select name = "ceo_name">
    <option select> Bill Gates @ microsoft.com
    <option> Larry Ellison @ oracle.com
    <option> Scott McNealy @ sun.com
    <option> Andrew Grove @ intel.com
</select>
<p>
<input type = "button" name = "Convert" value = "Convert name to
                                                email">
<p>
<input type = "text" size = "70" name = "Address">
</form>
</html>
```

20

The bulk of the work of the script is performed in the few lines of the function **Mailer::Convert_onClick**. This function simply takes the value selected from the combo box and removes the spaces, finally displaying the result in the text box. The tricky part is figuring out how to get the text out of the combo box. For situations like this, because the PerlScript documentation is practically nonexistent, you have to use another reference, such as Microsoft's documentation for VBScript. The objects and methods VBScript uses are very close to PerlScript's objects and methods; the main differences are in the syntax differences between Visual Basic and Perl.

The Web page for picking famous CEOs is displayed in Figure 20-7.

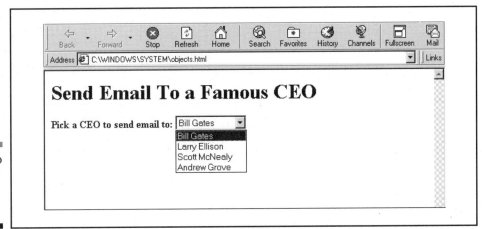

Using a combo box to get user input

Figure 20-7.

Creating Dynamic Web Pages

Now that you understand many of the basics of using PerlScript for working with Web pages, you are ready to see how the language can be used to create new Web pages "on the fly". You can do this without any processing at the server. Before you learn how to build Web pages from the browser itself, you first need to understand how to alter the content of a Web page as it downloads into the browser.

Adding Content at Download Time

You can use PerlScript to change the content of a Web page as it is being downloaded by the browser. A common example of this is a dynamic document footer. The information you can store in a footer can include things like the date and time, the browser that is viewing the Web page, and other variable information.

The following script shows you how to create a footer that can be added to every Web page. This footer accesses several PerlScript variables to list the date the Web page is being viewed and the type of Web browser the user is using. Here is the script:

```
<html>
<head>
</head>
<body>
<center>
<h2>Creating Variable Web Content</h2>
</center>
<p>
<font size = 2>
<blockquote>
<b>
You can add variable content to a Web page by accessing the proper
variables
in your PerlScript script. In this example, the footer information
includes the current date and the type of Web browser viewing the page.
</b>
</blockquote>
<hr>
<center>
<font size = 1>
<script language = "PerlScript">
($sec, $min, $hour, $mday, $mon, $year, $wday, $yday, $isday)
```

```
        = localtime(time);
$mon += 1;
$window->document->write("This page was generated on:
    $mon/$mday/$year.");
$window->document->write("<br>");
$user = $window->Navigator->userAgent;
$window->document->write("You are viewing this page with: $user.");
</script>
</form>
</html>
```

The script section of the code above accesses two variables to get the current
date and the user's Web browser type. To get the date, the script calls the
PerlScript function **localtime**, which is split up to get the month number,
day number, and year. To determine the user's Web browser, the script calls
the *Navigator* object, which has a property—*userAgent*—that contains the user
agent string, such as "Mozilla/4.0 (compatible; MSIE 4.0; Windows 95)".

An example Web page running the HTML code above is shown in
Figure 20-8.

20

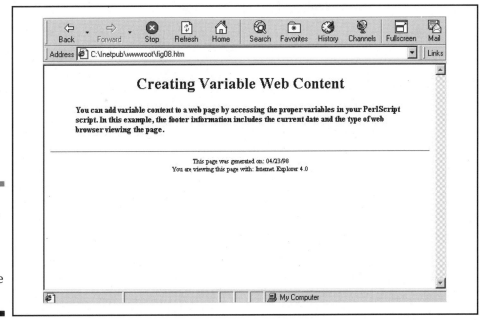

The footer on
this Web page
was created
with variable
data at
download time

Figure 20-8.

Creating New Web Documents "On the Fly"

The discussion above on creating dynamic Web content at download time was just a preliminary step toward the more interesting thing you can do with PerlScript: creating completely new Web documents without storing them on the server.

The key to creating Web documents "on the fly" is using the **open** method of the *Document* object. This method creates a new Web document, making it available to write content to it. The code to create a new document is quite simple:

```
$document->open;
```

Of course, you have to put something on the new Web page, so you will have to call the **write** method, like this:

```
$document->write("A new Web page");
```

With these two methods you can create new Web documents from the browser, perhaps in response to user input. Beware, however, of the fact that when you call the **open** method, the Web document that is currently being viewed will be overwritten by the new Web page.

```
<html>
<head>
</head>
<body>
<center>
<h2>Creating New Web Pages</h2>
</center>
<p>
<form action = " " name = "Dynamo">
Enter your name:
<input type = "text" size = "70" name = "User">
<input type = "button" name = "NewPage" value = "Create New Page">
<script language = "PerlScript">
sub Dynamo::NewPage_onClick() {
    $newpage->document->open;
    $userName = $top->newpage->document->User->{'Value'};
    $newpage->document->write("<html><head><title = 'New Web Page'>")
    $newpage->document->write("</title></head><body><h1>")
    $newpage->document->write("$userName's New Web Page");
```

```
        $newpage->document->write("</h1>");
        ($sec, $min, $hour, $mday, $mon, $year, $wday, $yday, $isday)
            = localtime(time);
        $mon += 1;
        $newpage->document->write("This page was generated on:
            $mon/$mday/$year.");
        $newpage->document->write("<br>");
        $user = $window->Navigator->userAgent;
        $newpage->document->write("You are viewing this page with: $user.");
}
</script>
</form>
</html>
```

The initial Web page is shown in Figure 20-9. The new Web page this code generates is shown in Figure 20-10.

20

Summary

PerlScript is a solution for situations in which you need to be able to perform client-side scripting from the user's Web browsers. Two of the major reasons for wanting to do this are user input validation and creating new Web pages "on the fly". Other scripting languages, such as JavaScript and VBScript, can also be used for client-side scripting. PerlScript, however, is the scripting language of choice if you want to utilize the power of Perl for such scripting.

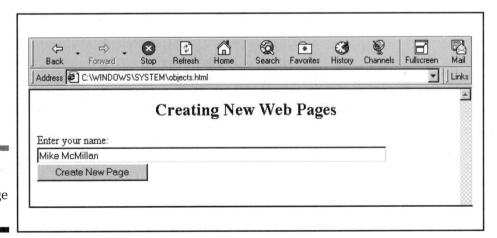

A Web page that creates a new Web page

Figure 20-9.

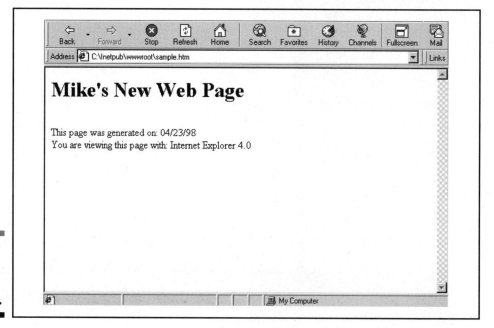

A dynamically
created Web
page
Figure 20-10.

You can download a copy of PerlScript from the ActiveState Corp.'s Web site
(**http://www.activestate.com**). There you will find the latest version of
PerlScript and some PerlScript examples. While you're there, you might also
want to grab the latest version of their Perl for Win32.

CHAPTER 21

The Perl
Standard Library

417

Included in the Perl distribution is a set of programs that extend Perl's functionality: the Perl Standard Library. Each program in the library is called a module. A module is like a C/C++ library file that includes a set of subroutines that perform some particular function. This file is often installed as a separate package so that its variable names and subroutines don't interfere with the objects in your program. A module file is brought into a Perl program at compile time through the **use** directive.

The Perl Library Modules

This chapter presents some of the modules that make up the standard library. The modules presented in this chapter are separated by function into the following categories:

◆   General Programming Modules

◆   File Access and Handling Modules

◆   Text Processing and Screen Interface Modules

◆   Mathematics Modules

◆   Networking and Interprocess Communication Modules

Bringing a Module into Your Program

As was discussed earlier, a Perl module is brought into a Perl program with the **use** directive. Modules are usually added at the beginning of a script, though this isn't a requirement. The following code fragment shows how modules are brought into a script:

```
use Carp;
use strict;
# perl code follows
```

If you are a C/C++ programmer, the **use** directive looks and performs similarly to the **include** directive in C/C++. Of course, they are not exactly the same, but if you want an analogy of the **use** directive in another language, **include** is a good model to use.

The following sections provide examples of the Perl modules, divided into the function categories listed at the beginning of this chapter.

General Programming Modules—Miscellaneous

The modules in this section are used to supplement program development and provide some useful features not found in standard Perl.

The Config Module—Getting Perl Configuration Information

The Config module contains information pertaining to your particular Perl configuration. This information is obtained from the *configure* script that is built into your version of Perl. There are three functions in this module you can use to retrieve configuration information:

◆   **myconfig**   A summary of the major configuration values

◆   **config_sh**   The original config.sh assignment script

◆   **config_vars(@names)**   Returns specific configuration variables

21

The following script shows you how to use the **myconfig** function to return the major configuration values of your Perl environment (the resulting output follows the script):

```
use Config qw(myconfig);
print myconfig();
```

This script produces the following output:

```
Summary of my perl5 (patchlevel 1) configuration:
Platform:
    osname=MSWin32, osver = 3.51, archname=i386-win32
    uname=' '
    hint=recommended
Compiler:
    cc='cl', optimize = ' '
    cppflags= ' '
    ccflags = ' '
    ldflags = ' '
    stdchar = 'char', d_stdstdio=, usevfork=false
    voidflags=15, castflags=0, d_casti32=, d_castneg=
    intsize=4, alignbytes=4, usemymalloc=n, randbits=15
Libraries:
```

```
    so=dll
    libpth=
    libs=
    libc=
Dynamic Linking:
    dlsrc=dl_win32.xs, dlext=pll, d_dlsymun=
    cccdlflags=' ', ccdlflags= ' ', lddlflags= ' '
```

The English Module—Replacing Perl Variables with English

As you have seen throughout this book, Perl has some very strange looking variable names, such as @_, $!, etc. The experienced Perl programmer usually has no problem with using these variables, but for newcomers or the occasional Perl programmer, they can be awfully hard to remember. The English module, when used in your scripts, replaces the cryptic variable names with an English alias. The variables still have the same meaning; they just have a different name.

To use the English aliases, just include the module in your program and start using the alias instead of the variable. Here is an example:

```
use English;
my $a = $ARG[0]; # assigns the first command-line argument to $a
```

The following table lists Perl variables along with their English aliases:

Variable	Alias	Variable	Alias
@_	@ARG	$?	$CHILD_ERROR
$_	$ARG	$!	$OS_ERROR
$&	$MATCH	$!	$ERRNO
$`	$PREMATCH	$@	$EVAL_ERROR
$'	$POSTMATCH	$$	$PROCESS_ID
$+	$LAST_PAREN_MATCH	$$	PID
$.	$INPUT_LINE_NUMBER	$<	$REAL_USER_ID
$.	$NR	$<	$UID

Variable	Alias	Variable	Alias
$/	$INPUT_RECORD_SEPARATOR	$>	$EFFECTIVE_USER_ID
$/	$RS	$>	$EUID
$l	$OUTPUT_AUTOFLUSH	$(	$REAL_GROUP_ID
$,	$OUTPUT_FIELD_SEPARATOR	$(	$GID
$,	$OFS	$)	$EFFECTIVE_GROUP_ID
$\	$OUTPUT_RECORD_SEPARATOR	$)	$EGID
$\	$ORS	$0	$PROGRAM_NAME
$"	$LIST_SEPARATOR	$]	$PERL_VERSION
$;	$SUBSCRIPT_SEPARATOR	$^A	$ACCUMULATOR
$;	$SUBSEP	$^D	$DEBUGGING
$%	$FORMAT_PAGE_NUMBER	$^F	$SYSTEM_FD_MAX
$=	$FORMAT_LINES_PER_PAGE	$^I	$INPLACE_EDIT
$-	$FORMAT_LINES_LEFT	$^P	$PERLDB
$~	$FORMAT_NAME	$^T	$BASETIME
$^	$FORMAT_TOP_NAME	$^W	$WARNING
$:	$FORMAT_LINE_BREAK_CHARACTERS	$^O	$OSNAME

21

The Strict Module—Avoiding Unsafe Programming

The Strict module is used to help you avoid making mistakes in your code. For example, because Perl is a weakly typed language, you can easily make assignments to variables without the variable first being declared (in fact, this process is encouraged for many quick-and-dirty programs). The Strict module forces you to predeclare all variables as well as subroutines. This module also forbids you from using symbolic references.

The following script provides an example of how the Strict module can be used to force good programming practices:

```
use strict;
$foo = 23; # this won't work and will cause the compiler to com-
plain
```

If you want to restrict certain types of "lazy programming" but allow other types, you can import in only the restrictions you want to enforce. For example, the following scripts restricts subroutine use but not variables:

```
use strict 'subs';
$func_out = SomeFunction; # fails because function SomeFunction not
predeclared
$foo = 23; # this is okay because variables aren't restricted
```

The Vars Module—Predeclaring Global Variables

A related module to the Strict module is the Vars module. This module allows you to predeclare global variables that can then be used under the strict module. For example:

```
use strict;
use vars qw($foo @list);
$foo = 23; # this works since it is predeclared as a global
$bar = 32; # this doesn't work
```

General Programming—Files

A lot of programming related to system administration tasks involves working with files. Perl provides several modules in the standard library for working with files. Some of these are described in the next sections.

The Cwd Module—Getting the Current Working Directory Path

This module is useful for determining what the working directory path is currently set to. Of course, knowing the proper path is necessary for working with files. Using the Cwd module, you can check the current directory path before saving a file or trying to read from a file.

This module has just one function, **cwd**. You call it without any arguments, and its return value is the current working directory path. Here is an example of using this module:

```
use Cwd;
$dirpath = cwd(); # dirpath might get something like "c:\perl\bin"
chdir "c:\\"; # be sure to double any backslashes
$dirpath = cwd(); # dirpath now becomes "c:\"
```

The File::Find Module—Finding a File in a Directory

The File::Find module looks for a file from a set of directories you specify and then performs a set of operations you define in a subroutine named **wanted( )**. A simple example will make this clear:

```
use File::Find;
find(\&wanted, 'c:\bin\include', 'd:\bin\include');
sub wanted {
    if (/.h/) { print "$File::Find::name\n"; }
}
```

In this example, the function **find** is taken from the File::Find module to look for files in the subdirectories 'c:\bin\include' and 'd:\bin\include'. The other argument to the function, **\&wanted**, is called so the function will know what operations to perform on the files it searches through in the subdirectories. The subroutine looks for files that have a .h in their extensions, and if it finds one, the file is printed.

The **find** function traverses directory trees using a breadth-first search order. If you want to perform depth-first search instead, use the function **finddepth**.

The File::Path Module—Building and Removing Directories

The File::Path module can be used to either create or remove a directory. If you want to create a directory, you will use the function **mkpath**. If you want to delete a directory, you will use the function **rmtree**. The **mkpath** function takes three arguments:

◆ The name of the path to create or a list of names of paths.

◆ A Boolean value that causes the function to print the names of the directories (defaults to false).

◆ The numeric mode of the directory (defaults to 0777).

The **rmtree** function also takes three arguments:

◆ The root directory to delete or a list of root directories.

◆ A Boolean value that causes the system to print a message each time it comes to a file (defaults to false).

◆ A Boolean value that will cause the function to skip any files you don't have write access to.

Here's a script that creates a new directory:

```
use File::Path;
mkpath('/my/path/');
```

Here's a script that creates several directories:

```
use File::Path;
mkpath(['/a/new/path', '/my/other/path'],1); # this one
            prints messages
```

Finally, here's a script that deletes a path:

```
use File::Path;
rmtree('/a/new/path',1,1); # won't delete it if I don't have write
access
```

Text Processing

Of course, Perl is a language chock-full of built-in functions for text processing. There are, though, certain functions that weren't practical for inclusion as built-ins, and these can be imported through the library. The following sections cover some of the modules you can use for text processing.

The Text::Abbrev Module—Building an Abbreviation Table

This module takes a list of words and builds an abbreviation table by finding all the unambiguous abbreviations for the words in the list. For example, the word "kite", if it is the only word starting with "k" in the list, can have the following abbreviations: "k", "ki", "kit", and "kite". If there is another word starting with "k" in the list, the abbreviation "k" cannot be used. Likewise, if there is another word that starts with "ki", then "ki" for "kite" cannot be used. And so on.

The function within the module that does the work is **abbrev( )**. It takes two arguments: a hash to store the abbreviation table and a list of words. Here is a sample script that shows a simple abbreviation table for four words:

```
use Text::Abbrev;
@words = qw(hello hi grant grieve);
%abbrev_table = (); # set up the hash
abbrev(*abbrev_table, @words); # send the hash as a typeglob
foreach $key (keys %abbrev_table) {
    print "$key-> $abbrev_table{$key}\n"; # print the table
}
```

This script produces the following output:

```
gran-> grant
hel-> hello
hi-> hi
gra-> grant
gri-> grieve
grant-> grant
hello-> hello
he-> hello
griev-> grieve
hell-> hello
grie-> grieve
```

The Text::ParseWords Module— Parsing Lines of Words

This module is used to take lines of words and parse them into individual tokens. The words are broken up based on whatever delimiter you specify to the function (it can even be a regular expression).

The function that does the work in this module is **quotewords**. The function takes three arguments: the delimiter for parsing, a Boolean value that determines whether or not the function will keep the quotes on the words it parses, and the list of lines to parse.

Here's a script that parses three lines of text:

```
use Text::ParseWords;
@old_quotes = ("now is the time for all good people",
               "four score and seven years ago our forefathers",
               "take my wife please");
```

```
@parsed_words = quotewords(" ", 1, @old_quotes);
```

When this script is run, the array @parsed_words will hold "now", "is", "the", "time"..., "four", "score", ..., "take", "my", "wife", "please". If the second argument had been 0 instead of 1, the quotes would have been left off the words in the new array.

The Text::Soundex Module—Creating a Word Hash

This module creates a hash out of a word, or list of words, using an algorithm described by Donald Knuth. The algorithm uses a model that is supposed to approximate the sound of the word when spoken. A hashed word is reduced to a four-character string, the first character being the first letter of the word, and the last three characters being digits. Let's look at a simple example first:

```
use Text::Soundex;
$scode = soundex 'McMillan'; # $scode gets M254
```

You can just as easily hash a whole list of words, like this:

```
use Text::Soundex;
@names = qw(Grant Lee Custer Stewart);
@scodes = soundex @names;
foreach $name (@scodes) {
   print "$name\n";
}
```

This script will produce the following output:

```
L000
C236
S363
```

The Text::Tab Module—Changing Tabs to Spaces and Back

This module is used to expand tabs into spaces and to unexpand spaces into tabs. Tabs and spaces can be at the beginning, in the middle, or at the end of a line.

The two functions of this module, **expand** and **unexpand**, take just one argument: an array of strings. The functions return the strings with their tabs and/or spaces transformed by the function. The following script shows how these two functions work:

```
use Text::Tabs;
$tabstop += 2;
print expand("hello\tworld\n"); # this changes the tab to spaces
print "hello\tworld\n"; # this is a regular tab
print unexpand("hello        world\n"); # this changes the spaces
to a tab
```

This script produces the following output:

```
hello     world
hello   world
hello        world
```

The Text::Wrap Module—Formatting Text Into Paragraphs

This module is used to format text into paragraph. The **wrap** function takes three arguments: a string to prepend to the first line of the text, a string to prepend to each subsequent line of text, and the string itself. You can set a property of the module, the columns property, to the size (in characters) of the paragraph you are formatting.

Here is a script that formats a line of text into a paragraph of 26-character lines:

```
use Text::Wrap;
$ppend1 = "";
$ppend2 = "";
print wrap($ppend1, $ppend2, "Fourscore and seven years ago our fa-
thers
                brought forth on this continent a new nation,
conceived in liberty
                and dedicated to the proposition that all men
are created equal…");
```

This script will print the following text:

```
Fourscore and seven
years ago our fathers
    brought forth on this
continent a new nation,
conceived in liberty
    and dedicated to the
proposition that all men
are created equal…
```

Mathematics Modules

For most calculations, Perl's mathematics functions work just fine. However, there are times when you might need to override these functions, say to perform only integer arithmetic with floating-point numbers. There are several modules that allow you to change how Perl does mathematics; these are described in this section.

The Integer Module—Overriding Doubles

This module is used when you want to perform all mathematical operations in integer mode, regardless of the data type of the number. Most of today's computers can easily handle floating-point numbers, but if you happen to be stuck using a computer without floating-point hardware, this module can come in handy.

Here is a script describing how the integer module works:

```
$x = 11/4; # $x gets the value 2.75
use integer;
$x = 11/4; # $x now gets the value 2
```

You need to be aware that this module doesn't force all mathematical objects to become integers, just arithmetic operations. Here is another script illustrating the difference:

```
use integer;
$x = 11/4; $x gets the value 2
print sin(1); # prints the value 0.841470984807897
The Math::BigFloat Module - Arbitrary-length Floating Point Math
```

This module lets you create and work with floating-point numbers of arbitrary length. The numbers created with this module are also called number strings (NSTR). This module works by creating a floating-point object and then performing the module's operations on the object. The following operations are supported by the module:

◆ fadd(NSTR)   Add NSTR to floating-point object

◆ fsub(NSTR)   Subtract NSTR from floating-point object

◆ fmul(NSTR)   Product of NSTR and floating-point object

◆ fdiv(NSTR)   Quotient of NSTR and floating-point object

◆ fneg( )   Returns negative of floating-point object

◆ fabs( )   Returns absolute value of floating-point object

◆ fcmp(NSTR)   Compares NSTR to floating-point object

◆ fround(SCALE)   Rounds floating-point number to SCALE digits

◆ fnorm( )   Returns the normalization of floating-point object

◆ fsqrt(SCALE)   Returns square root of floating-point object to SCALE places

Here are some examples of doing math with Math::BigFloat:

```
use Math::BigFloat;
$f = Math::BigFloat->new("23.123456789123456789"); # create a new
                                                    # object
$g = $f->fmul(2.5); # BigFloat math yields the value
+57808664197280866419725E-19
$h = $f->fround(10); # $h gets the value 2312345679E-8
```

When you import this module into your program, its operations overload Perl's standard operations, so that when you do regular arithmetic, as in:

```
$g = $f * 2.5;
```

21

the math that is performed uses the *Math::BigFloat* operators.

The Math::BigInt Module—Arbitrary-length Integer Math

This module allows you to perform arithmetic operations on integer numbers of an arbitrary length. Like the Math::BigInt module, this module has a set of operations you can perform on the objects you create with the module. The operations are:

◆ badd(NSTR)   Returns the sum of integer object and NSTR

◆ bsub(NSTR)   Returns the difference of integer object and NSTR

◆ bmul(NSTR)   Returns the product of integer object and NSTR

◆ bdiv(NSTR)   Returns the quotient of integer object and NSTR

◆ bmod(NSTR)   Returns the integer object modulus NSTR

◆ bgcd(NSTR)   Returns the greatest common divisor of integer object and NSTR

◆ bnorm   Returns the normalization of integer object

◆ bneg   Returns the negative of integer object

◆ babs   Returns the absolute value of integer object

◆ bcmp(NSTR)   Compares integer object to NSTR

Here are some examples of using the Math::BigInt module to do arithmetic:

```
use Math::BigInt;
$int = Math::BigInt->new("99912121244444222222");
$g = 23;
print $g * $int; # prints the value +2297978788862217111106
print $int->bnorm; # prints the value -99912121244444222222
```

As you can see from the examples, this module overloads Perl's standard math operators also.

Networking Modules

The standard library provides several modules to help support network programming. These modules include functions for pinging, getting hostnames, and socket programming.

The Net::Ping Module—Pinging a Host

This module implements the *ping* system command to allow you to ping a host from within your Perl program. Net::Ping has just one function, **pingecho**, that has two arguments: the hostname and a timeout for trying to ping the host. The hostname will hold the host you are trying to ping, of course, and the timeout argument holds the length of time (in seconds) to attempt to ping. Here is a script that shows you how to use Net::Ping:

```
use Net::Ping;
$hostname = "perl.com";
$timeout = 50;
if (pingecho($hostname, $timeout) {
    print "perl.com is up.\n"; # prints if perl.com is up
}
```

The $timeout argument is optional and if it is not used, the function will ping for five seconds. Also, instead of using a hostname, you can use an IP address instead, like this:

```
use Net::Ping;
$hostname = "203.22.13.405"; # if this is your IP, sorry
$timeout = 50;
if (pingecho($hostname, $timeout) {
    print "The host at 203.22.13.405 is up.\n"; # prints if IP
                                                 # address is up}
```

21

The Sys::Hostname Module—Getting a Hostname

This module is used to find your system's hostname. The function used, **hostname( )**, simply returns the hostname if it can determine it. If not, the function will complain. Here's an example:

```
use Sys::Hostname;
$myhost = hostname(); # try to get the hostname and store it in a
variable
```

If the function can't determine the hostname, you will get an error message like this: "Can't get host name of local machine at gethost.pl line 2".

The IO::Socket Module—Networking Via Sockets

It is beyond the scope of this book to talk in depth about sockets, but suffice it to say that a socket is simply an interface to the network in much the same way that a filehandle is an interface to the filesystem. Like a filehandle, you open a socket, read from a socket, and write to a socket. Of course, for more advanced network programming this model isn't sufficient, but to illustrate how the IO::Socket module works, it's fine.

Much of the network programming you will probably be doing will involve the Internet. As you may know, the Internet uses a client/server model for networking. For example, when you connect to a Web site using your browser, the Web site is the server and the browser is the client. When you do socket programming, you also use a client/server model. For example, you can write a very simple socket programming that mimics a tiny bit of the functionality of your Web browser. In this section you'll build a simple browser-like program that can request a Web page from a Web server.

The first thing you have to do to create a Perl program that mimics a Web browser is open a socket that will connect to a Web server. The following program fragment imports the IO::Socket module and opens a socket:

```perl
use IO::Socket;
$browser = IO::Socket::INET->new(
   Proto => "tcp" ,
   PeerAddr => "www.osborne.com" ,
   PeerPort => "http(80)" ,
);
```

The first line, of course, imports the module. The second line names the socket "$browser" and begins to create a new socket for that name. The third line sets up the protocol to use as TCP. This is the standard protocol for the Internet. The fourth line sets the address we are going to connect to: **http://www.osborne.com**. An IP address could have been used instead. The fifth line sets the port that the socket is going to connect to: 80. Port 80 is normally used as the Web server port, though another port can be used.

The next section of this program sends some data to the Web server and waits for a result. Here's the code:

```perl
$browser->autoflush(1);
print $browser "GET /about.htm HTTP/1.0\n\n";
```

```
while ( <$browser> ) {
   print;
}
close $browser;
```

The first line of this fragment flushes out the socket. The next line sends the GET command to the Web server, along with the document to get. This line is standard HTTP. The next line sets up a **while** loop that will print data from the socket as long as the server is sending data. Finally, the last line closes the socket.

This simple program will print the contents of the Web page requested, or, if the page requested can't be found, a message like the following will be printed:

```
HTTP/1.0 404 Object Not Found
Content-Type: text/html
<body><h1>HTTP/1.0 404 Object Not Found
</h1></body>
```

With just a little more work (okay, a lot more work) you can write a full-featured Web browser in Perl. You can also write your own FTP and Telnet clients in Perl too if you're big on reinventing the wheel.

21

Summary

The Perl Standard Library extends the power of Perl beyond the language's built-in functions. There is a module for everything from database programming to Internet programming to benchmarking your code. These modules can save you a lot of work because, as you know, the kinds of problems solved by the function in the standard library come up again and again.

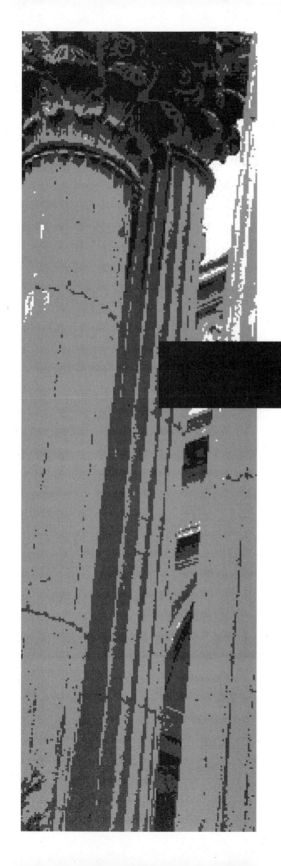

CHAPTER 22

Creating User Interfaces with Perl/Tk

As you have probably noticed by now, the Perl programs you have written so far haven't had a user interface. A major reason for this is because Perl scripts are often part of other programs that do have a user interface, such as CGI scripts where the web is the user interface. Many other Perl programs don't really need a user interface because they're supposed to be launched from the command line and are used more like utilities than full-blown applications.

You can, however, create programs in Perl that give your users a graphical user interface (GUI) that will make your program easier to use. The Perl language doesn't come with its own user interface (or at least not yet), but there is a module, Tk.pm, that will give you access to the Tk toolkit for building graphical user interfaces. This chapter will provide a brief introduction to Tk, provide you with some details on the widgets that are part of the toolkit, and show you how to use these widgets in combination with a Perl program. An important part of this chapter will be to show you how to combine Perl/Tk widgets with Perl code so that when a widget is selected, a command is performed.

A Tk Overview

The Tk toolkit was initially designed to provide a toolkit for building graphical user interfaces in another scripting language, Tcl (tool command language). Tk provides a set of widgets (or controls, in Micro-speak) and commands that you can use to build very powerful GUIs. A widget can be a window, a text box, a list box, a radio button, or any other feature that is normally found in a GUI. Actually, widgets are specialized windows that take different shapes based on what they are used for.

The best way to use Tk with Perl is to get Gurusamy Sarathy's distribution of Perl from CPAN. This version of Perl has the Tk toolkit built in so that all you will have to do is import the Tk module.

Tk's Widgets

Table 22-1 lists the different types of widgets available using Tk.

Widget	Description
button	Creates a command button
checkbutton	Creates a toggle button
radiobutton	One of a set of radio buttons
menubutton	A button that pops open a menu
menu	Creates a menu
canvas	A window for drawing graphics
label	A read-only text label
entry	A one-line text box
message	A read-only multiline text message
listbox	A scrolling text widget
text	An editable text widget
scrollbar	Scrollbar that can link to another widget
scale	A scale widget that can adjust the size of a variable
frame	A container widget for holding other widgets
toplevel	A new top-level window

The Tk
Widgets
Table 22-1.

22

Manipulating Widgets

As you will learn, widgets must be manipulated to be used. Commands have
to be given to widgets to place them on the screen, as well as to get them to
respond to the user's commands. Table 22-2 describes the commands that
you can use to manipulate Tk widgets.

Command	Description
bell	Ring's the terminal bell device
bind	Binds a Perl command to an event
bindtags	Creates binding classes
clipboard	Manipulates the clipboard

The Tk
Commands
Table 22-2.

Command	Description
destroy	Deletes a widget
event	Defines and generates virtual events
focus	Controls the input focus
font	Sets font attributes and measurements
grap	Takes the focus away from other widgets
grid	Places widgets in location on grid
image	Creates and manipulates images
lower	Lowers a window in the stacking order
option	Sets and queries the resources database
pack	Positions a widget in a window
place	Places a widget in a window
raise	Raises a window in the stacking order
selection	Manipulates a selection
send	Sends a Perl command to another application
tk	Queries or sets the application name
tkerror	Handler for background errors
tkwait	Waits for an event
update	Updates the display by going through the event loop
winfo	Queries the state window
wm	Interacts with the window manager

The Tk
Commands
(*continued*)
Table 22-2.

The following sections will explain in great detail how to use many of these commands to create and control your Perl/Tk user interfaces.

Designing and Programming the User Interface

Just in case you've spent the last eight or nine years stuck with character-based applications, this section will explain briefly the event-driven paradigm that controls applications that utilize a GUI.

When you get ready to create a GUI-based application, the first task you will normally perform (after all the analysis, of course) is to design the user interface. If you have experience with a programming language like Visual Basic, you are very familiar with designing a user interface. Interface design in Visual Basic involves dragging and dropping widgets (controls) on a window or set of windows until you have a complete GUI. Using Perl/Tk, however, you cannot drag and drop widgets. You will instead have to program the widgets to place them in a window using one of Tk's geometry managers. The geometry manager is responsible for the layout of the user interface window, and until you've properly programmed the geometry manager, you won't be able to see any widgets on the screen.

Once widgets are placed on a window using a geometry manager, you will have to write some code to get them to respond to the user's commands. These types of applications are called event-driven applications because the program responds only to events initiated by the user. For example, when you hit the Submit button on a Web-based order form, that button's Click event is activated and whatever code is written to respond to the user clicking that button will run.

The overall control of a GUI-based application is run by an **event** loop, which takes over when your application starts. After each widget event is handled, control is passed by to the **event** loop, which mostly just makes sure the application is ready to respond to the next event.

With this basic explanation of GUI-based applications, you now know enough to get started creating your own user interface. In the next section you will create a main window and begin adding widgets to the window to see how easy it is to work with Perl/Tk.

22

Creating a Simple User Interface

Unlike a lot of other code-based user interface systems, creating a simple user interface using Perl/Tk is quite easy. The first step is to learn how to display a window on which you will eventually place widgets to make a user interface.

To create a window and display it on the screen, you have to follow these steps:

1. Import the Tk module
2. Create a main window object
3. Create a title for the main window
4. Display the window

The script that implements these steps isn't much more complex. Here it is:

```
use Tk; # imports the Tk module
$win_main = MainWindow->new(); # creates a window object
$win_main->title ("Main Window"); # creates a title for the
window
MainLoop(); # display the window
```

The window that this script produces is shown here:

The first line of this script imports the Tk module. The second line creates a new *window* object and assigns it to the variable $win_main. The third line sets the title property of the window object to Main Window. This title is displayed in the title bar of the main window.

The only mysterious line of code in this example is the last line: "MainLoop( )";. This command executes the event loop that controls the user interface. If you ran the script without this line, the window would not be displayed. Also, because the command executes as a loop, the only way to close the window is to push the Close button in the upper right-hand corner of the window.

Adding Widgets to a Window

Now that you know how to create a window, the next step is to add a widget to the window. Once a main window is defined, you can define a widget in terms of the main window. This means that the widget you create will be placed somewhere within the main window. The geometry manager you use will determine how the widget is placed; you will determine where.

The simplest geometry manager to use for a basic user interface is **pack**. The **pack** method calculates the proper position, height, and width of the widget based on the controls already on the window. In just a minute you will see how to use the **pack** method.

Adding a Button Widget

The first widget you will learn how to work with is a button. You create a button by calling the **button** method. You can also set properties for the button, like what text is to be displayed on the button, by passing them as arguments to the **button** method. The following script adds to the previous script by adding a button to the window:

```
use Tk;
$win_main = MainWindow->new();
$win_main->title ("Main Window");
$button = $win_main->Button(text => 'OK');
$button->pack();
MainLoop();
```

A button widget is added to the window using the two next-to-last lines in the script. First, a *button* object ($button) is created by calling the **button** method. In the script, the label "OK" is added to the button, which is then placed on the window by the **pack** method. In this example, the method is called without any arguments. Calling **pack** this way leaves it up to the method to determine exactly how to place the widget on the window. Later you will see how you can provide arguments to **pack** to customize a window.

The window that results from this script is shown here:

The reason the window is so small is because **pack** made the window fit around the screen. The following script changes the size of the button, and, subsequently, the size of the screen also (see the following illustration):

```
use Tk;
$win_main = MainWindow->new();
$win_main->title ("Main Window");
$button = $win_main->Button(text => 'OK',
```

22

```
                                    width => 10,
                                    height => 4);
$button->pack();
MainLoop();
```

Now is a good time to mention that, because you're working with a window, you can resize a Perl/Tk window by hand, by dragging one of the sides with your mouse, just as with any other standard window.

The last thing to mention about Tk buttons is that when they have focus, or when you place the mouse over the button, the button becomes highlighted. This is a visual cue that the button currently has focus and pressing the left mouse button will cause the event that is bound to the button to occur.

Adding a Label Widget

The next widget type you will add to the window is a label. A label widget is used to hold text and, naturally, label things. A label widget is added just like a button widget, using many of the same properties, as well as some of its own properties that can customize the look of the button. The following code fragment, once placed with the rest of the previous script, will add a label to the main window:

```
$label = $win_main->Label(text   => 'This label labels a button',
                                    width   => 20,
                                    height => 2);
$label->pack();
```

This code adds a label object ($label) that has text placed in it ("This label labels a button") and has a width of 20 and a height of 2. The following illustration shows the main window when this code is added to the current script.

Notice how the main window has stretched a little wider to accommodate the width of the label. Also notice how **pack** automatically placed the label beneath the button.

There are several ways you can enhance the look of labels. For example, sometimes you will want a label to have a certain type of border around it. One popular border style is *sunken*. To change the border style of a label widget, you specify the relief property. Adding this property to our property list for the label ("relief => 'sunken') will change the label to look like the one shown here:

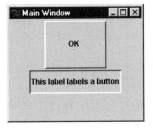

Adding a Text Box

The text box widget is another widget you will have in almost every user interface you design, since you almost always have to gather some sort of free-form input from the user. Like a label widget, text boxes have a width, height, and can have a border style. The following code fragment creates a text box with a *ridge* border style (see the following illustration):

```
$text = $win_main->Text(relief => 'ridge',
                        width  => 30,
                        height => 4);
```

You can insert text into the text box by using the **insert** method. The following code fragment inserts text into the text box created above:

22

```
$text->insert('Some text inserted');
```

If you want to insert text at a specific place in the text box, you can give the method an index of where to insert text. The index is a string that indicates the row and column of where to insert the text and takes the form of a decimal number. For example, if you want to insert some text at line 1 column 4, you would use the index "1.4".

You can also insert text at relative positions in the text box. Three relative positions you will use a lot are *insert* (put text where the insert cursor is), *current* (the character closest to the mouse pointer), and *end* (at the end of the insert cursor's line). The following code fragment inserts some text at the beginning of the text box (see the following illustration):

```
$text->insert('current', 'Some text inserted);
```

Adding a List Box

A list box displays a list of items that is usually presented so the user can pick one or more items from the list. Like a text box, a list box is created by first creating a list box object with its parameters and then inserting the items in a separate line of code. The following code fragment creates a list box for choosing among several automobile brands:

```
$list_box = $win_main->Listbox(width  => 25,
                               height => 5,
                              )->pack();
$list_box->insert("end", "Buick", "Oldsmobile", "Volvo",
"Chevrolet");
```

This code fragment uses a slightly different technique for packing the list box. Instead of putting the **pack** method on a separate line, it is added to the line that creates the list box object. This is just a convenient shorthand notation.

Also, notice in the line that inserts items into the list box that an insertion place is named before the added items. An insertion place (normally "end") is required, and if left out will cause an error.

There are several modes you can use for implementing how the user will pick items from the list box. The list below explains each mode:

◆ **Single**   Only one item can be selected at a time.

◆ **Browse**   Only one item can be selected at a time, but you can drag the mouse over each selection.

◆ **Multiple**   One or more items from the list box can be selected.

◆ **Extended**   One or more items can be selected by dragging the mouse, but a single click will deselect the current selection.

The following illustration displays the main window with a list box (in browse mode) added.

22

Here is the whole script that has been built for displaying the user interface:

```
use Tk;
$win_main = MainWindow->new();
$win_main->title ("Main Window");
$button = $win_main->Button(text   => 'OK',
                            width  => 10,
                            height => 4);
$button->pack();
$label = $win_main->Label(text   => 'This label labels a button',
                          relief => 'sunken',
                          width  => 20,
                          height => 2);
$label->pack();
$text = $win_main->Text(relief => 'ridge',
```

```
                        width  => 30,
                        height => 4);
$text->pack();
$text->insert('current', 'Some text inserted');
$list_box = $win_main->Listbox(width  => 25,
                               height => 5,
                              )->pack();
$list_box->insert("end", "Buick", "Oldsmobile", "Volvo",
"Chevrolet");
MainLoop();
```

Now that you know how to add widgets to a window, the next step is to learn how to place them in the window in some sort of order, not just one after the other, which is the subject of the next section.

Some Other Tk Widgets

While the widgets you've just seen are some of the more common ones you will use when creating user interfaces, there are others you will also find useful. The following sections will cover these other widgets, showing you how to add them to a window.

Radio and Check Buttons

When you want the user to make a single selection out of a range of choices, you can use radio buttons. A *radio button* is a widget that displays a diamond-shaped button along with text beside it. Each radio button has a value and variable associated with it that can change based on which radio button in the group is chosen. In other words, a radio button is synchronized with the other buttons in the group so that when a particular radio button is chosen, only its value property is "on". You do this by providing the radio button group with a synchronizing variable.

The following code creates a main window with a group of radio buttons:

```
use Tk;
$win_main = MainWindow->new();
$win_main->title ("Main Window");
$choice = "printer1";
$printer1 = $win_main->Radiobutton ( variable => \$choice,
                                     text     => "Printer 1",
                                     value    => "printer1");
$printer2 = $win_main->Radiobutton ( variable => \$choice,
                                     text     => "Printer 2",
```

```
                                                value    => "printer2");
$faxdriver = $win_main->Radiobutton ( variable  => \$choice,
                                      text      => "Fax Driver",
                                      value     => "faxdriver");
$printer1->pack(side => 'left');
$printer2->pack(side => 'left');
$faxdriver->pack(side => 'left');
MainLoop();
```

The radio button group created by this code is shown here:

In the code above, the synchronizing variable is $choice. It is initially set to "printer1", and that is the choice that is highlighted when the main window is displayed. Any of the three radio buttons could have been selected.

A variation on the radio button is the check button. A *check button* makes it possible for the user to choose more than one selection. Instead of being diamond-shaped, check buttons are square. The following code creates a group of check buttons (shown in the following illustration):

```
use Tk;
$win_main = MainWindow->new();
$win_main->title ("Main Window");
$printer1 = $win_main->Checkbutton ( variable => \$choice,
                                     text     => "Printer 1",
                                     );
$printer2 = $win_main->Checkbutton ( variable => \$choice,
                                     text     => "Printer 2",
                                     );
$faxdriver = $win_main->Checkbutton ( variable  => \$choice,
                                      text      => "Fax Driver",
                                      );
$printer1->pack(side => 'left');
$printer2->pack(side => 'left');
$faxdriver->pack(side => 'left');
MainLoop();
```

22

The Canvas Widget

The special-purpose canvas widget is normally used for drawing graphics. If you want your user interface to have a place where graphs can be drawn, or some other type of graphics, the canvas widget is the place to do that.

Like any other widget, a canvas is generally placed on a window with a height and a width. After that you will add graphics objects of your own design, as well as some of the widget's built-in graphics objects. Objects that come with the canvas widget include:

◆ Circles

◆ Rectangles

◆ Arcs

◆ Lines

◆ Text

◆ Bitmaps

◆ Polylines

The following example shows you how to draw an oval on the canvas widget. To do so, you simply have to specify that you want to draw an oval object and then give the object its coordinates for where to start drawing and how large to make the oval. Here's the script:

```
use Tk;
$win_main = MainWindow->new();
$win_main->title ("Main Window");
$canvas = $win_main->Canvas(width => 400, height => 250)->pack();
$canvas->create('oval', 100, 10, 150, 80);
MainLoop();
```

This code will create an oblong oval. If you want to create a more "circular" oval that is filled with a color, you can add a line like this:

```
$canvas->create('oval', 10, 10, 80, 80, fill => 'red');
```

You are not limited to oval shapes either. If you'd like to draw a rectangle on the canvas, you can add this line:

```
$canvas->create('rectangle', 170, 10, 250, 40, fill => 'blue');
```

This line will create a black rectangle, as shown with the other shapes created here:

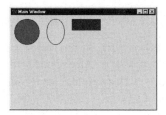

Creating Event Bindings

To make a widget programmatically perform a command, you have to create what is called an *event binding*. This simply means that, for example, when you press a button, some event will occur. A button widget has a command property that you will set so that pressing a button runs a subroutine, causing something to happen.

A simple example of an event binding is displaying text in a label when a button is pushed. The first thing to do is create a window that holds a label and a button. Here is the code to do that:

```
use Tk;
$win_main = MainWindow->new();
$win_main->title ("Main Window");
$label = $win_main->Label(width => 20, height => 2)->pack();
$button = $win_main->Button(text => 'Display Text')->pack();
MainLoop();
```

The next step is to add a command to the button widget. The property for doing this is called *command*. The code fragment that creates a command looks like this:

```
command => \&display_text
```

This line simply says that when the button is pushed, the command to run is a function called **&display_text**. The function is called through a reference, hence the backslash prefacing the subroutine name. Functions called this way are called callback functions.

The function itself is very basic. All that has to be done is simply to reconfigure the label to have text on it. Perl/Tk widgets have a method

22

associated with them called *configure*, which is used to change the properties of a widget. Here's the code for the function:

```perl
sub display_text {
    $label->configure(text => 'Text displayed here');
}
```

That's all there is to it. Here's the complete script for creating a simple **callback** function:

```perl
use Tk;
$win_main = MainWindow->new();
$win_main->title ("Main Window");
$label = $win_main->Label(width => 20, height => 2)->pack();
$button = $win_main->Button(text => 'Display Text',
                            command => \&display_text)->pack();
MainLoop();
sub display_text {
    $label->configure(text => 'Text displayed here');
}
```

When this script is run, the window first looks like the window on the left. Then when you push the "Display Text" button, the label is filled with text as shown in the illustration on the right.

Here's another example, this time using a different method of tying a **callback** function to the event. The method used in this example is called an **event binding**. The **bind** keyword tells Perl: when a certain event occurs, perform a callback function. The events that can be bound include things like double mouse clicks, single mouse clicks, pressing a combination of keys, etc.

The script below creates a binding based on a list box. The list box displays a selection of cars to choose from, just like in the example list box above. When you double-click on one of the selections, your choice is displayed in the label above the list box. Here's the script:

```
use Tk;
$win_main = MainWindow->new();
$win_main->title ("Main Window");
$label = $win_main->Label(relief => 'sunken',
                          width  => 40,
                          height => 2);
$label->pack();
$list_box = $win_main->Listbox(width  => 25,
                               height => 5,
                               )->pack();
$list_box->insert("end", "Buick", "Oldsmobile", "Volvo",
"Chevrolet");
$list_box->bind('<Double-1>', \&car_choice);
sub car_choice {
   my $car = $list_box->get('active');
   if (!$car) {
      return; # no active choice
   }
   $label->configure(text => "You have chosen to purchase a
$car.");
}
MainLoop();
```

22

The event binding occurs in the line:

```
$list_box->bind('<Double-1>', \&car_choice);
```

Here, a double mouse click, designated as <Double-1> (the 1 stands for the left, or first, mouse button), is bound to the callback function **&car_choice**.

The **callback** function then gets the active list box choice with this line of code:

```
my $car = $list_box->get('active');
```

Then the value that is held in the scalar $car is displayed in the label. The following illustration shows the window after a choice has been made:

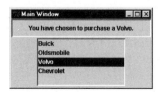

Summary

Perl is often viewed as a character-based language that isn't suitable for creating user-friendly applications. Combining Perl and the Tk toolkit gives you the option of creating a graphical user interface that will make your Perl programs look better and will make your users enjoy using your programs. And if your users enjoy using your programs, they'll use them more and maybe even ask you to create additional programs.

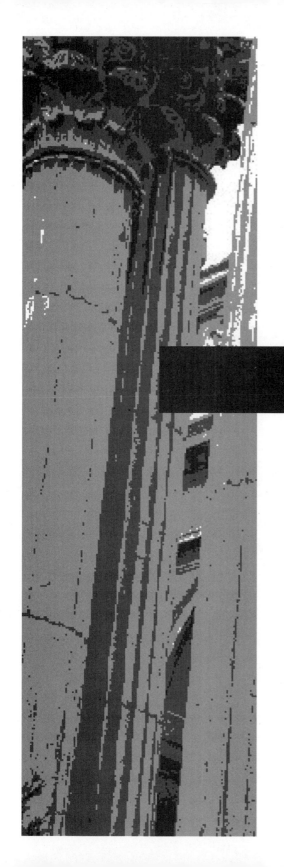

APPENDIX A

Perl
Error Messages

There are seven classifications of error messages that Perl can generate. These classifications are listed in Table A-1.

Error messages that are labeled as optional warnings (W) can be seen if you use the *-w* switch when you run your Perl scripts. You can usually ignore these warnings and still get your script to run properly, but you should at least look over the code that caused the error. Error messages that are labeled as deprecations (D) also do not necessarily mean the demise of your script. Depracations, however, occur because a newer Perl construct has been developed, and you are really encouraged to change your code to match the new Perl form, whatever it may be.

The following section lists all the possible error messages in alphabetical order, followed by their classification, and provides an explanation of what the error message means.

The Perl Error Messages

When you see the string ***** in the error messages below, this means an object from the code in question will replace *****. When you see NNNNN in

Error Class	Meaning
W	An optional warning
D	An optional deprecation
S	A mandatory severe warning
F	A fatal error
P	An internal error (also called a panic)
X	A very fatal error
A	An alien error message indicating an error not generated by Perl

The Perl Error Message Classifications

Table A-1.

the error messages below, this means a numeric object from the code in question will replace NNNNN.

The following abbreviations are also used in the messages below:

◆ **SV** Scalar variable

◆ **HV** Hash variable

◆ **AV** Array variable

Error Message	Meaning
"my" variable ***** can't be in a package (F)	Occurs when you try to declare a lexically scoped variable within a package. To localize a package variable, use local.
"no" not allowed in expression (F)	Perl displays this message when the no keyword is recognized by the compiler but doesn't return a meaningful value.
"use" not allowed in expression (F)	Perl displays this message when the **use** keyword is recognized by the compiler but doesn't return a meaningful value.
***** may only be used in unpack (F)	Appears when you try to pack a string by supplying a checksum value. This causes an error because the checksum process loses information about the string.
***** (. . .) interpreted as function (W)	Perl issues this warning because any list operator followed by parentheses yields a function.
***** argument is not a HASH element (F)	Perl displays this message when the argument is not a hash element.
***** did not return a true value (F)	This message appears when a file loaded with require or use doesn't load properly.
***** found where operator expected (S)	Occurs when the Perl lexer expects an operator but gets something else instead.

A

Error Message	Meaning
***** had compilation errors (F)	This message is displayed as the summary message when Perl -c fails.
***** had too many errors (F)	Issued when the parser gives up trying to parse a program. This occurs after ten tries.
***** matches null string many times (W)	Issued when the pattern you're trying to match will end up in an infinite loop.
***** never introduced (S)	Issued when a symbol goes out of scope before it has been used even though it was introduced.
***** syntax OK (F)	Appears as the summary message when Perl -c is successful.
*****: Command not found (A)	Appears when you try to run your script in **csh** instead of Perl. This error message occurs only in Unix.
*****: Expression syntax (A)	Appears when you try to run your script in **csh** instead of Perl. This error message occurs only in Unix.
*****: Undefined variable (A)	Appears when you try to run your script in **csh** instead of Perl. This error message occurs only in Unix.
*****: not found (A)	Appears when you try to run your script in the Bourne shell instead of Perl. This error message occurs only in Unix.
-P not allowed for setuid/setgid script (F)	Issued because the script would have to be opened by name by the C preprocessor, which is a security break.
-T and -B not implemented on filehandles (F)	Caused because Perl can't open the **stdio** buffer if it doesn't know the type of **stdio**.
500 Server Error	Indicates a CGI error and not a Perl error.
?+* follows nothing in regexp (F)	Perl issues this message when you start a regular expression with a quantifier.
@ outside of string (F)	Occurs when a pack template is specified with an absolute position outside the string being unpacked.

Error Message	Meaning
accept ( ) on closed fd (W)	Indicates an accept was attempted on a closed socket.
Allocation too large: ***** (F)	Issued when you try to allocate more than 64K in MS-DOS.
Arg too short for msgsnd (F)	Occurs when the string argument to **msgsnd** isn't at least **sizeof(long)**.
Ambiguous use of ***** resolved as ***** (W) (S)	Issued when Perl interprets an expression in a way you might not have intended.
Args must match #! line (F)	This message appears when the switches Perl was invoked with don't match the switches on the #! line.
Argument ***** isn't numeric (W)	Perl issues this message when it expected a numeric argument to an operator but found a string instead.
Array @***** missing the @ in argument ***** of *****( ) (P)	This message is displayed when you leave the @ off of an array variable name.
Assertion failed: file "*****" (P)	This message is issued when a general assertion fails.
Assignment to both a list and a scalar (F)	Perl displays this message when the second and third arguments to a conditional operator are not either both lists or both scalars.
Attempt to free non-arena SV: *****	This message occurs when you allocate an SV object from outside an arena that will be garbage collected upon exit.
Attempt to free temp prematurely (W)	This message appears when a scalar value is freed before the internal **free_tmps( )** routine had a chance to free it.
Attempt to free unreferenced glob pointers (P)	Perl issues this message when the symbol aliases get their reference counts mixed up.
Attempt to free unreferenced scalar (W)	This message occurs when Perl tries to decrement the reference count of a scalar and finds the reference count is already at 0.
Bad arg length for *****, is *****, should be ***** (F)	Perl displays this message when you try to pass a buffer of the wrong size to **msgctl**, **semctl**, or **shmctl**.

A

Error Message	Meaning
Bad associative array (P)	This message is displayed when a null HV pointer is passed to one of Perl's internal hash routines.
Bad filehandle: ***** (F)	Perl issues this message when a symbol was passed to something that wanted a filehandle.
Bad free( ) ignored (S)	This message occurs when an internal routine calls **free( )** on an object when **malloc( )** had not been called.
Bad name after ***** ::(F)	This message is displayed when a symbol that is named by a package prefix isn't finished.
Bad symbol for array (P)	Perl displays this message when an internal request tried to add an array entry to an object that wasn't a symbol table entry.
Bad symbol for filehandle (P)	Perl displays this message when an internal request tried to add a filehandle entry to an object that wasn't a symbol table entry.
Bad symbol for hash (P)	Perl displays this message when an internal request tried to add a hash entry to an object that wasn't a symbol table entry.
Badly placed ( )'s (A)	This message occurs when you try to run your script through **csh** instead of Perl. This error message occurs only in Unix.
BEGIN failed—compilation aborted (F)	This message is displayed when an untrapped exception was raised while executing a **Begin** routine.
bind( ) on closed fd (W)	Perl issues this message when you try to bind a closed socket.
Bizarre copy of ***** in ***** (P)	This message occurs when Perl detects an attempt to copy an uncopyable internal value.
Callback called exit (F)	This message is displayed when a subroutine invoked from an external package exited by calling the exit function.

Error Message	Meaning
Can't "last" outside a block (F)	This message is caused by trying to break out of the current block by issuing the last statement outside of the current block.
Can't "next" outside a block (F)	This message is caused by trying to reiterate the current block with a next statement outside of the current block.
Can't "redo" outside a block (F)	This message is caused by trying to restart the current block with a **redo** statement outside of the current block.
Can't bless non-reference value (F)	Perl issues this message when you try to bless a symbolic, or soft, reference.
Can't break at that line (S)	This debugger warning message indicates that the line number specified contains a statement that can't be stopped.
Can't call method "*****" in empty package "*****" (F)	This message is displayed when you try to call a method in a package that doesn't have anything it.
Can't call method "*****" on unblessed reference (F)	This message is displayed when you try to call a method without supplying an object reference.
Can't call method "*****" without a package or object reference (F)	This message could be displayed when you try to call a method by supplying an expression that doesn't evaluate to a package or an object reference.
Can't chdir to ***** (F)	Perl displays this message when you specify a directory that you can't get to with **chdir**.
Can't coerce ***** to integer in ***** (F)	This message will be displayed when you try to force certain scalar values to be an integer.
Can't coerce ***** to number in ***** (F)	This message will be displayed when you try to force certain scalar values to be a number.
Can't create pipe mailbox (P)	This message occurs only in VMS.

A

Error Message	Meaning
Can't declare ***** in my (F)	Perl issues this message when you try to declare something other than a scalar, array, or hash variable as a lexical variable.
Can't do inplace edit on *****: ***** (S)	This message is displayed when the creation of a new file fails because it can't be edited in place.
Can't do inplace edit without a backup (F)	This message occurs with certain operating systems that can't work with deleted yet still open files (MS-DOS).
Can't do inplace edit: ***** > 14 characters (S)	This message occurs when a filename doesn't have enough characters to make a backup filename.
Can't do inplace edit: ***** is not a regular file (S)	Perl displays this message when you use the **-i** switch on a special file.
Can't do setegid! (P)	This message is displayed when a **setegid( )** call fails.
Can't do seteuid! (P)	This message is issued when the **seteuid** emulator fails.
Can't do setuid (F)	This message is displayed when Perl tried to execute **suidperl** to do **setuid** emulation, but the execution failed for some reason.
Can't do waitpid with flags (F)	Perl issues this message when the machine running the script doesn't have either **waitpid** or **wait4**.
Can't do {n,m} with n > m (F)	This message occurs when the **minima** is greater than the **maxima** in a regular expression.
Can't emulate -***** On #! line (F)	This message is displayed when the #! line specifies a switch that doesn't make sense in the current context.
Can't exec "*****": ***** (W)	This message occurs when a system, exec, or piped open call can't execute a named program for the reason indicated by the second *****.
Can't exec ***** (F)	Perl displays this message when it can't execute the program named by ***** on the #! line.

Error Message	Meaning
Can't find label ***** (F)	This message is displayed when you issue a **goto** to a label that isn't defined.
Can't find string terminator ***** anywhere before EOF (F)	This message occurs when Perl can't find the closing delimiter to a string.
Can't fork (F)	This message is displayed when an error occurs trying to fork while opening a pipeline.
Can't get filespec - stale stat buffer? (S)	This message occurs in VMS because of the difference between access checks under VMS and Unix.
Can't get pipe mailbox device name (P)	This message occurs only in VMS and is displayed when Perl can't retrieve a mailbox name after creating one to act as a pipe.
Can't get SYSGEN parameter value for MAXBUF (P)	Another VMS message that occurs when Perl asks $GETSYI how big to make the mailbox and doesn't get an answer.
Can't goto subroutine outside a subroutine (F)	Perl displays this message when a **goto** doesn't have subroutine to go to.
Can't localize a reference (F)	This message is displayed when you try to make a reference variable local.
Can't localize lexical variable ***** (F)	This message is displayed when you try to make a lexical variable local.
Can't locate ***** in @INC (F)	This message occurs when you try to load in a file that couldn't be found in any of the libraries of @INC.
Can't locate object method "*****" via package "*****" (F)	Perl displays this message when you try to call a method that doesn't exist in the package.
Can't locate package ***** for @*****::ISA (W)	This message is displayed when the @ISA array contains the name of a package that doesn't exist.
Can't mktemp( ) (F)	This message occurs when the **mktemp** routine fails while trying to process an -**e** switch.
Can't modify ***** in ***** (F)	Perl displays this message when you try to make an assignment to the item *****.

Error Message	Meaning
Can't modify non-existent substring (P)	This message is displayed when Perl's internal routine that does assignment to a **substr** was handed a NULL pointer.
Can't msgrcv to readonly var (F)	This message occurs when the target of a **msgrcv** cannot be modified.
Can't open *****: ***** (S)	This message is displayed when an in-place edit can't open the original file for the reason indicated.
Can't open bidirectional pipe (W)	Perl displays this message when you write something like open(PIPE, "|PIPE|").
Can't open error file ***** as stderr (F)	A VMS error that occurs when Perl can't open the file after 2> or 2>> on the command line.
Can't open input file ***** as stdin (F)	A VMS error that occurs when Perl can't open the file specified after < for input.
Can't open output file ***** as stdout (F)	A VMS error that occurs when Perl can't open the file specified after > or >> for output.
Can't open output pipe (name: *****) (P)	A VMS error that occurs when Perl can't open an output pipe.
Can't open Perl script "*****": ***** (F)	This message occurs when the specified script can't be opened for the reason indicated.
Can't rename ***** to *****: *****, skipping file (S)	Perl displays this message when an **-i** switch rename fails for some reason.
Can't reopen input pipe (name: *****) in binary mode (P)	A VMS error that occurs when Perl tries to reopen STDIN as a pipe in binary mode.
Can't reswap uid and euid (P)	This message occurs when a **setreuid** call fails in the **setuid** emulator of **suidperl**.
Can't return outside a subroutine (F)	This message is displayed when a return statement is executed outside of a subroutine.
Can't stat script "*****" (P)	Perl displays this message when Perl won't allow you to **fstat** the script even though it is already open.

Error Message	Meaning
Can't swap uid and euid (P)	This message occurs when a **setreuid** call fails in the **setuid** emulator of **suidperl**.
Can't take log of NNNNN (F)	This message is displayed when you try to take the logarithm of a number that is either not positive, or real, or both.
Can't take sqrt of NNNNN (F)	This message is displayed when you try to take the square root of a negative number.
Can't undef active subroutine (F)	Perl displays this message when you try to undefine a subroutine that is currently running.
Can't unshift (F)	This message occurs when you try to unshift an array that can't be unshifted.
Can't upgrade that kind of scalar (P)	This message is displayed when Perl tries to convert one of the specialized SV types.
Can't upgrade to undef (P)	This message is displayed when Perl tries to upgrade an undefined SV.
Can't use "my *****" in sort comparison (F)	Perl displays this message when the variables $a and $b are used in a comparison after they've been declared as lexical variables with **my**.
Can't use ***** for loop variable (F)	This message occurs when you try to use something other than a simple scalar as a loop variable on a **foreach**.
Can't use ***** ref as ***** ref (F)	This message is displayed when you mix up the reference types.
Can't use \1 to mean $1 in expression (W)	This message is displayed when you try to use the \1 backreference to a matched substring outside a regular expression.
Can't use string ("*****") as ***** ref while "strict refs" in use (F)	Perl displays this message when a soft reference is used when "strict refs" is declared.
Can't use an undefined value as ***** reference (F)	This message occurs when you try to use an undefined value as a hard or soft reference.

A

Error Message	Meaning
Can't use global ***** in "my" (F)	This message is displayed when you try to declare a special variable as a lexical variable.
Can't use subscript on ***** (F)	This message is displayed when the object to the left of ***** isn't an array reference.
Can't write to temp file for -e: ***** (F)	Perl displays this message when the write routine fails while trying to process an **-e** switch.
Can't x= to readonly value (F)	This message occurs when you try to repeat a constant value with an assignment operator.
Cannot open temporary file (F)	Perl displays this message when the **creat** routine fails while trying to process an **-e** switch.
chmod: mode argument is missing inital 0 (W)	This message is displayed when the mode argument to **chmod** isn't interpreted to be an octal number.
Close on unopened file ***** (W)	Perl issues this message when you try to close a file that was never opened.
connect( ) on closed fd (W)	This message is displayed when you try to do a connect on a closed socket.
Corrupt malloc ptr NNNNN at NNNNN (P)	This message occurs when the **malloc** package that comes with Perl has an internal failure.
corrupted regexp pointers (P)	This message is displayed when the regular expression engine gets confused by what it received from the regular expression compiler.
corrupted regexp program (P)	Perl displays this message when the regular expression gets passed a regular expression program without a valid magic number.
Deep recursion on subroutine ***** (W)	This message occurs when a subroutine calls itself more than 100 times more than it has returned.
Did you mean &***** instead? (W)	This message is displayed when you refer to a subroutine with a dollar sign, as in $sub when you meant &sub.

Error Message	Meaning
Did you mean $ or @ instead of %? (W)	Perl issues this message when you refer to an individual hash item with %, as in %hash{$key}.
Do you need to predeclare ***** ? (S)	This message occurs when a subroutine or module name is referenced when it hasn't yet been declared.
Don't you know how to handle magic of type '*****' (P)	This message is displayed when the internal magic variables are mishandled.
do_study: out of memory (P)	This message indicates that the condition that caused the message should have been caught by **safemalloc** instead.
Duplicate free( ) ignored (S)	Perl displays this message when an internal routine has called **free( )** on an object that has already been freed.
Elseif should be elsif (S)	This message occurs when you use **elseif** instead of the keyword **elsif**.
END failed — cleanup aborted (F)	This message is displayed when an untrapped exception was raised while executing an **end** subroutine.
Error converting file specification ***** (F)	This VMS error occurs when you pass an invalid file specification to Perl.
Execution of ***** aborted due to compilation errors (F)	This message is displayed as the summary message when a Perl compilation fails.
Exiting subroutine via ***** (W)	Perl issues this message when you try to exit a subroutine using a nonstandard technique.
Editing substitution via ***** (W)	Perl issues this message when you try to exit a substitution using a nonstandard technique.
Fatal VMS error at *****, line NNNNN (P)	A VMS error that indicates something in VMS caused the program to fail.
Fcntl is not implemented (F)	This message is displayed when your machine doesn't implement **fcntl**.

A

Error Message	Meaning
Filehandle ***** never opened (W)	This message occurs when an i/o operation is attempted on a filehandle that was never initialized.
Filehandle ***** only opened for input (W)	This message occurs when you attempt to write to a read-only filehandle.
Final $ should be \$ or $name (F)	Perl displays this message when a $ comes at the end of a string and Perl can't decide if what to follow should be a reference or a scalar.
Final @ should be \@ or @name (F)	Perl displays this message when an @ comes at the end of a string and Perl can't decide if what to follow should be an array reference or an array name.
Format ***** redefined (W)	This message is issued when you redefine a format.
Format not terminated (F)	This message occurs when a format isn't terminated with a single dot (.).
Found = in conditional, should be == (W)	This message is displayed when you assigned and you meant to test for equality.
gdbm store returned NNNNN, errno NNNNN, key = "*****" (S)	Perl displays this message when a **store( )** from the GDBM_File extension module failed.
gethostent not implemented (F)	This message occurs if your C library doesn't implement **gethostent**.
get{sock, peer}name( ) on closed fd (W)	This message is displayed when you try to get a socket or peer socket name on a closed socket.
getpwnam returned invalid UIC NNNNN for user "*****" (S)	A VMS error that indicates the call to **sys$getuai** underlying the **getpwnam** function returned an invalid UIC.
Glob not terminated (F)	Perl issues this message when the lexer finds a left angle bracket when it was expecting a term.
Global symbol "*****" requires explicit package name (F)	This message is displayed when you try to use a global variable when you've declared use **strict vars**.

Error Message	Meaning
goto must have label (F)	Perl issues this message when you try to go to an unlabeled destination.
Had to create ***** unexpectedly (S)	This message is displayed when Perl has to create a symbol that should have been in the symbol table but wasn't.
Hash %***** missing the % in argument NNNNN of ***** (D)	This message occurs when in an old Perl script you left out the % of a hash name.
Illegal division by zero (F)	Perl displays this message when you try to divide a number by 0.
Illegal modulus zero (F)	Perl displays this message when you try to divide a number by 0 to get the remainder.
Illegal octal digit (F)	This message occurs when you use an 8 or 9 in an octal number.
Illegal octal digit ignored (W)	This warning message occurs when Perl finds an 8 or 9 in an octal number and interpretation of the number stops before the 8 or 9.
Insecure dependency in ***** (F)	This message is displayed when you use something the tainting mechanism doesn't like.
Insecure directory in ***** (F)	Perl issues this message when you use system, exec, or a piped open in a **setuid** or **setgid** script if $ENV{PATH} contains a directory that is writable.
Insecure PATH (F)	Perl issues this message when you use system, exec, or a piped open in a **setuid** or **setgid** script if $ENV{PATH} comes from data supplied by the user.
Internal inconsistency in tracking vforks (S)	A VMS warning that occurs when Perl loses track of calls to **fork** and **exec**.
Internal disaster in regexp (P)	This message occurs when something goes wrong with the regular expression parser.

A

Error Message	Meaning
Internal urp in regexp at /*****/ (P)	This message also occurs when something goes wrong with the regular expression parser.
Invalid [ ] range in regexp (F)	This message is displayed when the range specified in a character class had a minimum character greater than the maximum character.
ioctl is not implemented (F)	Perl issues this message when your machine doesn't implement **ioctl**.
junk on end of regexp (P)	This message occurs when the regular expression parser is mixed up.
Label not found for "last *****" (F)	This message is displayed when you try to break out of a loop by name but you're not currently in the named loop.
Label not found for "next *****" (F)	This message is displayed when you try to continue in a loop you're not currently in.
Label not found for "redo *****" (F)	This message is displayed when you try to restart a loop you're not currently in.
listen( ) on closed fd (W)	Perl displays this message when you try to do a listen on a closed socket.
Literal @***** now requires a backslash (F)	This message occurs in old Perl scripts because Perl used to try to decide if a bare @ meant a literal "at" sign or to interpolate an array.
Method for operation ***** not found in package ***** during blessing (F)	This message is displayed when you try to specify an entry in an overloading table that doesn't point to a valid method.
Might be a runaway multi-line ***** string starting on line NNNNN (S)	This message is an advisory indicating that the previously reported error may have been caused by a string or pattern that wasn't terminated properly.
Misplaced _ in number (W)	Perl displays this message when an underline in a decimal constant wasn't on a three-digit boundary.
Missing $ on loop variable (F)	This message occurs when a loop variable is introduced without a $.

Error Message	Meaning
Missing comma after first argument to ***** function (F)	This message is displayed when you try to specify a filehandle or an indirect object before the argument list.
Missing operator before ***** ? (S)	This message is displayed when a string is found when an operator was expected.
Missing right bracket (F)	This message appears when the Perl lexer counts more opening curly braces than closing curly braces.
Missing semicolon on previous line? (S)	This message is a guess by Perl that the problem may be that you left off the semicolon on the previous line.
Modification of a read-only value attempted (F)	Perl issues this message when you try to modify a constant.
Modification of non-creatable array value attempted, subscript NNNNN (F)	This message is issued when you try to directly make an assignment to an array and there was something wrong with the subscript (e.g., it was negative).
Modification of non-creatable hash value attempted, subscript "*****" (F)	This message is issued when you tried to create a hash and it couldn't be.
Module name must be constant (F)	Perl issues this message when you try to use a fancy module name when a bare module name is required.
msg ***** not implemented (F)	This message is issued because you don't have System V message IPC on your computer system.
Multidimensional syntax ***** not supported (W)	This warning is issued when you try to use C-like syntax to refer to a multidimensional array.
Negative length (F)	This message is issued when you try to perform a **read**, **write**, **send**, or **recv** operation with a negative buffer length.
Nested *?+ in regexp (F)	Perl issues this message when you try to write something like ** or ?* in a regular expression.

A

Error Message	Meaning
No #! Line (F)	This message occurs when the #! is not well formed as required by the **setuid** emulator.
No ***** allowed while running setuid (F)	Perl issues this error when you try to do something that it considers too insecure for a **setuid** of **setgid** script to even attempt.
No -e allowed in setuid scripts (F)	This message occurs because a **setuid** script can't be specified by the user.
No comma allowed after ***** (F)	This message is displayed when a list operator that contains a filehandle or other indirect object has a comma between that and the following arguments.
No command into which to pipe on command line (F)	A VMS error that occurs when Perl finds a | at the end of a command line, since Perl performs its own command-line redirection.
No DB::DB routine defined (F)	Perl issues this error when a script was compiled with the **-d** switch but a routine can't be found to call at the beginning of each statement.
No dbm on this machine (P)	This is a Perl internal error.
No Dbsub routine (F)	Perl issues this error when a script was compiled with the **-d** switch but a DB::sub routine can't be found to call at the beginning of each subroutine call.
No error after 2> or 2>> on command line (F)	A VMS error that occurs when Perl finds a 2> or a 2>> on the command line but can't find a file to write the data.
No input file after < on command line (F)	A VMS error that occurs when Perl finds a < on the command line but can't find a file from which to read data.
No output file after > on command line (F)	A VMS error that occurs when Perl finds a lone > on the command line and doesn't know where to sent the output.

Error Message	Meaning
No output file after > or >> on command line (F)	A VMS error that occurs when Perl finds a > or a >> on the command line but can't find a file for which to write the data.
No Perl script found in input (F)	This message is displayed when Perl is called with perl -x but no line was found with"#! perl" in it.
No space allowed after -I (F)	This message occurs when at least one space separates -**I** and its argument.
No such pipe open (P)	A VMS error that occurs when an attempt is made to close a pipe that hasn't been opened.
No such signal: SIG***** (W)	This warning is issued when a signal name is specified as a subscript to %SIG but wasn't recognized.
Not a CODE reference (F)	Perl issues this error when it tries to evaluate a reference to a code value but gets something else to evaluate instead.
Not a format reference (F)	This message appears when you try to create a reference to an anonymous format.
Not a GLOB reference (F)	This message is issued because Perl was looking for a reference to a **typeglob** but got something else instead.
Not a HASH reference (F)	This message is issued because Perl was looking for a reference to a hash but got something else instead.
Not a Perl script (F)	Perl issues this error when the #! line isn't well formed, as required by the **setuid** emulator.
Not a SCALAR reference (F)	This message is issued because Perl was looking for a reference to a scalar but got something else instead.
Not a subroutine reference (F)	This message is issued because Perl was looking for a reference to a subroutine but got something else instead.

A

Error Message	Meaning
Not a subroutine reference in %OVERLOAD (F)	This message occurs when an attempt to specify an entry in an overloading table doesn't point to a legal subroutine.
Not an ARRAY reference (F)	This message is issued because Perl was looking for a reference to an array but got something else instead.
Not enough arguments for ***** (F)	Perl issues this error when more arguments to a function are needed than are specified.
Not enough format arguments (W)	This warning is issued when more picture fields than value lines are specified in a format.
Null filename used (F)	This message is issued when you try to require a NULL filename.
NULL OP IN RUN (P)	This message is displayed when an internal routine called **run( )** with a null **opcode** pointer as an argument.
Null realloc (P)	Perl issues this message when an attempt is made to **realloc** null.
NULL regexp argument (P)	This message occurs when the internal pattern-matching routines get messed up.
NULL regexp parameter (P)	This message occurs when the internal pattern-matching routines get messed up again.
Odd number of elements in hash list (S)	Perl issues this message when you try to create a hash with an odd number of elements.
oops: oopsAV (S)	An internal Perl warning that indicates the grammar is messed up.
Operation '*****' *****: no method found (F)	This error occurs when you try to use an entry in an overloading table that no longer points to a valid method.
Operator or semicolon missing before ***** (S)	This message is displayed when you use a variable or a subroutine call where an operator is expected.

Error Message	Meaning
Out of memory for yacc stack (F)	Perl issues this error when the **byacc** parser doesn't have enough memory to make its stack larger.
Out of memory! (X)	This error is returned when **malloc** indicates there is not enough memory to satisfy the request.
page overflow (W)	This warning indicates that a call to write produced more lines than can fit on one page.
panic: ck_grep (P)	This message is displayed when an internal consistency check fails while trying to compile a **grep**.
panic: ck_split (P)	This message is displayed when an internal consistency check fails while trying to compile a split.
panic: corrupt saved stack index (P)	Perl issues this message when an attempt is made to store more localized values than there are on the stack.
panic: die ***** (P)	This message occurs when the context stack is popped to an **eval** context, but the context wasn't really an **eval** context.
panic: do_match (P)	This message occurs when the internal **pp_match( )** routine was called with invalid data.
panic: do_split (P)	This message occurs when a split is not set up properly.
panic: do_subst (P)	This message occurs when the internal **pp_subst( )** routine was called with invalid data.
panic: do_trans (P)	This message occurs when the internal **pp_trans( )** routine was called with invalid data.
panic: goto (P)	Perl displays this message when the context stack is popped to a context with a label, and the context is not one that can do a **goto**.

A

Error Message	Meaning
panic: INTERPCASEMOD (P)	This message occurs when the lexer has trouble with a character case modifier.
panic: INERPCONCAT (P)	This message is displayed when the lexer has trouble parsing a string with brackets.
panic: last (P)	Perl displays this message when the context stack is popped to a block context, only to discover it's not really a block context.
panic: leave_scope clearsv (P)	This message occurs when a writable lexical variable becomes read-only within the scope.
panic: leave_scope inconsistency (P)	This message is displayed when the savestack gets out of sync.
panic: malloc (P)	Perl issues this message when a request is made to **malloc** for a negative number of bytes.
panic: mapstart (P)	This message indicates that something is wrong with the compiler's **map** function.
panic: null array (P)	This message indicates that one of the internal array routines was passed a null array value pointer.
panic: pad_alloc (P)	This message is displayed when the compiler gets confused about which scratchpad it is using.
panic: pad_free curpad (P)	See **pad_alloc**.
panic: pad_free po (P)	Perl issues this message when an invalid scratchpad offset is detected internally.
panic: pad_reset curpad (P)	See **pad_alloc**.
panic: pad_sv po (P)	See **pad_free po**.
panic: pad_swipe curpad (P)	See **pad_alloc**.
panic: pad_swipe po (P)	See **pad_free po**.
panic: pp_iter (P)	Perl issues this message when the **foreach** iterator is called in a nonloop context.
panic: realloc (P)	This message occurs when **realloc** is requested with a negative number of bytes.

Error Message	Meaning
panic: restartop (P)	This message indicates that an internal routine requested a **goto** without supplying a destination.
panic: return (P)	Perl displays this message when the context stack is popped to a subroutine or **eval** context, only to find it wasn't really a subroutine or **eval** context.
panic: scan_num (P)	This message indicates the **scan_num( )** routine was called on an object that wasn't a number.
panic: sv_insert (P)	This message occurs when the **sv_insert( )** routine is called to remove more of a string than exists.
panic: top_env (P)	This message is displayed when the compiler tries to do something crazy.
panic: yylex (P)	This message indicates the lexer got messed up trying to process a character case modifier.
Parens missing around "*****" list (W)	This warning indicates you meant to do an assignment with parentheses instead of without them.
Perl ***** required — this is only version *****, stopped (F)	This error indicates that the module in question uses features from a more recent version of Perl than you are currently using.
Permission denied (F)	This error indicates the **setuid** emulator didn't like what you were trying to do.
pid NNNNN not a child (W)	A VMS warning that indicates that **waitpid** was asked to wait for a process that isn't a subprocess of the current process.
POSIX getpgrp can't take an argument (F)	This message indicates your C compiler uses POSIX **getpgrp**, which takes no argument.
Possible memory corruption: ***** overflowed 3rd argument (F)	Perl issues this error when a sentinel byte in **ioctl** or **fcntl** gets fouled up and Perl thinks memory is corrupted.

A

Error Message	Meaning
Precedence problem: open ***** should be open(*****) (S)	This message indicates you used **open...|| die**, when you should have used **open(...) || die**.
print on closed filehandle ***** (W)	This warning indicates you tried to print on a closed filehandle.
printf on closed filehandle ***** (W)	This warning indicates you tried to print on a closed filehandle.
Probable precedence problem on ***** (W)	This warning indicates that the compiler found a bare word where it expected a conditional.
Prototype mismatch: (*****) vs (*****) (S)	This message indicates the subroutine specified had a forward declaration with a different function prototype.
Read on closed filehandle <*****> (W)	Perl issues this warning to tell you the filehandle you're reading from was closed before the read.
Reallocation too large: NNNNN (F)	This error indicates you tried to allocate more than 64K on an MS-DOS machine.
Recompile Perl with -DDEBUGGING to use -D switch (F)	This message indicates you need to recompile Perl with -DDEBUGGING in order to use the **-D** switch in your code.
Recursive inheritance detected (F)	Perl issues this error when more than 100 levels of inheritance are used.
Reference miscount in sv_replace( ) (W)	Perl issues this warning when the internal function **sv_replace( )** is handed a new SV with a reference count other than 1.
regexp memory corruption (P)	This message occurs when the regular expression engine can't use what the compiler gave it.
regexp out of space (F)	This error message is displayed when **safemalloc** doesn't catch a bad regular expression.
regexp too big (F)	This error results from a regular expression that compiles to a size larger than 32767 bytes.

Error Message	Meaning
Reversed *****= operator (W)	This warning is issued when the assignment operator (=) isn't written last.
Runaway format (F)	Perl generates this error when a repeat-until-blank sequence generates 200 lines at once, and the 200th line looks just like the 199th line.
Scalar value @*****[*****] better written as $*****[*****] (W)	Perl issues this warning when you've used an array slice to indicate a single array element.
Script is not setuid/setgid in suidperl (F)	This error message is generated when the **suidperl** program is invoked on a script that doesn't have its **setuid** or **setgid** bit set.
Search pattern not terminated (F)	This error is issued when the lexer can't find the final delimiter of a / / or an **m( )** construct.
seek( ) on unopened file (W)	This warning is issued when a seek is attempted on an unopened filehandle.
select not implemented (F)	Perl issues this error when the select system call isn't implemented on the current machine.
sem ??? not implemented (F)	This error is issued when your system doesn't have System V semaphore IPC.
semi-panic: attempt to dup freed string (S)	This message is displayed when the **newSVsv( )** internal routine tries to duplicate a scalar that had been marked free.
Semicolon seems to be missing (W)	This warning is issued when a syntax error was probably caused by leaving off a semicolon.
Send on closed socket (W)	This warning is issued when you try to send to a filehandle that is closed.
Sequence (?#... not terminated (F)	Perl generates this error when a regular expression comment isn't closed with a parenthesis.
Sequence (? ***** ...) not implemented (F)	This error is issued when a proposed regular expression extension has the character reserved but has not been written.

A

Error Message	Meaning
Sequence (? ***** ...) not recognized (F)	Perl issues this error when a regular expression extension doesn't make sense.
Server error	Also known as "500 Server error", this is a CGI error and not a Perl error.
setegid( ) not implemented (F)	This error is generated when you try to assign to $) but your operating system doesn't support the **setegid( )** system call.
seteuid( ) not implemented (F)	This error is generated when you try to assign to $> but your operating system doesn't support the **seteuid( )** system call.
setrgid( ) not implemented (F)	This error is generated when you try to assign to $(but your operating system doesn't support the **setrgid( )** system call.
setruid( ) not implemented (F)	This error is generated when you try to assign to $< but your operating system doesn't support the **setruid( )** system call.
Setuid/gid script is writable by world (F)	Perl generates this error because the **setuid** emulator won't run a script that is writable by the world.
shm ***** not implemented (F)	This error is issued when you don't have System V shared memory IPC implemented on your machine.
shutdown( ) on closed fd (W)	This warning is issued when you try to do a shutdown on a closed socket.
SIG***** Handler "*****" not defined. (W)	This warning is generated when the signal handler named in %SIG does not really exist.
sort is now a reserved word (F)	In older versions of Perl, the sort keyword could be used as an object name.
Sort subroutine didn't return a numeric value (F)	This error is generated when a sort subroutine doesn't return a number.
Sort subroutine didn't return a single value (F)	This error is generated when a sort subroutine tries to return a list value with more or less than one element.

Error Message	Meaning
Split loop (P)	This message is displayed when a split loops infinitely.
Stat on unopened file ***** (W)	Perl issues this warning when you try to use the **stat** function on a closed filehandle.
Statement unlikely to be reached (W)	This warning is issued when you issue an **exec** with a statement after it other than die.
Subroutine ***** redefined (W)	This warning is generated when you redefine a subroutine.
Substitution loop (P)	This message is displayed when a substitution is looping infinitely.
Substitution pattern not terminated (F)	Perl issues this error when the lexer can't find the delimiter of an **s/ / /** or an **s{ }{ }** construct.
Substitution replacement not terminated (F)	Perl issues this error when the lexer can't find the final delimiter of an **s/ / /** or an **s{ }{ }** construct.
substr outside of string (W)	This warning is issued when you try to reference a **substr** that is outside of a string.
suidperl is no longer needed since . . . (F)	This error is generated when the **setuid** emulator is run when your version of Perl was compiled with the -DSETUID_SCRIPTS_ARE_SECURE_NOW switch.
syntax error (F)	Perl generates this error when there is something wrong with your script syntax.
syntax error at line NNNNN: '*****' unexpected (A)	This error is issued when you run your script through the Bourne shell instead of Perl.
System V IPC is not implemented on this machine (F)	Perl issues this error when you try to execute an IPC function on a machine that can't run IPC functions because IPC is not implemented.
Syswrite on closed filehandle (W)	This warning is generated when the filehandle you are trying to write to is closed.

A

Error Message	Meaning
tell( ) on unopened file (W)	This warning is generated when the tell function is executed on a filehandle that is closed.
Test on unopened file (W)	This warning is generated when you try to invoke a file test operator on a filehandle that is closed.
That use of $[is unsupported (F)	Perl issues this error when an old Perl script tries to do multiple assignment to $[.
The ***** function is unimplemented	This message is displayed when the function indicated isn't supported by the architecture in use.
The crypt( ) function is unimplemented due to excessive paranoia. (F)	Perl generates this error when Configure can't find the **crypt( )** function on your system.
The stat preceding -1 _ wasn't an lstat (F)	This error is generated when you test the current **stat** buffer for a symbolic link when the last **stat** that wrote to the **stat** buffer went past the symbolic link to get to the real filename.
times not implemented (F)	This error is issued when your version of the C library doesn't support the **times( )** function.
Too few args to syscall (F)	This error is displayed when there isn't at least one argument passed to the **syscall** function.
Too many ('s (A)	This message is displayed when you run your script through the **csh** shell instead of Perl.
Too many)'s (A)	This message is displayed when you run your script through the **csh** shell instead of Perl.
Too many args to syscall (F)	Perl generates this error when you pass more than 14 arguments to **syscall**.
Too many arguments for ***** (F)	This error is issued when you pass too many arguments to the function indicated.
trailing \ in regexp (F)	This error is generated when a regular expression ends with a naked backslash.

Error Message	Meaning
Translation pattern not terminated (F)	This error is issued when the lexer can't find the delimiter of a **tr/ / /** or **tr[ ][ ]** construct.
Translation replacement not terminated (F)	This error is issued when the lexer couldn't find the final delimiter of a **tr/ / /** or **tr[ ][ ]** construct.
truncate not implemented (F)	Perl generates this error when your machine doesn't implement a known file truncation mechanism.
Type of arg NNNNN to ***** must be ***** (not *****) (F)	This error is issued when the argument to a function is not of the correct type.
umask: argument is missing initial 0 (W)	Perl displays this message when a **umask** of 222 is issued, when it should be 0222.
Unable to create sub named "*****" (F)	This error is issued when you create or access a subroutine with an illegal name.
Unbalanced context: NNNNN more PUSHes that POPs (W)	This warning is issued when the exit code detected an internal inconsistency in how many execution contexts were entered and exited.
Unbalanced saves: NNNNN more saves than restores (W)	This warning is issued when the exit code detected an internal inconsistency in how many values were temporarily localized.
Unbalanced scopes: NNNNN more ENTERS than LEAVEs (W)	This warning is issued when the exit code detected an internal inconsistency in how many blocks were entered and exited.
Unbalanced tmps: NNNNN more allocs than frees (W)	This warning is issued when the exit code detected an internal inconsistency in how many scalars were allocated and freed.
Undefined format "*****" called (F)	Perl generates this error when it can't find the format called.
Undefined sort subroutine "*****" called (F)	Perl generates this error when it can't find the sort subroutine called.

A

Error Message	Meaning
Undefined subroutine &***** called (F)	Perl generates this error when it can't find the subroutine called because the subroutine either wasn't defined initially or was undefined.
Undefined subroutine called (F)	Perl generates this error when it can't find the anonymous subroutine called.
Undefined subroutine in sort (F)	Perl generates this error when a sort subroutine is declared but hasn't been defined.
Undefined top format "*****" called (F)	Perl generates this error when the format specified doesn't exist.
unexec of ***** into ***** failed! (F)	This error is issued when the **unexec** routine fails.
Unknown BYTEORDER (F)	This error is generated when there are no byte-swapping functions for a machine with this byte order.
unmatched ( ) in regexp (F)	This error message is generated when bare parentheses are not balanced in a regular expression.
Unmatched right bracket (F)	Perl issues this error when the lexer finds more opening braces than closing braces.
unmatched [ ] in regexp (F)	This error is issued when the brackets around a character class don't match.
Unquoted string "*****" may clash with future reserved word (W)	This warning is issued when you use a word that may be used as a reserved word later.
Unrecognized character \ NNNNN ignored (S)	This message is displayed when an illegal character is found in the input is ignored.
Unrecognized signal name "*****" (F)	This error is generated when you give the **kill** function a signal name Perl can't recognize.
Unrecognized switch: -***** (F)	This error is issued when you give Perl an illegal option switch.
Unsuccessful ***** on filename containing newline (W)	This warning is generated when a file operation fails, probably because the filename contained a newline character.

Error Message	Meaning
Unsupported directory function "*****" called (F)	Perl generates this error when your machine doesn't support **opendir** and **readdir**.
Unsupported function ***** (F)	This message is generated because your machine doesn't support the specified function.
Unsupported socket function "*****" called (F)	This error is issued because your machine doesn't support the Berkeley socket mechanism.
Unterminated <> operator (F)	This error is generated when the lexer finds a < but can't find a >.
Use of $# is deprecated (D)	This message is displayed when you try to use an **awk** feature instead of **printf** or **sprintf**.
Use of $* is deprecated (D)	This message is displayed when $* turns on multiline pattern matching and the /m or /s modifiers should have been used instead.
Use of ***** in printf format not supported (F)	Perl generates this error when you try to use a feature of **printf** that is only supported in C.
Use of ***** is deprecated (D)	This message is displayed when the old Perl construct specified can now be done in a better way.
Use of bare << to mean <<"" is deprecated (D)	This message is displayed when you use << to terminate a *here* document instead of the more current <<"" form.
Use of implicit split to @_ is deprecated (D)	This message is displayed when you should have explicitly assigned the results of a split to an array.
Use of uninitialized value (W)	Perl issues this warning when an undefined value is used as if it were defined.
Useless use of ***** in void context (W)	This warning is issued when something is evaluated without a side effect in a context that does nothing with the return value.
Variable "*****" is not exported (F)	Perl generates this error when you refer to a global variable that you thought was imported from a module but wasn't while use strict is in effect.
Variable name "*****::*****" used only once: possible typo (W)	This warning is generated when you have a typo in a unique name.

A

Error Message	Meaning
Variable syntax (A)	This message is displayed when you run your script through **csh** instead of Perl.
Warning: unable to close filehandle ***** properly. (S)	This message indicates that an implicit close performed by an open failed.
Warning: use of "*****" without parens is ambiguous (S)	This message indicates you forgot to enclose an argument to a function in parentheses.
Write on closed filehandle (W)	This warning is generated when you try to write to a closed filehandle.
X outside of string (F)	This error is generated when you try to specify a relative position in a pack template that is outside the beginning of the string to be unpacked.
Xsub "*****" called in sort (F)	Perl issues this error because an external subroutine cannot be used as a sort comparison.
Xsub called in sort (F)	This error is issued when an external subroutine is used as a sort comparison.
You can't use -1 on a filehandle (F)	This error is generated when you try to open a symbolic link with a filehandle.
You haven't disabled set-id scripts in the kernel yet! (F)	This error is generated for the reason specified in the message. To get around it, you should use the **wrapsuid** script in the eg/ directory.
You need to quote "*****" (W)	This warning is issued when you assign a bareword as a signal handler name.
[gs] etsockopt( ) on closed fd (W)	Perl generates this warning when you try to get or set a socket option on a closed socket.
\1 better written as $1 (W)	This warning is issued when you use \1 as a backreference when you should have used $1.
'l' and '<' may not both be specified on command line (F)	A VMS error that is caused because you tried to use both l and < as a STDIN stream when only one is allowed.
'l' and '>' may not both be specified on command line (F)	A VMS error that is caused because you tried to use both l and < as a STDOUT stream when only one is allowed.

APPENDIX B

Perl Module Extensions

This appendix discusses how to use the modules that extend Perl much as C's libraries extend the C language. Perl modules are special types of packages that exist as separate files. Many of them are implemented using object-oriented techniques, which by now you are familiar with. Perl modules can be found in the lib subdirectory, though some of them are placed in their own subdirectory as well. Perl modules for Windows systems in the ActiveState distribution are in the lib/win32 (lib\win32) subdirectory.

Packages

A *package* is a group of Perl code that exists within its own namespace. This means that the code within the package cannot access the variables and functions of code outside the package, and code outside the package cannot access the variables and functions within a package.

The most basic package in Perl is called *package main*, which is the standard Perl script. You can bring in another package to your program through the *use* or *require* operators. These operators are called *package declarators* and can be placed anywhere in your script, though by convention package declarations are placed at the beginning. You can also switch into a package in more than one place in your program.

When you switch into a package, the set of variables and functions that make up the package are imported into your program. They are available for use just as if they had been written into the main program. The scope of a package begins with the declaration and continues until the innermost closing block of code in the package, or until another package is declared. While the package is in scope, all variables and function references refer to the contents of the package. Trying to reference a function or other object outside the package will trigger an error.

Modules

With this brief, though sufficient, definition of packages in place, you can now learn what a module is. A *module* is simply a package that has been placed in a separate file and stored under a name that is the same as the module. Using a module, you can import its variables and functions into any other package, including, and especially, package main.

Modules can be thought of as very similar to library files in C. To import a module, you declare it with the *use* operator. Once the module is declared, you can use its variables and functions freely in your program.

The Structure of a Module File

To understand how to work with modules, it helps to understand how Perl modules are structured. Here are the contents of a very simple Perl module, the integer module:

```
package integer;

=head1 NAME

integer - Perl pragma to compute arithmetic in integer instead of
double

=head1 SYNOPSIS
    use integer;
    $x = 10/3;
    # $x is now 3, not 3.33333333333333333

=head1 DESCRIPTION
```

This tells the compiler that it's okay to use integer operations from here to the end of the enclosing block. On many machines, this doesn't matter a great deal for most computations, but on those without floating-point hardware, it can make a big difference.

```
See L<perlmod/Pragmatic Modules>.

=cut

sub import {
    $^H |= 1;
}

sub unimport {
    $^H &= ~1;
}

1;
```

To be better able to work with modules, you need to understand how they are structured. Since they are written by different programmers, module files are not always structured in the same way, but most well-written modules

B

will contain certain sections that can help you pick out the functions contained in a module and use them.

For the integer module, the most important place to look for information is under the heading "Synopsis" within the module file. You can use any text editor to open a module file. It is here that the usage of the module is explained, along with an example. For this module, there aren't any functions, and to use the module you simply have to declare it, as shown in the documentation under "Synopsis".

After reading this example, it is easy to test this module. Here is a Perl script to do just that:

```
$x = 3;
print 10/$x; # Perl prints 3.333333333333
use integer;
print 10/$x; # Perl prints 3
```

As you can see, when the module is declared, it gains control over the script and, in this example, changes the way Perl performs integer arithmetic.

Let's look at another example, this time from the Win32 environment. One Perl for Win32 module that comes with the ActiveState distribution of Perl is the Win32 module. This module includes several functions that allow you to obtain basic system information concerning your computing environment. Here is a listing of the Win32 module:

```
package Win32;
require Exporter;
@ISA = qw(Exporter);
@EXPORT =
    qw(
    NULL
    WIN31_CLASS
    OWNER_SECURITY_INFORMATION
    GROUP_SECURITY_INFORMATION
    DACL_SECURITY_INFORMATION
    SACL_SECURITY_INFORMATION
    MB_ICONHAND
    MB_ICONQUESTION
    MB_ICONEXCLAMATION
    MB_ICONASTERISK
    MB_ICONWARNING
    MB_ICONERROR
    MB_ICONINFORMATION
    MB_ICONSTOP
```

```
);

# Routines added in ntxs.cpp:
# Win32::GetLastError
# Win32::PerlVersion
# Win32::LoginName
# Win32::NodeName
# Win32::DomainName
# Win32::FsType
# Win32::GetCwd
# Win32::GetOSVersion
# Win32::FormatMessage ERRORCODE
# Win32::Spawn COMMAND, ARGS, PID
# Win32::LookupAccountName SYSTEM, ACCOUNT, DOMAIN, SID, SIDTYPE
# Win32::LookupAccountSID SYSTEM, SID, ACCOUNT, DOMAIN, SIDTYPE
# Win32::InitiateSystemShutdown MACHINE, MESSAGE, TIMEOUT, FORCE-
CLOSE, REBOOT
# Win32::AbortSystemShutdown MACHINE

# Win32::GetTickCount
# Win32::IsWinNT
# Win32::IsWin95

# We won't bother with the constant stuff, too much of a hassle.
Just hard
# code it here.
sub NULL { (0);}
sub WIN31_CLASS { &NULL;}
sub OWNER_SECURITY_INFORMATION {(0x00000001);}
sub GROUP_SECURITY_INFORMATION {(0x00000002);}
sub DACL_SECURITY_INFORMATION {(0x00000004);}
sub SACL_SECURITY_INFORMATION {(0x00000008);}

sub MB_ICONHAND         { (0x00000010); }
sub MB_ICONQUESTION     { (0x00000020); }
sub MB_ICONEXCLAMATION    { (0x00000030); }
sub MB_ICONASTERISK     { (0x00000040); }
sub MB_ICONWARNING     { (0x00000030); }
sub MB_ICONERROR    { (0x00000010); }
sub MB_ICONINFORMATION    { (0x00000040); }
sub MB_ICONSTOP         { (0x00000010); }

1;
```

B

The main difference (besides their functions) between the Win32 module and
the integer module is that the Win32 module is comprised of several functions

that must be called to obtain data. For example, the first function in the module is **Win32::GetLastError**. This function pulls out information from the Windows NT error log concerning the last error in the log. Another function in the list is **Win32::PerlVersion**. This function returns the version of Perl that is running the current script. Here's how to use this function in a program:

```
use Win32;
$pver = Win32::PerlVersion;
print "The current version of Perl is $pver.\n";
```

A last example involves a module that includes object-oriented methods. In the standard Perl distribution is a group of modules that perform specialized mathematical functions. One of these is the BigInt module, which allows Perl to perform integer operations on big integers. The BigInt module is too large to print here, but you can open the file in your text editor to see how it is structured.

To perform big integer operations using BigInt, you first have to create big integer numbers. You do this with a method called **new**. Here is a small script that imports the BigInt module and creates two new big integer objects:

```
use Math::BigInt;
$num1 = Math::BigInt->new("20 000 000 000");
$num2 = Math::BigInt->new("-22222");
```

The **new** method always takes a string and returns a big integer object from the string.

You can then perform normal integer operations using the familiar operators (*, /, +, −) because these operators are overloaded with big integer routines from the module. In other words, the standard operators have been redefined to perform big integer math. With that in mind, here is a script that does big integer addition:

```
use Math::BigInt;
$a = Math::BigInt->new("20 000 000 000");
$b = Math::BigInt->new(-22222);
$c = $a + $b;   # $c gets the value +19999977778
```

The key to using the Perl modules successfully is to be able to read through them to understand how they operate. To quote a familiar phrase from the Unix world, "Use the source, Luke".

APPENDIX C

Special Perl Variables

Perl has a set of system variables that have special meaning when used in a Perl script. Generally, these variables hold commonly used data that are referred to so often that having a special variable hold the value is the best way to handle the data. Also, many of the shell programs Perl is based on used these type of variables, and many programmers have found them useful.

These special variables have two names: a mnemonic name and a longer name. In this book, special variables have been referred to using their mnemonic names, but you can use their longer names by adding the English module to the beginning of your program, like this:

```
use English;
```

Once this module has been added to your program's namespace, you can refer to a special variable using its longer name, as in:

```
use English;
print $ARG; # where $ARG is the long name for $_
```

The following table defines each of the special variables in Perl. You will also notice that there are special arrays in Perl, such as @ARGV, which holds the arguments passed to a Perl program from the command line. Each special variable (or array) is defined and its longer name is given also.

Variable	Meaning
$_ ($ARG)	This variable holds the default input and pattern-searching space. If you don't specify another variable in a context, Perl assumes you are referring to this variable.
$. ($INPUT_LINE_NUMBER)	This variable holds the current line number of the last filehandle that a program read. If your program opened a filehandle and read in five lines from the file, $. would be equal to 5.
$/ ($INPUT_RECORD_SEPARATOR)	This variable holds the input record separator, which is set by default to the newline character.

Variable	Meaning
$, ($OUTPUT_FIELD_SEPARATOR)	This variable holds the output field separator, which is what gets printed between fields when the *print* operator is called. Set this variable when you want to specify something to be printed between fields. The default for this variable is the empty string.
$\ ($OUTPUT_RECORD_ SEPARATOR)	This variable holds the output record separator, which is what gets printed after a record is printed. You might use this variable if you want Perl to automatically print a newline after each record without having to specify "\n" in your code. The default for this variable is the empty string.
$" ($LIST_SEPARATOR)	This variable holds the separator for values interpolated into a double-quoted string. The default value is a space. If you want fields in a double-quoted list to be separated with something besides a space, you can use this variable to change the default.
$^L ($FORMAT_FORMFEED)	This variable holds the formfeed character that is output when a format sends a formfeed command. The default is "\f".
$: ($FORMAT_LINE_BREAK_ CHARACTERS)	This variable holds the characters after which a string can be broken to fill continuation fields in a format. The default is "\n-".
$^A ($ACCUMULATOR)	This variable holds the value of the *write* accumulator for *format* lines.
$? ($CHILD_ERROR)	This variable holds the value returned by the last pipe close or *system* operator.

C

Variable	Meaning
$! ($OS_ERROR)	This variable holds the value of the last error code returned by the system.
$@ ($EVAL_ERROR)	This variable holds the value of any syntax error returned from the last eval command. If there was no syntax error, the value is null.
$$ ($PROCESS_ID)	This variable holds the process number of the version of Perl running the current program.
$< ($REAL_USER_ID)	This variable holds the real user ID (uid) of the current running process.
$> ($EFFECTIVE_USER_ID)	This variable holds the effective uid of the current running process.
$(($REAL_GROUP_ID)	This variable holds the real group ID (gid) of the current running process.
$) ($EFFECTIVE_GROUP_ID)	This variable holds the effective gid of the current running process.
$0 ($PROGRAM_NAME)	This variable holds the name of the program that is currently running.
$] ($PERL_VERSION)	This variable holds the current Perl version plus the current patchlevel divided by 1000.
$^D ($DEBUGGING)	This variable holds the current value of the debugging flags.
$^H	This variable holds internal compiler hints.
$^I ($INPLACE_EDIT)	This variable holds the current value of the inplace-edit extension.
$^O ($OSNAME)	This variable holds the name of the operating system the current Perl binary was compiled for.
$^P ($PERLDB)	This variable holds an internal flag so the debugger doesn't execute on itself.

Variable	Meaning
$^T ($BASETIME)	This variable holds the time (in seconds) the current program began running, using 1970 as the base time.
$^W ($WARNING)	This variable holds the current value of the warning switch, which will be either true or false.
$^X ($EXECUTABLE_NAME)	This variable holds the name that the current Perl binary was executed as.
$ARGV	This variable holds the name of the file being read from <ARGV>.
The following variables are special global arrays and hashes:	
@ARGV	This array holds the command-line arguments being passed to the current program.
@INC	This array holds a list of where to look for Perl scripts to be evaluated by the following Perl constructs: *do EXPR*, *require*, or *use*. This array usually contains the default Perl libraries, as well as the current default directory.
@F	This array holds input lines that are split using the -a switch.
%INC	This hash holds the entries for filenames of the files included in a Perl program. The key is the filename specified, and the value is the location of the file.
%ENV	This hash contains the settings of the current environment. The key is an environment variable and the value is the value of that environment variable.
The following variables are global special filehandles:	
ARGV	This variable is used to refer to command-line arguments, usually written as <>.

C

Variable	Meaning
STDERR	This variable is used to refer to the standard error filehandle.
STDIN	This variable is used to refer to the standard input filehandle.
STDOUT	This variable is used to refer to the standard output filehandle.
DATA	This variable is used to refer to the filehandle that refers to whatever follows the __END__ token.
_ (Underline or underscore character)	This variable is used to refer to the filehandle used to cache information from the **stat**, **lstat**, and **file** commands.

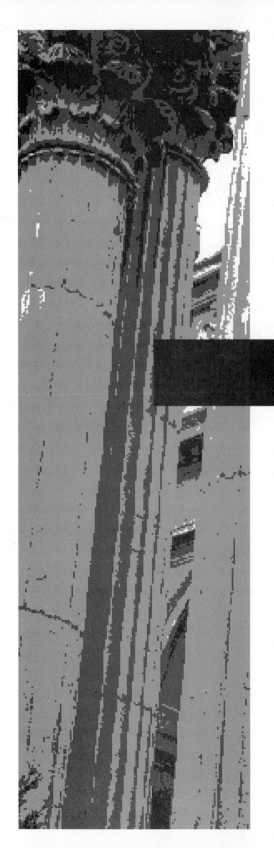

APPENDIX D

Where to Find Perl and Get Help about Perl

Where to Find Perl

Perl is available in many different places, but there is now one central location where you can find Perl and Perl code for any platform it is available on—the Perl home page. The address is **http://www.perl.com**. There are links on this page to both the Perl binaries and to source code for all the Perl implementations.

If you are looking for Perl on a 32-bit Windows platform, you can find it at the home page, or you can go directly to the ActiveState company home page, **http://www.activestate.com**. ActiveState provides and supports the most popular Win32 distribution of Perl. You can also download a version of PerlScript and PerlIIS from this site.

How to Get Help for Perl

The best place to get help for Perl is through the Perl Usenet newsgroups. There are several:

◆ **comp.lang.perl.announce**   For announcements concerning new Perl version releases, bug fixes, new modules, etc. This is a moderated newsgroup.

◆ **comp.lang.perl.misc**   Where most Perl-related traffic occurs. Anything and everything related to Perl programming is discussed here.

◆ **comp.lang.perl.tk**   For people using Perl with the Tk toolkit for Perl.

◆ **comp.lang.perl.modules**   For discussing the creation and use of modules in Perl.

◆ **perl-win32-users**   Where issues concerning the Win32 versions of Perl are discussed.

◆ **comp.infosystems.www.authoring.cgi**   Not specifically about Perl, but concerns CGI programming. Perl-related issues with CGI are discussed here.

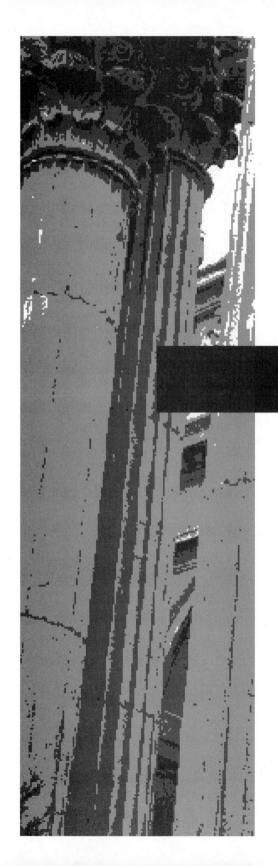

APPENDIX E

The Comprehensive Perl Archive Network (CPAN)

The Comprehensive Perl Archive Network (CPAN) is a worldwide network of sites that contain the entire set of Perl source code, scripts, modules, utilities, and documentation that make up the Perl software community. This set is available as individual files that you access through FTP (file transfer protocol).

The CPAN files are contributed by individuals and groups who submit a proposal to the CPAN administrators. If the administrators decide the proposal is useful and hasn't already been done, they allow the contributor(s) to post their contribution to the master CPAN site, FUNET, the Finnish University Network. From this site, the files are mirrored to sites all over the world, making CPAN truly a worldwide distribution of Perl information.

CPAN Sites

At the time of this writing, there are over 70 CPAN sites. Here is a list of just the North American sites:

◆ California   **ftp.cdrom.com, ftp.digital.com**

◆ Calisota   **ftp.perl.org**

◆ Colorado   **ftp.cs.colorado.edu**

◆ Florida   **ftp.cis.ufl.edu**

◆ Illinois   **uiarchive.uiuc.edu**

◆ Manitoba   **theory.uwinnipeg.ca**

◆ Massachusetts   **ftp.ccs.nev.edu, ftp.iguide.com**

◆ New York   **ftp.rge.com**

◆ North Carolina   **ftp.duke.edu**

◆ Oklahoma   **ftp.ou.edu**

◆ Ontario   **enterprise.ic.gc.ca, ftp.utilis.com**

◆ Oregon   **ftp.orst.edu**

◆ Pennsylvania   **ftp.epix.net**

◆ Texas   **ftp.metronet.com, ftp.sedl.org, ftp.sterling.org**

◆ Washington   **ftp.spu.edu**

CPAN Site Structure

A CPAN site is organized by Perl announcements, contributing authors, distributions, documentation, ports, and scripts. The files themselves are usually compressed into either tar or gzip format.

The following list outlines the content of a typical CPAN site. Since the structure of CPAN is standardized, you will find this same structure no matter which CPAN site you access. Here is the CPAN listing for **ftp.cs. colorado.edu:**

◆ Current directory is /pub/perl/CPAN

◆ Cpan.html   The CPAN documentation

◆ ENDINGS   Describes the .tgz file extension

◆ Mirrored.by   Sites mirroring CPAN

◆ Mirrored.from   Sites mirroring CPAN

◆ README   What to find on CPAN

◆ Readme.html   The README file formatted in HTML

◆ RECENT   Recent additions to CPAN

◆ Recent.day   Recent additions to CPAN (added daily)

◆ Recent.html   The RECENT file formatted in HTML

◆ Recent.week   Recent additions to CPAN (added weekly)

◆ ROADMAP   What to find on CPAN and where to find it

◆ Roadmap.html   The ROADMAP file formatted in HTML

◆ SITES   List of CPAN sites

◆ Sites.html   The SITES file formatted in HTML

◆ authors   List of CPAN authors

◆ clpa   Archive of the **comp.lang.perl.announce** news list

◆ doc   Perl FAQs, documentation

◆ indices   All indexed sources

◆ ls-lR.gz   The latest Perl distribution

◆ misc   Miscellaneous things related to Perl

E

- ◆ modules   Modules for Perl (version 5)
- ◆ ports   Perl ports to different operating systems
- ◆ scripts   Sample Perl scripts
- ◆ src   Various versions of Perl source code

You can find a comprehensive description of CPAN and its sites at the Perl home page: **www.perl.com**.

APPENDIX F

Glossary of Terms

argument   Data supplied as input to a program, subroutine, or function.

ARGV   The array that holds the command-line arguments.

array   A list of values, where the key is either numeric (for a normal array) or a string (for a hash or association array).

array variable   A named array that can be used as the argument of a function.

associative array   The old Perl name for a hash (see **hash**).

autosplit   Splitting a string automatically on whitespace.

backtracking   Perl does this in regular expressions when it backs up on an expression to try another match.

base class   A generic object class from which other classes are derived.

bless   A declaration that declares something as an object.

BLOCK   A group of Perl statements surrounded by curly braces.

Boolean context   A scalar context where the value returned by an expression is either true or false.

character class   A list of characters surrounded by square brackets used in regular expressions.

class   A package that either declares methods that work with objects of the class, or that derives methods from other packages to work with objects of the class.

class method   A method that treats a class as an object.

constructor   A class method that creates an object.

context   The environment that an object is considered to be part of.

CPAN   The Comprehensive Perl Archive Network.

current package   The package within which the current statement is compiled.

cwd   The current working directory.

DBM   A set of database routines that emulate an associate array using disk files.

derived class   A class that inherits its methods from a generic class.

destructor   A method a class calls to destroy itself.

directory handle   A name that represents an instance of opening a directory for reading.

dynamic scoping   Refers to variables that are visible throughout the block of code they are defined in, as well as any subroutines that are called from that block.

environment   A set of variables a process inherits from its parent.

environment variable   Key/value pairs that are passed down to a process from its parent.

EOF   end of file.

false   In Perl, the value false is represented by the null string or 0.

file glob   A wildcard match on files.

filehandle   A name given to a file that is opened for read/write operations.

format   A specification of how data and other information should be laid out for reporting purposes.

function   An operation that returns a value. Also called a *subroutine* in Perl.

glob   The * (asterisk) character, which matches a "glob" or everything in pattern matches.

hard reference   A scalar value containing the actual address of a native Perl object, such as a variable.

hash   A named list of key/value pairs, also called an *associative array*. It is called a *hash* because a hash table is used to implement this data structure.

interpolation   Inserting one piece of text in the middle of another string of text. Variable interpolation involves substituting the value of a variable within another string. Can also refer to the automatic conversion of one variable type to another, such as a string to a number, during evaluation.

key   A piece of data used to locate another piece of data, called the *value,* in a hash.

label   A name to give a line of code for reference in another part of a script.

lexical scoping   Storing the value of a variable in a private table that is only visible to the subroutine the variable is located in.

F

LIST   A syntactic construct representing a comma-separated list of expressions, which are evaluated to form a list value.

list context   The environment within which an expression returns a list of values rather than a single value.

list operator   An operator that does something to a list.

list value   A list of scalar values that are passed to a function to provide a list context.

lvalue   A location (variable, array element) that you can assign a value to.

method   An action that an object can perform if told to.

module   A package that contains code for reuse in Perl scripts.

newline   A character that represents the end of a line (\n).

numeric context   The environment in which an expression is supposed to return a number as a value.

object   A "thing" that knows what kind of thing it is and knows what to do because of the kind of thing it is.

package   A grouping of code that prevents other code from obtaining its variables and values by making its contents private.

pattern matching   Taking a regular expression and comparing it with a string to see if they contain the same contents.

pointer   Perl doesn't use them; it uses references instead.

procedure   See **subroutine**.

reference   Something that points to information that is stored elsewhere.

regular expression   A pattern of characters that is used to find other characters that match them.

rvalue   A value that is assigned to an *lvalue*.

scalar   A simple data type, such as a number or a string.

scalar context   The environment in which an expression is expected to return a scalar.

scalar literal   An actual value in a Perl script, as opposed to a scalar variable.

scalar value   A value that is a scalar, as opposed to a list value.

scalar variable   A variable that holds a scalar value.

scope   The range with which a variable is visible to a Perl script. See **dynamic scoping** and **lexical scoping**.

script   A Perl program.

slice   A selection of array elements.

standard input   The default input stream for your Perl scripts, usually the keyboard.

standard output   The default output stream for your Perl scripts, usually the screen or display.

STDIN   An abbreviation for standard input.

STDOUT   An abbreviation for standard output.

string   A sequence of characters.

string context   The environment in which an expression is expected to return a string value.

subroutine   A named grouping of code that can be stored in one part of a program and invoked somewhere else in the program by calling the subroutine name.

subscript   A value that indicates the position of an array element.

substring   A smaller string inside a larger string.

switch statement   A construct that evaluates a conditional expression and branches to a particular part of a program.

symbol table   An internal storage space for keeping track of variables, filehandles, and subroutines.

text   A string or file containing printable characters.

typeglob   A single identifier, prefaced with an asterisk (*), to refer to a group of things with the same name, such as *var for $var, @var, and %var.

unary operator   An operator with only one operand, such as ++ or --.

variable   A named storage location for holding different types of values.

variable interpolation   See **interpolation**.

whitespace   The blank characters that exist between words, operators, etc.

working directory   See **cwd**.

F

Index

V

W

X

Z